THE KEEPER'S BOOK

Peter Jeffrey Mackie writes in his introduction to *The Keeper's Book* that 'Sport and love of sport is part of the great heritage of our race.'. He believes that sport and sportsmanship are what keeps society thriving and is undoubtedly one of our most powerful social forces in this day and age. This book pursues the sport of the hunt and the social interactions associated therein. This particular past time requires not only a love of adventure, but also self-discipline, patience and technical skill. Not only does Mackie discuses the pursuit and conquest of wild animals, but he also describes how to preserve them, covering all matters in great detail. Mackie goes on to cover everything from hunting to angling in astounding detail. Although first published in 1929, this timeless classic is sure to peak the curiosity of anyone interested in outdoors amusements and their impact today.

www.keganpaul.com

KEGAN PAUL LIBRARY OF COUNTRY AND COASTLINE PURSUITS

THE KEEPER'S BOOK • SIR PETER JEFFREY MACKIE

AMID THE HIGH HILLS • HUGH FRASER

THE AUTHOR

THE KEEPER'S BOOK

A Guide to the Duties of a Gamekeeper

BY

PETER JEFFREY MACKIE

LONDON AND NEW YORK

First published 2005 by
Kegan Paul Limited

2 Park Square, Milton Park, Abingdon, Oxon OX144RN
711 Third Avenue, New York, NY 10017, USA

Routledge is an imprint of the Taylor & Francis Group, an informa business

First issued in paperback 2016

ISBN 978-0-7103-1158-0 (hbk)
ISBN 978-1-138-97397-8 (pbk)

British Library Cataloguing in Publication Data

Library of Congress Cataloging-in-Publication Data
Applied for.

PREFACE TO THE 16th EDITION

THAT a Sixteenth Edition of this book is required after seventeen years implies little credit to the ability of the Author-Editor. It must be remembered that there is always growing up a new generation of young sportsmen who require to go through the Mill of Learning to " Play the Game," and that without this teaching they are a danger alike to themselves and their neighbours.

There is no finality to knowledge, and although in other respects this edition may not differ greatly from previous ones, it has been carefully revised and brought up to date as far as the knowledge of the Editor and of the various writers permits. As before, there are wide margins left for personal notes.

That many sportsmen may differ with the views expressed is to be expected, yet if this work forms the foundation on which other sportsmen of greater knowledge may add their experience, the object of the book will not have been sought in vain.

PETER J. MACKIE.

ACKNOWLEDGMENTS

I BEG to acknowledge my gratitude and thanks to Lord Glenconner, Mr. Archibald Thorburn, and Mr. Philip Rickman, and to Nobel Industries Limited and Messrs. Eric Nobel, and Rowland Green, for permission to use the copyright illustrations. Also to my friend Mr. John Geddie for his laborious work of reading and correcting my proofs.

P. J. M.

ACKNOWLEDGEMENTS

[illegible]

CONTENTS

CONTENTS

LIST OF ILLUSTRATIONS

REPRODUCED IN COLOUR

IN TEXT

INTRODUCTION

SPORT and love of sport is part of the great heritage of our race, and it is a far more important factor than many people realise. The Briton does not question his own conventions. It would be hard to frame a concise definition of all that we understand in the simple term "sportsman"; yet not only our own race but the civilised world in general, has learnt to take this word, divorced from its simple relationship to field sports, and to apply it as descriptive of a code of conduct, a standard of behaviour or a rule of life governing in a wide sense a man's relationship to his fellow-men. Sportsmanship is in essence the adhesion of self-disciplined individuals to a collective code, and it is perhaps the most powerful of all our modern social forces. It is the spirit which has regulated, maintained and cemented the bonds of our own commonwealth of nations. Interpreted in a myriad ways, adapted to meet the needs of complex situations and difficult and wayward races, it has served us as statecraft, as diplomacy, as a code of justice, and above all as a code of honour and social service. Imperial Rome may have left on the world the impress of its laws and its roads. Imperial Britain has evolved this curious but entirely admirable code of sportsmanship.

One cannot deny the utility of ball games as distinct from sport in fostering something of the same spirit, but there is in these games a competitive or a team play spirit which, admirable in itself, is something apart from the essential quality of real sport. We must not be led to confuse the narrower and more specialised outlook and training of the athlete with the very much higher craft of the hunter. The one is an accomplishment, the other in a much wider sense a liberal education.

There are few better schools for a youngster than a good training on moor and hill, covert and marsh. He learns not only to shoot, but to shoot—clean. He learns not only the pursuit and conquest of wild creatures, but how to preserve them. He learns self-discipline, patience, and technical skill, and he learns how to use his eyes and how to see for himself. This is a book about shooting and the arts, crafts and responsibilities of our hunters of to-day, but I who write and you who read, know full well that no book can be more than a guide or a reminder. It can at best help you to know what to look for—but you must see and do for yourself.

In a quarter of a century there has been progress not only in methods and the technical development of sport, but in its economic importance and to a certain extent in the opposition to it. The growth of the English industrial town populations and the journals which cater to this class have accentuated the difference of outlook which exists between the town-dweller and the country-man. An extremist group of misguided and unduly imaginative folk are definitely against all "blood sports," *i.e.,* shooting, hunting and fishing. Their avowed object is the legal prohibition of all sport. They are blind to any side of the case but their own, and they do not at the moment represent a serious menace. On the other hand, it would be idle to suggest that all the measures on our Statute Books have been placed there because they represented the genuine opinion of the majority of voters. Political experience suggests that any organised minority with funds may succeed in pressing through legislation which affects an unorganised majority. The mass of voters are uninterested in a question which so far as they can see does not affect them personally, and in any intensive political campaign fact and truth are apt to be lost sight of in a mist of distortion and propaganda.

The economic side of shooting is far more important than the average townsman knows. He does not realise that sporting rights are proportionately as valuable to the farmer freeholder as the greatest estate owner. Still less does he realise that, except for the amenities of sport, the countryside would lose many of its residents. The local shopkeeper may not realise to what extent the claims of sport affect many of his best customers. It is not a matter which one can definitely balance in account books, but in general it is a matter which should be borne in mind by all concerned—and mentioned whenever casual conversation swings round to anti-sport talk.

It would be difficult to assess the amount of general unemployment caused if shooting were to be prohibited. It is not only a matter of a catastrophic fall in land values and, so far as many parts of Scotland are concerned, ruin to landowners and keepers alike, but it affects gunmakers and the steel factories, and the men who make the raw metal from which the guns are fashioned by hundreds of skilled craftsmen. Millions of cartridges are fired in a year ; we can put our pen through so many tons of paper, and the people who make it : the smokeless powder and lead shot industries—felt wadding. We can wipe out the game food industry, we can take a substantial load of traffic and passengers off the railroads, reduce motoring a little, hit the sale of tweeds, and generally carry the ever-widening ripples of our devastation farther and farther afield.

Viewed in this light we can count the probable cost of sentimentality ——?, but it is also fair to question whether any direct benefit would occur to the animal world in general by the relaxation of our present system of preserving. The experience of the war years was that lack of keepering meant an entirely disproportionate increase of vermin—who did not confine their attention to game but made matters worse for the farmer. Nature is a good deal more cruel than man, but the sentimentalist seldom knows anything about Nature at first hand.

It is, I think, wise and timely to stress the economic importance of sport as well as its educative and character-forming side, and when we come across these people who know nothing about it and are therefore ready to condemn the pleasures of others, it is as well to put to them points of view they have not taken into consideration. You will probably not convince the fanatic, but you will certainly win over the ordinary moderately intelligent but badly-informed man who has only heard one side of the case. This I would put among the duties of a modern gamekeeper, that he should make clear to all and sundry that he is not only a skilled keeper of game, but a preserver of wild life in general, and that but for the keenness and sportsmanship of owners and keepers, eagles and wild cats, and even the noble red deer, would be as extinct as wolves in Britain within a generation.

A second and a more serious menace to sport might arise from legislation designed to attach the small farmer's vote to a Party programme. The problems raised by the question of sheep *versus* grouse are difficult, but it is undeniable that in the great majority of cases it is the value of the grouse rather than the sheep which has brought moors under good management, which has enhanced the farming value as well as the game value of the land. Here again an appreciation of the underlying economics of sporting estates is the best argument, and a clear conception of the value and function of sport in our present state of social development is in itself the best safeguard for the continuance of things as they are and have been in our father's time.

NOTES.

NOTES.

NOTES.

CHAPTER I

GAMEKEEPERS

SOME years ago when visiting a school in the West Highlands, and after having listened for some time to a cross-examination of one of the classes on powers of observation, the writer asked the question, " What is a gamekeeper ? " and the answer received from a bright-eyed, sandy-haired Celt of about ten years of age was, " A big man that gangs aboot in a braw suit of claithes wi' a dug and a gun, and daes naethin'." Now, though out of the mouths of babes and sucklings one should expect wisdom, one must not attempt to justify humour at the expense of justice. The little Highlander's answer was very much on the line of the street boy's definition of a Club as " A house where gentlemen read newspapers on Sunday." No doubt there is more of actual truth in the latter than in the former reply. But both indicate a real impression made upon a fairly observant youngster, and neither reply is to be despised as a subject for reflection.

There are three classes of keepers—good, bad, and indifferent : by indifferent we mean inefficient.

It must be admitted that there are many keepers whose chief occupation up till the 12th of August, or even till the 1st of September or the 1st of October, seems to consist in going about with a dog and a gun, and in virtually doing nothing—that is, nothing of real value to the shooting under their control. In no other class of men do we find such extremes: on the one hand of skill, energy, and efficiency, and on the other, of stupidity, laziness, and incapability. Taking the occupation as a whole, and regarding it as a department of skilled labour, we must admit, though the admission may give offence, that it does not reach the average level of efficiency of other skilled labour.

The fact that an outstanding minority of keepers are more than efficient, and combine the qualities of patient and intelligent keepers of ground and stock with all the instincts and capacities of thorough sportsmen, does not get rid of the truth of the general criticism. Of course no one would insult the profession of gamekeeping by placing it in the same category with any branch of unskilled labour in the industrial community. It is because we believe the duties of a keeper demand a high standard of observation, skill, patience, and energy, that we have to admit the failure, in the common run of the calling, to reach that standard. Viewing them on the side of moral character alone, we readily recognise that, for probity and general temperance, gamekeepers compare favourably with any other section of society. In fifty per cent. of cases they are sober, honest, good-tempered, and naturally generous, and to all these qualities they add, as a rule, an exceptionally keen sense of humour. But, considering the responsibilities of their work, the percentage of efficient and trustworthy workmen is very much smaller than the figure quoted above.

This book is written for " all good keepers who know their work, and for the indifferent ones who do not." How competent a person is the good keeper ! He is not only a grand sportsman, but a splendid servant—a man who knows nearly everything that is to be learnt of the habits and habitats of game, and of the necessary methods of managing and improving the ground, stock, and shootings under his care, and yet is always on the outlook to learn more. The really first-class keeper is a precious jewel in the crown of sport—a man who often puts to shame the knowledge and skill of the best-read and most keenly observant master. This capable servant is the man of all others who deplores the fact that the status of his craft is lowered by infusion of men with the sporting knowledge of farm labourers, the energy of vagabond hucksters, the initiative of village boors—and who are thoroughly convinced that they know everything.

It has been said that the ideal keeper combines skill with energy, but even in ordinarily good keepers the combination is rare. An ideal keeper, in our view, would combine the sporting capacities of the Highlander with the energy and perseverance of the Lowlander. The first has probably more insight and general intelligence, the latter more initiative and energy. As Mr. Stuart Wortley has so aptly said: "Highlanders are, as all the world knows, a very fine race of men, courageous and loyal, courteous and amiable—they make the best sportsmen and the best soldiers in the world; but they are neither so practical nor so energetic under ordinary conditions as the northern Englishman, and laziness is their great failing."

The fact of the matter is that the Highlander is a born hunter, and the descendant of a long line of hunters. His ancestors having been brought up under the clan system, "sporting" blood runs in his veins, and his instincts are still strong for fighting and hunting, not for butt-building and draining. He is a lineal descendant of men of the type of Maclean of Ardgour, "strong Donald the hunter, Macgillean Mohr."

> Low down by yon burn that's half-hidden with heather,
> He lurked like a lion, in the lair he knew well;
> 'Twas there sobbed the red deer to feel his keen dagger;
> There pierced by his arrow, the cailzie cock fell.
> How oft when at e'en he would watch for the wild fowl,
> Like lightning his coracle sped from the shore;
> But still, and for aye, as we cross the lone lochan,
> Is Donald the hunter, Macgillean Mohr.

Time and circumstances of civilisation have done much to modify the Highland spirit and instincts, but the independence, pride, and tradition, which make a Highlander naturally antagonistic to that manual labour which is a necessary accompaniment of a gamekeeper's duties, still remain to a marked extent, especially amongst the keepers of the Western Highlands and Islands of Scotland. Give a keeper of this breed a gun or rod in his hand, or let him be spying out your deer in the forest, or tracking your birds on the moor, and there is no man in the world to compare with him. But put him to drain your water-soaked ground, repair or rebuild your butts, or to do any of the innumerable prosaic duties inseparable from a gamekeeper's responsibilities, and he is not to be compared with either the Yorkshire or Norfolk keeper, or with the man from the Lothians.

The pride and other characteristics of race, which so long confined the Highlander's instincts to hunting and fighting, also assert themselves in a marked way in his relations to his master. If the latter is " the laird "——one of a line of fifty Campbells, a hundred Mackintoshes, or a thousand Grants—then the Highlander is a much more satisfactory workman than if his master comes of a branch of what he still regards as virtually an alien people. In the former case he is one of a family : in the latter he has an instinctive feeling of resentment against being reduced to a position of servitude. He is slow to come into line with modern social conditions.

But though these reflections on the abilities and disabilities of race may be allowable, it is dangerous to generalise further, and, while admitting the marked distinctions between Highlander and Lowlander, it would be idle to shoot their characters as keepers into separate pigeonholes. We have in our mind many Highland keepers who combined keen sporting instincts and capacities with indomitable energy and perseverance in the pursuit of their more irksome duties; and can also recall many Lowlanders and English shire keepers who were preternaturally lazy.

It is to be regretted that the qualities of charm and laziness so often go together. Some of the most interesting keepers we have known have been the most indolent. We have in remembrance particularly a keeper in Perthshire, whose knowledge of sport and whose capacity for narrative made of him a fascinating companion in the chase, yet who invariably neglected such duties as the killing of vermin, the digging out of springs, the proper burning of heather, and the hundred little duties for which, more especially, he was paid. Of course he knew all about the rights and wrongs of these matters, but, in dealing with subjects of the kind he spoke in the vaguest generalities, and promptly turned the conversation to some famous day on the hill when, late in the season, "the Captain," his master, killed forty brace to his own gun, or to a story of some record stalk in the forests of Ross-shire or Aberdeenshire. There was not an experience of the new master that he could not cap with a story of brilliant shooting on his old master's part, or equally skilful manœuvring on his own, and his exploits were all told with such a power of picturesque description that any criticism of his constant disregard of the moor and stock improvement was disarmed.

The net result of this keeper's inequalities has been a sad deterioration of the shooting capacities of the moor which was under his control—a deterioration which it will take many years for a new, and probably more reticent, keeper to repair. The particular moor in question is loaded with vermin, the heather is long and rank, the springs are clogged with undergrowth, and a thousand-acred shooting now realises about ten brace of grouse a year. In our younger days, before we began to understand the science of maintaining a moor as breeding-ground for grouse, we considered this old keeper infallible. He could cast a better line than any other man : he seemed to know the actual capacity of every fly. We can vouch to the brilliance of his shooting, to his knowledge of the habits and haunts of birds, and to his skill in leading his master through the intricacies of the most difficult stalk. But, sad to say, on reviewing in cold blood the inefficiencies of his character as a responsible keeper, we have had to dethrone him from the pedestal on which he had been placed.

Let it be frankly admitted that the blame of the prevalence of inefficiency lies, to a great extent, at the door of the owners or occupiers of the shootings. There has been, and there is, too little recognition of the services of good keepers. There is in general not sufficient of a slide in the scale of wages to urge on the keeper to improve his knowledge and his capacity for work. Remuneration for labour is on all too stereotyped lines : the efficient keeper is too often paid the same wage as the inefficient. There is too little recognition of superiority and too little condemnation of the reverse ; and, this being the case, the result is obvious. The keeper has little stimulus to improvement, outside his own personal self-respect, and, in consequence, the standard of general efficiency is kept lower than it should be.

Much of the inefficiency of the keeper is also due to the ignorance or indifference of the master or his factor. Except in a few cases of prominent land-agents, this profession is lacking in efficiency, which accounts largely for the deplorable state into which land has drifted of late years ; in land, where the margin of profit and gain is so narrow, thoroughly capable and efficient men are required. Where the property is managed by the lawyer-factor in a large town efficient supervision cannot be expected, and so the estate drifts on from bad to worse without the proprietor being able to get clear himself. The lawyer-factor has been the curse of Scottish landowners ; they cannot supervise or check the work of the keeper and other estate employees. There are few men in this world, even among the best of us, who can be trusted to do their work efficiently and well, and for the love of the work, without proper supervision.

But it must be pointed out that, if the ignorance or carelessness of a master may account for a keeper's slackness and inefficiency, it does not excuse it. Even taking the master on the highest plane, he can seldom be more than a very good amateur. The keeper is, or ought to be, a specialist. Within the limits of his duties, a keeper should know all that is to be known, and, in the majority of cases, should know infinitely more than his master. Not only should he be independent of any chance instruction from his employer, but he should also be in the position, when called upon to do so, to give advice and convey information on all points. In fact, the highest state of perfection can only be reached if a keeper bases his knowledge and his work on the possibility of his master being an absolute ignoramus on all matters connected with sport, not even excepting the handling of a gun. Another cause of inefficiency of the keeper arises from so many shootings being let, and from the constant change of tenants, many of whom know little of sport; the keeper naturally takes advantage.

The relationship between master and keeper varies largely on all shootings. In some cases the master takes little or no concern with the details connected with the improvement and management of his ground and stock, and is only interested in the sport of the days on which he or his friends may shoot. In other cases he assumes meticulous direction of, and dictation regarding, all matters affecting his sport, and requires that his keeper should make him conversant with every step he takes in the pursuit of his calling.

Between these two extremes are found masters whose interest and attention are keen on some and indifferent on other points. It is chiefly in dealing with these that the keeper will have to use such discretion and tact as he possesses, discerning when and where he is expected to seek or give advice, and when and where this is not required of him. In those cases where the masters virtually assume the whole control of the details connected with their shootings, it is often found that, through a desire to please—especially developed in the courteous Highland race—keepers often hold back definite knowledge or valuable advice which may be of essential importance to their employers. The intelligent and responsible keeper can always give information, or make suggestions, without being dogmatic, and he is but a poor gamekeeper who hides his knowledge and his opinions in order to curry favour, or out of fear of meeting contradiction. Civilly, quietly, yet firmly he should state his facts and express his views, and he will find that he is seldom misunderstood and always more highly respected. The man who prevaricates for the sake of pleasing, who pretends to know when he is ignorant, or pretends to be ignorant when he knows, is a bad servant, and a keeper who is sure in the long-run to get into difficulties.

It will be gathered from what has been said that we are dealing with the keeper as a skilled specialist. There is not much to say concerning that anomaly—the "occasional" keeper. We mean the man who is not really a gamekeeper at all, but a farm-hand who goes out with the guns, and who is the only person in charge of the shooting. To attempt to instruct such a person would be a waste of energy and a squandering of sensible advice. Such a man may learn a little, but he has neither the time nor, as a rule, the instincts for sport. And yet how many of our so-called keepers are but mere unskilled labourers! They might possibly know the difference between a grouse and a grey hen, but as to the habits and habitats of game, as to the destructive capacity of vermin, or as to the tempers and temperaments of dogs, they are as ignorant as the sedentary Cockney whose only knowledge of game has been obtained at the "Jungle" at Earl's Court.

There are three occupations which contain a specially large proportion of men of great charm and gentleness, and a superiority of tone and character to the general run of mankind: and they are all open-air pursuits—those of gamekeepers, shepherds, and gardeners. They are men who live in close touch with Nature, and are students of natural history; and, as someone has said, the closer to Nature the closer to God.

NOTES.

CHAPTER II

THE IDEAL KEEPER

THE good keeper, as has been said, is a treasure—generally one of Nature's gentlemen, and not too common nowadays. The bad keeper is a curse, luckily not a prevalent one—an affliction that should not be passed on to others by the help of a false or evasive certificate of character ; while the indifferent keeper comprises the greatest number of the calling, and must be " tholed " as one of the more or less inefficient.

What has been written will enable the reader to picture the main lines along which the good keeper may be evolved. Much will depend on the man's innate character—on his sense of responsibility, his sense of duty, his ambitions, his perseverance and persistence under difficulties, his determination to succeed in a career that has a history behind it of honour and fame. A good keeper should be an optimist. No man ever did much in this world who started in life with the resolution only to be as competent as his fellows. It is well to have the ambition to be better. The history of general progress is the story of personal endeavour. This is no doubt a truism, an oft-repeated commonplace, but commonplaces after all are the most valuable, and at the same time, most despised and neglected things in our modern world. If a keeper would only make up his mind that, in addition to the careful carrying out of his duties, he would add one single solid fact to our practical knowledge of the science of sport, he will have earned a claim to the gratitude of the great host of people who find in this form of recreation the best way to cultivate the *mens sana in corpore sano*.

There are so many curbs on human endeavour that it is impossible to reach perfection. It is good for us, however, to have practical ideals—signposts which point to success—even although we find in the long-run that our reach far exceeds our grasp. One thing is certain, that the good keeper seldom stands still ; he never stagnates ; his knowledge and his capacity ripen with the years. How many keepers there are who never seem to improve, who gradually forget all they have learned, and become impervious to new ideas, adding to this mental deterioration the slow disease of indolence.

The average gamekeeper is the most conservative man on earth. Not only does he cling to the long-practised methods of his father and his grandfather ; he is impatient of any suggestion that might interfere with his own settled convictions. Even the best of keepers is apt to be solid, stable, and stationary. It may be said of him, as of the old-fashioned Tory in politics : " Firmly rooted in the past, he draws his nourishment from the traditions of his fathers, submits himself willingly to the constituted authorities of the present, the heritage of the past, and finds his proper field of action in the administration of things as they are. His disadvantage lies in his blindness to the future, and in his systematic ignoring of the principles of change and progress in the universe. When all things are moving around him, from his want of adaptability to new circumstances, he is at last forced to accept, ungraciously, changes which it would have been his wisdom to anticipate."

On the whole, it must be admitted that very little has been learned of recent years beyond what was known to our progenitors regarding the habits and habitats of game. But much has been discovered as to its care and preservation, and more as to the best ways of bringing it to the gun. It is in dealing with these latter problems that the keeper should show himself amenable to ideas, and try to keep in touch with the newest views, and profit by them—not, indeed, by blindly accepting each new theory as gospel, but by testing it carefully in the light of his own experience—in other words, by giving it a fair trial. One has only to use one's eyes to observe how the old-fashioned and discredited practices of the past are still followed on some of our best shootings. The prehistoric butts on the skyline, the indiscriminate burning of heather, the smoking-out of rabbits, the bands of yelling beaters, advancing in a straight line to the guns—all remain with us as persistent monuments of the conservatism of the keeper, despite what comes to his ears of greater success achieved under newer methods. As far as some keepers—and their masters—are concerned, Lord Walsingham, Sir R. Payne Gallwey, Mr. Stuart Wortley, Mr. Lloyd Price, Mr. Harting, Mr. Tom Speedy, and The Mackintosh of Mackintosh, might never have made an experiment or written a word. They seem to forget that sport is not like doctrinal theology—final and irrevocable; but a branch of science, varying under the stress of thought and experience.

The mention of certain famed authorities on matters of sport leads us to observe how little advantage has been taken of the literature of sport by the gamekeeper class. No doubt the keen and intelligent master puts his keepers in possession of the ideas he has accumulated from books, but this is not in itself absolutely satisfactory. Keepers should be encouraged to read for themselves; in some cases to correct their own opinions, and in others to add to their own extensive knowledge. Many keepers are apt to despise books on sport as the writings of mere theorists, and to shun them accordingly. It would be as well for them to understand that this is an error of the first magnitude. Nothing is more fortunate for sport than that its literature emanates from some of its most practical exponents, for up till now there has been no valuable work on sport that has not been written by a great sportsman. A similar remark cannot be made of other branches of literature, and this fact should help to upset the prejudice amongst keepers against that which they regard as mere book-learning. It will be found that most masters are only too delighted to lend to their keepers such books as the volumes of the Fur, Feather, and Fin series ; those of the Badminton Library dealing with shooting ; the *Encyclopædia of Sport*, and the contributions of Mr. Speedy, Mr. John Colquhoun, Mr. Hutchinson, Mr. Bromley Davenport, Sir E. Grey, Mr. Innes Shand, Mr. Lloyd Price, Mr. Harting, Mr. Carnegie, and others. In fact, it is the master's duty to see that his keeper is put in possession—temporarily or otherwise—of some of the more practical of these writings, and to insist that advantage be taken of the advice there put forward.

Not that all the knowledge of sport is to be found in the brains and memories of the writers of books. There are skilful arts, practised by some of our best keepers, that have never yet been put down in black and white. There are many "tricks of the trade" that are still sacred to particular shootings. For sport, in its widest sense, as embracing the preservation of game, is, like shooting, not only a science—it is an art. A man may know much about law without being a great lawyer ; a man may be conversant with most of the facts of medical science, and yet be a poor physician. A keeper, like a poet, is "born," not "made." But a belief in this fact often leads to the most disastrous results. The men who are thoroughly convinced *in their own minds* that they are heaven-born keepers are apt to be conceited, opinionative, dogmatic, and imperious, "given to run riot in idolatries, drifting into vanities, congregating in absurdities, planning short-sightedly, plotting dementedly." They regard with disdain the suggestions of the man who has learned his business by mere patient plodding. Let even the man who is a sportsman by instinct, and a keeper by nature, not hesitate to learn of men who are his inferiors, perhaps, in everything except a little knowledge.

Enthusiasm, although it is not everything, is an invaluable quality in the good keeper. It inspires enthusiasm not only in his underlings, but in the sportsmen themselves. Nothing is more depressing to a day's shooting than to have a keeper who seems bored by his work. Such a day is bound to be a failure, or, at best, an imperfect success. The joy of sport; the keenness for a good bag; the evident and just pride in knowledge which the keeper is only too willing to impart; the calm, firm, and deliberate manner in carrying out a plan, skilfully and patiently constructed—these are the conditions that inspire confidence in, and respect from, the sportsman. But seeming indifference; evident ignorance; a noisy, changeful, aimless plan of campaign; shouting at his dog—these are the conditions that make for the irritation of "the guns" and for a general feeling of dissatisfaction. When these conditions exist, it will in all likelihood be found that the courtesy of the keeper is in proportion to the size of his "tips" and his geniality to the number of his "nips."

Such a man is a disgrace to an historical and responsible calling. He can be of no satisfaction to himself, and he is a nuisance to everybody else. He quarrels with the farm servants ; he indiscriminately shoots every suspicious dog that he meets ; he is outwitted by poachers, and is hated by his assistants. Knowledge, skill, perseverance, discrimination, firmness, order, courtesy, and enthusiasm—these are the eight primary requirements for a good keeper. Knowledge of the technicalities of his craft, skill to carry them out, perseverance in face of difficulty and failure, discrimination in dealing with superiors, equals, neighbours, and inferiors, firmness in all he does, order in all his methods—in his books, his kennels, and his sporting arrangements—and enthusiasm to carry out what he has carefully planned, modified by a gracious civility—all these will tend to his own, his master's, and his assistants' satisfaction.

Above all things the ideal keeper is *humane*. His humanity is shown by his careful consideration not only of his fellow-men, but of those faithful servants of the chase—the horse and the dog ; and if his humanity is of the right quality he will extend his gentleness and consideration so as to prevent unnecessary suffering to the quarry itself. The hunting song says : " Though we all hunt reynard, we love him." In the same way the instinct of love and pity also extends to the birds of the air and the beasts of the field. A cruel keeper is a monster.

NOTES.

CHAPTER III

THE APPRENTICE KEEPER

WHAT we have already said should give the young man who aspires to be a gamekeeper some idea of the qualities of character and temperament, and of the knowledge and skill, that go to make a successful servant. There are one or two other points that we may indicate which may be of use to the uninitiated at the threshold of his career.

A boy brought up in the town is not likely to make a good keeper, and, let it be stated, that the sooner a boy starts his work the easier it will be for him to learn.

It goes without saying that no man deficient in power of observation or in ordinary intelligence should ever think of giving his life up to the care and the pursuit of game. The 'prentice hand must not only have a good groundwork of the common rudiments of reading, writing, and arithmetic, but he must also be keenly interested in natural history. For, unless he be careful in reading up and noting the haunts, habits, and peculiarities of the various beasts and birds which people his district, he will never be a success in the sphere he has selected for his life's work. And having noted the facts, he will never attain to any great height of trustworthiness and dependence unless he is able to put them together in his mind and make the necessary deductions. How often do we find a keeper whose brain is well stored with facts and experiences, yet so arranged that each item seems to be pigeonholed in a separate compartment in his brain, and not on speaking terms with any other ?

Let, therefore, the wise apprentice start in life with the belief that everything is done for a purpose, and that there is some connecting link between cause and effect. Let him always be asking in his own mind the question—why ? At first he may have great difficulty in finding an answer, and then the question must be repeated aloud to those who know, whose duty it will be to explain, and to direct the eyes and the brain of the 'prentice to observe facts and reasons which have eluded him. Let him remember this law—that everything is done either from reason or from experience, and that the rule-of-thumb gospel is only for the inefficient and incapable workman. There are very few things in this world that should be done merely from routine and habit.

The 'prentice must therefore get into the practice of using his eyes, his memory, and his power of reasoning. In saying so much, let us recall what was expressed in the first chapter. On no account should he pretend to know when he is ignorant, or pretend to be ignorant when he knows. The man who is too conceited to admit his ignorance will never learn anything, and the man who is so good-natured or complaisant as to hide his knowledge for the sake of being pleasant, may be a good courtier, but he is a dishonest servant.

Generally speaking, the first duty of the apprentice gamekeeper is to be kennel-boy. Simple as it may appear, the keeping of a kennel requires a good deal of attention and intelligence. It is sad to see how often a valuable kennel of dogs is subjected to neglect. Unless the head-keeper has a knowledge and a keen love of dogs, it is impossible that the kennel-boy can be properly trained. It will add to his store of knowledge if he can borrow or acquire books written on the subject, provided he has sufficient intelligence to discriminate what is practical from what is not. There are two or three points which may be briefly noted—(1) The kennels should be kept scrupulously clean, and periodically disinfected with weak carbolic and water ; (2) the bedding, which should consist of clean straw, should be shaken up every day and any dust swept out of the benches. Let the 'prentice keeper note the appearance of a dog that sleeps in a stable among clean straw, and he will at once understand the necessity for cleanliness in the bedding of dogs. There is nothing a dog seems to revel in more than a roll among clean straw when it is put into his bed. (3) After the kennel has been washed, or during very hot sunshine, dogs should not be allowed to lie upon the pavement, as their bodies are apt to draw damp from it and rheumatism to result. Many dogs are rendered unfit for work by neglecting this important precaution. (4) The dogs should get plenty of fresh water, and be fed regularly, and have daily exercise.

The 'prentice keeper should always be out with the head-keeper when he is training his dogs. As to the management of dogs in the field, experience can only be gradually acquired, but the perusal of books on dog-breaking by such authorities as General Hutchison, Sir Henry Smith, and others, may be useful in giving hints. Still, without observation, common sense, patience, and perseverance, he will never become a practical dog-breaker. However pure the breed, and however satisfactory the condition in which dogs are kept, perfection in breaking is neither to be secured nor expected unless with very considerable experience amongst game. The proportion of keepers who handle dogs well is small.

The 'prentice keeper must also, as soon as possible, be put in contact with ferrets. He must be instructed as to the cleaning of their sleeping and their feeding quarters, and learn in detail the whole question affecting their breeding, their feeding, and their working. Next to these, the management of hill ponies, and other horses used in sport, must come under his observation.

Of other matters for early observation, mention must be made of the burning of heather, the improvement of soil, and questions of draining, fencing, and planting. In all these matters the 'prentice keeper should be compelled to use his hands as well as his brains. His early days must be jointly those of a labourer, a carpenter, and a forester. He will find that, having dealt with these matters in a practical way, he has laid a better foundation for his position as keeper than if his knowledge were only based on observation and theory. Let him have an accurate knowledge of the use of the spade, the saw, and the hammer, long before he knows the use of a gun.

The third part of his training should be concerned with the " engines " of sport—with the construction and use of snares, traps, and nets, and, finally, of guns. He must not only see the snares and traps set by others, but he must be allowed to set them himself; great care being taken that he understands the why and wherefore of his procedure, and to see that he acts, not from theory or imitation merely, but from his knowledge of the habits and habitats of game.

While he is learning these branches of his craft, he will, of course, be out with the guns, acting as beater, driver, stop, flank, or marker, and thus slowly accumulating valuable knowledge as to the questions of finding birds and bringing them to the guns.

At this stage the present book, it is hoped, will be intelligible to him, and he will be well on the road to become a qualified keeper.

NOTES.

CHAPTER IV

RELATIONS WITH FARMERS, ETC.

THE war, together with Socialistic legislation, has made the duties of the keeper more difficult, farmers having in many cases taken advantage of the situation by making inroads into the rights of proprietors, as steps towards abolishing the Game Laws.

However skilful and energetic a keeper may be, however brilliant his qualifications, or original his ideas, he will find himself considerably handicapped unless he be able to keep at peace with his neighbours. It is not only the cantankerous " fathead " or the uncouth barbarian who butts against the susceptibilities and prejudices of others. It is often the man of character and ideas. Knowledge is apt to breed impatience with stupidity and irritation against ignorance. The clever man is by no means the most popular one. The one thing to remember is that every man looks out upon the world from a distinct and individual point of view, and that, to earn friendship and sympathy, it is necessary to gauge your opponent's standpoint when dealing with what may seem his prejudices and wrong-headed convictions. As in heaven, so on earth, there are more mansions than one, and the keepers who start with the motto, "We are the people, and wisdom will die with us," will soon find that they are going to have a very poor time of it indeed. Let them remember the old definition: "A gentleman is a man who combines a high and well-grounded self-esteem with an habitual nice and delicate regard to the rights and feelings of others." Let us admit that this is no easy matter. But as John Stuart Blackie said: "Difficulties are the true test of greatness: cowards shrink from them; fools bungle them; wise men conquer them." And again: "Prudence yields to circumstance; folly quarrels with it; pride defies it; wisdom uses it; and genius controls it."

So far as the keeper in his official position is concerned, his principal neighbours are the shepherd, the farmer and his labourers, the neighbouring keepers, and the townsfolk and villagers. In dealing with these, let us remember that a little tact is worth a world of bullying, a little give-and-take more powerful for good than endless protestation and argument. In all his relations the main point to be remembered is, that consideration for a neighbour's interests is the first step towards the security of one's own. And if serious difficulties do present themselves, say with prejudiced and unreasoning farmers, it is better for the keeper to refer the matter to his master, who can speak and act with greater authority than he, than to undertake a campaign which might make his position unpopular, if not untenable. There is nothing more difficult to learn than the art of correction, unless it be the discipline of accepting it in the right spirit. The work achieved in this direction by the Services and our public schools is noteworthy and admirable. But we must remember that it is only the minority who have served with the colours, or who have learned manly self-control at the great public schools.

Let us take the case of a shepherd or his master, the sheep-farmer, who may have the grazing on a moor on which the keeper is in charge of the game. Enmity or tactlessness can only result in more damage to the interests of the owner of the game than to those of the owner of the sheep stock. A resentful shepherd has a tantalising habit of destroying nests and of making friends with poachers, and, by a curious coincidence, it may somehow happen that he collects his sheep on the very days when we wish the hill to be kept quiet. During the breeding and nesting season, his dog has a habit of ranging the moor, with the result that many eggs are destroyed, many young birds perish, and the moor is generally disturbed. Heather is badly burned : oftentimes butts and springs are tampered with. All of which unsatisfactory state of affairs might have been different if a little tact had been used, and a friend made of the shepherd, and this friendship shown in many little acts of consideration, as helping an occasional sheep or lamb in distress, or giving information to the shepherd as to their possible danger, or as to the whereabouts of a sheep that has gone astray. An occasional present of rabbits—of course with the consent of the master—may also be recommended.

A great number of farmers are not easy to satisfy, and many have been spoiled by rich shooting tenants meeting them much more than half-way. Farmers should be treated justly, yet firmly. In many cases the harm done is overrated, and is used as a threat to blackmail wealthy Sassenachs, innocent of other open-air conditions than those of Piccadilly or the Park. Good relations with the farmers are more important in low ground than on moor shootings. Here, antagonism between keeper and farmer, owner or shooting-tenant and farmer, may possibly be disastrous to good sport. Of course, farmers have no right to enter coverts, if these are, as they should always be, strictly reserved in the lease to the landlord.

As for the farm labourers, they possess opportunities of poaching which render them particularly dangerous. They can with ease set traps, nets, and snares without being observed. Their presence in the fields seldom arouses suspicion, and they may take the opportunity of following the principle of every man for himself, unless a friendly sentiment towards the master and the keeper has stimulated their interest in sport and in justice. Far too little is attempted by the average keeper in the direction of conciliating the farm labourer, either by common sympathy and kindness, or by an occasional present, say of rabbits or hares. The keeper is often too apt to be oppressed by the idea of his own dignity, and to despise the mere clod of the fields. Let him remember that dignity does not necessarily mean austerity. A keeper can be firm, and even suspicious, without being " a pompous ass."

We remember once, at a big covert shoot in the north of England, taking particular note of the relationship that existed between the head-keeper and his corps of beaters—chiefly made up of farm labourers, hired at 2*s*. 6*d*. a day, plus a scratch lunch of bread and cheese. The month was December, it may be added, and the temperature stood not very far above zero. At a glance one discovered that not only was the keeper feared—not a bad condition of affairs—but that he was actively hated. One or two stray remarks dropped by the beaters in highly flavoured Yorkshire dialect soon convinced us of this. As for the keeper, he ordered his rank and file about as if all of them combined roguery with stupidity and laziness. No doubt many of his beaters were brainless, lumbering louts, but it is not always wise in this sensitive world to call a fool a fool, especially if numerous adjectives of a sanguinary and condemnatory nature are prefixed.

Nobody expects the keeper to proceed in this style: " Would you mind, my dear sir, kindly accompanying the rest of the men in beating out this cover?" But there is a medium between this and the not uncommon, " Nah, then, ye ——, stir yer —— legs and look sharp, you —— —— ——." Not only does such gross want of common consideration, such absolute ignorance of human nature—which in all its manifestations has some form of pride and self-respect at its base—tend to the detriment of a particular shooting ; it has in the long-run a damaging effect on sport in general. It is not suggested that the keeper's attitude should be one of obsequious fawning for favour ; but he should remember that, apart from the question of taste, there are elements in society which are daily becoming more antagonistic to the Game Laws, and that there is no need for him to emphasise the antagonism of class against class.

Let it be repeated that on all occasions when the help of farm-hands is called in for the purposes of sport, the keeper should, where such is needed, give the master a gentle hint as to the advisability of ministering well to the stomachs of these temporary employees. Irish stew or hot-pot, with, in cold weather, a glass of whisky, does not cost much, and at most would be but " a drop in the bucket " of shooting expenses.

Even in shootings where farm-hands are not engaged, much valuable information may be at the disposal of the farm servant, and this is likely to be given or withheld in proportion to the popularity of the master, but more particularly of the keeper. Where an amicable feeling exists on all sides, sport is cleared of many of its handicaps. Good relations with the farmer may lead to the latter acquiescing in the desire that he should cut his corn *towards* the cover, so as to keep the birds upon the sportsman's ground. On the other hand, enmity will in all likelihood deter him from assisting the keeper, as, for example, by leaving a strip of uncut corn in the middle of a field so that he may drive out the game that remain in it before the reaping be finished.

A good understanding with the farmer may also checkmate the poaching propensities of his underlings. Despite his powers under the Ground Game Act, hares and rabbits will not be overshot, and orders may be given that the driver of the mowing-machine should keep a good look-out for birds, so that any possible damage may be averted. Information as to the movements and whereabouts of poachers will be placed at the keeper's disposal, and an altogether intelligent interest taken in, and considerable assistance given to, the sporting capabilities of the land. Surely so satisfactory a return is worthy of more outlay than mere condescension or indifference.

Let there be, at all costs, some considerable respect for the pets of the neighbourhood. The keeper should not treat all dogs and cats as vermin. If he does he will not only break the law, but also cause offence to the neighbourhood. In another chapter he will get some hints as to the law of the matter. It is only necessary to say here that, while as a rule the collie and the pet tabby should be respected, no mercy should be shown to the stray lurcher, or that king of poachers—Tom the vagabond. An intelligent keeper will soon discover the ownership of every living creature on his ground, and be able to judge fairly well as to the way they should be treated. There are many other points at which the interests of keeper and farmer meet, and which may suggest problems to the thoughtful man. Those we have indicated may assist him in endeavouring to encounter any other possible clashing of interests in a spirit which combines tact with firmness, and justice with not too sacrificing nor yet too niggling a form of generosity.

Friendship with neighbouring keepers is an absolute necessity where there is much interchange of shooting. In most cases, where an owner or tenant finds a difficulty in getting assistance for his drives or beats in a not over-thinly populated country, he may safely set this down either to the indolence or the unpopularity of his keeper.

It will be to the interests of the employer for the forester and keeper to be friendly, and work together.

If black game in Spring are plucking the buds of newly planted Scots fir, or if rabbits are in a newly planted cover, and the forester asks the keeper's attention, he should at once make matters right. We have known stupid keepers refuse to take orders from a forester who happened to be in charge, there being no resident factor, the result being that the plantations were ruined.

Every keeper who is worth his salt will, of course, soon have a good general knowledge of the character of every man and woman, dog and cat, that comes within the radius of his shootings. He will have fairly well gauged the potential poacher, and know whom to appease, of whom to seek favour, and whom to control. And, of all general rules, he should keep this one foremost in his mind : Let him not make a habit of drinking with his neighbours. There is a curious notion abroad in some parts of the earth that a man's courtesy should be judged by his acquiescence in an expressed desire that he should have a drink. To drink habitually with any man diminishes authority, and no keeper can ever afford to lose that most valuable of assets. No person who counts will value a man less because he is temperate or because he refuses to give way to the harmful habit of promiscuous "treating." The keeper is to be warned even of the occasional glass with the suspicious stranger. If a man must have his glass, let him have it at home, or with men with whom he is thoroughly acquainted—men whom he respects and by whom he is respected—men who will neither misunderstand him nor inveigle him into slackness of duty or active mischief. The man who to-day seems a friend, and is laughing with us, may turn out to-morrow to be a poacher who is laughing at us. There is no law in the country, outside the laws of physiology and the law of any religion he may profess, that prevents a man from taking a fairly good "skinful of liquor," but the general rule must be emphasised—that no drunkard, or even habitual "nipper," can retain respect, and without that priceless jewel in the chaplet of authority, a keeper had better change his occupation and take to breaking stones.

NOTES.

CHAPTER V

POINTS IN LAW A GAMEKEEPER SHOULD KNOW

By H. Burn-Murdoch, Advocate and Barrister-at-Law

Master and Servant.—Fortunately the relations existing between gamekeepers and their employers are very often so satisfactory, and even so cordial, that questions as to the legal rights of parties rarely have to be discussed. It is always well, however, to know the nature of one's legal rights : they form part of the general law of master and servant which may be found explained in many large volumes. Only a very short statement can be given here. As to the contract of service, this will follow any conditions upon which both parties agree, as to length of service, wages, notice, etc. If no mention is made of the duration of employment, this is presumed in *Scotland* to be by the year, and whether by the year or half-year, forty days' clear notice must be given before the end of the time, in order to end the contract. In *England*, disputes on such subjects are usually settled by a jury, and the results of this are so uncertain that no rule can be exactly stated. It has, however, been decided that a head-gardener falls into the large class of employees who are engaged on the common terms of a month's notice or a month's wages. A keeper's employment may be presumed to be on the same terms in *England* and *Ireland*, unless a different bargain is made.

But the contract will be broken and ended without any period of notice in certain cases. These may be shortly expressed as—(1) Disobedience of lawful orders, or want of proper respect; (2) Dishonesty, drunkenness, insubordination, or other serious misconduct; (3) Incompetence, general neglect, or absence from work. Where a servant breaks his contract by some such misbehaviour, he loses his right to any wages for the time since the last period of service, and the date when wages were last due. Thus, if a keeper were employed and paid by the half-year, ending say at Whitsunday, but was *justifiably* dismissed a few months or weeks before, he would not be entitled to any wages for the incomplete period. On the other hand, if *un*justifiably dismissed, he would be entitled to the whole wages up to Whitsunday, even if dismissed months before. The employer must keep his side of the contract by paying the wages agreed upon, at the proper time. He must be a reasonable master, and, for example, must not expect a head-keeper, employed as such, to serve as under-keeper. These principles are recognised by the common law (i.e. non-statutory law) in all three countries.

It would perhaps be harsh to refuse to give a written "character" to a good servant, but it must be said that a master is under no legal obligation to do so. Indeed, he becomes responsible if he does, and, if some other employer were deceived by a false and flattering testimonial, might be held liable in damages for any resulting loss. But a communication regarding a servant's character which a master makes to a prospective employer is privileged, that is to say, the writer will not be held legally liable for anything said honestly and without malice, even if it be uncomplimentary and incorrect.

Should a keeper suffer personal injury by an accident arising out of his employment and in the course of his work, he will be entitled to recover compensation from the master under the Workmen's Compensation Acts if any loss of wages results. Formal notice of the accident, preferably in writing, must be given at once to the employer, unless the latter has full knowledge of the accident at the time. Within six months from the occurrence a definite claim must be made for a specified amount of compensation. He will have no right to compensation where the accident was due to his own " serious and wilful misconduct " unless it causes serious and permanent disablement. It is desirable for the employer to insure against liability for compensation : heavy liabilities may be suddenly incurred without anyone being to blame.

Keepers, like many other agents and employees, frequently have to trade with dealers and tradesmen on behalf of their employers. Tempting opportunities are sometimes given by dealers and others to make a profit by a " commission " or " discount " on the account, or in some similar way. It is necessary to keep in mind that all such secret profits by a servant or agent are improper, and that now anyone who " corruptly " offers or accepts such secret commissions is liable under the criminal law. A keeper should accept nothing of the kind without the full knowedge of his master. He will then be all right, not only with the law of the land, but also with his own self-respect.

The whole subject of game, in regard alike to its preservation and its destruction or capture, is so fenced about by law, that no keeper can properly do his work without knowing at least the main restrictions which the law places on himself and others. Space forbids that more than an outline be given here, but for the sake of those wishing more detailed information a list is given at the close of this chapter of the leading books on the subject. The law on the subject is in rather a confused state, owing to the careless wording of Acts of Parliament. Those who are fond of abusing lawyers and the law should remember that these laws have been manufactured in Parliament by laymen.

Game, in its general sense, means all birds and beasts which are both used as food for man and are usually shot or hunted by man for sport. But the word is also used in the narrow sense of the birds and beasts mentioned in the leading Game Act of each of the Three Kingdoms. These are hare, pheasant, partridge, grouse, heath or moor game, black game, and bustards. (Heath game and moor game only mean black game and grouse respectively.) For Ireland add deer, landrails, and quail. In Ireland " moor game " is also supposed to mean black game and ptarmigan. Many Acts of Parliament use the word game in this sense when they state that the provisions of the Act apply to " game and rabbits, teal, widgeon, deer," etc. By various Acts it has been made illegal to kill birds during the nesting season. A table of the close times for each species of game is given at the end of this chapter.

Ownership of Game.—There is no property in game or other wild animals in their natural state. In Scotland they become the property of anyone who captures them (in the legal phrase, " reduces them into possession "), even if the captor breaks the law in taking them, unless forfeiture of the game is made a part of the penalty for the offence. In England and Ireland the law is more complicated. There, if game is flushed and killed on the ground of one proprietor, it becomes his property. If it is flushed on the ground of one man and killed or captured on another's ground, it becomes the property of its captor. Young game unable to leave the nest, or, at least, the soil of its home, is the property of the owner of the soil. In all three countries tame animals (or those which have been tamed) are the property of the person who keeps them. Young pheasants, hatched from a setting of eggs by a barn-door hen, are considered to be tame so long as they follow their foster-mother. To steal them is therefore punishable as theft, and they do not require the protection of the Game Laws. Dead game also does not fall under the provisions of the Game Laws, which do not make it a special offence to appropriate dead meat. But it is not ordinary theft to take game before it has become the property of someone, that is to say, in the usual case, before it is killed and bagged. This leads to a curious result : if, for instance, a man, passing along a public road while pheasants are being shot on the adjoining land, picks up a dead bird that falls at his feet and walks off with it, he is not guilty either of theft or of breaking the Game Laws. The Courts have so decided in Scotland, and although there is no decision quite so clear in England or Ireland, the law is understood to be the same.

In England and Ireland the property in game is sometimes affected by the peculiar privileges belonging to Royal forests, chases, purlieus, parks, free warrens, and manors. The keepers on such estates have also exceptional powers, but such privileged places are not so numerous as to require notice here.

Shooting Rights.—The right of hunting and shooting game (which is a different thing from the property in the game) belongs naturally to the owner of the ground. In Scotland this right remains with the proprietor, though he lets the land on an agricultural lease, unless the lease contains an express stipulation that the tenant should have the game rights. In England and Ireland the agricultural tenant has the game rights, unless the lease contains a contrary stipulation. This, however, is subject to what must afterwards be said about the

Ground Game Acts, which apply to all three countries. Of course the owner of the land may let the game rights to a sporting tenant, and the farming rights to an agricultural tenant. In such a case disputes may easily arise between the two tenants if either exercises his rights in such a way as to interfere with the rights of the other. The law is, that each is fully entitled to exercise his rights, provided he does so in such a manner as not to interfere unduly with the rights of the other. For example, the sporting tenant must not tramp through a field of standing corn, but he is quite entitled to walk through turnips after partridges, provided he does not unnecessarily trample down the turnips, or go so frequently through them as to damage the crop seriously. The rights of the game tenant (or the landlord, when the shooting is in his own hands) include a right to enter on the land during the close time for game, for the purpose of killing vermin and otherwise protecting the game, provided he does not unnecessarily or unduly interfere with the agricultural tenant. Of course, each case must be judged by itself, but the rule for the keeper to remember is that the Courts will only protect him in his duty if he acts with reasonable consideration for the farmer's rights.

Damage Done by Game.—When a landowner lets a farm to an agricultural tenant, reserving to himself the game rights, he becomes liable for damage to the farmer's crops by game unless he shoots the game regularly, so as to prevent the stock becoming excessive.

This does not apply to hares and rabbits, because all farmers are entitled to kill these for themselves, and by doing so can remove any cause of complaint. In the case of damage by deer, pheasants, partridges, grouse, or black game, amounting to more than one shilling's worth of harm done per acre over the area damaged, any tenant in England and Wales, or Scotland, can now claim an arbitration with his landlord to recover money compensation. In order to do so he must give the landlord written notice of the damage, and of his claim, and must provide sufficient opportunity for an inspection of the damage upon the landlord's behalf before the crop is raised or cut, or if a reaped crop is damaged, before it is removed from the field. There is no right to compensation for damage done by any kind of deer or game which the tenant himself has written permission to kill. This right to compensation is statutory, and the tenant cannot contract to do without it, but in fixing the amount payable there must be deducted any sums-of-money compensation which the tenant is entitled to independently, under his contract or lease. Any compensation which the landlord has to pay under this law may be recovered by him from the shooting tenant.

Farmers' Rights of Shooting and Trapping.—Any farmer or agricultural tenant may also possess such rights of shooting as he has contracted for with his landlord under the lease. Apart from this, the Ground Game Acts give to every occupier of land the right (of which he cannot divest himself) to kill the hares and rabbits on his holding. The right may be exercised by the occupier or persons authorised by him in writing. The occupier and one other person so authorised are the only persons who may use firearms. No person shall be authorised by the occupier to kill ground game except—(1) Members of his household resident on the land; (2) Persons in his ordinary employment on the land; and (3) One other person *bonâ fide* employed by him for reward to kill ground game. The keeper, if authorised in writing by the landlord or game tenant (who has a concurrent right to kill ground game), may require any person killing game for the occupier to produce his written authority. If he has none, he may be prosecuted as a poacher. These Acts also forbid the use of firearms at night (i.e. from end of first hour after sunset to beginning of last hour before sunrise), and the use of spring-traps except inside rabbit-holes. The right of killing ground game under this Act must not be exercised on moors or unenclosed lands which are over 25 acres in area and are not arable, except from the 1st day of September in any year till the 31st day of March in the following year, both dates inclusive, and no *shooting* is permissible on such lands until 11th December—a provision probably designed to favour the grouse.

Heather Burning.—In Scotland and Ireland, but not in England, farmers are accustomed to burn the heather and old grass, or bent, on the moorland pastures periodically. This operation, known as "muirburn," is also beneficial to the grouse, as they feed on the young shoots of the heather or ling which come up afterwards. Obviously a moor cannot be burned without risk of damage to growing woods, etc., by the fire spreading, and the certainty of some damage to wild birds' nests on the ground burned. To burn too large an area in any one year is unnecessary for the sheep farmer and very bad for the stock of grouse. Many leases of such ground in Scotland therefore regulate the amount which can be burned in any one year; and by a statute of 1772 such burning may not be done from 11th April to 1st November in any year, except in the case of high, wet moorlands, which may be burned between 11th and 25th April by the proprietor if they are in his own occupation, or otherwise by the tenants with the proprietor's written permission. Under some farming leases the landlord contracts to do all necessary burning himself. In such cases the farmer is entitled to have a proper proportion burned regularly, and may recover compensation if too much ground has been left under old heather. In Ireland the burning is permitted only between 14th June and 2nd February. In both countries a penalty is incurred if the Act is broken.

A war-time regulation permitted an occupier of land in Scotland to make muirburn between 1st October and 30th April, after giving due notice and taking due care to prevent damage to woodlands. The Report of a Departmental Committee in 1921 stated "that heather-burning has been greatly neglected in many districts of Scotland and that there is much lack of knowledge of the advantages of burning in a systematic rotation." It recommended that the ordinary burning season should be altered to run from 1st October to 15th April, with an additional period to 25th April subject to the proprietor's consent as before. Up to the present time (1924) this alteration of dates has not been effected.

Gun Licences, etc.—These being the leading conditions as regards the persons legitimately on the lands which the sportsman must observe, the conditions in regard to the Government are chiefly contained in the provisions as to licences. The second table at the end of the chapter shows all the licences required in the Three Kingdoms, and the times during which they run. In the remarks following it is assumed that the reader has that table before him. A licence as a male servant is not required for a servant who is *bonâ fide* employed in a capacity not requiring such a licence (as, e.g., a farm labourer), though he should be taken for an odd day to beat a covert or to kill vermin, or to do any duty for a gamekeeper. Similarly, a gun licence is not required by a person sent out with a gun to kill vermin—i.e. animals of a purely noxious kind, such as weasels, stoats, etc. At one time it was thought that rabbits were vermin, but it has now been settled that no one can shoot rabbits, even under the Ground Game Act, without a gun licence. The only exceptions from the need of a game licence which require notice here are—(1) The taking or destroying of conies (rabbits) in Great Britain; (2) the killing of hares—(*a*) in England, by one person authorised in writing by the occupier of the land ; (*b*) in Scotland, by the owner or lessee of any land ; or any person authorised by him in writing ; (3) the killing or taking of ground game under the Ground Game Act ; (4) coursing or hunting hares or deer with hounds ; and (5) the taking of woodcock or snipe with nets or springes in Great Britain. A keeper's game licence can only be taken out by his employer, who has himself a full licence to kill game. Such a licence is not available except on the land on which his employer has the right to kill game. Such a licence may be transferred to a new keeper, if the keeper for whom it was taken out dies or leaves his employment while the licence is current. The officer of excise who issued the licence must endorse the name of the new keeper on the licence before the transference can take effect.

Gamedealers' Licences.—Only persons who hold the licence to deal in game may sell it retail or buy it wholesale, whether alive or dead. (" Game " includes hares but not rabbits). The only persons entitled to sell to such licensed dealers are those who have taken out the full £3 licence to kill game. It is supposed that a gamekeeper holding a £2 licence may lawfully sell game to a dealer on the account and with the written authority of his master (who must have the full £3 licence), provided that he only sells game killed on lands over which his employer has the right of shooting. (The statutory sections, which on this point are confused, are 23 and 24 Vict., c. 90, ss. 2, 7, 13, and 1 and 2 Will. IV, c. 32, ss. 17,

25, 29: see Highmore's *Excise Laws*, 3rd ed., 1923, vol. 2, pp. 155–63.) Another exception is introduced by the Ground Game Act, 1880, in favour of persons killing ground game under that Act, who may sell such game killed by them to a licensed dealer, though they have not a licence to kill game.

Possession of Live Game.—To deal in, or have possession of, live game is an offence under the Game Act, 1831, except that persons holding a gamedealer's licence or a game licence are entitled to possess game for sale alive or for breeding purposes.

Showing Licence.—Any person doing any act in Great Britain, for which a licence to kill game is necessary, must show his licence to, and allow a copy of it to be taken by, any officer of Inland Revenue, or any person duly licensed to kill game, or the owner, occupier, or gamekeeper of the land on which he then is, who demands to see his licence. If the licence is not produced, the person must give his true name and address, and state the place where he took out the licence, under a penalty of £20 in case of refusal or of the information proving false.

Licences in Ireland.—The laws of Ireland in regard to this part of the subject are too complex to be stated in detail in the space at our disposal, nor is this necessary in a book expressly for keepers. No reference, therefore, is made to such questions as property qualification, manorial privileges, and those of " persons not under the degree of an esquire," and, in short, all matters with which an ordinary keeper is not concerned. No licences as male servants are required in Ireland. Licences for dogs must be got on 31st March in each year, from the Petty Sessions Clerk of the district. Duty, 2*s*. for each dog and a 6*d*. stamp on the certificate of registration. A gamekeeper in Ireland, instead of taking out a *licence* to kill game, registers his deputation or appointment (which is chargeable with a 10*s*. stamp duty) with the supervisor of excise within whose district the lands are situated, and the officers of excise thereupon, on payment of the duty (i.e. £3), grant a *certificate* to such gamekeeper to kill game. Such certificate may be transferred to a new keeper if the keeper to whom it is granted dies or quits the service, just as in the case of a keeper's licence in England and Scotland. There is a provision in Ireland about showing a certificate to kill game on demand similar to that in England and Scotland, with two differences, viz.: (1) The person making the demand must show his certificate, which is not necessary in England or Scotland, and (2) the penalty for refusing to show the certificate is £50, not £20.

Rifles, Pistols, etc.—The Firearms Act, 1920, was intended to check the possession of pistols by undesirable characters. It applies to all firearms and explosives, except smooth-bore shot-guns, or ordinary air-guns, and shot-gun ammunition. It is illegal for young people under fourteen to possess, use, or carry firearms or ammunition at all, and it is illegal for anyone else to do so unless he has obtained a firearms certificate. This must be obtained from the chief officer of the district police. The certificate must be renewed every three years or else it expires. A firearms certificate does not dispense with the need for the usual game licence or gun licence. Any constable may demand possession of the certificate by any person in possession of a firearm or ammunition, and he may confiscate these on failure to produce the certificate. In such cases, if a person refuses to give his name and address, or is suspected of giving them falsely, he may be arrested on the spot.

It is not an offence for anyone over fourteen years old, for example a gamekeeper, to carry a firearm or ammunition belonging to a person holding a firearms certificate for it, by the latter's instructions and for the latter's use for sporting purposes only.

Selling a firearm or ammunition to anyone but a registered firearms dealer, or even giving or lending or transferring possession, are also illegal except upon production of the firearms certificate of the purchaser, borrower, etc., and immediate intimation of the transfer by registered letter to the chief police officer by whom the certificate was issued.

Laws against Poaching.—The keeper's legal powers and duties in regard to persons who come on the ground with no legitimate title to be there (whom we may call generally "poachers"), cannot be stated intelligibly without first giving a short outline of the legislation for the protection of game against such persons. For all practical purposes the law is contained in a very few

Acts of Parliament, the first of which was passed in 1828 and the last in 1862. The subject is divided into three parts—(1) Trespassing in pursuit of game in the night-time; (2) trespassing in pursuit of game in the day-time; and (3) the prevention of poaching.

Night Poaching is forbidden by two Acts, which both apply to the whole United Kingdom, viz. the Night Poaching Acts, 1828 and 1844.

For the purpose of both Acts, "night" is defined as the period between the expiration of the first hour after sunset and the commencement of the last hour before sunrise, and "game" is defined as including hares, pheasants, partridges, grouse, heath or moor game, black game, and bustards.

An offence under these Acts is committed by any person who, during the night, (1) unlawfully takes or kills any game or rabbits on any land, or on any public road or path or the sides thereof, or at the openings or gates from any such land into such road or path; or (2) unlawfully enters, or is on such *land* (no mention of *roads*, etc.), with any instruments for the purpose of taking or destroying *game*. Entering land for the purpose of taking *rabbits* is only punishable under these Acts when at least three persons are together, and any of them are armed with firearms, bludgeons, or other offensive weapons. But this does not make it lawful for single individuals to trespass by night in pursuit of rabbits. A person caught on the ground with poaching instruments, such as nets, and charged with being there in pursuit of game, could hardly defend himself by saying he only meant to take rabbits.

Arrest of Night Poachers.—Any person committing the offence first mentioned may be arrested and given into custody by the owner or occupier, or by his gamekeeper or servant, or anyone assisting such gamekeeper or servant, wherever he may be seized, provided the pursuit started on the land. Anyone committing the offence second mentioned may be similarly arrested and given into custody, provided the seizure be made, or the pursuit begun, on the land on which the offence is committed. In either of these cases an assault by the offender on any person authorised to arrest him is a serious aggravation of the offence. A person authorised to make such arrest may, without being guilty of assault, use *sufficient* violence to effect this arrest. In Scotland a person not so authorised would commit an assault by the attempt to arrest, and be liable in damages to the poacher, if he used violence, while the poacher who violently resisted the unauthorised attempt to arrest him would be justifiably acting in self-defence. In England and Ireland the Prevention of Offences Act, 1851, s. 11, authorises any person whatsoever, to apprehend any person found committing an indictable offence in the night; and this has been held to authorise anyone to arrest a person found committing an aggravated offence against the Night Poaching Acts. It is an aggravation of these offences if they are committed by three or more persons acting in concert, provided any of them be armed with gun, bludgeon, or other offensive weapon.

Day Poaching.—Trespassing in pursuit of game by day, i.e. between the commencement of the last hour before sunrise and the expiry of the first hour after sunset, is a less serious offence than night poaching, and the law is different in each of the Three Kingdoms.

Day Poaching in Ireland.—Trespassing in pursuit of game in daylight is prohibited by the Game Trespass Act, 1864. This needs no further mention here, as it confers no special power on anyone to enforce it, or turn trespassers off the ground, but merely provides a penalty for such trespass. The keeper there must rely on his common law right to turn trespassers off the land on his master's orders.

Day Poaching in Scotland.—The law is fixed by the Day Trespass Act, officially called the Game (Scotland) Act, 1832. This Act imposes a penalty on anyone who trespasses on any land in the daytime (as defined above) in pursuit of game or of deer, roe, woodcocks, snipes, quails, landrails, wild ducks, or conies (i.e. rabbits). The penalty is larger if the offender have his face blackened or is otherwise disguised. A man who remains on the high-road may commit a trespass by sending his dog into a field to chase rabbits, or by acting in concert with others who are in the fields in pursuit of game, etc.

A man who has a perfect right to be on the lands for another purpose may be convicted under this Act of "unlawfully entering," if he takes game when on the lands. For example, a farm servant whose employment requires him to be on a particular field to plough, becomes a trespasser if he takes game on that field.

Any such trespasser may be required, by the person having the right to kill game on the land, or by the occupier, or the gamekeeper, or other person authorised by either of them, to quit the land and give his full name and address. If he refuses to do either of these things, the gamekeeper, or other such person, may apprehend the offender and take him before the Sheriff. If the offender cannot be brought before the Sheriff within twelve hours of his arrest, he must be discharged, but may be proceeded against for his offence by summons or warrant. The gamekeeper (or other) may also require the offender to give up any game he has with him, and, if he refuses, may take it from him.

The gamekeeper cannot be sued for anything wrong he has done in carrying out the Act after six months have elapsed since the act complained of.

A trespass to pick up dead game is not an offence under this Act.

Day Poaching in England.—The law as to day poaching is contained in the Game Act, 1831. By that Act a penalty is imposed on anyone who trespasses in the daytime (defined above) on any land in pursuit of game or woodcocks, snipes, quails, landrails, or conies. The penalty is increased if five or more persons so trespass together. As in Scotland, the offender or offenders may be ordered to quit the land and to give their names and addresses, and, on refusal, may be arrested and taken before a Justice of the Peace. If they cannot be brought before a Justice within twelve hours, they must be discharged, but may be proceeded against for the offence by summons or warrant. They may also be required to give up any game in their possession. The persons authorised in England to make and enforce these demands are the persons having the right of killing game on the land, the occupier of the land, any gamekeeper or servant of either of them, or any person authorised by either of them ; or, where the offence takes place in a Royal forest, park, chase, or warren, the warden, ranger, verderer, forester, master-keeper, under-keeper, or other officer thereof. Armed resistance aggravates the offence. In England, persons who unlawfully hunt, wound, or kill any deer in parks or enclosed lands are guilty of felony, whether by night or by day.

The Poaching Prevention Act, 1862, applies to Great Britain and Ireland. For the purposes of this Act, " game " includes any one or more hares, pheasants, partridges, woodcocks, snipes, rabbits, grouse, black or moor game, and eggs of pheasants, partridges, grouse, and black or moor game. The Act empowers any constable or peace officer in any highway, street, or public place, to search any person whom he may have good cause to suspect of coming from any land where he was unlawfully in pursuit of game, or any person aiding or abetting him, and having in his possession any game unlawfully obtained, or any gun, part of a gun, or nets or engines used for killing or taking game, and also to stop and search any cart or conveyance in which such constable shall have good cause to suspect that any such game or such articles are being carried by any such person, and if he (the constable) find such game or articles, to seize and detain them. It must be noted that the powers of search and seizure conferred by this Act are conferred on constables and peace officers only. Consequently, all that the keeper can do to carry out the Act is to give information to the constable, if his covers have been disturbed by poachers, or if he has other reasons for supposing that poaching is going on.

Things Forbidden by Law

What the gamekeeper must not do may be stated more briefly.

Poison.—In all three countries it is absolutely forbidden to put poison in any shape or form upon any land, enclosed or unenclosed. This prohibition is not only contained in many Acts relating to game, but is also extended by other Acts to the use of poison for any purpose—with the sole exception of the use of poison, under very strict precautions, about a house or steading for the destruction of rats, mice, and such small vermin. In connection with this exception, the gamekeeper must see that all precautions are taken to prevent any dog, cat or fowl or other domestic animal, from getting at such poison.

Shooting on Sunday or at Night.—In England and Ireland it is illegal to kill game on Sunday or Christmas Day. There is no such direct prohibition in Scotland, but the Act 1661, c. 18, prohibits salmon-fishing and *all other profanation* of the Sabbath day. This Act is still in force, as regards Sunday shop-keeping at all events, but conviction for shooting on Sunday could not probably be obtained if the shooting did not go on so near to houses or churches as to cause serious annoyance.

The use of firearms by night to kill ground game is forbidden in all three countries, but the Acts forbidding this in regard to other game do not extend to Ireland. In England no one may use firearms within fifty feet of the centre of a public roadway. In Scotland no one may use firearms on, or in, any exposed situation near a public roadway, so as to cause annoyance to any passenger thereon.

The Wild Birds Protection Acts.—One of the ordinary duties of the keeper is the destruction of vermin which might destroy the game which it is his duty to preserve. These Acts, which extend to all three countries, contain three main provisions. (1) From 1st March to 1st August no one except the owner or occupier of land, or persons authorised by him, may shoot, trap, or snare, etc., any wild bird. (2) A schedule is provided of seventy or eighty kinds of wild birds which are not, during that period, to be taken or killed by anyone whatever. (3) This schedule or list of birds may be added to or varied in respect of particular counties. The taking of eggs may also be prohibited. The keeper, before killing any birds between these dates in order to preserve the game, should therefore ascertain, by application to the county clerk, that such birds are not included in the schedule for his county. A Departmental Committee reported in 1919 in favour of considerable amendment of these Acts, including absolute protection, all the year round, for certain rare or useful birds. So far (1924) no change has been made.

Pole-traps etc.—An Act of 1904 forbids the use of pole-traps for the purpose of bird-catching. Every person " who on any pole, tree, or cairn of stones or earth shall place any spring-trap or gin, calculated to cause bodily injury to any wild bird coming in contact therewith," commits an offence punishable with a fine of 40*s*., or £5 on a second conviction. Anyone who knowingly permits this to be done is equally liable. By an Act of 1908, any person " who shall attempt to take any wild bird by means of a hook or other similar instrument " is made liable to the same penalties.

Daily Inspection of Traps.—Spring-traps for hares or rabbits must be inspected by some competent person at reasonable intervals, and at least once every day between sunrise and sunset. The Protection of Animals Act, 1911, imposes a fine of £5 on anyone who either sets or causes to be set any spring-trap so as to be likely to catch a hare or rabbit, unless it is so inspected.

"*Poaching*" *Dogs and Cats.*—The ordinary gamekeeper has no right to kill a dog or cat which is poaching on the land under his charge. By so doing he makes himself liable to have a civil action brought against him by the owner, to recover the value of the dog or cat. If the dog or the cat is in the act of killing a valuable bird or animal, the keeper might be held entitled to kill such dog or cat, provided this were the only means of saving such valuable animal or bird. The cases in which this defence has been upheld are so rare that it would be safer for the ordinary keeper to refrain from such killing. Special powers, however, are given to the gamekeepers of any lord of the manor, lordship, or royalty, duly appointed under the hand and seal of said lord on a ten-shilling stamp, and registered with the clerk of the peace for the county. A keeper so appointed may seize and take for his master's use any dogs, nets, and other instruments for taking game as shall be used within such manor by any person not authorised to kill game.

Similar privilege is conferred upon the gamekeepers duly appointed in the same manner upon any lands in Wales of the clear annual value of £500. By the Dogs Act, 1906, " any person who takes possession of a stray dog " must either return it to its owner, or else send written notice to the chief police officer of the district, stating full particulars, under penalty of 40*s.*

Spring-guns.—A keeper must not set any spring-gun or any trap which might be destructive either to men or dogs, but it is quite lawful to set a spring-gun with a detonating cartridge, which can only act as an alarm-signal.

It is hardly necessary to say that a gamekeeper who fires a gun at a poacher may be tried for assault or murder, as the case turns out. Keepers, like policemen, are sometimes placed in a very difficult position when they have to deal with dangerous characters. The legal rule is strict—that in preventing crime the guardians of law and order must use no more violence than is absolutely necessary for the purpose. But anything is legal which is really required in self-defence, and even the killing of the wrongdoer is justifiable, if nothing else can save the life of an innocent person.

The question sometimes arises how far a person shooting may follow his wounded game on to the land of a neighbouring proprietor. The rule is that he may follow game which is dead or on the point of death. In this connection it may be noted that to enter land for the purpose of taking dead game is not a breach of the Day Trespass Act.

In regard to fishing, the law lays no special duties on the gamekeeper and confers on him no special privileges so nothing need be said on that subject in this chapter. Angling law is dealt with in Chapter XXI.

Separate legislatures have now been established in Northern Ireland and the Irish Free State. The laws previously in force remain operative until changed by local legislation. Up to the present time (1924), no important change has been made, so far as concerns the topics dealt with in this chapter, but changes must be expected. For example, the Land Act, 1923, of the Irish Free State provides that in future statutory sales of land the sporting rights are to become vested in the Land Commission.

Leading books on the game laws in the different countries are :

Scotland—*The Law of Scotland on the Game Laws, Trout and Salmon Fishing* J. H. Tait. 7*s*. 6*d*. Edinburgh : William Green & Sons, Ltd. 1902.

England—Oke's *Game Laws*. Lawrence Mead. 17*s*. 6*d*. London : Butterworth & Co. 1912. *Law of Sporting Rights*. R. S. Nolan. 5*s*. London : The Field & Queen (Horace Cox) Ltd. 1914.

Ireland—*The Irish Game Laws*. M'Carthy Conner. 6*s*. Dublin : Hodges & Figgins. 1891. Supplement. 1*s*. 1903. (Out of print.)

No. I.—Table of Close Times

(All dates inclusive)

Creature Protected.	England.	Scotland.	Ireland.
Ptarmigan.	None.	11th December to 11th August.	11th December to 19th August.
Grouse, or moor-fowl.	11th December to 11th August.	11th December to 11th August.	11th December to 11th August.
Bustard, or wild turkey.	2nd March to 31st August.	2nd March to 31st July.	11th January to 31st August.
Partridge.	2nd February to 31st August.	2nd February to 31st August.	2nd February to 31st August.
Pheasant.	2nd February to 30th September.	2nd February to 30th September.	2nd February to 30th September.
Black game, or heath-fowl.	11th December to 19th August. In Somerset, Devon, and New Forest, 11th December to 31st August.	11th December to 19th August.	11th December to 19th August.
Landrail. Quail.	2nd March to 31st July.	2nd March to 31st July.	11th January to 19th September.
All other wild birds.	2nd March to 31st July.	2nd March to 31st July.	2nd March to 31st July.
Fallow deer (male).	None.	None.	30th September to 9th June.
Other male deer.	None.	None.	21st October to 9th June.
Hare.	1st March to 31st July. (The prohibition here is only against selling or exposing for sale.)	1st March to 31st July. (The prohibition here is only against selling or exposing for sale.)	21st April to 11th August.

No. II.—Table of Excise Licences

Licences Required.	Duties to be Paid for them. £ s. d.	Dates on which they Terminate.	Penalties which may be incurred in respect of them.
1. For each gamekeeper or under-gamekeeper a licence for a male "servant."	0 15 0	31st December following issue.	For not taking out sufficient licences . £20 For making a false declaration, or no declaration £20
2. For each dog above six months old.	0 7 6	31st December following issue.	For keeping a dog without a licence, or for refusing to produce licence on demand of excise-officer or police-constable . . . . . £5 and costs
Irish Free State: For any dog Northern Ireland: "	0 5 0 0 2 6	31st March following.	For keeping a dog without a licence, or permitting it to remain in house . £2
3. Gun licence (only required by persons who have not a game licence).	0 10 0	31st July following issue.	For using or carrying gun outside house, or for refusing to produce licence on demand of excise-officer or police-constable . . . £10
4. Licence to kill game— (*a*) Full period of a year (*b*) To expire on the 31st October, if taken out before that date. (*c*) To expire on 31st July following, if taken out after 31st October.	 3 0 0 2 0 0 2 0 0	 31st July following issue. 31st October following issue. 31st July following issue.	For taking or pursuing game without licence, or for failing to produce licence on demand of excise-officer, gamekeeper, person with proper licence to kill game, owner, lessee, or occupier of the land, or for giving false answer to such demand . . £20
Irish Free State: Full period of a year.	1 0 0	do.	do.

No. II.—Table of Excise Licences—*continued*

Licences Required.	Duties to be Paid for them.	Dates on which they Terminate.	Penalties which may be incurred in respect of them.
	£ s. d.		
(*d*) For a continuous period of fourteen days.	1 0 0	Fourteen days after date specified in licence.	
(*e*) For a gamekeeper for whom the "male servant" licence is paid.	2 0 0	31st July following issue.	
5. Licence to deal in game	2 0 0	1st July following issue.	For dealing in game without excise licence, whether he shall have a justices' licence or not . . . £20 For every head of game sold or offered for sale without the licence of the justices being granted to the seller. £2 and costs For every head of game bought by a person not licensed to deal in game from anyone except a licensed dealer . . . . . . £5 and costs For a licensed dealer buying from other than a person licensed to kill game, or selling without the sign up, or putting the sign at more than shop, or selling game at any other place than the shop where his sign is up . . . . £10 and costs

Note.—The special licensing provisions applicable to Ireland are dealt with in the text. See pages 59, 60.

No. III.—Firearm Certificates

Firearms and Ammunition Certificates.	Duties to be Paid for them.	Dates on which they Terminate.	Penalties which may be incurred in respect of them.
	£ s. d.		
6. Firearms Certificate (required in addition for any firearms or ammunition except smooth-bore shot-guns and their ammunition).	0 5 0	Three years after issue.	Imprisonment 3 months with hard labour and £50 fine. (Purchase, possession, use, etc., of firearms or ammunition not authorised by certificate.)
Fresh renewal of the certificate.	0 2 6	Three years from renewal.	

NOTES.

NOTES.

CHAPTER VI

THE POACHER

In the last chapter we have dwelt on several points of the laws of sport which affect poaching. In studying the various kinds of game which it is the object of the poacher to secure illegitimately, more will be said on this subject. The days are past when a halo of sentiment hung round this law-breaker. Seldom now does he inspire the song-writer or the writer of romance. "The Lincolnshire poacher" and his contemporaries were no doubt men with a glamour about them—instinctive hunters, impatient of the trammels of game legislation, and lineal descendants of a breed of sportsmen—beginning with Robin Hood—that knew not Acts of Parliament, and had no fear of the power of the constable and the police court. But the glamour has passed, like many other illusions of simpler and freer days. The twentieth-century poacher, taking him "by and large," is an ill-conditioned, lazy, drunken, and slinking scoundrel, an enemy to law and order, without a particle of true sportsmanlike feeling in his veins. As a class, poachers are a set of hardened criminals, careless of everything but their own besotted lives. The occasional poacher is a much rarer bird, and is the uncurbed expression of the natural poaching tendency which exists in human nature. He may be a farm hand, a village loon, or even a medical student home for the vacation; but whatever he may be, he is, in the majority of cases, an amateur and not so dangerous as his professional brother, who is a cast-off from honest trades—a grain in the lower sediment of society. He is the friend of no man and an enemy to most, and, in the majority of cases, will be found an arrant coward. Remarkably ignorant on most questions, he is terribly acute on all matters affecting the poaching of game, and coward though he be, may be ready at a pinch to get rid of another life rather than risk his own.

There used to be a popular impression that the best man to secure as a keeper was one who had been a poacher. If the word "poacher" be applied to the occasional and not the habitual offender, there may once have been some truth in the idea. But, for our purposes, there is much more wisdom in the reverse statement—that the best poacher is the man who has been a keeper. A gamekeeper discharged for drunkenness or dishonesty is a dangerous man to deal with, especially if he continues to hang about the district in which he formerly had respectable employment. He is thoroughly conversant with every preserve in the county, and knows to a nicety the habits and habitats of the game in the district. The inference is obvious. He is the very man to lead a gang of poachers. It is therefore unwise to allow a discharged keeper to remain on the property.

Generally speaking, the only way to put down poaching is by firm determination and constant action against the wrongdoer. "Softness" or remissness in the keeper, in overlooking the inroads on his preserves, only encourages the poacher to increase his depredations. The poacher must be kept in order by fear, and not by kindness. With most dishonest people of his class kindness is mistaken for weakness.

Indication has been given in a previous chapter of the line of conduct which it is advisable for keepers to pursue in dealing with men who are potential poachers—farm servants and the like—and it will not be necessary to say more on the subject. In dealing with the professional poachers, individually or in gangs, in addition to such usual procedure as the bushing of fields to prevent partridge-poaching, the construction of wire and bells in pheasant coverts and by pheasant coops, and other forms of special protection, it will be necessary that the keeper should institute a regular system of watching, and a system which is flexible enough to stand modification in time and season. The nesting season, and the days when birds are young, should be periods for particular alertness. A cloudy, windy night should at once suggest to the keeper the idea of more than usual vigilance, for this condition of weather offers an especial chance to the plans of the poacher. The artful keeper should also not get into the habit of making regular rounds—he should vary them daily.

When a district is habitually invaded by gangs of poachers, the keepers of neighbouring estates should work in unison, and should lay their heads together to carry out a joint plan of campaign, to frustrate the designs of the trespassers in pursuit of game, who, as a rule, take to their heels on the faintest suspicion of danger. It is advisable not to give too long notice to beaters regarding the locale of a shoot, as poachers are apt to mature their plans for another part of the ground. Late on the night before, or, better still, early in the morning of the day on which the shooting is to take place, is soon enough.

Finally, let gamekeepers be feared. There is nothing like a reputation for strength to keep off the intruder. There is much to be gained when the keeper is held in awe. To illustrate the truth of this remark, an experience of our younger and more irresponsible days may be quoted. The present writer had a lease of a shooting in the Upper Ward of Lanarkshire, an estate with excellent coverts, in which were preserved a large stock of pheasants. He had been much troubled by the inroads of poachers, and had a suspicion that their boldness was stimulated by the " softness " of the head-keeper. Mr. Gaiters was a mild-speaking, humorous, patient, and godly man, and despite his honest endeavours to get the better of his unscrupulous enemies, the victories were generally on their side. Things went from bad to worse till one eventful night.

The tenant had retired to his smoking-room for the evening, when a servant came running in to inform him that a big tussle was going on at the end of one of the coverts, owing to the fact that a gang of poachers had been surprised in their work by the head- and under-keepers. From the account he had received, one might imagine an encounter of the first magnitude. He was about to set out for the field of action when an eccentric idea came into his brain. He went to the gunroom, took down his gun, put some cartridges into his pocket, and "rushed into the night." As soon as he got within fifty yards of the covert in which the "fun" was proceeding, he loaded his gun and began to empty cartridge after cartridge on to the top of the trees. He could hear the tramp of feet in the distance and other evident sounds of struggle. When he ceased firing, the sounds ceased also.

Another servant at this moment came running up, and then the second part of the *coup* was carried out. A sheep had been killed that very day, and the tenant immediately gave orders that some of the blood should be brought to him. This he mixed with water in a bucket. Accompanied by his servant, he now set out for the cross-roads near to the point where the encounter had taken place. In a few moments the watered blood had been scattered indiscriminately here and there about the road, and two pair of feet began to trample the dust. The night was so dark that the immediate effect was not discernible. Having completed his piece of work, he returned to the house, and, warning his attendant to keep a quiet tongue in his head, retired to bed.

Next morning there was " the devil to pay." An early visitor in the shape of a constable found an unusually early riser in the shape of the shooting tenant, who listened with keen attention to a story of the strange doings of the night before. The constable suspected manslaughter, though no body had been found. The listener, evidently much impressed with the seriousness of the situation, accompanied his visitor to the cross-roads, where already a small crowd had collected, peering into hedges and over dykes to find a mutilated corpse. For the roadside presented a gruesome spectacle. Even the practical joker was impressed by the ghastliness of the experiment. As for the head-keeper, he was quite nonplussed. The fight had been a severe one, but he could not account for the roadside shambles. The constable was, of course, sceptical at his mild protestations, and the crowd voted him a new quality of humour. To cut a long story short, there was a private interview between tenant and constable, and " the smile on the face of the bobby " was partly inspired by the fact that he discerned a new way of keeping the law. The moral of the tale is—that a reputation as a fighting man, and one whose blows do not merely go skin deep, is not an objectionable adjunct of the character of a keeper. There was no more poaching on that shoot for many a long day.

NOTES.

NOTES.

CHAPTER VII

THE DOG—FROM A GAMEKEEPER'S POINT OF VIEW

By Dr. Charles Reid

Time was when the dog was perhaps of greater importance in the field than it is now ; when our grandfather sallied forth at break of day adorned in those quaint and wondrous garments which still excite our admiration, if not our envy, with his trusty Joe Manton, and all the varied paraphernalia deemed necessary accompaniments, and with—by no means least—a dog, most probably trained by himself, from whose prowess and excellence a large measure of his enjoyment was sure to be derived. And in the evening, over his pipe and his home-brewed, did not the mighty deeds of " Don " and " Carlo " figure much more prominently in the conversation than in these degenerate days ?

Most of us can recall and picture the satisfaction of Charles St. John, when, after watching the futile efforts of a brother sportsman on the other side of the River Findhorn, trying to retrieve in vain several active " runners " in a turnip-field, he crossed the river, politely offered his assistance, and, with the aid of his " poodle," brought them to bag. Other men, other ways. Still, the conditions are not so changed that we can get through a day's sport without the assistance of our canine friends, and it is in the hope of bringing their importance still more prominently before a very intelligent class of men that we are encouraged to write these few pages. The average sportsman is a tender-hearted man, of sensitive disposition, and nothing mars the day's pleasure more than the feeling that, owing to having inferior dogs, a number of wounded animals have not been picked up ; and if, as is probable, he be a man who shoots a good deal, he cannot help contrasting the situation with that at such and such a place where he has just been shooting, where the superior training of his friend's dogs was the source of much comment and much satisfaction to the various " guns." How often has the present writer heard in the smoking-room this remark, made, too, by one who, from his experience, was a capable judge : " I have only known three keepers in my life to whom I could entrust a dog to train for me."

This, if true, shows how little the subject is attended to by gamekeepers as a class, and the present writer can sufficiently endorse it by remarking that the attention paid to it by gamekeepers as a whole is far below what it ought to be. He does not altogether blame them, but, on the contrary, believes that owners and shooting tenants are almost solely responsible for this state of affairs. Not one in ten of shooting men takes any interest in this subject, and it has become too common for tenants to depend on getting their dogs from dealers at the beginning of each season, regardless alike of their appearance or their qualifications—in fact, they probably never set eyes on the animals till they, the sportsmen, arrived at their shooting quarters. Still, apart from your peripatetic sportsman, we have a large class who are more interested in their dogs, and who wish to see them not only better looked after, but better trained, who do not wish either to have their sensitive feelings disturbed and their sport marred by the unnecessary loss of wounded birds, or to have their minds haunted by the frantic yells of " Carlo " under the lash, even though the flagellation may be well merited.

Even from a commercial point of view, it is important to consider this question, because the value of game *unnecessarily* lost at the end of the season may represent a total which would exceed many times the value or keep of a good dog.

It is part of a good keeper's duties to be able to train a dog both for the moor and the covert, as well as rear pheasants or trap vermin. But how many do we find thoroughly proficient in these latter arts who have the most elementary ideas on the subject of the former? By contrast, and not by any means in the way of disparagement, we would point out another class, who, with no better material to work upon, if so good, get, on the whole, better results. We refer to shepherds and their collies. We hear of the sagacity and cleverness of the collie, but feel certain that the great majority of gamekeepers will bear out the statement that the average sporting dog, pointer, retriever, or spaniel, is capable of a higher education than his much-vaunted canine brother, although placed, as a rule, under more adverse conditions.

The explanation why the average collie is better trained than the average sporting dog is not far to seek. More work is put on him, but so gradually, that his brain can absorb and remember—he is kept up to the mark by having to do certain things daily, and not allowed to forget; he is not taken out on a string half a dozen times a year and expected to do a dozen different things of which he never learnt the rudiments. Many keepers may suggest: "But we have not the shepherd's time to do this, with so many other duties." Quite true, but it is not necessary. Much can be done at odd times in the spring before the nesting season, and again in the early autumn before shooting begins. A few lessons during ordinary exercise, and at odd times, have a wonderful effect; lessons should not—a mistake often made—be left till the shooting day, when the excitement caused by the appearance of game and the shooting is sufficient to absorb the dog's whole mind. Later on we shall refer to this subject more fully.

For some reason the average keeper dislikes exercising dogs. This neglect is cruel, and accounts for many of the ailments they suffer from. I have seen keepers doing their daily rounds without even a retriever in attendance. This man should not be a keeper.

Exhibition of Dogs

It is not necessary, in a work of this kind, to discuss the vexed question of the influence of canine exhibitions on the sporting dog. Much good has been done by these ; but, alas ! also much evil. The sporting dog, however, has suffered less than most other breeds, and on the whole, in the writer's opinion, distinct benefit has accrued, except in the case of the spaniel breed. This is due to the fact that dogs of other breeds have not been tampered with to the same extent as the spaniel has been by "fanciers," whose handiwork is seen in the numerous grotesque creatures which appear on the bench, and, with considerable difficulty, are able to walk a few times round the judge's ring. With these, however, the gamekeeper has nothing to do. The breed is right enough, but by selection a non-sporting class has produced an animal unfitted for work owing to the exhibitors' want of knowledge and the apathy of other classes. One must remember, however, that those are selected specimens, and that it is possible to find animals of the same breed which are quite fit and able for field-work.

The majority of our judges of sporting dogs are men who are good sportsmen, and who judge the animals from a working point of view. So also are the majority of the exhibitors of sporting dogs. For this reason, the type of our best animals which win on the bench is an improvement on the dog of thirty years ago, and there is undoubtedly greater uniformity. We would therefore advise the discerning reader to attend these exhibitions—not to walk round when the dogs are benched, but to make a point of being present at the judging, to plant himself stolidly down opposite the ring, and to scrutinise carefully every animal in it. If, in addition, he can get a friend with more knowledge than himself to point out the good and the bad points, he will find that his few hours have not been mis-spent, and have their own reward in the future, when he comes to select a puppy from a litter to train himself. He will then appreciate what a heavy-loaded shoulder, slack loins, or bad feet mean in a hard day's work. This is by no means learnt in a day, though some people have an instinctive eye for the points of an animal. Still, the average gamekeeper is an intelligent man, and, given the interest and the fact that the knowledge is going to be useful to him in his profession, he will soon be able to select a dog whose outward appearance at least, fits him for the purpose required. As to the breed of dog, this must depend on the countryside. Retrievers and spaniels are the most companionable sporting dogs. The Labrador breed has been overdone, and the fashion is changing back to the flat-coated retriever; while nothing is prettier to watch than a brace of Springer spaniels working.

Selection of Dog

Without going into unnecessary details, perhaps a few of the salient points which occur to the writer may be of

service in choosing a sporting dog, whether pointer, setter, or retriever. Suppose you have the choice of a litter of puppies old enough to train, and therefore of an age to enable you to judge what the future animal will develop into—ask the owner to let them all run free in a paddock, and carefully watch their movements. Assuming that the puppies are all in good health, not only do you learn very quickly which is the best mover, but you note also the disposition and temperament of the various animals. Look at that bold young scamp, full of life, racing round at the head of the others, chasing every butterfly, leaf, or moving thing, and contrast him with this other timid, nervous creature, afraid of his own shadow. It doesn't require an expert to tell you which will give you most trouble and which will develop into the better animal.

If you find several of the right kind, then so much the better. You can now look over them at close quarters. Let us hope your fancy has a bright, full, intelligent, dark eye. As in the higher animals, including human beings, the eye is a real index to the character. Most judges object to a light yellow eye or a small sunken eye ; and rightly so, because, as a general rule, you will find the former wild, erratic animals, and the latter dour and stubborn. The head should be big, with plenty of room for brains ; one nicely rounded over the skull proper is preferable to an angular shape. The tendency at the present time is to have a long head in all our breeds, but the fallacious and evil part of it is that this elongation is made at the expense of the skull proper. It began with collies, then fox-terriers and Scotch terriers, and has even invaded our sporting breeds.

The moment a dog shows some width between the ears, and he naturally gets thicker somewhat as he gets older, he is supposed by certain breeders to be "past." In the same manner, when he develops some muscle at the sides of his head to use those long jaws, he has become "coarse" and unfit for exhibition. Could anything be more absurd? We, however, have something different in our eye—we require all the brains we can get in our dog, and we are going, therefore, to select that puppy with the big head, skull nicely rounded, with a muzzle of moderate proportions, terminating in a nose of good size and open nostrils. Whether retriever or pointer, we want a level mouth, neither undershot nor overshot—the former condition is almost never seen, but the so-called snipey muzzle is a common defect in our retrievers at the present time, and a bad one.

The *neck* should be of a good length to give "carriage" to the animal, and set on *shoulders* which slope well back, and the tops of the shoulder-blades should come high up and fairly close together. As in a hunter, you cannot, these points wanting, have pace and staying-power.

The *chest*, looking at it from the front, should be narrow; but behind, the shoulders should be deep from above downwards, and the ribs springing well outwards, giving a good " barrel." This should be continued right back to the free or short ribs. If deficient there, and with great apparent length in the loins, you have a " slack " animal, without endurance.

The *loins* should therefore be firm, almost slightly arched, with plenty of room from the projecting *iliac* bones to the root of the tail.

The *thighs* should be strong and muscular, with hocks well let down—neither " cow-hocked " nor bending outwards and short below. If your dog is to gallop freely through heather, or jump a fence—as in the case of a retriever—he must be good in his hind-quarters.

And the *feet*, too, are of prime importance. No matter how good he may be in the foregoing points, with bad feet he will be a failure. See that these are of a suitable size, compact, toes close, not spreading and arched.

The chief points, therefore, to be desired in a working dog are a good head and eye, light shoulders, strong loins, powerful thighs, and compact feet. Given these in our chosen puppy, and we start well with an animal better than our neighbour's, while we hope to make him above the average in other respects.

Training a Dog

It would be quite impossible, in our limited space, to give full instructions on this matter ; and, moreover, there exist so many capital treatises on the subject that it is unnecessary. In our opinion, therefore, it will serve a more useful purpose to point out some of the errors which many trainers make in the training of their dogs, and, if possible, to suggest the remedy. At this stage, we would like to recall to the novice the importance of an aid of great value in the hands of our grandfathers, which, unfortunately in our opinion, has fallen into disuse. We refer to the use of the *check-cord.* By its means the most refractory puppy can be brought to reason in a third of the time and with a minimum of labour, and certainly with greater comfort to the pupil and his master. We shall refer to this again.

" Down " and " Down Charge."—It does seem a simple matter to put a dog down and to keep him there, but in actual practice, what do we find ? Not one in ten will obey and remain till he is ordered otherwise. In the old muzzle-loading days, of course, this was absolutely essential to give the guns time to reload, and, in our opinion, it should still be strictly enforced, particularly in the case of pointer or setter. In training any dog, including retrievers, by teaching him this habit early you obtain a command which makes succeeding lessons infinitely more simple. Begin by putting the puppy down at your feet, gradually increasing the distance ; if he move take him back to the same spot. You may move about, keeping your eye on him at first till you are able to go any distance without movement on his part. On no account must the dog be allowed to move till he gets a command either by " signal " or " call."

The value of this lesson is appreciated when the dog is taken first among game. The trainer must be consistent, and what is at first very irksome to your excitable and high-couraged youngster, in a very short time becomes a mechanical habit. Sometimes you will have difficulty with a timid, nervous puppy in preventing him from running into your feet. In such a case avoid any punishment, but patiently return him to the original spot. If he persist and you punish him, then he probably bolts. Rather than punish, try the cord and hitch it round a peg or post, so that when he moves, a pull in the other direction will show him what you wish.

From this to "down charge" becomes a very easy step indeed, so long as you keep remembering that he is not to be allowed to move till commanded by "signal" or "call." The advantage of firing some caps or small charges during this early training is twofold—you decrease the risk of causing gun-shyness, and you avoid the excitement of inexperience in the presence of game. A very common mistake is to take a young dog to the second part of his education before the first is complete, and to endeavour to teach those primary lessons in the field. This is undoubtedly wrong, and renders difficult a task that is otherwise so simple. The advantages of having a dog which drops to hand or "shot" in the field are sufficiently obvious. In practice, what do we usually find? "Duke" or "Don," if he obeys "down charge," does so only for a moment, and then he is off to have a look at a dead bird, putting up some others on the way ; or the repeated shouts of his trainer effectually do this. In extreme cases we perhaps have a race between master and dog, who is to get the bird first, and if " Don " wins the feathers begin to fly.

Use of "Call" or "Whistle."—We cannot too strongly impress also the proper use of a suitable call instead of the human voice. It is too heart-breaking for words to find a whole hillside cleared of grouse, covey after covey responding to the frantic shouts of " Don," " Don," " Heel," " Heel," or to witness a fine " show " of partridges, which you have with infinite labour driven into the " roots," " clearing " out in all haste at the end. Even more marked is the result of the human voice in snipe-shooting. A dog readily answers, but once he knows its use, if he fail to respond to a second call, a little gentle reminder is necessary. The two most common mistakes made are the *too frequent use of the call,* which causes negligence on the dog's part ; and secondly, *failure to moderate the volume* according to the distance between master and pupil. Naturally, if the sound be used to its full extent when the animal is a few yards off, it does not impress him when he is at a distance, perhaps, of one hundred yards. The most successful dog-trainers whom we have met were very quiet in their manner, and used signs as much as possible—only resorting to the call when it was impossible to attract the dog's attention by hand.

Range.—Most young dogs will run out freely, and if not, then the example of an old dog will soon be followed.

Where many err is in allowing the dog at first to pursue his erratic course, and to imagine that he is hunting for his own amusement, and not theirs. Make a point of starting the dog to range to one side or other, and see that he does it. For some reason or other, many dogs will run a short distance and then turn sharp to the other side, thereby missing a particular piece of ground which you wish them to take. Call your dog up at once, and see that he does what you wish. In the same way, get him into the habit of mechanically crossing his ground thoroughly, and later, when he increases in wisdom, you may permit him more freedom of judgment. Neither is it good to allow your dog to be working half a mile away, either on the beat below you or on the one above, which you intend to take next. By teaching the proper "range" thoroughly at first you avoid this, nor do you find him at the far end of a field of "roots" before you have entered it. The nature of the work required will determine the requisite training: you require a more bold and free-running dog for a moor where birds are few and far between than for a well-stocked moor, or on low ground, where you are working in enclosures. For this reason your training will be different on a well-stocked moor on the mainland from what it would be if moor shooting were on the Western Islands.

Pointing.—As a rule this is not a difficult matter to teach—most puppies will stand on scenting game, and the example of an old dog may be useful. Here the use of the check-cord is of the greatest value, for it enables you to steady him for any length of time you wish and effectually prevent him from chasing birds when they rise, thus rendering excessive punishment unnecessary. A good plan is to find your birds with an old steady dog, which the young one is quick to observe, then with the end of the cord in your hand you " steady " him also for a few minutes—the chances are that he also gets their scent ; then flush your birds, putting both dogs " down," and carefully mark them down. Now take up the old dog, go to the place where you know the birds are, and allow the young one to find them, taking care that the end of the cord is within reach. As soon as he winds them, repeat " Steady ! " or " To ho ! " and repeat the previous performance. Having done this, the rest is easy. Two lessons of this kind are often sufficient, and, assuming that this has been done in the spring, when birds sit so well before the nesting season, it will only require a few points before the Twelfth to produce a dog that is fit to take his turn with the others. The only precaution necessary is not to run him too long and too much. No man can have really good dogs who keeps them going when they are tired—nothing spoils his ranging sooner.

When on this subject, we would again point out the importance of thoroughly teaching a dog those preliminary lessons before he is taken to game. Very little is then necessary before he is fit to be shot over—much less than most persons imagine. Many owners and tenants of shootings refuse to allow their keepers to train dogs on their ground, in the belief that it disturbs and injures their sport. That it does so is undoubtedly the case if a brace, perhaps, of well-grown lively puppies are taken on to a moor and allowed to career wildly after every moving object. But knowing as we do, and have tried now to show, that so little is necessary if the greater part of the training is done, as it should be, *before they see game*, we think that keepers should be allowed considerably more latitude in this matter of taking out the dogs. A benefit to the owner in having better dogs would be the immediate result, with a handsome addition to his servant's yearly income.

"*Heel.*"—It seems also necessary to give instructions how to keep a dog to heel; but again in practice how unsatisfactory is the observance of this simple rule! As we have already pointed out in the abuse of the "call," constant repetition produces neglect to obey. The dog is called to "heel"; he obeys, perhaps, for thirty seconds, till he finds something attractive to his eyes, or more frequently his nose; he is allowed to do this with impunity till a little more confidence and freedom on his part attracts attention, when he is again called to "heel." Few things are more irritating to good sportsmen who understand the "game" than the misuse of "heel" and the abuse of the "whistle"; and if the user is armed with one of those instruments usually seen in the hands of our friend "Robert," then good-bye to a pleasant day's sport. And yet the remedy is so simple —namely, a little suitable reminder, or, in the case of a shy, timid dog, the use of the check-cord till the habit is fixed. The importance of this it is almost unnecessary to point out, for how often does not the necessity of keeping to " heel " arise in a day's sport either to save the dog himself unnecessary work or for the welfare of the sport.

Running in to "Shot."—Of all errors in the training of a dog this is the most common, and probably the worst. Unfortunately, too, when once it has become a confirmed habit, it is almost impossible to remedy it. Of course, in the case of a " setting " dog, it is not usually so marked, because, unless he has been taught to retrieve, he rarely bolts in at once on his game. But even in the case of a setter, it may mean a diminished bag through flushing other birds before the guns have reloaded. By insisting on the " down charge," we find, as we have already pointed out, the prevention; and the sole cause of the trouble is want of consistency on the part of the trainer. On no account should the dog be allowed to move without word of command, and if he does move, then let him be punished more or less severely according to the particular temperament of the animal. The punishment may only be a verbal reproof or something more tangible, *but escape one or other he must not.* Here, again, the check-cord is of great value, and if a dog is interrupted when half-way to his game, the effect is more salutary than a dozen severe thrashings.

Over-training.—Occasionally one sees a retriever trained most thoroughly, who does everything he is commanded perfectly, and yet he is of small value at work. Why? Because he is a machine—the dog has no confidence in himself. If put on to find a bird, he gives in at once and returns to heel; or the moment he loses the scent he looks to his master for guidance. This, of course, is pure habit. Had the dog been allowed to use his own judgment—i.e. had his master, even though he knew the dog was wrong, allowed him to find out this for himself a few times—a better dog would have been produced.

Use of Eyes instead of Nose.—Also a common error made by many. To save trouble, or, it may be, from delight in seeing the young dog carry so well, he is allowed to retrieve what he *sees*—he does this, perhaps, thirty times for once that he is asked to find something which he hasn't seen fall, or, worse still, which is not in his view all the time. Should one be astonished, therefore, that the dog's first idea is to use his eyes, and continue to do so, while that cock pheasant is making tracks for the next county, or that winged partridge has made a dozen sharp doubles in the rank turnips? Had he used his nose at first, he ought to have had that bird in twenty yards, instead of delaying the guns for ten minutes or more, probably losing his game altogether.

Another common fault is in allowing a young dog to run too far out to retrieve his game—he sees the bird fall, and is allowed to go; in many cases he overruns the spot in his keenness. To remedy this he ought to be taken near the place and given the advantage of the wind before he is told to "seek dead." All this should be done *quietly*, and, if too impulsive, he should be cautioned with the word " Steady ! " Undoubtedly some dogs are from the outset better than others at marking birds down, but the chief fault lies with the trainer in not inculcating on the animal this habit of " seeking close " at first till he strikes the trail, and then giving him a chance of doing the rest himself. The less the young retriever sees of " fur " at first the better ; indeed, many good trainers refuse to allow their dogs to touch hares or rabbits for at least two seasons, and the practice has much to commend it. Probably one sees better-trained retrievers at covert-shoots than elsewhere, because, if he is a wise man, the owner does not produce his worst on these occasions, and possibly the temptation to " run riot " is not so great. To make a really good retriever requires much more time and patience than with either pointer or setter. Begin early, but be careful not to put so much work on the animal as to produce an effect such as I have already described under " Over-training."

Temperament.—To be really successful with his dogs, the trainer ought to study their characters as he would that of a human being. Like the " higher animal," a dog has his peculiarities, which must be recognised ; otherwise a half-trained animal, or even failure, will be the result. How often do we hear that So-and-so is a " good man," but very severe with his dogs ? In no litter will you find two alike, and to mete out the same treatment to all spells failure at once. The trainer who recognises this early saves himself an incalculable amount of trouble and produces better animals.

Choice of Particular Breed

It is unnecessary to give advice as to the choice of a particular breed. Owners of pointers advance many reasons on behalf of their favourites as against the various breeds of setter, while the owners of the latter are equally strong on the other side. While it may be that, on an exceptionally dry moor, the shorter-coated animal has a slight advantage, we do not think that this is of great importance ; and fancy may be allowed to determine the preference. On similar grounds decision is usually made between the curly and the heavy-coated retrievers, and between the various breeds of spaniel.

Of much greater importance is it to satisfy oneself that the particular animal springs from a *good kind*, and that from his structure he is fitted for the work required. There is no reason why a dog should not be both good-looking and a good worker. Many of our best dogs on the bench are capital workers, and only ignorance would hold the whole of our exhibition dogs are useless for sporting purposes.

Assistance can be got from Books.—The great body of our gamekeepers are intelligent men, and thoroughly capable of understanding what is written on this subject, and they have scope in the numerous and inexpensive books which have been published on dogs and their training. Unfortunately, the majority are content to follow in the footsteps of the " head " with whom they served their apprenticeship—a " head " who, however capable in conducting a grouse-drive or rearing pheasants, had neglected this branch of his trade. This is not as it should be, and we would again impress on every keeper who takes a pride in his work the necessity and the advantages of being " a good man with dogs." We would advise him to study works such as *Dog Breaking*, by General Hutchison, or *Training of Retrievers*, by Colonel Henry Smith, and not merely to rest content to teach a dog obedience, but by patience and perseverance to develop to its utmost the natural intelligence of the animal. His experience in course of time will tell him that some of his protégés will not be capable of attaining high level ; but he will meet with others which responds, to all his care, and in developing whose good qualities he will feel that he has had a well-merited return apart from the many encomiums bestowed by his confrères.

The More Common Ailments of Dogs

We have not space to treat this subject as fully as its importance would justify. But probably our purpose will best be served if we mention the more common ailments met with in the dog, and capable of being intelligently treated by the average gamekeeper. In this category we include such diseases as Distemper, Dyspepsia, Rickets, Chorea or St. Vitus's Dance, Fits, Paralysis, Mange, Disorders of Kidneys, Heart Disease, Dropsy, Congestion of Brain, Constipation, Diarrhœa, etc.

It may be more convenient at this stage to give some remarks on the ailments of puppyhood, which, as a rule, are simple and not numerous. Many a good puppy is lost from want of a little care. Occasionally it happens that a puppy is born " tongue-tacked," and unable to suck properly, which is only remedied by a " snip " with sharp scissors. The writer also has known a whole litter lost within a week of birth owing to the teats of the dam being so enlarged that the puppies could not get suitable nourishment. This would be likely to happen only in the case of a dam that had had several litters ; and if she brought other litters up successfully, on this occasion the true cause might be more easily missed. The remedy on a future occasion is easily found by providing a foster-mother.

Constipation at this early period sometimes gives trouble, for which a little castor oil is advisable, and it is good practice at any time during this treatment to administer the same whenever a puppy is seen to be restless, whining, or not sucking with the others. The common mistake made is delaying until too late. The use of an enema syringe, even the small glass ear-syringe, with soapy warm water, may be found of great value in an urgent case.

Your intelligent and careful keeper will do much to prevent the ordinary ailments of puppyhood by attention to the dam before parturition, and we would specially point out the advisability of allowing her to run about during at least two weeks before the expected arrival of the litter. If asked, however, to what the excessive mortality in puppyhood is due, we would unhesitatingly say—*worms*. Here, again, prevention is better than cure. See that the dam is treated for worms before impregnation. Recollect, also, that vermin may be the means of introducing these pests, for it has recently been proved conclusively that the " flea " acts as a host during an intermediate stage of the development of the parasite, and it is obvious that both the dam and the puppies can be thus infected. It may be advisable to wait till the puppies are weaned before treating for worms, but, if action is necessary, treatment should not be delayed. The most common worm at this period is the " round " worm, pointed at both ends, whose habitat is the stomach and small intestine. Their presence may be noted in the vomit, or later in the fæces, and it is safe to assume that they are present if the puppy be dry in his coat, more or less emaciated, with abdomen overdistended, and, in an extreme case, taking fits. Santonin is the remedy, given *fasting*, in doses of ½, 1, or 2 grains, according to age and size of puppy. An equal amount of calomel given with it seems to increase the action of the drug, and a similar result is obtained if the santonin be followed by a small dose of castor-oil. If necessary, this should be repeated in a few days.

Rickets is also another common ailment of puppyhood, caused usually by errors in diet and, secondarily, insanitary or unsuitable surroundings. In our experience the mode of dieting is the chief cause, i.e. the food is given in too large quantities and seldom, instead of *small and often.* A puppy, after being weaned, ought to be fed *at least* four times a day till he is three, or even four, months old, and thrice daily till six months. Milk should form the chief portion, and the solids be increased with his age. If skim milk only can be used, then the lack of fat must be remedied by the addition of cod-liver oil or other fat. Where size is of importance, as in most sporting dogs, great benefit will be derived from the addition of a preparation of hypophosphates, such as the popular Parrish's syrup, or chemical food. We would here emphasise the importance of using new milk as much as possible ; no other article of diet can replace it if you wish to do justice to your puppies. The starchy foods, meat, potatoes, etc., may be introduced gradually, but very sparingly at first.

Under the *secondary cause* of rickets we would include a damp or cold bed, want of exercise, etc. But while many breeders consider these as the primary cause of the disease, in our opinion this is to be found in errors of diet such as we have mentioned, though the other injurious influences are often contributory. In many otherwise capital kennels the arrangements for the rearing of puppies are too often defective, and if the owner can possibly manage it, we would advise him to send them out to " walk " at a farmhouse or with a cottager who possesses a cow. At the critical period—between the second and fourth months—the keeper can inspect the puppies every fortnight at least, and remedy any faults in overfeeding, etc. Where possible, also, board them out in pairs for the sake of the additional exercise they got in playing with each other.

Distemper is the greatest scourge of the canine world, and, unfortunately, the treatment is also far from what it should be. Here again space will not allow us to go fully into the matter. As in most things where you find sharp difference of opinion, the probability is that the right view has still to be discovered. Vaccination with calf-lymph has had many advocates, but the balance of opinion is against its being of any value, though we must live in hope that a serum will be found which will do for distemper what antitoxin now does for diphtheria.

We would here point out to keepers that distemper is a specific fever caused by the presence of a poison in the system; that the symptoms vary according to the virulence of the epidemic and the particular animal affected; and that, therefore, to treat the patient intelligently, one must not pin one's faith to So-and-so's ball or powder, but rather skilfully prescribe for each step of the disorder. When the animal is first affected it is good treatment to give a dose of opening medicine, but not a severe purgative; and to feed often with light, sloppy food chiefly of milk or broth. To get rid of the poison is the first essential. For medicine, 10 to 20 grains of aspirin according to age and size of dog should be administered at once; strength maintained by whisky and milk; dog kept quiet and warm; and dose repeated if necessary; or half to one tablespoonful of spirit of mindererus twice or thrice daily, and even oftener if fever is high.

If powder is preferred, then 5 to 10 grains of nitrate of potash may be given at several intervals. In the majority of cases this is sufficient, and a recovery takes place. If cough is troublesome, or the animal be "wheezy," 5 to 10 drops of ipecacuanha wine may be added to the mindererus spirit. In bad forms you may get head symptoms early, when the dog becomes restless, even delirious, and to treat this you may give 10 to 30 grains of bromide alone or with tincture of hyoscyamus, 10 to 30 minims.

Pneumonia is, however, the usual complication in fatal cases, occurring, too, most frequently *after* the acute symptoms have subsided. The ignorant owner thinks that a walk would do the animal good, or even a wash, and the result is disastrous. Prevention here again is the first essential; but if the presence of such a complication is recognised by the rapid and laboured breathing, then apply hot fomentations—remembering, too, that the animal usually lies on the affected side—mustard and whisky. Turpentine sprinkled on the hot cloths may be applied, and if necessary, when the case demands, don't hesitate to remove the hair over that side before applying the counter-irritants. Whatever doubt one may have about giving stimulants at the onset of an ordinary pneumonia, there can be none in this form, and we would give them, freely, new milk and whisky, whisky, port, beef-tea, eggs, etc., in small quantities and at regular intervals. For medicine, strychnia, carbonate of ammonia, etc., have great value, but the former should only be given under skilled advice.

Chorea, or St. Vitus's Dance, is a very common sequel to distemper, and much more intractable than in human beings. When the spasmodic, jerking movements occur during the attack, bromide of potash, in doses already stated, would be useful; and recently salicylate of soda in 10-grain doses, with twice the amount of bicarbonate of soda, has been found valuable. This should be given three or four times daily, and the dose gradually increased. Iron and arsenic later as a tonic, and the latter alone pushed, may cure. Fowler's solution in doses of 2–10 minims may be given twice daily and increased till it begins to cause redness of eyes, or symptoms of irritation of the alimentary tract, such as vomiting, diarrhœa, etc.

For *Fits or Convulsions* occurring in distemper, the treatment already given above under *Distemper* will suffice, as, indeed, in all cases where the cause is not known. The keeper will remember that these are only symptoms, not necessarily an organic disease, and to treat them intelligently he will try to find what is causing them, remembering that worms are a very common cause. Again, if the fit occur soon after a meal in a dog of gross appetite, the treatment is obvious. If in an old dog, and if the keeper has noticed blindness on one side, he may suspect some pressure on the brain from tumour or other cause; and he should find this cause, if possible. Bromide of potash again will be valuable, and may be combined with iodide of potash.

It is unnecessary to go fully into *diseases of the heart, kidneys*, etc., which really belong more to the veterinary surgeon. A simple diuretic, such as mindererus spirit or nitre, is useful in relieving kidney irritation, such as dogs often suffer from after hard work.

Mange.—This malady is far too common in most kennels, especially when one knows that it is preventable. The so-called red, or virulent, form is as easy to check if treated *at once*, as it is difficult later, and we have found the various mercurial ointments the most efficacious. The green oxide of mercury ointment, one part to two of lard, when applied daily, on the appearance of the patch of mange, generally cures, and a dressing of sulphur and oil, followed by a good washing with carbolic or Jeyes' fluid properly diluted, generally effects a cure. Paraffin-oil is also very valuable, but should be diluted with other oil or an emulsion made with soft soap.

Eczema.—For patches there is no better remedy than white precipitate ointment, which may be diluted with an equal part of zinc ointment. If dry and scaly and more chronic, some tarry preparations may be added. The food also should be changed, more vegetables given, and Fowler's solution tried in obstinate cases.

Rheumatism.—The salicylates are now so well known in the treatment of this complaint, that every keeper ought to be able to administer them at once. The salicylate of soda is perhaps the most easily procurable and the most easily administered, both horses and dogs taking it readily in their food. From 5 to 15 grains twice daily, or every four hours in acute cases, will "work like a charm." In more obstinate cases 5 to 10 grains of the iodide of potash, given twice daily for some weeks, is very good treatment. Milk also should form a considerable proportion of the diet, and mild occasional doses of aperient medicine should be given.

Wounds.—A keeper ought to be able to sew up wounds when necessary, and an outfit comprising a few surgical needles, with ligature silk, horsehair, or stout fishing gut, will often come in useful. He should, of course, wash the wound thoroughly with a weak solution of carbolic, Condy's fluid, or other antiseptic, and muzzle the animal to prevent him tearing open the wound.

Inflammation of Eyes.—Inflammation of eyes can easily be treated satisfactorily at the outset with weak lotions of boracic acid or alum—just sufficient to make it perceptible to one's own taste. For more chronic cases, yellow oxide of mercury, 2 grains to an ounce of simple ointment—a small piece of the size of a pea rubbed along the eyelids—is valuable. Here also, the strength of the ointment may be increased considerably if found necessary.

Kennels.—Most of the diseases from which our dogs suffer are preventable. Bad damp kennels are responsible for as many of the diseases as the negligence of the keeper. It is difficult to determine whether to pay the keeper for feeding the dogs by the week, or simply to order in for him a stock of feeding stuffs. In the latter case the dogs are generally sure of getting the feeding (the number of keeper's hens should be strictly limited); while in the former case a keeper often tries to make profit off the dogs, and we have known instances of starving and improper feeding. Wooden floors, which one sometimes sees in kennels for the purpose of preventing rheumatism, are an abomination; they are very difficult to keep clean. The ideal kennel to our mind faces south, and alongside stands the keeper's house. The building, in the particular case in my mind, is surrounded by a wire fence 7 ft. high, covered with 3-in. mesh wire netting, enclosing a small park of 3 acres, where the dogs can have exercise, and into which they are turned when the kennels are being cleaned. A burn also runs through this enclosure, where they can bathe in warm weather. This, to our mind, is an ideal situation.

Iron roofs should not be used for kennels, as they are extremely hot in summer, and insufferably cold in winter. Where roofs of the kind at present exist, it is a good plan to cover them with sods of grass, which in time grow together. Such a covering, with a little top dressing, will last for ten or fifteen years, and will keep the kennels warm in winter and cool in summer.

Poles, 18 in. high and 4 in. in diameter near the gutter, should be fixed in the floor of each run for dogs to lift their legs against. The gutter drained to the lowest end should run the whole length of the kennels, with an outlet pipe which falls into a tank or cesspool with two divisions, the second of which is filled with coke to act as a septic tank. From the top of the second chamber a small fireclay pipe should run to take the water away, and discharge itself at some distance into the ground, which can be improved by a few cartloads of gravel. This will form a second filter for the water before it enters the stream, and will keep the outside of the kennels clean and dry. Water should always be led into the kennels. In each run there should be a wooden platform or bench, 8 in. off the ground, for dogs to sit out on.

A very good plan to stop dogs from the bad habit of wetting their beds is to have a folding lid of light spars shutting down about 1·7 above the bench, according to size of dog, so that there will just be room for dogs to get in, but not space enough to stand up in. If this is done, dogs will not be able to continue the bad habit. The kennels should be scrupulously clean, both outside and inside, and twice a year the inside should be lime-washed with a little carbolic mixed.

NOTES.

NOTES.

CHAPTER VIII

VERMIN

By Tom Speedy

The first essential condition, in order to increase a stock of game on an estate, is the destruction of vermin. As soon as game begin to increase, vermin will arrive upon the scene, although how and from what quarter they have introduced themselves is among those mysteries in natural history which are as yet unexplained. As bearing somewhat on the subject, it may be mentioned that in a recent visitation of a plague of voles, when these rodents threatened to devastate the pasture-lands in the Border-counties, foreign owls—of the short-eared species, which, though an occasional winter visitant to this country, has only on rare occasions been previously known to breed with us in any numbers—congregated in hundreds in the vole-invested districts and nested in the heather. Whence they came in such numbers must ever remain a mystery; but they suddenly appeared. I have noted a similar coincidence with regard to game. I have introduced hares to an island, where they at first rapidly increased. The eagle and the buzzard soon made their appearance, and nested on the island, when the hares vanished at an alarming rate. It must therefore be manifest that a fundamental principle in game-preserving is—keep a sharp eye on the destruction of vermin.

There are few things more interesting than the trapping of vermin, and no keeper will prove very successful in this task, unless he makes a careful study of the object of his pursuit. By keeping a diary in which to note carefully the kinds of vermin got, and by duly recording the contents of their stomach, or crop and gizzard, the young keeper will, with a few years' experience, possess an amount of knowledge which will give him power among his fellows. So much nonsense is written on this subject, that, without practical acquaintance with the habits of the various kinds of vermin, he may be very easily led astray by non-practical writers promulgating their fanciful theories. When man first appeared on the scene there was, presumably, what some are pleased to call the "balance of nature." Man, however, was given dominion over the beasts of the field and over the fowls of the air; and by gradually reducing those which were useless and those which preyed on others which were useful to him, a somewhat different state of things was by and by arrived at.

A few hundred years ago, wolves, foxes, and other vermin were so plentiful in this country that sheep-farming was out of the question. By killing down the wolves and other large beasts of prey, sheep-farming became a comparative success. It was found, however, that a similar crusade had to be waged against birds as well as against beasts of prey. Sir William Jardine, in his "Naturalists' Library," tells us regarding eagles: "Such was the depredation committed among the flocks during the season of lambing that every device was employed and expense incurred by rewards for their destruction. From March 1831 to March 1834, in the county of Sutherland alone, 171 old birds, with 53 young and eggs were destroyed."

Now that in many districts sheep-farming scarcely pays and grouse have become so valuable, it is necessary to cultivate the latter by destroying their natural enemies, in the same manner as it was necessary to destroy the wolves, etc., for the sake of the sheep. Of ground vermin, we have the badger, otter, fox, pole-cat, stoat, weasel, hedgehog, and rat. Among winged vermin we have the hawk species, from the eagle down to the merlin. The game-preserver has chiefly to guard against the peregrine falcon, the sparrow-hawk, and the merlin; also the corvidæ—ravens, carrion-crows, and magpies. There are other species which do very considerable destruction to game, but not on the same scale. Amongst these may be mentioned rooks, jays, jackdaws, kestrels, and owls.

It is with a feeling of regret that I classify the badger with vermin. Being brought up in the historic Borderland, and inheriting the hunting spirit of my ancestors, I, in my boyhood, regarded badger, fox, and otter hunting as the chief end of man. Badger hunts on the banks of the lower reaches of the Tweed are still to me a pleasing remembrance. Of late years the badger has in many places disappeared, in consequence of the common use of the steel trap. Many gentlemen, however, and notably the Earl of Rosebery, are preserving them, and have reintroduced them on their estates, so that it is to be hoped that the day is yet far distant when the disappearance of this, the largest, strongest, and fiercest of our British wild beasts, will have to be deplored.

The ravages of the badger among game are generally confined to the devouring of eggs and the digging-out of rabbits' lairs. Their scenting-power is remarkable, as they dig down perpendicularly to a depth of 3 ft. straight to the spot. I was recently interested in an illustration of their scenting-powers through poison being inserted in a dead hind calf, and placed on an island in the centre of a deer forest, for the purpose of destroying carrion-crows. The water round the island was deep and 20 yards across, yet the badger had scented the carrion, and swam over to its certain doom. This is the only illustration of badgers swimming that has come under my observation. They are very destructive among eggs, and, as a consequence, their presence cannot be tolerated in a game-preserve. I have frequently trapped them with eggs as a bait ; but they are practically omnivorous, wheat in harvest-time being found in their excrements. They are likewise attracted by any sort of carrion.

The otter may also be classified as a poacher. It is generally believed that he preys only upon fish, but instances have come under my observation of his killing rabbits and grouse, especially the former, which fact can be corroborated by an examination of the excrements.

But a much more dreaded enemy of the game-preserver than either the badger or the otter is the fox—though here one must speak with bated breath, fox-hunting being regarded as a national sport. In hunting districts the fox lives the life of a licensed freebooter, feasted on the best, from the farmer's geese and turkeys and all kinds of winged and ground game down to the smallest of birds, and protected even by the " ruthless " gamekeeper. It is quite otherwise where no fox-hounds are kept ; yet despite the co-operation for his destruction of farmers, gamekeepers, and shepherds, he holds his own against his numerous enemies among the barren waste lands of our Scottish mountains. Notwithstanding every device employed, the fox is still to be found in great numbers in the Highlands of Scotland, many cubs being dug out and sent to hunting districts every year.

When a den is found containing cubs, the usual method employed is to bolt them with terriers and then shoot them down like rabbits. Frequently, however, cubs find their way into crevices in the rocks where they cannot be followed by terriers. Keepers conceal themselves in different places and wait till the old ones approach with food for their progeny. As it is the invariable habit of the fox to approach from leeward, and as his scenting-powers are so keen, it is difficult to take up a position. The love of foxes for their offspring, however, is so great that they run great risk to reach them, and, in avoiding one keeper when approaching the den, they frequently go within range of another, and are shot. I have, when watching a cairn, known the vixen steal in unobserved and remove the cubs under cloud of night, when she must have passed within a few yards of where I lay. On one occasion she appeared on an eminence above me, and seeing her outline distinctly against the sky, I fired with fatal effect, though she ran a considerable distance before dropping dead. The piteous howling of the dog fox all through that night is still fresh in my mind. This incident indicates a love of offspring which might be an example to higher animals.

In such circumstances, and where the nature of the den or cairn admits, the cubs can be caught in traps. It is a common method to do this, and as fox cubs are in many cases a considerable source of income to the keeper, I would recommend that a good patent rubber-jawed trap be used, in order to prevent the legs being broken. Any lady can put her hand on the plate and spring the trap without injury. Of course, the keepers have to watch all night in the vicinity to take the cubs out as they are caught.

Trapping is a common method of destroying foxes in mountainous districts. The usual way is to utilise a pool of water, and, making a road into the centre of it,

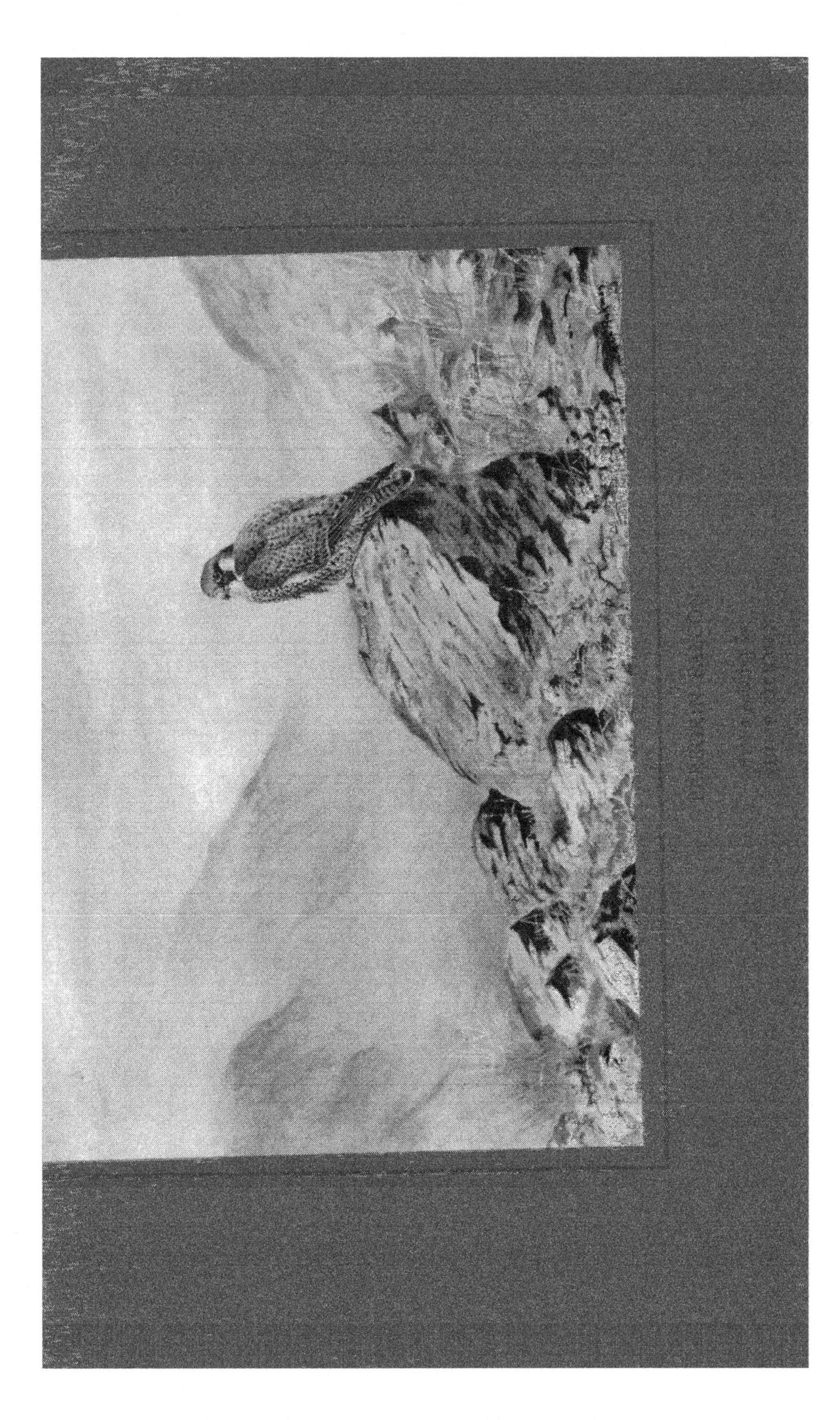

to place a bait with the trap skilfully covered on the road. It is necessary that the pool of water be near a spring, in order that a summer's drought may not interfere with it. Any carrion will do for a bait, and, so far as my experience goes, nothing is better than the carcass of a fox or cat, as reynard is almost certain to be attracted by the smell, and so venture on to the treacherous trap. It may be well to mention here that the traps should only be set for foxes in places where they can be seen by the telescope from a distance, so that the keeper need never go near them except when he sees that the trap has been sprung. The cunning of the fox is proverbial, and he quickly associates the smell of the keeper with the trap, and thus suspects danger. When, however, the scent of man evaporates, he becomes bolder, and ventures to the bait which attracts him.

A successful way of trapping old foxes in early spring is, when one is caught, to take out the bladder, bury the carcass—if possible among peat hags, or in such places likely to be frequented by foxes—make a mound like a large mole-heap for a grave, set a few traps round the base, and sprinkle the contents of the bladder on it. So soon as human scent has disappeared, foxes are certain to pay this mound a visit.

Sometimes a couple of foxhounds are got to scour the valleys in the early morning, in order to take up the scent and follow Reynard to his mountain fastnesses. On such occasions the co-operation of a large number of keepers is secured, and all the principal passes in the mountains guarded by guns. Many foxes are killed in this way.

Another animal most destructive to game is the cat. The wild cat is now so rare that it is almost superfluous to refer to it as an enemy of game. Still, on one estate, not many years ago about a dozen wild cats were trapped. As they were sent on to me, I had them stuffed and exhibited at a meeting of the Field Naturalists' Society in Edinburgh, when I read a paper on Wild Cats to the members. This paper found its way into the newspapers, and endless discussion ensued, when it was asserted by no mean authority that the genuine wild cat has been long extinct, having crossed with the domestic cat, and that we no longer have the original *Felis catus* of Scotland. Sir Herbert Maxwell, in his *Memories of the Months*, states, however, that he had some specimens sent from Argyllshire to Dr. Oldfield Thomas, of the British Museum, who pronounced them indistinguishable from the pure *Felis catus*. As cats have not the sagacity and cunning of foxes, they are easily trapped, and quickly fall a victim to the gamekeeper. The same remark applies to the domestic cat: having no suspicion, it is easily trapped. The destruction of cats by gamekeepers is a continual source of discord between them and their neighbours. Once cats begin to hunt for game, their presence cannot be tolerated, and it is desirable that they be kept down. Great judiciousness, however, should be exercised by the gamekeeper, and when a domestic cat is trapped it ought quickly to be put out of sight and its fate kept secret.

The stoat, or ermine weasel, is a species of vermin that the gamekeeper has good reason to fear. He is a merciless tyrant, a meaningless murderer, shedding blood from mere wantonness. Both ground and winged game fall victims to his bloodthirstiness. Even wood-pigeons are not exempt from his rapacity, as I have seen one in a pigeon's nest 10 ft. from the ground, and watched him throw the young birds over the nest and carry them off. The climbing capacity of the stoat can scarcely be credited : in a pole-trap, 7 or 8 ft. from the ground, on the moor at Castle Menzies, in Perthshire, I witnessed a number of stoats captured. Whether they had scented the blood of birds that had been caught, or by what motive they had been impelled to climb the pole, I cannot say, but the fact remains that the stoats climbed that pole and were secured in the trap at the top of it.

It is bootless for a keeper to think that he has vermin trapped down on his estate ; for the stoat is ubiquitous. Some years ago I collected five hundred stoats and weasels to transport to New Zealand, in order to cope with the rabbit plague. There were no rabbits and no stoats there till man introduced some rabbits, and with the most ruinous results. It was therefore found necessary to introduce the natural enemy of the rabbit, hence the transportation of stoats and weasels. Before they had been long in the colony, it was discovered that stoats had travelled a distance of ninety miles. Their scenting-power enables them to track their prey like a beagle, and I have seen both rabbits and young hares lie down and squeal through sheer terror, before a stoat was within many yards of them. In an instant the stoat would spring on to the back of its victim, and, with that unerring instinct peculiar to the weasel tribe, seize it behind the ear, when, I am disposed to think, in many cases it sinks its tusks into the spinal cord. Fortunately the stoat is easily trapped, and nothing makes a better bait than one of their own species, their cannibalistic tendencies being a gruesome trait in their character.

In the rabbit-warren, in the covers, on the grouse-moor, or by the hedgerows, the stoat demands the vigilance of the keeper. Some years ago a brood of magpies made their appearance in a strip of plantation where a couple of broods of young pheasants had been frequently seen. Drilling holes in the side of three eggs and inserting a small quantity of strychnine, I had them placed in the strip late at night, in the hope that they would be seen by the magpies in the early morning. On going round, however, the eggs were gone, but there was no trace of the magpies. After a diligent search, I saw something white under some spruce branches, and on lifting them, found the eggs, two of them intact and one broken, while a large stoat, stiff-dead, lay beside them. How it had removed the three eggs a distance of 62 yards, I cannot explain.[1]

[1] More than one writer in the *Scotsman* has suggested that the eggs were pushed along the ground by the stoat's forefeet.

The weasel, though smaller in size, very much resembles the stoat. It is also very destructive among young game, and, like the stoat, bloodthirsty in its habits. Recently, while travelling over the moor of Tullymet, in Perthshire, in company with the keeper, we had our attention attracted by the peculiar action of a hen grouse jumping in the air. Approaching the place, we observed a weasel looking out of a hole among the heather. With the aid of our sticks we dug out the hole, and discovered five young grouse, about a week old, which had been killed and dragged in.

Another illustration in point. A neighbour's boy had a pair of rabbits confined in a house, with a brood of eight young ones nearly half-grown; and a second litter, seven in number, about ten days old. Hearing a noise, about seven o'clock one evening, in the rabbit-house, the boy went to ascertain the cause. On opening the door, a weasel made its exit by a small hole, and effected its escape. It was soon found that the entire fifteen young rabbits had been cruelly slaughtered, the speck of blood behind the ear revealing the spot where the weasel tribe, with unerring accuracy, seize their prey and quickly extinguish the lives of their victims. The noise which attracted attention was caused by the old pair of rabbits defending themselves as best they could; but there can be no doubt that had attention not been attracted, they would have shared the same fate as their progeny.

Yet another illustration. While collecting the stoats and weasels already referred to, I experimented with them for the purpose of acquiring knowledge at first-hand as to their bloodthirsty habits. It has been argued that wild predatory birds and beasts kill only to satisfy the cravings of hunger. Experience and observation, however, have taught me otherwise, as I have seen both ground and winged vermin kill for seeming amusement, or perhaps from innate ferocity. Should a weasel happen to come across a brood of young game before they are able to fly, every chick is certain to be ruthlessly destroyed. While experimenting with the weasels referred to, I procured a small-mesh net wire cage, 6 ft. long, 2½ ft. broad, and 2½ ft. high. Into a corner of this I introduced a box large enough to contain a weasel —the box having a sliding door over a small hole. A dozen sparrows were also introduced, and these kept fluttering about the cage in wild excitement. Looking through a window and at the same time pulling a string, the sliding door was drawn open. Immediately the weasel put out his head, while his eyes kept changing to all the colours of the rainbow. His course of action was quickly decided on, and out he bounded among his prey. The dexterity displayed by the little wretch was amazing, as in a few seconds the twelve sparrows lay dead in the bottom of the cage. The way in which he jumped up and caught them in the air proved to my mind the dangerous nature of this class of vermin in a game-preserve. I afterwards regretted that I had not timed the slaughter of the sparrows by my watch, but I saw enough to convince me that the gamekeeper who neglects the trapping of weasels is " not worth his salt."

Recently I observed a weasel with something in his mouth, the brilliant yellow hues of which excited my curiosity. Giving chase, he soon dropped the object, and on picking it up, it turned out to be a frog which he had killed. This is the only occasion I have known a weasel to kill a frog.

Most keepers who have had experience in rearing pheasants are aware of the bloodthirsty habits of the weasel when it finds its way into the rearing-field. As an invariable rule, precautionary measures should be adopted by having traps set in every likely spot around. Care must be taken, when the pheasant-chicks extend their rambles, that small conduits are made with stones, in which the traps should be placed, in order to secure immunity from the danger of the birds getting into them. Weasels are easily trapped, and nothing keeps them down better than rabbit-trapping, as they are frequently caught in running in and out of rabbit-holes. Where stoats and weasels abound, it is most desirable to have a few flat stones or flags in suitable places, propped up by pieces of stick set with the old figure-of-four trap. The slightest disturbance fetches the flag down, and the victim is at once crushed to death.

The hedgehog is another species of vermin destructive to game. Its depredations are chiefly confined to nest-harrying. The amount of mischief done in a game-preserve by hedgehogs is great. Again and again I have trapped them, using eggs as a bait, and have seen one in a pheasant's nest devouring the eggs. This was on the Ladykirk estate, in Berwickshire. The hen was sitting by the roadside, where she was seen daily by passers-by "in the know." On nearing the spot one evening, my attention was attracted by seeing the pheasant flying, or rather jumping up, flapping her wings, and making a chirring noise. On going forward, I found the eggs scattered in all directions, and some of them smashed in the scuffle, while a hedgehog was regaling himself in the nest. Discovering my presence, he gradually curled himself into a bristly ball ; but, needless to say, he got short shrift.

The hedgehog has been known to kill very young hares and rabbits, and even half-grown pheasants. Not only so, but it has frequently been found entering coops and killing barn-door hens while these were acting as foster-mothers to young pheasants. The hedgehog's staple foods are snails, slugs, and beetles, but, as already mentioned, it is fond of flesh and eggs. Many people assert that it devours fruit, but, so far as my experience goes—and I have dissected the stomachs of a large number—it does not eat anything of a vegetable nature except small quantities of grass, which, I presume, are swallowed when it is grubbing for beetles among the roots.

Another enemy of game is the rat. After the rat is full-grown it acquires an appetite for flesh, and kills any young game it may come across, whether this be winged or four-footed. Rats are becoming a much more formidable enemy of the game-preserver than they used to be, as now they are burrowing more in hedgerows, so that it is difficult for partridges to nest and successfully hatch their young. The reason for this is obvious : the modern use of cement has quite baffled them in trying to undermine granary and stable floors ; while sewer-pipes have displaced old-fashioned conduits, so that they no longer find farm-steadings a congenial home. They therefore take possession of rabbit-holes, where, in many cases, they are allowed to harbour and breed without restraint. Prior to the passing of the Ground Game Act, rabbits were in most cases killed by the use of traps, with the result that many rats were secured. Nowadays, rabbits on a farm are generally let to professional rabbit-catchers, who kill them in a simpler way, namely, by snares, with the result that rats get off scot-free. A large East Lothian farmer who had the shooting on his farm, informed me that he would not allow a snare to be set. In trapping the rabbits the previous year, the man he employed caught 114 large rats. What the result would have been had these rats been allowed to remain and breed, it is not difficult to imagine. No effort should therefore be spared in order to kill down this species of vermin.

Game also suffers, though not to a large extent, from adders. I have seen one kill very young grouse and black game. On dissection I have found that another had swallowed three nearly-fledged larks. As the hand of everyone is against adders, nobody misses a chance of killing them. As an incentive, the payment of one shilling for every adder's tail is a good plan, and generally yields favourable results among shepherds and keepers.

At the head of the list of birds of prey stands the golden eagle. As already said, this bird has suffered much persecution on account of its depredations among lambs, and is now so scarce that many of our largest proprietors are preserving it. It is gratifying to all lovers of natural history that this should be so. At the same time, a pair of eagles do incalculable damage to a grouse moor, and more especially a driving moor. I have frequently seen drives destroyed by an eagle crossing the moor in aerial circles in the distance. The circumstance of their flying about drives the grouse from that locality, as they shrewdly regard the presence of the eagle to be incompatible with their security.

Some years ago I introduced seventeen mountain hares, from Dalnaspidal and Castle Menzies moors in Perthshire, to Hoy, the loftiest isle of the Orcadian Archipelago. Being very prolific, the hares soon increased to considerable numbers, when a pair of eagles made their appearance and nested in the Kame Rock, at the north end of the island. They had long before deserted Hoy as a nesting-place, but the introduction and increase of hares again attracted them to this rock-bound island. The hares were quickly decimated, yet the proprietor continued anxious that the eagles should there find a congenial home.

Whether by unscrupulous egg-collectors who regularly visit Orkney, or by farmers enraged at the loss of their lambs, it is difficult to say, but the fact remains that eagles' nests are systematically robbed in Hoy. Recently, however, a pair nested in a perpendicular precipice near the crofter township of Rackwick, where they hatched their eggs and reared their young in safety. But it is difficult to preserve eagles where farmers, shepherds, and egg-collectors have access to the eyrie. It is therefore only in those wildernesses which are afforested that the species can be preserved in this country, as there they are allowed to harbour and breed without restraint.

It is now some years since a pair of eagles nested on sheep ground outside the deer forest of Strathconan, at that time the property of Mr. (now Earl) Balfour. As a number of lambs had disappeared during the previous year, and an eagle had even been seen in the act of carrying one off, the farmer vowed vengeance upon these robbers of his flock. After a number of such depredations, it was at last reluctantly agreed to destroy the eagles. Being consulted in the matter, I suggested that if we could manage to rob the nest, the parents could be spared, seeing it is only when they have to provide for their progeny that they carry off lambs.

The keepers thought that to rob the nest was impossible, as the eyrie was in an inaccessible rock. However, taking with us a cart-rope, we wended our way towards the place. Getting above the eyrie, I tied one end of the rope round my waist and prepared to descend. Though very steep, we all managed to get down to a birch tree, to which my companions fastened the other end of the rope, in order partly to relieve them of the strain of my weight. I then managed to crawl feet foremost to the edge of the precipice, where I could see the sticks on the outer edge of the nest, though to reach it some 10 ft. of sheer descent intervened. On being let over, I looked like Mohammed's coffin, suspended between heaven and earth. The rope now assumed a rotary motion which for me was anything but pleasant. Reaching the ledge, I called up to slacken the rope, and proceeded to examine the place, which went some distance backwards, forming a sort of cavern. Closely cuddled together were two little downy eaglets, evidently only a day or two hatched. Exploring the cavern, I saw what was evidently the larder of previous years, as the bleached remains of lambs, red-deer calves, hares, rabbits, grouse, black game, ducks, etc., lay all around in profusion ; while a newly-killed grouse, neatly plucked and partly devoured, lay near the nest, doubtless supplying the rusks of eagle babyhood.

Putting an eaglet in each coat-pocket, I hallooed to be hauled up. This was by no means a pleasant process, as I was several times roughly jolted against the rock, with the result that the little eaglets were both crushed to death. They may, however, still be seen as stuffed specimens in the Royal Scottish Museum. I am no advocate for the destruction of eagles, but, being gluttonous birds, they are frequently captured in traps set for foxes.

Next to the eagle the buzzard is the largest bird of prey in this country. It lives a good deal on carrion, and, as a consequence, is easily trapped. It, however, kills grouse, as I have found their legs and feet beside a buzzard's nest. How it seizes them I have never been able to understand, but I imagine it must snatch them off the nest, as never to my knowledge has a buzzard been seen in pursuit of grouse on the wing. Judging from the castings of the young birds at the nest, the buzzard preys largely upon rabbits, leverets, mice, moles, beetles, and caterpillars. As mentioned, however, I have seen the remains of grouse at their eyries. At the same time, the buzzard is not very destructive to winged game, so that, as with the kite and hen-harrier, which are both now rare, I do not urge its extermination.

The peregrine falcon is a very difficult bird to deal with, as it generally nests in inaccessible precipices out of reach of the keeper. As it scorns to be attracted by any bait unless killed by itself, it is exceedingly difficult to get rid of this most dreaded enemy of grouse. I know of places where peregrines breed, and even if one is shot off her eggs, the male immediately starts in search of another mate. I have known five hen birds killed out of the same nest in succession, so mates must be plentiful somewhere. When they are allowed to rear their young, a heavy toll is taken from the grouse on the surrounding moor. The fastest cock grouse that ever flew has no more chance before the peregrine than a rat has before a terrier in an open field.

Only those who have concealed themselves near the eyrie of this bird, and with a telescope watched the number of victims brought to the nestlings, have any conception of the havoc it commits among winged game. I once sat for hours with a glass and watched what was carried to the eyrie by the peregrine. In five hours I saw five grouse brought, and it was interesting to note how dexterously the male bird transferred them to his mate, which flew out of the eyrie and met him in mid-air. When the young are able to use their wings, they fly out and snatch the prey from their parents in the same manner. Notwithstanding the depredations among grouse, when in coveys, by the peregrine when providing for its nestlings, it is in the spring months that most damage is done, as it then breaks up the pairs, and it is almost certain that either the cock or the hen of the pair attacked will fall a victim.

The peregrine falcon is by far the noblest and most dashing of our British birds of prey. He is a bold and pitiless marauder, and Highland lairds will never know what rentals their estates can realise so long as this merciless tyrant among grouse life is allowed to harbour. Endless discussion has from time to time taken place in the columns of sporting and other papers between falconers, naturalists, sportsmen, and keepers, as to how a falcon strikes his prey. Falconers determinedly adhere to the theory that it is done by means of the talons. It is difficult to reconcile this with the fact that some of the victims have not even a scratch on them—

only a blue mark on the spine, the result of a severe blow. One can hardly understand how this blow could be struck by those terrible talons, at the terrific pace of a falcon swoop, without the skin being broken. At other times, when making a quarry, the peregrine cuts the head clean off his victim, the head and body being sometimes found yards apart. Sometimes the head is found hanging to the body by a bit of skin.

Most keepers of my acquaintance who have spent their lives among the mountains are agreed that the peregrine strikes with his wing. Falconers, on the other hand, deny this, and, as has been said, assert that the blow is struck with his talons. Their experience, however, is unfortunately only derived from birds kept in confinement. It has been noted by careful observers that when young peregrines begin to hunt for themselves, they clutch their prey; but, as can easily be understood, it would be dangerous to clutch and "bind" to a heavy bird such as a blackcock or a duck flying at its utmost speed, and they soon give up clutching. I have myself seen a blackcock, several grouse, a golden-eye drake, and a mallard, struck down by the peregrine, the victims in every case being dead except the last mentioned, which was only stunned, and flew off when approached. Major Morant, who spent ten years of his life in the wilds of Ardnamurchan, after describing birds killed in the air by wild hawks, says: "The grand sudden death of these birds is certainly very different to the descriptions one reads of the way tame hawks take herons. After getting above them, they seem to settle on their backs (binding is, I believe, the correct term), and they descend to the earth together, scratching and fighting like a bagful of cats."

Mr. Knox, in his charming book, *Game Birds and Wild-Fowl*, says: "It is because the breast-bone of the hawk is protected with such strong pectoral muscles that the concussion which deprives its victim of life can have no injurious effect upon the author of the momentum which causes the injury."

How, then, are peregrines to be got rid of? This is the question pressing for solution, on a moor where they take up their abode. Preparatory to nesting, these birds are sometimes seen flying about the top of a cliff. I have recommended a number of cairns to be built with stones to a height of from 4 to 5 ft., so as to be out of the way of sheep—these cairns to taper at the top, and be capped with a turf or divot, in which a hole could be cut out. When a trap was placed in this hole and covered as carefully as possible, it was found that the peregrine was frequently caught. I have known many peregrines killed in this manner. As these traps were generally set in high altitudes, exposed to the sweeping blasts, there was difficulty in keeping them covered with earth or other suitable material. The peregrine is a cute bird, hence the necessity for careful covering.

To see the falcon "making a quarry" is something to be remembered. He is, however, a meaningless murderer, shedding blood from mere wantonness. I have seen him strike down a blackcock and continue his flight without taking the trouble to look after his fallen victim. Few have the slightest idea how destructive he is. As is well known, grouse indigenous to Britain sometimes realise a pound per brace, and shooting rents pay a large percentage of local taxes. The peregrine pays neither rent nor taxes, but it would be interesting to ascertain how many grouse one pair annually destroy. This will never be ascertained, as every grouse killed between February and June means the destruction of a covey; and, as already mentioned, I have seen them, when catering for their young, bring five grouse to one eyrie in five hours. At Rackwick, in Hoy, the peregrine frequently swoops down and carries off domestic chicks close to the cottages. Would any lover of birds tolerate this? Much as this dashing bird of prey may be admired, its presence must be regretted, though, with such spots as the stupendous cliffs of Hoy to breed in, it will probably baffle human ingenuity to get rid of the species.

The sparrow-hawk, the merlin, and the kestrel are the only other birds of prey it is necessary to refer to here, other species being now regarded as *raræ aves*.

The two first mentioned are both very destructive among young game, and it is most essential that they should be kept down. Sparrow-hawks are exceptionally destructive, and whenever they make their appearance in the "warbling grove it is only for the purpose of depredation, and they are gloomy intruders on the general joy of the landscape." I have found the remains of over twenty young pheasants at the nest of a sparrow-hawk. I have frequently seen it carrying off blackbirds and thrushes, and it was painful to hear the piteous screams of the victims, as they were borne off in the cruel talons of the hawk. It will thus be seen that the successful rearing of game is impossible when this bird is allowed to exist. The vigilance of the keeper is therefore necessary to find out the nesting-place. When this is accomplished the destruction of the pair of birds is a simple matter. To put the hen bird off the nest, then conceal oneself within range and shoot her as she returns, is the general mode of procedure. If this can be done at night, so much the better, as, by being in concealment before daylight the following morning, the cock bird will make his appearance, generally affording an easy shot. Many prefer to trap the cock bird on the nest, which is easily done. On dissecting the last sparrow-hawk I shot, the crop was found to contain the entire wing and other parts of a young grouse, while in the gizzard were the remains of small birds and other matter partly assimilated.

Though this hawk skims along and seizes birds as above described, it also lifts its quarry from the ground, but, with the exception of carrying off young pheasants in the rearing-field, it is seldom seen in the act. I have, however, witnessed it strike down a wood-pigeon after the manner of a falcon. In this instance the pigeon was flying across a field, when the hawk dashed down with lightning speed on its victim. I saw the hawk distinctly for a hundred yards before it struck. It is difficult adequately to describe its mode of attack, further than to say that the hawk assumed the shape of a wedge, the wings being taut "as sails filled with a stiff breeze." In an instant the blow was given, a cloud of feathers flew from the pigeon, and it fell lifeless to the ground. On my running up and hallooing, the hawk flew off. Picking up the pigeon and plucking it, not a scratch was visible; but death was evidently due to what appeared to be a severe bruise along the backbone. Those who have noted the sharp claws of the sparrow-hawk will have difficulty in believing that the blow is struck with them; otherwise some part of the skin must necessarily be torn.

The merlin—the smallest British bird of prey—is a handsome creature. It is, however, a merciless tyrant among small birds and young game, and its presence cannot be permitted by the game-preserver. Though destructive to game, it is more of a small-bird destroyer, and a pair of merlins are computed to kill a thousand birds in a year, including, of course, those carried to their young. I have never seen a merlin kill a bird larger than a thrush, but Major Morant says: "We once put up a hen grouse in the month of February, which was immediately pursued by a merlin. On coming over a ridge which had concealed the birds from our view, the merlin rose from the heather; and on going to the spot we picked up the grouse, which died in our hands. The grouse weighed twenty-four ounces. The skin was not broken, but she had a tremendous bruise over the spine." The merlin, as far as my experience goes, breeds on the ground, generally in the bank of a gully in the open. It is asserted that it occasionally breeds in rocks and trees, but this has never come under my observation.

The kestrel is the most common of our British hawks. He is a pretty object, for who does not love to see him hover? I am unwilling to shoot kestrels, as in the crop and gizzard of those I have killed I have found that mice, beetles, and caterpillars were usually present. It cannot be denied, however, that when catering for their hungry nestlings young game are carried off in large numbers. That distinguished naturalist, the late Duke of Argyll, instructed his keepers not to kill kestrels, as they were harmless to game. His Grace, however, changed his mind on the head-keeper showing him the remains of many grouse at a kestrel's nest. When the kestrel makes a practice of visiting a field where pheasants are being reared, he is even worse than the sparrow-hawk. The latter comes at pretty regular intervals, and the keeper can depend upon his coming. Unless he be fired at, he will return to the same part of the field, frequently to the same coop, so that, as a rule, he is easily shot. The kestrel, however, is quite different in his habits. He may come twice within an hour, and perhaps not for a day or two. He is much more wary, perches on a tree and surveys the scene, or hovers to mark his prey, darts upon it with unerring aim, and is then off like an arrow. The least movement alarms him, and he suspects any unusual object. If fired at and missed, it takes some ingenuity to get him. Fortunately, he does not take young pheasants after they are about a fortnight old, in this being unlike the sparrow-hawk, which takes them till they are as large as he is fit to carry. Still, I do not advocate the destruction of this beautiful bird. Let the keeper find the nest, watch what is brought to it, and use his judgment as to whether or not the death-warrant should be pronounced.

It is because some naturalists attempt too much that they are not listened to. What is the good of talking to ignorant keepers, and asserting that kestrels do no harm to game, when most of these men have shot them in the act?

The raven is the largest of the corvidæ, and well known for its cruel rapacity on sheep farms. It is not uncommon to find the eyes of sheep and lambs pecked out, on the hills where these birds are allowed to exist. They are by no means so scarce as people believe, being still found in large numbers in the mountainous districts of Scotland. I have a couple of them as pets, and dirtier or more cruel ones I never possessed. Strange to say, some of our County Councils are protecting ravens, which act savours of ignorance on their part as to the habits of these birds. Ravens nest very early, and with their young broods may be seen flying about from daylight till dark. Indeed, it is surprising how anything escapes them. I have seen a brood of ptarmigan, while enjoying themselves on the mountain-tops, suddenly attacked by these sable butchers. The peculiar cry of the old birds, as they tried to lure the ravens away, was of no effect. The young brood squatted out of sight as best they could, but the keen eyes of the ravens soon discovered them, and the helpless ptarmigan were duly gobbled up. I managed to shoot one as they circled near my place of concealment, and in the gizzard I found a brace of young ptarmigan which had been swallowed whole. The same tactics are followed with a covey of grouse, and it is easy to see that a heavy toll must be taken by ravens in those districts where they abound.

A curious but none the less popular belief regarding the raven ascribes to these historic birds the credit of having fed the prophet Elijah in his hiding-place "by the brook Cherith that is before Jordan." The story that the raven, of all birds of prey, should have shown humanitarian instincts has not seemed too strange to be imparted to children with that delightful simplicity which characterises many a mother with her child on her knee. As a matter of fact, it is established that the "ravens" who fed Elijah were a wild tribe of Bedouins inhabiting the deserts of the Jordan Valley. This dark and cruel race were famed for their mercilessness towards captives. It was naturally a matter of popular astonishment that these desert nomads should not merely have spared the man of God, but provided him with bread and meat, morning and evening.

The writer has seen this tribe. They are called the "Ravens" to this day.

The hoodie-crow and the carrion-crow may be bracketed with the raven as enemies of game. The destruction to grouse eggs by these birds is incalculable. Sometimes a hoodie's nest will escape the vigilance of the keeper. In such a case I have seen the shells of hundreds of grouse eggs at a spring a short distance from the nest. It will thus be evident how impossible it is for game to be reared with carrion-crows in the district. Young grouse are picked up by these birds, even after they are half-grown. I have seen a pair of hoodies endeavouring to get at young grouse which were pretty well grown, and had got their tail feathers. So resolute were the savage birds in their purpose, that they never observed me, though I was concealed within forty yards. The old grouse succeeded in driving the crows off before they got a young one. The siege continued for fully twenty minutes, when one of the crows, in circling round, at last got his eye on me, and uttered that peculiar call of his mate; and then they both quickly winged their way up the glen. On going to the spot, I found a lot of feathers lying about, and certainly, but for my presence, they would have succeeded in their merciless work.

Setting the game-preserver aside, the destruction of these birds is necessary in the interest of the stock-farmer. Recently, on the farm of Cardon, in Peeblesshire, shortly before lambing, a blackfaced ewe had both her eyes pecked out by a hoodie-crow. Fortunately she was discovered alive, and with careful nursing the animal recovered and gave birth to a lamb, which she successfully reared. When the shepherd called her, it was interesting to see her run and eat porridge out of a basin. Writing on a subsequent occasion, the owner of the ewe said: "This spring a blackfaced ewe hogg has been treated in the same barbarous way, and had to be destroyed."

The magpie feeds much in the same manner as the hoodie, though it searches amongst underwood more, in order to get at the nests of small birds. The nests of the pheasant and partridge are very frequently discovered by the magpie's sharp, piercing eyes, after which shells will be found minus the contents. The vigilance of the keeper should never relax so long as his ground is infested by any of the corvidæ species. Though he should manage to shoot the hen bird off her nest, he must not imagine that he has destroyed the brood for that year. Another mate will soon be found, and hatching will go on. I have repeatedly shot a magpie off her eggs, and in a few days a second one shared the same fate. There appears to be a registry for unmarried magpies somewhere, as no sooner is one shot than another is secured, and domestic arrangements go on as before.

A pair of magpies nested in a tree close to my home. When the process of hatching was commenced, I had the bird disturbed and shot as she flew from the nest. Early the following morning, a number of magpies appeared, and a great deal of hilarious chattering around the nest indicated to my mind that, in " pyet " language, a wedding was going on. The hilarity was brought to a sudden termination by a shot from the centre of a holly bush, when they quickly dispersed, minus one, which fell to the ground. This continued in the early morning for a week, during which no fewer than six magpies were secured. Though I have all my life trapped crows and magpies with bits of rabbit and other flesh, I have found that eggs have an irresistible attraction for these birds.

With regard to owls, much diversity of opinion exists as to the damage they do to game. Many naturalists declare that they are perfectly harmless, but, as the result of practical observation, I fearlessly assert that they are wrong. I would not shoot an owl on any consideration, and they are in great numbers at my home, where they breed in holes in the old trees. (The tawny species is here referred to.) At the same time, were pheasants or partridges being reared, or a large head of game expected owls would not receive the same generous treatment. In Sir Herbert Maxwell's book already alluded to, the *Memories of the Months*, when writing on owls the author dwells at considerable length on the habits of these birds. Much as I respect this distinguished writer, I regret that, as a Scotsman, he does not give us the result of practical observation in his native country. Instead of this, he prefers to quote from a German author, Dr. Altum. He states that this German doctor examined 210 pellets of the tawny owl and 706 pellets of the barn-owl, and goes on to enumerate the number of mice, amounting to thousands, found in these pellets.

Why such a recognised authority should go to the Continent, where birds of the singing class are conspicuous by their absence, in order to find the pellets of owls, requires some explanation. Surely this Scottish naturalist could have found owls and made his observations on his own extensive estates, instead of having them " made in Germany." I have all my life picked up the pellets of owls to examine them, and have found the remains of all song-birds. One I picked up contained the feet and feathers of a thrush.

A sentence in the book above quoted would seem to indicate that the author had been nodding. He says he does not doubt that if any young chick or pheasant " comes in the way, the owl will pounce on it and enjoy it mightily. But," adds Sir Herbert, "young chicks are not, or ought not to be, abroad in the night, which is the only time that most kinds of owls can hunt." It is exceedingly unfortunate that distinguished authors should record their opinions instead of their observations. I have no desire to dogmatise on this subject, but I have again and again watched tawny owls at the nest, as well as taken them from the nest and placed them in a box, when from a window I could observe what the parent birds brought to them for food. They usually commenced to carry food to the young between three and four in the afternoon.

I therefore exhort all young keepers to follow my example in this particular—to watch and carefully note the victims of the owl, and so explode the theories of mere litterateurs. It will be no use for the young keeper to do this for one season only, as the abundance or scarcity of mice depends largely on climatic influences, and when mice are plentiful there is no doubt that large numbers are devoured by owls. The results of my observations as to the food of owls compel me to include the following: young hares, young rabbits, bats, young pigeons, both wild and tame, ducklings, thrushes, blackbirds, sparrows, and all the smaller birds, moths and beetles. It is right also to mention that in some seasons a very large number of mice—both the vole and the long-tailed field-mouse—are included in the owl's bill of fare.

The tawny owl has also been known to kill full-grown pheasants. In a large open pheasantry at Inveraray, Mr. Cameron, the head-keeper to His Grace the Duke of Argyll, and an observant naturalist, discovered that hen pheasants were being killed and eaten by some animal, though he could not at first make out which. He suspected rats, and had traps set to try to secure the depredator, but without success. One morning, however, after a fall of snow, he found another dead pheasant, when the mark of the feathers revealed the fact that owls had been the murderers. He therefore baited a trap with the partly-eaten pheasant, and erected a pole near by, on the top of which he placed a pole-trap. By seven o'clock that night a tawny owl was caught in the pole-trap, and in the morning another was in the baited trap.

At the same place a number of ducks were being hand-reared, and enclosed by wire netting to prevent them straying. The ducklings were fed at six o'clock in the morning, and between nine and ten in the forenoon ten of them were missing. Two keepers concealed themselves, and, very shortly, a hen gave the alarm which made them look out. So stealthily and noiselessly did an owl glide in, that he was not seen or heard till he was in the act of pouncing on a lot of ducklings which were clustered together, basking in the sun. He was so near his quarry that the keeper could not shoot without killing the ducks. But his sudden movement frightened the owl off, when he made straight for a tree near where the other keeper was concealed and perched above him. Needless to say, his ravages among ducklings were avenged. As I recorded in the *Scotsman* at the time, a tawny owl picked up a squirrel on the public road at midday ; and I have discovered, by placing weasels and short-eared owls together, that the weasels were killed and devoured by the owls.

The short-eared owl is a winter visitor, and as it is only on rare occasions that it breeds in this country, and has a chance of seeing young game, I would plead for its protection. During the vole plague on the Border pasture-lands scores were to be seen nesting in the heather like grouse, each laying as many as ten and twelve eggs. While studying these birds in Ettrick Forest, I took a couple of young ones home in my pocket for the purpose of finding out as much as possible about their habits. It has been demonstrated beyond all doubt that in whatever part of the world a plague of mice appears, short-eared owls, impelled by a powerful instinct, are sure to follow and devour them. How they make the discovery is one of those mysteries in nature upon which we can only speculate. Capital was made out of the mice plague by farmers, on the ground that the destruction of pasture by the mice was traceable to the destruction of hawks, owls, etc., by gamekeepers, in the interests of game-preservation. Unfortunately for the advocates of this theory, mice plagues had periodically appeared in different parts of the country centuries before game-preservation was ever thought of, and, strange to say, the mice were followed and devoured by short-eared owls. Perhaps the earliest record we have of mice plagues is found in 1 Samuel vi, where it is stated that the Philistines made golden images of "the mice that mar the land."

I would also spare the barn-owl, for the following reasons: he is a splendid mouse-destroyer, is now rare, and is a beautiful object in nature. The long-eared owl is common in most parts of the south-country, especially amongst spruce woods, where it sits screened from observation during the day. It is easily known by the "horns" or tufts of feathers on its head. Usually selecting the old nest of a pigeon or carrion-crow, it deposits its eggs therein, generally five in number. Few birds display more faithfulness and bravery in defence of their nest and young. After a heavy shower of snow and severe frost, the following night, in the month of March, I have seen one frozen to the nest, though, life-like, covering her eggs.

Long-eared owls are very destructive among pigeons and occasionally among young game, but the sparing of them must be left to the good sense of the keeper, who should endeavour to satisfy himself as to how far their destruction would be justified. The same remark applies to the jay, the rook, and the jackdaw.

Legislation for the protection of birds has cut some very queer capers. An Act was passed some years ago abolishing the pole-trap, or any trap put on a tree or in an elevated position. It reads thus—

(1) From and after the passing of this Act, every person who on any pole, tree, or cairn of earth or stones, shall affix, place, or set, any spring, trap, gin, or other similar instrument calculated to inflict bodily injury to any wild bird coming in contact therewith, and every person who shall knowingly permit or suffer, or cause any such trap to be so affixed, placed, or set, shall be guilty of an offence, and shall be liable on summary conviction to a penalty not exceeding 40*s*., and for a second or subsequent offence to a penalty not exceeding £5.

(2) Every offence under this Act may be prosecuted under the provisions of s. 5 of the Wild Birds Protection Act, 1880; and

(3) This Act may be cited as the Wild Birds Protection Act, 1904, and shall be construed with the Wild Birds Protection Acts, 1880 to 1902.

This pseudo-humanitarian legislation has for its object the prevention of cruelty. No one will deny that trapping in any shape is cruel, but a modern pole-trap is more exempt from the charge of cruelty than any other form of gin or snare. Mr. C. M. Pelham-Burn, the inventor of the humane pole-trap, used it with great success on his moors in Morayshire. It differs from the ordinary pole-trap in that the jaws strike high and catch the bird by the middle, so causing instant death. By the Act in question, however, the trapping of a sparrow-hawk on her nest, or of a peregrine on a cairn, has become illegal, so that these tyrants among bird life, especially the peregrine, have practically free scope to butcher the beautiful grouse, which constitute one of the greatest attractions of our Scottish Highlands.

It was surprising that this measure found support in both Houses of Parliament from members who possess a large amount of territory in the Highlands of Scotland. The many hundreds of thousands of acres which constitute the rugged background of our Scottish scenery, and are in many cases owned by members of the Legislature, might at all events have been regarded as a sufficient sanctuary for the protection of rare birds and beasts. Such, however, has not been the case, and the smaller landowners who possess a few thousand acres of heather must submit to their grouse, which in many instances constitute their means of livelihood, being torn to pieces by birds of prey. We have here an instance of selfishness on the part of certain large Scottish proprietors of which I, for one, feel ashamed. Surely they might have protected birds of prey in their own forests, and left it to the discretion of their poorer neighbours to do as they pleased. Whether the few pseudo-humanitarian M.P.'s who brought in the Bill abolishing the pole-trap, instructed their keepers to act in accordance with law, and to refrain from setting traps in " an elevated position," had better not be asked. In conversation with a keeper to one of those who voted for the abolition of the pole-trap, I remarked that he would have to set an example and refrain from trapping hawks. With a peculiar twinkle in his eyes, he significantly replied —" Imphm ! "

After a fall of snow the young keeper should be out at daylight to note his observations of footprints. When the ground is covered as with a sheet of soft white paper, impressions of all birds and beasts are easily made upon its surface, and can then be read as in a book. A study of the tracks of the various kinds of vermin is most interesting, and every keeper should be able to discriminate at once what made the impression. Many traits in the habits of birds and animals, unobserved at other times, can then be accurately noted. A study should also be made of the disturbed cries of every denizen of the wood, as these constitute a valuable guide in detecting the enemies of game. The intelligent keeper knows at once if a stray cat, dog, or fox is in the wood. The warning cackle of a cock pheasant, the screeching of a jay, the excited piping of blackbirds and other birds, indeed the disturbed movements of any living thing, quickly notify to his practised ear that an enemy is abroad.

I am a game-preserver and a lover of birds. As man has dominion over the fowls of the air and beasts of the field, the destroyers of the birds we value most must be kept in check. As I have tried to show, a pair of peregrines, sparrow-hawks, or merlins, must be reckoned to kill about a thousand birds annually, so no one can affirm that bird-preservation and hawk-preservation are synonymous terms.

Properly understood and judiciously carried out, man's dominion over the beasts of the field and the fowls of the air is merciful as compared with the ordinary operation of the laws of the struggle for existence and the survival of the fittest. In the interests of the food-supplies of the nation, and having regard to the pleasure and profit of mankind, it is the duty of all to preserve birds and animals which are useful by destroying those that prey upon them.

Vermin Clubs

District or County Vermin Clubs are great incentives to keepers to do their work in killing vermin. The results are published and circulated among the members every quarter, giving the names of keepers, shoot averages, and different kind of vermin killed. In Argyllshire during the war there was so great an increase of vermin that game decreased, and the shooting values of properties were seriously depreciated. A Vermin Club was started, with a secretary, to whom returns were made, and proved a great success, with the result that in two years there was a marked increase of game.

The publishing of returns from the various properties caused emulation amongst the keepers. Their returns were checked by the factor or proprietor ; more thorough work was done, with beneficial results to the shoot.

We strongly advise the starting of these Vermin Clubs. The work of starting them will take some doing, as opposition will probably be offered by lazy keepers, but energetic, efficient keepers will favour them, because they know that no matter how hard they trap, if their neighbours neglect their duty, the ground suffers from the inroad of vermin from across the boundary.

NOTES.

NOTES.

CHAPTER IX

VERMIN CLUBS

By A. S. Leslie, C.M.G.

One of the results of the war was the wholesale exodus of gamekeepers to serve their country, and as a consequence the balance of nature began to reassert itself. Vermin of all kinds increased and as vermin increased game decreased, until in many districts there was more vermin than game. On the return of peace it was realised that organised efforts would be required to deal with the situation, and in several districts in Scotland Vermin Clubs were established with a view to combined action against the common enemy.

One of the first Vermin Clubs to be formed was in the wild and remote district of Lochaber where foxes, in particular, had become so numerous as to be a serious menace to the sheep stocks in the district. This Club was started on the initiative of a group of public-spirited proprietors who raised a fund to pay head-money on the following scale :

Old fox	10*s*.
Hoodie-crow	1*s*.
Greater blackbacked gull	1*s*.

The initial efforts of this Club met with considerable success, but it was found that the quantity of vermin was so large that the financial strain upon the members had become very severe, and that if the Club was to be continued the amounts of the premiums to be paid to the vermin-killers would either have to be curtailed or the subscriptions increased. Undoubtedly there is a marked decrease in the numbers of vermin now to be seen in Lochaber, more particularly in the case of foxes. A gratifying feature of the Club is that farmers are now beginning to realise the beneficial results of the Club's operations and to subscribe, in some instances very liberally, towards its funds.

In the beginning of 1921, a Vermin Club was formed in Argyllshire under the auspices of Sir Peter Mackie, Bart., of Glenreasdell; the late Mr. J. R. Moreton Macdonald of Largie; Captain Ian Ramsay of Kildalton, and Mr. Colin Campbell of Jura, with Mr. A. S. Leslie, C.B.E., as Secretary.

The promoters of this Club decided against the payment of vermin-money, but relied instead upon the zeal of the gamekeepers in the employment of members. In this decision the gamekeepers themselves concurred, for they were the first to realise that it was merely their duty to kill down the vermin, and they asked for no further reward than recognition of work well done.

Until the Vermin Club was started many gamekeepers were inclined to feel that they did not receive sufficient encouragement; that their employers were often absent during the trapping season and did not know or care whether the vermin was being killed or not; that the expense of traps was something grudged, and that even when a gamekeeper killed down his own vermin conscientiously his efforts were of little avail unless the gamekeepers on adjoining estates were equally zealous.

In order to meet these difficulties it was decided that all gamekeepers employed by members should make a monthly return of vermin killed. These returns, after being checked by employers, were published in the form of a bulletin which was privately circulated among the members of the Club and their gamekeepers. The success of the scheme was immediate; many gamekeepers who had felt that the task of reducing vermin was almost hopeless, plucked up new courage when they found that other gamekeepers in the county were seconding their efforts; a spirit of co-operation and emulation was aroused, and new and improved methods were devised for the destruction of the principal enemies of game.

It is an interesting feature of the record of the Argyll Vermin Club that, although the quantity of the vermin in the county has been greatly reduced since the Club was established, the quantity killed during the third year of its existence does not show a very marked decrease on previous years, thus indicating that the methods of trapping and the skill of gamekeepers have improved.

The actual figures are as follows :

	1921	1922	1923
	81 estates, or game-keepers	93 estates, or game-keepers	99 estates, or game-keepers
Foxes	339	366	305
Stoats	2938	2566	2383
Weasels	1946	1483	1283
Cats	969	906	913
Rats	5321	5789	5584
Hedgehogs	791	901	735
Squirrels	43	130	101
Hawks	738	838	990
Hoodie-crows	3351	3789	3573
Rooks	1679	2193	1717
Jackdaws	1813	1924	1589
Ravens	341	366	335
Blackbacked Gulls	2151	2538	3292
Wood-pigeon	67	361	507
Various	1254	813	718
Total	23742	24948	23963
Total Area in acres	643844	776464	928932
Total head per 1000 acres ..	36·8	32·1	25·8
Average per Estate or Game-keeper	293	268	242

As an example of the result of improved methods of trapping, the case of the blackbacked gull may be noted. This ferocious bird is only too common on many parts of the West Coast, and special efforts were made to devise means for its destruction. One of the members of the Club, assisted by his gamekeeper, invented a trap of a special design ; a description and sketch of this trap was sent to all gamekeepers in the Club, and as a result the number of blackbacked gulls killed rose from 2,151 in 1921 to 3,292 in 1923. In the five months from July to October 1923, the number killed was 888 as compared with 421 in the corresponding period of the previous year.

The success of the Argyllshire Vermin Club is a vindication of the theory that the zeal of the gamekeeper, when properly organised, is capable of producing as good results as the payment of vermin-money. The costs of the Argyllshire Club, including printing, postages, and other standing charges, average less than £150 a year, equal to about 1½*d.* per head of vermin recorded as killed, whereas if vermin-money had been paid, even on a moderate scale, the expense could not have been less than £1,000 a year.

In July 1921, a Ross-shire Vermin Club, and in January 1923, a Perthshire Vermin Club, were formed : both these Clubs work on the same lines as the Argyllshire Vermin Club and have done much towards reducing the quantity of vermin in these counties. The Perthshire Club, in particular, though it has only been in operation for eighteen months, is already beginning to prove its efficiency by the test of diminishing returns from the districts which were formerly most heavily infested with vermin.

The figures for the first year were as follows :

Foxes	182
Stoats	2774
Weasels	1570
Cats	689
Rats	5509
Hedgehogs	1590
Squirrels	236
Hawks	634
Hoodie-crows	1120
Rooks	899
Jackdaws	739
Blackbacked Gulls	430
Wood-pigeons	806
Mergansers & Gooseanders ..	41
Various	976
Total	18195
Area in Acres	424037
Total Head per 1000 acres ..	45·2
Average per Estate or Gamekeeper	254

Vermin Clubs are capable of almost unlimited development, especially in districts like Argyllshire, Ross-shire and Sutherlandshire, where valuable sporting properties lie in close proximity to the sea and to large areas of deer forests, which are not preserved for game and which form sanctuaries for the breeding of vermin ; in such districts it is almost impossible to make a permanent reduction in the quantity of vermin since the stock is being constantly replenished by immigration from outside. Where these conditions prevail a constant warfare against vermin must be waged year after year and when funds permit an endeavour should be made to carry the war into the enemy's country by periodical raids into the unpreserved sanctuaries. In other districts, such as Inverness-shire, Morayshire, Banffshire, Aberdeenshire, Forfarshire and Perthshire, where the proportion of unpreserved estates is smaller, Vermin Clubs are only necessary as a temporary measure to meet special conditions. Where such necessity arises a few years of organised work would reduce the stock of vermin sufficiently to enable it to be controlled by the individual efforts of gamekeepers.

The areas embraced by Vermin Clubs should be large in order to justify the overhead charges required for each separate organisation; for example the Ross-shire Club might include the adjoining northern counties of Sutherland and Caithness; the Perthshire Club might be extended to Stirling and Dumbarton; the Argyllshire Club to Arran and Bute.

Other counties in the North of Scotland do not at present require special organisation, but in the South of Scotland, including the counties of Kirkcudbright, Wigtown, Lanark, Dumfries, Roxburgh, Ayr, Selkirk and Peebles, and in the northern counties of England, vermin has recently increased to an alarming extent, chiefly owing to the breaking-up of estates. It is understood that the formation of a Border Vermin Club is under consideration.

NOTES

CHAPTER X

GROUSE—BLACK GAME—PTARMIGAN

By Sir Peter J. Mackie, Bart.

The migrating of grouse is now pretty well accepted as among the causes of scarcity of birds on a moor, in addition to grouse disease, which used to bear the sole blame. In the case of grouse disease, the dead birds found on the moor leave no doubt as to its existence; but when no dead birds are found, other causes of scarcity of birds must exist.

I think the last few very wet, stormy winters, especially on the West Coast of Scotland, where the moors are wind-swept, have had the effect of driving the birds off to sheltered and more congenial quarters. Food is also a factor in the carrying capacity of a moor, and where there has been over-burning of heather, leaving no shelter, it is not to be wondered at that birds will not stay. The result has been that while some moors have been greatly depleted of stock, others, in the north of Scotland, have been overstocked to such an extent that, the food becoming deficient, birds have again migrated, and in many instances have no doubt returned to their old moors, in the hope of finding more room and better food conditions.

It is well for the gamekeeper never to lose sight of the fact that upon his diligence and skill in attending to the moor depend to a large extent the success of the shooting season, in as far as it is affected by the amount and the condition of the stock of birds. So clearly is this recognised by all sportsmen, that a well-known authority[1] has laid down the following dictum: "I have always observed that where there are really first-rate and honest keepers, there is always a pretty good stock of game. Of course seasons will vary, and anyone used to the moors will know pretty well when to make the allowance for bad weather, etc., but it is astonishing how lightly moors will suffer from this cause, or from disease, when the keeper and his subordinates are thoroughly trustworthy. Of course you cannot gather figs of thistles; and when you have a bare, grassy, waterless, or rank heathery moor, it is useless to look for birds in any amount, but in an average case, with favourable conditions, the number and health of the birds will be affected by the conduct and care of the keeper in charge."

The main points to be attended to by the keeper in the management of a moor are:

1. The judicious burning of the heather.
2. The regulation of the water-supply.
3. Draining.
4. The elimination of vermin.

[1] Mr. A. Stuart Wortley.

5. The suppression of poachers.

6. The feeding of the birds in hard weather.

7. The introduction of new blood.

8. The destruction, in the autumn, of old cocks.

9. Judicious planting round and upon lower parts of the moor, useful shelter for sheep and birds.

10. Careful and reasonable control of the number of sheep ; overstocking means dirty ground, and deficient food for both sheep and grouse.

11. The laying down of grit and lime, if deficient, and the making of paths, where land is not peaty ; birds like paths and roads ; they supply grit and dusting-ground.

12. The removal and burning of all dead matter, such as dead grouse, dead crows, dead vermin of all kinds, but particularly the carcasses of sheep.

13. The careful bushing of wire fences and the placing of discs of metal on any telegraph wires that may be near.

14. The keeping down of bracken by cutting in June and July.

These points may be considered *seriatim ;* the personal supervision of the proprietor or tenant being the best guarantee of their receiving attention :

1. *Judicious Burning of the Heather.*—Good heather is essential to a large stock of grouse, as it is their food. Good heather depends on burning regularly. It is an excellent plan to allow bee-keepers to put their bees on the moor, when the heather is coming into bloom—as

they carry the pollen and fertilise the flowers without which the seed cannot be fertile. The burning of the heather depends, of course, upon the conditions of the weather in different parts of the country in different seasons, but it may be laid down as a general rule that the best time for burning is as soon after the legal day, 1st November, as possible. I know it is a disputed point, yet my experience has been that heather burns more thoroughly in the autumn than in the spring, if one can get a spell of dry weather. Though it may appear green, there seems to be an oil that keeps it alight, and one can burn against the wind, the flame slowly eating up everything as it goes. On no account put off to the last few days, as many keepers do.

During the period of burning advantage should be taken of every dry day. Heather-burning is controlled in Scotland by an Act passed in 1773, whereby any person setting fire to heath or moor between 11th April and 1st November is, on conviction, liable to a penalty of £2 for the first offence, £5 for the second, and £10 for the third and every subsequent offence, or, failing payment, imprisonment. The owner, tenant, or occupier of the lands shall be found guilty, unless he can prove that the fire originated on other lands, or was caused neither by his tenants nor members of his household. An extension of time until 20th April may be obtained by proprietors of wet or high moorlands which are in their own occupation. As, however, this is about the date when birds generally start laying, great care should be

exercised, and if there are any signs of eggs, no more burning should be done. If the lands are let, proprietors may authorise their tenants to burn under the terms of this extension. Notice must be sent, before commencing operations, to the sheriff-clerk of the county, along with a fee of 1*s*. No tenant-farmer should have power to burn a moor as he likes. Landlords should, in granting leases, limit the sheep stock, and stipulate that the farm tenant shall only burn the hill or moor jointly with the proprietor's keepers, both he and the tenant supplying an equal number of men—the keepers directing the burning. Keepers should never be off the moor in time of heather-burning.

When a moor has been badly neglected and is covered with acres of thick, old, and rank heather, burning should be carried out in a more radical fashion than is necessary on ground that has been carefully attended to in the past. In the former case, heather may be burned in long narrow strips of a width of some 25 to 30 yards. These strips should, if possible, be spread fairly over the moor. In exceptional and very bad cases, it may be necessary to burn a very large tract of old rank heather. But, excluding these badly neglected cases, the best method is to burn the heather in small patches, uniformly, all over the moor. The reason for this is fairly obvious. The necessary cover must never be at too great a distance from the feeding-ground of the young birds, which is generally young heather of some few years' growth. Fair play is thus given to the younger birds, which are liable to be evicted from their feeding-ground amongst the young shoots by the older birds, when the heather has been burned in long strips. When small patches of heather are burnt, it is more difficult for the old birds to see their younger brethren—or cousins or nephews or nieces, as the case may be—when they are feeding and sunning themselves. In proceeding to burn the heather, the keeper must take into consideration the dryness of the moor and the direction of the wind. He should always be accompanied by at least two assistants, to control the fire and to prevent it from extending too far.

The keeper must always remember that the danger lies not in over-burning but in under-burning. Old heather, whether dry and rank, or, as is usual, very damp underneath, is a plague to any moor, supplying healthy food neither for birds nor sheep. It seems hardly necessary to add that it is also liable to elicit many a curse from the tired sportsman, who is either patiently following the dogs or is " finding " his own birds. On no account is the burning to be left to the absolute discretion of the shepherd. A moor should be burned on a 10 or 12 years' rotation, according to the ground. A problem to be solved is the increase of grass and the dying out of heather on many moors, one reason being overstocking by sheep and cattle, with the result that their droppings fertilise the ground and bring up grass which kills the heather. As proof, I know of a hill-side facing south, once covered with heather, that gradually became grass or "white" land. A large number of bilberry or "blae-berry" plants growing on it were eaten close and never bore fruit. These berries, as is well known, are a favourite food of grouse. To test whether they would come to fruit if left uneaten, a square of 8 or 9 acres was fenced off. After 7 or 8 years all within the fence was clothed with beautiful heather and blae-berries; while all without was white grass.

In regard to heather-burning, it may be added that if the moor is to be chiefly shot over dogs, the heather may be allowed to grow a little longer than on a moor used for driving purposes. In the former case it is more necessary to preserve good cover than in the latter, and there is no doubt that the radical heather-burning practised on a "driving" moor tends to make the birds wilder.[1]

2. *The Regulation of the Water-supply.*—There is no subject so much neglected by gamekeepers as that of the efficient water-supply of the moor. On the driest moor the keeper hesitates to be seen with anything but a gun, whilst during certain weeks of the year he should carry only a spade. In fact, it may be laid down as a general rule that, omitting the pairing and nesting seasons, the spade should be a constant companion of the diligent and skilful keeper. Springs and streams need continual clearing to prevent the moor getting boggy and damp. Streams have to be dammed here and diverted there, so

[1] A useful heather-burner, sold by MacPherson, Inverness, is now on the market; it answers admirably, and ensures a great saving of time and trouble compared with the older methods.

that an equal distribution of water may be supplied to the moor, for there is no greater handicap to the preservation of game than a deficient grit and water-supply. Every keeper should remember that this subject is as important as the burning of heather. It is a question upon which he will have to utilise as much brain as he possesses, for its proper solution calls for the careful application of varied methods to individual cases. Here, for example, is a spring that is absolutely clogged by undergrowth ; there, again, is one that is obscured by heather and other overgrowth ; whilst elsewhere we find a stream that has too free a fall and that requires judicious damming, so as to supply the small pools which experience has shown to be necessary as water-troughs for the birds. It must not be forgotten, too, that a series of well-cleared and generously flowing springs add much to the pleasures of a shooting-party, and often indicate to the sportsman the competency and efficiency of the keeper.

Not only do the springs require attention and consideration, but the condition of the larger streams must be carefully inquired into. It may be necessary to divert the flow of a stream on to a tract of ground that requires water. It may also be the duty of the keeper to get rid of those many deep undermining pools which are apt to form in the course of streams, and which are death-traps for young birds, not to mention sheep. The undermined parts must be filled in and the sides of the pool shelved. This ought really to be done by the careful shepherd, but the shepherd is no more fond of the spade than is the keeper.

3. *Draining.*—The question of the efficient draining of the moor is of equal importance. The old-fashioned way of draining was up and down the hill as indicated in the illustration. A better way is to run them on a slope, as also shown: these sloping drains gather the water more thoroughly. Another way is to "herring-bone" them, as seen in the middle distance of the picture. No definite laws can be laid down as to the nature and extent of the drains. Each case must be judged on its individual merits. Many keepers are apt in this matter to proceed upon some stereotyped line, and to miss the idiosyncrasies of the moors under their control. Drains should, as a rule, be wide and shallow, and should be formed with sloping sides. They should never be too deep.[1] On no account must there be over-draining; but this is not a danger that need generally be feared. I have tramped over many a moor that has been swampy and boggy and waterlogged, and have noted on these the gradual disappearance of the heather. Such moors are destined to become useless as breeding or holding ground for birds.

All wet holes covered with green vegetation are most unhealthy both for birds and sheep, and should be drained. They are common on every moor, but with a

[1] Deep drains may be "roaded," which is done by making a short incline 2 feet broad at right angles to the main drain, at intervals of a hundred yards. The "roading" is of assistance to the birds in getting to the water.

little care their disappearance is only a matter of time; their presence denotes a careless keeper. Owing to the war and the scarcity and high price of labour, the draining of the moor has, in many instances, been greatly neglected, with a consequent deterioration of pasture and heather. This problem is more likely to get harder than easier in the future, and, as labour-saving machinery has been introduced in other departments of agriculture, sheep-farmers will have to look about for a labour-saving apparatus to do the draining in a mechanical way, otherwise the consequences will be serious.

The low rental of many of the large sheep-farms will not allow any margin of expenditure by the landowner for labour. Take Argyllshire, where there are farms with magnificent buildings on them, running up to 4,000 acres in extent, with a sheep-rental of, say, £250, = 1*s.* 7*d.* per acre; there is no margin here to do draining by hand. Some sort of machine or implement could surely be invented[1] for cleaning out the old sheep-drains which are getting closed up—something that could be drawn, say, by a couple of ponies, one on each side of the drain—something after the style of a

[1] I have offered a prize of £100 through the Highland and Agricultural Society, for the best implement or machine for the purpose, the prize to be awarded by a Committee of that Association after a practical trial. Here is a chance for the many clever men who are always ready to criticise any new invention, and I hope to see, very shortly, an inexpensive machine that will thus save hand labour, and be of great use both on the sheep-runs and the grouse-moors. Two draining-machines were shown at the Royal Show at Stirling, but neither of them were awarded the prize; with a little trouble one of them could have been improved. My offer is still open.

plough—guided by a man ; with adjustable arrangement to rise and fall with the qualities of the ground, and which would scoop out the drains and thus keep a free run for the water. An implement like this should be able to cover a large tract of ground in a day—ten times what one man could do by hand. Of course it would not be possible on all grounds, but the ground where it could be worked can be selected, and the remainder, either on high hard grading or soft peaty places where the ponies could not go, could be done by hand. Such an implement as this would be of great service, and should stir the inventive genius of practical sheep-farmers and country smiths.

4. *The Elimination of Vermin.*—This subject is dealt with in a special chapter by the late Mr. Tom Speedy, than whom no one could speak with greater authority.

5. *The Suppression of Poachers.*—The laws in regard to poaching must be carefully remembered. They are summarised in Chapter V. The greatest care must be observed at two seasons : first, at the nesting season and for some time afterwards ; and, secondly, just before the Twelfth, when marauders are apt to be abroad to procure an early supply of grouse for the market.

It is most essential that the moor be kept quiet and free from trespassers from 15th April, when the birds begin to lay, until the time when young birds are able to fly. The keeper himself should have all his work on the moor done by the time the birds are laying, and should not cross it more than is necessary, and never with dogs.

The goodwill of the shepherd is specially valuable at this time.

6. *Feeding of the Birds in Hard Weather.*—The stock of grouse on a moor depends to a great extent on the supply of food. In addition to plenty of young heather, grouse are very fond of blae-berries (bilberries); these should be encouraged to grow, and roots from woods and rough ground should be lifted and planted at intervals on the moor. Women and children should be prevented from gathering the ripe berries on the moor. The artificial feeding of the birds in hard weather is not only considered unimportant, judging from experience, it is a point absolutely neglected. It is necessary chiefly on high ranged moors, the tendency being for birds to emigrate to the lower reaches during severe weather. Mr. Stuart Wortley writes on this point: "It is quite worth while to feed them a little at such times. It is chiefly when the snow is caked or frozen over with a very thin coating of ice, and they cannot scratch through it to get food, that they are most pinched and may leave the ground, never to come back. I remember Mr. Walter Stanhope telling me that, in the very hard winter of 1859-60, the grouse on his Dunford Bridge moor left the ground in hundreds. Many were killed in the fields in a half-starved state, and even one or two in the Barrack Square at Sheffield, some fifteen miles off. He then sent men up to the moor with long rakes, and as they raked the snow off, the grouse followed them close, as gulls will follow the plough. Your keeper should see to these methods of

helping them to feed in severe weather, and not, as is too often the case, helplessly gape at the half-starved packs sitting on walls or scratching at the ground in the fields below the moorland, until, forced by hunger, they rise and fly clean away in search of milder conditions." This may account for recent migration of birds, while keepers do nothing.

Of course, the feeding of the birds must not be carried out unless under dire necessity, for there is possibility of some uncharitable neighbour considering the action unsportsmanlike, in so far as it may draw away the birds from his moor. But there is not much danger of this misunderstanding taking place. Stooks of corn judiciously planted in the most desirable places is the best method of supplying food. It is an ill wind that blows nobody any good, and at such a time the keeper may be in a position to judge of the number of old cocks left on the moor. Their greed will be easily discernible, and an apparently mean advantage might be taken to rid the moor of these voracious, ill-mannered, domineering tyrants. This is a practice recognised by all experienced poachers, and it is well that keepers should profit from the skill of law-breakers. There is a good deal to be learnt from rogues and vagabonds.

7. *Introduction of New Blood.*—The evil effects of interbreeding must be remembered, and there is much to be said in favour of the occasional introduction of new blood, either by interchange with other owners, or, in Scotland, by the purchase of Yorkshire grouse and vice

versa. The first point to be made certain is that the new birds come from a healthy stock, which has not had disease for three years. In putting down the new birds, the long feathers of a wing may be clipped or the outside long feathers may be soaped, unless the weather is very wet. The most satisfactory method, however, is to pull two of the outside feathers off each wing. This keeps the birds on the moor for six or eight weeks, till they get accustomed to their surroundings, and take up with the other birds. The new birds, when they begin to fly, can generally be noticed in a pack by being behind and having a more laboured action in flight. Unless the birds by some method are kept on the moor, their usual tendency is a homing one, and they generally make for the moors from which they have come. Whether they reach these or not is another matter, but without some of the above safeguards—the last-mentioned preferably—it is useless laying down grouse.

There is, however, one very serious warning that must be repeated here. If birds are introduced from strange moors, on no account should they be purchased from suspicious sources. The important correspondence that took place some time ago in *The Field*, as to the dastardly manner in which certain moors were depleted of their grouse by netting near the marches, ought to make every true sportsman suspicious of the dealer in live game. I see no reason why a man should not rent a moor, and, instead of shooting it in August or September, leave it quiet till the end of the season and supply from it shootings which want fresh blood, and are willing to pay for it. Such sources exist, and the trade is openly carried on as a business in a perfectly straightforward manner. My own experience of several importations of such birds is that a high percentage arrive safe and in good condition. It is necessary, however, to stipulate the sex proportion when purchasing, and to get two hens to every cock. When laying the birds out on the various parts of the moors as far away from the march as possible, it is also advisable to note carefully the sex, keeping a record of the same in a book, in order to see that you have got what you paid for. Otherwise you may be stocking a moor with a lot of useless old cocks, which will do more harm than good. This is a point seldom considered by keepers, who as a rule simply turn the birds down on the moor, and let them take their chance.

The practice of exchange of eggs between keepers is one which is most easily carried out, if they will only take the trouble, and it is the least objectionable, as a fair exchange is no robbery.

Considering the evils of the other system, and the difficulty of keeping the imported birds on the ground, it is better that eggs should be exchanged. One or two placed in each nest is the most reliable method of laying them down, though it entails more trouble to the keeper than placing a large number in one or two nests ; or they may be put under domestic hens. The hatching of grouse eggs under hens is very similar to that of pheasants. Twelve or thirteen eggs are the best number to set. A small hen should be chosen and the nest set in a clod of turf, thus keeping as close to nature as possible. Twenty-five days is the length of incubation. The coops should be placed on short heather, and after hatching they should be moved daily, to prevent the ground getting foul. The same feeding should be given as to pheasant chicks, with a little variation, but too much should not be given at one time, so as to encourage the birds to take the natural feeding on the ground. They soon begin to take the tender shoots of heather and other plants, and, with a little study as to what agrees and what disagrees with them, they soon thrive.

Notwithstanding the fact that grouse are absolutely wild birds, they are easily reared, and are a most interesting study. When old enough to fly and take care of themselves, they should be at once moved to different parts of the moor, where they will soon become acclimatised. If left too long on the ground where they have been reared, they will continue packed there, in a semi-domesticated state, and refuse to move. The sooner they mix with the wild birds the better. It is absolutely necessary not only in the rearing of grouse, but of all other young birds, that they have a fresh supply of clean water several times a day, and that all dishes and utensils should be absolutely clean, otherwise they will be apt to contract disease. No food should be put inside the coops on any account, as it soon gets contaminated, and deaths follow. (*See* Artificial Rearing.)

Another method is the exchange of coveys with moors eight or ten miles off. This method, however, is not to be recommended, as it sets a bad example to the countryside, and may lead to poaching. In July, when the coveys are fairly strong, the keeper should take a steady pointer (on a hot day when the birds will lie close), and, having located the covey, should throw a net over the same. Carefully catch all the birds in the covey, and transport them in a basket, laying them down on a part of the moor, which, if it be at all possible, should not be shot over that year. Birds were transported from Ronachan, in Kintyre, to Jura in this way with success, some years ago. To all these methods, however, the ordinary keeper is averse on the score of trouble. He prefers to muddle along, and content himself with the consolation, without any jot of proof to support it, that birds fly from one moor to another, and thus keep up a change of blood. All evidence, however, tends to show the opposite—that birds keep to their own moor, and, if removed, generally return, unless driven away by want of food and shelter.

8. *The Destruction, in the Autumn, of Old Cocks.*—This, one of the most important of the gamekeeper's duties, is nowadays so neglected as to be almost unknown. It is universally recognised that the presence of a large number of old cocks is in every way detrimental to a moor. Old cocks are pugnacious and quarrelsome, and they seem to take a special delight in interfering with the domestic arrangements of the younger birds.

They are, in every way, undesirable tyrants. They drive the younger birds from their selected nesting-grounds, and thus interfere with breeding. It is on this account that so many authorities advocate driving as a cure for such ill-fated moors, although many old-fashioned keepers are averse to driving. In driving, the old cocks are killed off in much greater numbers than in shooting over dogs. It is a matter of the commonest observation that the old birds and cocks lead the packs, and it is an established fact that a driven moor generally gives better breeding results than a moor that is worked by dogs alone ; for, in shooting over dogs, the guns are apt to take the nearest birds, which are generally hens and young birds.

No better example of this can be found than the Moy moor, which is about 11,000 acres in extent. When The Mackintosh started driving in 1871, the bag was 2,836 birds, while in 1893 it had risen to 4,480, and in 1901 to 7,127 ; what it was over dogs before the driving began we are not told. But whether the moor be driven or dogged, the keeper should be allowed in the late autumn, after the systematic shooting days are passed, to take occasional walks over his ground and endeavour to shoot down as many old cocks as he is able.

How much this precaution is necessary may be emphasised by an instance which came under the notice of the present writer, in the month of January 1903. He was one of a party of guns in an improvised partridge-drive in the county of Ayr, and in one of the beats, being an outside gun, he was stationed at the end of a field which lay on the fringe of the moor. He was surprised to find, as the beaters came towards the guns, that the air seemed filled with the calls of old cock grouse, and on looking to the right, he could see them rising and going away every half-minute or so. The climax was reached as the beaters were entering the last field, when, instead of partridges, six or eight old cock grouse came over his gun. He hesitates to prophesy what the condition of that moor will be in a few years. When the tenant discussed the point with the keeper, the only reply he received was the futile one, that he had tried for years to get near the cocks to shoot them. But not for a moment did he realise that their presence was a reflection upon his capacity as a keeper.

This matter of the killing of old cocks is one upon which the owner of a moor is himself generally ignorant or careless ; but every keeper, who has at heart the prosperity of the shooting under his care, should see that attention is paid to it. A good opportunity to stalk old cock grouse and blackcock is when there is a cornfield near the moor, and the corn is in stook. Get concealed in the evening or early morning and lie in wait, when you will find that the birds are so greedy that they cannot keep away, and take little notice of the shots.

Of course it must be understood that this shooting down of old cocks is no child's play. It requires both patience and skill. In the majority of cases the birds must be stalked. The stalker must go on to the moor alone, his trained dog being well under control, and behind him. He must proceed in absolute silence, taking advantage of any cover the moor may afford in the shape of old dykes and ditches. He will find that a well-choked barrel is best for his purpose, although it may even be necessary to use a rifle. He should never hesitate to kill the birds sitting. Some years ago, on a moor in Strathtay, the present writer indulged in a series of these stalking expeditions. He was very content, after a day's careful working of the ground, by creeping up burn-sides or crawling alongside old dykes, or often by coming upon his bird unexpectedly round a favourable knoll, to return at night with two or three brace of old cocks. He counted such a bag as of much more import to the future prosperity of the moor, than if he had returned with a larger one made up of younger birds.

But even despite such stalking expeditions there is often left on the moor a large number of these unwelcome "chronics." Where there is much hilly ground, they are to be found on the tops in late autumn and winter, from which fortresses they descend, to the detriment of their younger brethren in the plains. Even where driving is not practised as a general rule, it is as well that one or two drives, at least, be arranged over the tops. Such drives are not easy to manage, but a competent keeper, keeping in view the general law of driving which refers to the customary flight of birds, and observing the point at which the old cocks come nearest to possible " butts," can select his stations accordingly. This is a matter worthy of the careful consideration of master and keeper, but it is a matter generally neglected on a " dogging " moor.

It is even to be recommended that the old cocks on the tops be regarded as vermin and trapped. If such trapping were carried out on the very high ground alone, there would not be much danger of harm coming to the younger birds.

9. *Judicious Planting.*—It is advisable, where there is little cover of the nature of forest growth or shrubbery near the moor, that there should be a certain amount of planting on the lower parts of the ground, to act as cover for the birds in bad weather. This is also beneficial to the sheep and cattle stock on the moor, as not only does it serve as shelter, but it gives a more luxuriant growth of grass and heather. On a wind-swept moor, sheep and cattle never do so well, and require more food than on one which has good shelter, so that planting adds considerably to the value of the property and should be encouraged.

10. *Careful and Reasonable Control of the Number of Sheep.*—A separate chapter is devoted to the relationships between keepers and farm tenants. It is only necessary here to emphasise three facts: (1) The one already referred to, that in no case must the heather-burning be left to the discretion of the sheep-farmer; (2) that shepherds' dogs must be kept under control in the breeding season; and (3) that the keeper should,

where necessary, indicate to his master the palpable fact that the stock of sheep is too large, and interferes with the feeding material of the grouse. Most moors are habitually over-stocked by the farmer. This condition is the chief factor in the high death-rate among sheep and the small size of lambs, and is also detrimental, not only to proper shooting (especially when this is practised over dogs), but also to the food supply of the stock of game on the moor. When letting a farm a limit should be put upon both the cattle and the sheep stock. The number of sheep a moor will carry varies according to the feeding ; the same applies to the stock of grouse. Three acres to one sheep is, on average ground, a fair stock, and with good heather, one should kill one grouse to two acres. A clause should be inserted in the lease, exacting a penalty of a rent of one pound per sheep for every head in excess of the stipulated number. The farmer would get a better price for his sheep. A count of the sheep should be taken every few years at a gathering for dipping, in order to see that this clause is observed.

When the adjoining land is well stocked with sheep, it is altogether desirable that the moor should be fenced off. Some of the best-managed moors suffer not inconsiderably from the depredations of sheep from neighbouring lands. The feeding capacities of the moors under consideration may be, and in the event of there being only a small stock of sheep are sure to be, better than those of the adjoining lands, and on this account the sheep will naturally migrate to the best grazing-grounds, and will, as a result, injure their feeding capacity. The moors will also be constantly disturbed by the shepherds' dogs driving back the sheep to their legitimate ground. Along the march of a moor which is not fenced, it is advantageous not to burn the heather, but to leave it long and rank. Where such a condition exists, the sheep will not stray so readily across the march. Over-stocking both by cattle and sheep is short-sighted policy—it pollutes the land; deaths increase, stock are undersized, and they fetch a lower price in the market, so that it pays the farmer better to under-stock rather than over-stock. When will factors and land agents understand this?

On the question of sheep and grouse moors, Mr. Tom Speedy writes: "Let us assume that there is a good stock of game, and the nesting season all that can be desired. About the 20th of May hatching has commenced, and large broods are by this time following the parent birds. This is also the period for gathering the sheep, with the view of marking the lambs. Shepherds and their dogs are out betimes to the marches of their respective hirsels. The process commences, and the flocks are driven in a homeward direction. Eventually the shepherds meet and the sheep are concentrated in an immense flock, sometimes amounting to thousands, and driven towards the 'fanks.' Those who have witnessed the gathering of a flock as described, and have seen them driven in a solid line many hundreds of yards in width across a heathery hillside, must at times have speculated as to the probable fate of grouse eggs and newly hatched chicks. With this end in view, we have devoted many hours, accompanied by a dog, to the trail made by the flock, and have found both eggs and young game in large numbers trampled and destroyed. In the second week of June a similar course of congregating is adopted, for the purpose of clipping the old stock. Again, in the beginning of July, gathering is unavoidable for clipping the milk ewes."

During these repeated operations the sheep are generally driven over the same route to the fanks. We strongly advise keeping the heather short on the route, so as to facilitate the progress of the lambs. The shepherds will always select this way, and thus it will be a means of saving many birds. This is a point upon which the shepherd should be consulted.

Damage is often done by cattle lying down on nests, and we have known the eggs of both grouse and black game destroyed in this way.

11. *Improvement of the Feeding-ground of the Birds by Introduction of Grit and Lime Quartz.*—Grit is an essential and important part of the food of the grouse. It can be obtained by the birds usually in small quantities by the sides of streams and on paths. It will be found to the advantage of the moor, and the trouble will be fully repaid by the results, if a few sacks of lime and pounded shells be taken on to the moor every spring, and deposited in suitable places near to a stream, before the laying season.

12. *The Removal and Burning of all Dead Matter, such as dead grouse, dead vermin of all kinds, but particularly the carcasses of sheep.*—It has been recognised from the earli-

est ages on record that nothing leads more to pestilence than leaving dead animal matter exposed to the air, and in contact with the food and water-supply of mankind and other living creatures. This recognised fact must be borne in mind by the keeper in dealing with any dead matter that may be found on the ground under his control. Dead grouse, dead crows, dead vermin, are dangerous enough in their power of contaminating the air, the soil, and more particularly the watercourses, but dead sheep are infinitely more capable of mischief, not only to living sheep, but also to game. It will be found, on careful observation, that a high death-rate of sheep is due to two causes: (1) To overcrowding, and (2), and more specially, to the presence of, or the effect of the former presence of, the rotting carcasses of sheep. Some years ago an experiment was made on a certain moor in Scotland. The carcasses of two sheep were left to rot in the open. After decay had well set-in two sheep (a two-year-old wether and a ewe) were temporarily fenced in at different parts of the moor, each sheep being given two acres of good hill ground. Both the sheep died within six weeks, and there appears to be no doubt that death resulted from their having eaten grass contaminated by the carcasses of the dead sheep.

In these latter days, when the destruction of vermin is carried out with some thoroughness, the ravens and hoodie-crows—the natural scavengers of the moors—have not the chance of making a meal off any sheep that may have died, and so the carcasses are left to rot. Not only are the watercourses contaminated (courses which may be bringing water for domestic purposes), but in wet districts great areas of the moor may be poisoned by decaying matter, to the detriment of the sheep-farm, and, what is more important for us, of the grouse. The keeper should therefore impress upon the farmer the danger that threatens his stock by any neglect in removing this dead material. Shepherds as a rule will laugh at this warning, partly from ignorance, but chiefly because acting upon a belief in it will give considerable trouble; but they ought to be compelled to meet the wishes of master and keeper on the subject. Keepers and shepherds should be encouraged to carry off all dead birds and burn them. The yearly present to the shepherd will be a reminder. A clause should be inserted in the lease compelling farmers to bury every dead sheep not less than 2 ft. underground, and care should be taken that the grave be some distance from a watercourse. A penalty in a lease is a useful thing to make the tenant observe this stipulation.

13. *The Careful Bushing of Wire Fences, and the Placing of Metal Discs on any Telegraph Wires that may be near to the Moor.*—The great mortality that often occurs from birds being caught in their flight by wire fences or telegraph wires is known to every keeper, and yet measures to counteract these evils are not consistently carried out. All wire fences that are likely to be in the line of flight should be "bushed" with heather,

care being taken to see that the bushing is not removed. We have known instances of its removal by shepherds, one confessing to having picked up sixty grouse in one season along a line of several hundred yards. Notice should also be given to the Post Office authorities, if it be found that birds have been killed by coming in contact with their telegraph wires. These authorities will meet the wishes of the sportsman, and have discs of metal put at intervals along the wires, to warn the birds of their danger. In driving along a moor road in Argyllshire one spring, the present writer observed, within half a mile, three or four dead grouse and black game lying in the ditch-side in the line of the telegraph wires, and on examination there could be no doubt as to the cause of death.

14. *The Keeping Down of Bracken.*—The increase of bracken is a serious matter on many moors. It generally grows on good land which was formerly cultivated. No effectual cure has been found. Experiments by Colonel Ferguson-Buchanan of Auchentorlie, in spraying with a 5 per cent. sulphuric-acid solution in July, have been tried with some success. This costs one-third less than cutting. (For particulars, see Highland and Agricultural Society's Transactions, 1916, article by G. P. Gordon, B.Sc.) As bracken is said to grow on sour land, a good dressing of basic slag or lime—the winter after spraying—might be beneficial and prevent its return. The best way to get rid of this pest is to cut the bracken twice yearly, by means of an old reaper—it

does not need to be clean cut, only torn, so that the stem bleeds—or with the scythe, when it is about six inches high, and before it seeds. If this be continued for some years it will die down, but if left alone it is certain to spread, and ruin the hill both for sheep and game. Another suggestion, but one which we have not had tried, is that of fencing a bracken area with grazing pigs, as it is said that they eat the roots. It might be worth while to try this experiment, as the bracken curse is a serious one. Constant cutting, I think, weakens the plant, and it is certainly thinner in districts under our notice. I have not, however, heard of any effectual cure. Perhaps science will devise some use for the bracken. Proprietors might offer a handsome prize for such a discovery.

Artificial Rearing

Excellent reports have been received from various sources as to the success attending the "hand" rearing of grouse. Game-hens, and sometimes bantams, have been used for the purpose. The coops are placed on short heather, where a fresh shift can be got every day. "When the chicks are hatched," says Mr. Speedy, "they should at first be fed on hard-boiled eggs, with an admixture of 'Standard' meal, the makers of which have a preparation for the rearing of grouse and black game. Rice and seed may be added later, and maize—of which they are very fond—when they are large enough to swallow it. It is desirable to rear them in places where, besides heather, as much natural food as possible can be got, such as blackberries, cranberries, ribwort, bracken, etc. Hand-reared grouse keep well together during the autumn and winter months, and are easily known, so that they can be spared by the careful sportsman. On the approach of spring, they spread over the moor and pair off to propagate their species, thus disseminating broadcast fresh blood over the district." No doubt some difficulty will be experienced in procuring the eggs of grouse. One solution of the difficulty is to obtain them from deer forests, where the removal of eggs would be regarded more as a benefit than otherwise.

Shooting the Grouse

1. *Over Dogs*

The charm of seeing dogs work has been overlooked in the craze for driving and big bags. After the war there has been at least a partial return to the good old peaceful days, when sportsmen were satisfied with seeing the dogs work, and with a modest bag, and felt true content in breathing fine air amidst beautiful scenery.

There are several important points to be remembered by the keeper in shooting over dogs. Some of these points are dealt with in the chapter on dogs, others may be recalled here. As to whether pointers or setters are preferable on a grouse moor depends largely on the moor, and how it is watered. Setters require much water, but as a rule pointers are more steady than setters. Two guns are sufficient in each party ; there should never be more than three ; if a dangerous or young shot be in the party—better put him on the extreme left :

1. The guns must be kept in line, and should be warned not to walk too quickly, as that is fatal to good shooting.

2. Outside beats should be worked first, so as to drive in birds on to the lower grounds for the afternoon shooting.

3. The direction of the wind must be continuously studied, and the beats arranged accordingly, working the dogs against or across the wind.

4. A knowledge of the habits and habitats of the grouse must be taken into consideration. In the early morning, the birds are found on their natural feeding-ground—that is, on heather three to four years old. On the approach of the dogs the grouse generally seek cover in the thicker heather near. After feeding-time they return to their roosting-ground, where they remain during the middle hours of the day. In the evening they return again to their feeding-ground, and after that, a little before dusk, once more go back to their roosting-ground. In very hot weather the birds frequent the sloping sides of burns and streams, or seek the cover of mixed bracken and heather, or shelter themselves among the bog-myrtle. In wet weather the birds

ascend to the higher grounds. In boisterous weather they are generally found on the sheltered sides of hills.

5. Strict silence should, if possible, be maintained as the " guns " proceed. There must be no superfluous speech-making either to men or dogs. The attention of the guns should be drawn to a point by some simple ejaculation, such as " Mark, sir," or " Steady." The question of arresting the attention of the guns is important. Nothing is more tantalising to the keen sportsman than to be told in a casual, indifferent, or languid voice to " Look to your right, sir," and to find that a bird has gone away some hundred yards before the sentence is completed. When a bird rises independent of a point, the keeper should call out emphatically, " Mark, sir," indicating " right " or " left " or " behind," as the case may be. Sound carries far on a moor. Nothing spoils sport so much as a noisy keeper shouting to his dogs, or loud talking by the guns. This puts all the birds on the alert, so that they are off before the dogs come to a point. The first bird to rise is generally the old cock, and he should be shot first and not the bird nearest the gun, which is generally a " cheeper " at the beginning of the season.

6. The ground should be worked systematically. Towards evening every piece of ground must be carefully searched. The largest bags of the day may be made when the birds have retired to their roosting-ground.

7. In addition to what is said in the chapter on dogs, the following points may be remembered:

(1) Pointers and setters should not be overworked. To avoid this, they should be changed at least every hour.

(2) It is best to have one man whose duty it is, primarily, to hold the non-working dogs in leash. This man should walk some eighty yards behind the guns, and should act as a marker for the flight of coveys and for fallen, especially towered, birds. Where the number of men is limited, he receives the picked-up birds, and after carrying them for a sufficient time to allow them to cool, he hands them on to the man with the horse and panniers.

(3) Retrievers must be kept well in leash.

(4) If the scent is bad, the dogs must not be allowed to range too far, and the ground must be worked very slowly and carefully. If the point habitually fails, or if the birds are so wild as not to sit to the point at all, it is best to withdraw the dogs altogether.

(5) Plenty of time must be allowed for dogs to drink, but they must be discouraged from habitually taking to water. Where the ground is destitute of water and the day is very hot, water should be carried on to the moor in the panniers for their benefit.

(6) Dogs should be given some slight refreshment in the shape of a sandwich at the luncheon hour. Never give a dog a game- or chicken-bone.

(7) It is as well, at the beginning of the season at least, to soak the feet of the dogs in strong brine or other

hardening fluid, after the day's work. Plenty of exercise on the roads before the Twelfth hardens their feet. This is implied in the proverb—" An auld dog for a hard road ! "

(8) When a dog comes to a point, there should not be any " to-hoing " to it. If it has been properly taught, it should " hold up " without any words from the keeper ; an uplifting of the keeper's hand should be sufficient. If a dog has a habit of drawing too close on the birds, the keeper should come quietly to its side and hold it gently back till the guns are ready, directing of course the attention of the guns to the point. If the dog be too slow in drawing on the birds after the guns are ready, it should be encouraged by patting it on the back or even by dragging or pushing it on. The noisy old-fashioned keeper who shouts at his dogs should be reminded that birds can hear.

2. *Driving*

The keeper's duties in regard to grouse-driving may vary from the conducting of several improvised drives on a moor that is free from butts, and which is chiefly " dogged," or walked, or stalked, to the arrangement of systematic and elaborate drives. In preparing for the former, little is necessary beyond a study of the wind, a knowledge of the general flight of the birds, and the selection of points which might be used as natural butts, such as dyke- or burn-sides, rocks, or the backs of the crests of braes and hillocks. In dealing with an elaborate drive, however, the keeper is concerned with a very different business, and carrying through the campaign will require most of his arts and all his resources. But there are three important pieces of information, knowledge of which must underlie the whole of his plan of campaign :

(1) Accurate observation of the lie of the land. The keeper must carry in his mind a veritable Ordnance Survey map of the moor.

(2) The habits of the birds so far as the question of their customary flight is concerned.

(3) The principles underlying the forming, the marching, and the evolutions of the corps of beaters.

These three pieces of knowledge will lead him far to a successful solution of the problem before him, which is : how best to get the stock of birds over the guns. To successfully carry out a series of drives to the most perfect issue will, however, require not only careful consideration, but much elaborate manœuvring. On this account he will have to take into consultation, more closely than in most of his other duties, the man who should know a great deal about the sport he wishes to enjoy, viz. his master. Besides this, the keeper, who desires to learn the art of grouse-driving thoroughly, must seek information of a more elaborate nature than this book pretends to supply. If he desires to bring his results even approximately to the perfection attained at Moy Hall, Bromhead, Gannochy, High Force, or

Studley, he will buy, or borrow from his master, the writings of Lord Granby, Lord Walsingham, Sir R. Payne Gallwey, Mr. Tom Speedy, Mr. Horace Hutchinson, and Mr. Stuart Wortley—more particularly of the last-named. All these writers deal with their subject tersely, simply, and graphically, and any intelligent keeper will rise from the perusal of their writings with a fairly definite view as to the last and the best word on the subject. As has been said, one cannot pretend to deal with the matter so elaborately as well as so vividly as is done in Mr. Stuart Wortley's admirable work ; one can only absorb the best views and present them with the modifications of one's own experience.

Let us then deal further deal with the three points enumerated above :

(1) *Accurate Knowledge of the Conformation of the Land.*—From this knowledge the keeper will be able to lay the plan of his drives, so as to gain efficiency along with economy of time and of space. He will learn what parts of the moor should be driven first, so as to keep the birds on the ground for future drives, and how best to work the moor in order that the birds may be driven in from the outlying beats for the final flush over the guns. On hilly and rocky grounds he will discover where best to place the butts so that those different parts may be effectively worked. With a knowledge of the usual flights of the birds, added to the general information he may possess as to the lie of the land, he

will be able to judge as to the best general distribution of the butts.

(2) *The Flight of the Birds* —It is only by continuous and careful observation that the keeper will be able to gauge with fair accuracy the general direction taken by the birds in their flight. On this important data depends the question as to where the butts should be placed. Where driving is practised on a moor, the initial drives can only be regarded as experimental, and even when fairly accurate knowledge has been obtained, further experience may require the alteration of the position of the butts. The fact cannot be unduly emphasised, that no hesitation must be shown in making new lines of butts, or in shifting old ones. On many moors the butts of primitive days are treated like eternal monuments, not to be interfered with by any law or experience on earth. Truly these old stagers may be monuments—of ignorance; they are quite useless for sport.

(3) *The Formation, Progression, and Evolution of the Corps of Beaters.*—The art of driving is not easily learned, and the details are only perfected by experience. There are keepers who, despite the fact that birds are continually breaking back over the drivers or escaping at the flanks, persist with their primitive array of a more or less uncontrolled line of drivers, who are possessed of only three ideas: firstly, to make their way by a bee-line to the butts; secondly, to keep in line with their neighbours; and thirdly, to yell " Mark ! " whenever birds rise. Let it be reiterated that the formation of the

drivers should never be a straight line, but should be horseshoe-shaped, and that the length and the disposition of the flanks ought to vary according to the ground and the direction of the wind.

Having enumerated the three main points which must serve as the basis of the keeper's knowledge, let us glance for a moment at some of the practical duties which are the natural outcome of this knowledge.

The first thing to be considered is the placing and building of butts. The practical points connected with this procedure may be thus enumerated:

(1) The butts must be placed in the general line of flight of the birds, which, as we have shown, should be discovered by the keeper, after careful observation from experimental drives.

(2) Butts should never be placed on the skyline; but with some eighty yards or so of gently sloping ground behind the skyline, this ground constituting the main field of action. The best possible situation is just over a brae or small hill—the skyline being about eighty, and never more than one hundred, yards from the line of butts. Never, no never, on the skyline!

(3) Butts should never be placed where experience has shown that the birds usually fly too high for the guns—for example, at the bottom of a deep gorge between hills. Birds only dip their line of flight in traversing wide, shallow valleys. In passing over a deep gorge, they maintain their flight at the height of the first peak crossed,

and will be out of range of the guns at the bottom of the gorge.

(4) The distance between the butts should be regulated according to what experience has shown to be the width of the flight of the birds, after concentration by the drivers and flankers. On level ground they should be closer together than on rougher and more hilly ground —say 45 to 50 yds. apart. The old fashion of having butts at intervals of some eighty to a hundred yards is going out of vogue. The other extreme is practised by The Mackintosh at Moy Hall, where an allowance of only 15 to 20 yds. is made between the butts, on the principle that the concentration of birds is more marked than is generally believed, and that much good shooting material is thrown away when the butts are wider apart. This space is, I think, too little. The chief objection made to closely-placed butts has been that of the possible danger of accident. Where the nature of the ground necessitates that any butt is out of sight of that nearest to it, a stake, or better, a white stone, should be placed to indicate the fact of the proximity. This practice discounts any chance of temporary forgetfulness, which has been known to occur to the best of sportsmen. On rough and hilly ground the spread of the flight is wider, and here the butts should have a greater distance between them—a fair distance being from 50 to 60 yds.

(5) Butts must always be in a straight line and as inconspicuous as possible, and, except in very rocky and

very marshy country, practically 2 ft. above the surface of the moor. The old-fashioned high-walled " batteries " should in general be discarded. The best way to construct a butt is to dig a pit in the ground with a diameter of some 5 ft. at the bottom and 6 ft. across the top. The " gun," in standing in the pit, should be just able to see and shoot over the slight parapet at the top, which should be almost flush with the moor, and never more than 2 ft. above its level, the outside being so built with heather turf as to slope gently up to the mouth of the butt. It may be useful, for the sake of firmness, to line the inside of the butt with wire-netting, and also the outside of the slightly elevated portion above the level of the moor. The draining of the butt itself is of importance. An opening in the butt, with a drain which leads to a lower level than the floor, may be covered with stones. The floor of the butt may be covered with turf or stones. This ensures a fairly dry base for the shooter and his loader to stand upon. Wooden floors are objectionable as the " gun " is liable to slip, especially in wet weather. A board of wood, supported on two posts, as a seat at one side of the butt is advisable. A stake may also be inserted to which to tether a retriever.

(6) Butts should be well built, well drained, well in line, and kept in good repair. On no account must a very prevalent fashion be permitted to continue—of allowing the butts to take care of themselves, or leaving their repair to any energetic or practical hands that may

exist among the "guns." How often has one found oneself crouching behind a small turf dyke, or in badly built, tumble-down, draughty butts, flooded with three or four inches of water, from which one had to go scouring the land for stray slabs of peat or heather hummocks on which to kneel, for in no other fashion could one hide from view a cold and restless body! How often has one shivered and groaned in these pits of stupidity and gross carelessness! If newer-fashioned butts are not forthcoming, then, in the name of all that is sensible, let the keeper or his men patch up and drain the old ones, and save the "guns" from acute rheumatism, pneumonia, or shattered tempers. Let the "guns" at least have a chance of doing even their second best.

It is on moors that are let to shooting tenants for short periods that such criminal neglect of duty chiefly prevails. The proper remedy is to withhold altogether, or at least reduce, the tip to the keeper, and politely tell him the reason, when departing. Often it is the owner himself that is to blame. He knows he will have little difficulty in letting his shooting, and, if he is not a keen or unselfish sportsman, he is never particularly anxious for a lengthy lease of his moor. In such cases, the duties of a keeper are often allowed to slacken to an appalling extent, and with the decline of the sense of duty, the butts suffer first; after the butts, it is the turn of the springs and the drains—everything, in fact, that seems to the lazy or half-stupid keeper to have little bearing on the number of birds killed.

(7) It has been suggested by some writers that the heather should be burnt for some distance round the butts, so that the birds may be found without difficulty after the drive. The two great objections to this are (*a*) That the butts would stand out more conspicuously than when surrounded by heather; and (*b*) that the birds are apt to be badly broken up in falling on to hard ground. Young heather should surround the butts—it greatly assists in picking up the bag, and saves time.

The Drive

There are general principles in regulating the disposition and movement of the drivers which may be enumerated:

(1) Short drives are better than long ones.

(2) Where men are easily obtainable, and it is proposed to carry out the drive in as complete and elaborate a manner as possible, two companies of drivers should be employed, one taking up their position at the far end of the second drive, ready to come forward as soon as the first drive is over and the birds are picked up, if a return drive is intended, or as soon as the guns get into the next line of butts.

For the comfort of the party, the walk between the various lines of butts should be as short as possible. A beaten pad between the lines adds to the comfort of the guns.

(3) In a first-rate drive there should be from sixteen to twenty drivers, the best men being on the flanks.

The centre man of the horseshoe should also be an experienced man, while, to save expense, the main curve of the horseshoe may be made up of intelligent boys. Fewer beaters are required towards the end of the season, when the birds are wilder.

(4) If the head-keeper goes with the drivers he should be on that flank which it is necessary to hold in chief control, otherwise he may act as a stop; both ends of the line of butts should be stopped. They are also useful in marking birds.

(5) Drivers should walk slowly and silently, keeping their eyes open, their mouths shut, and their ears alert, to receive directions from the man under whose control they work. There is no earthly use in yelling "Mark" when the birds rise—this only frightens them, and is apt to make them break back; grouse in flight naturally cling to the hill-side. When birds are going forward to the butts, the head-keeper, or whoever is directing the drive, should blow his whistle to warn the guns to be on the outlook for birds; that is all that is required.

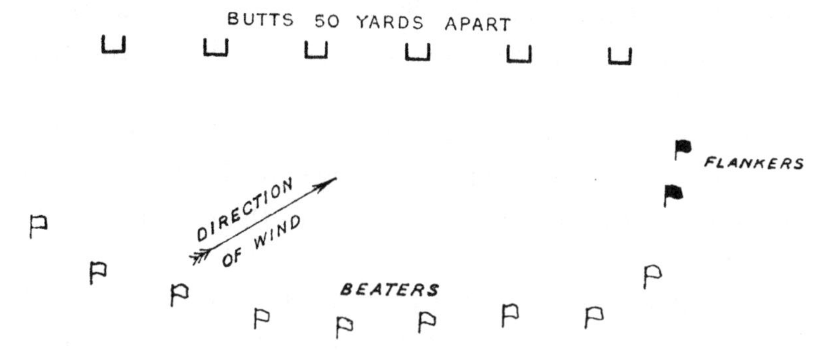

(6) When birds rise and show a tendency to break back or to pass over the flanks, the drivers and flankers should quietly stoop, so as to keep out of sight for the time, and then quickly rise again as the birds approach them. This plan is much better than the common one of shouting and gesticulating, and the probability is that the birds will sweep round in front of the drivers and go over the guns.

(7) In driving ground which is high on one flank and low on the other, the drivers on the lower ground should be a little more advanced than those on the higher ground.

(8) When there is a strong wind blowing across the drive, the downward flank should be well advanced. They thus form a screen to turn the birds. It may also be advisable to put more men on the downwind arm of the horseshoe, at the expense of the upwind one. It is really useless to attempt to drive grouse against a strong head-wind, so the drives of the day must be regulated by the direction of the wind, and not by rule of thumb, and the lines of butts arranged so as to drive when wind is not in the prevalent direction.

(9) Different coloured flags should be used by the different members of the drive. For instance—plain white for the rank and file, red for the centre or head man, and red and white for the flank men and points.

(10) Drivers should come to a halt about fifty yards in front of the butts, and stay there till all the birds are picked up by the keepers and their dogs. When going from one drive to another, both guns and beaters should talk as little as possible, and no shots should be fired.

Picking up and Packing of Birds

(1) Where dead birds can be seen they may be picked up by hand before the retriever is loosened, but in doing so, care should be taken not to spoil the scent for the dogs by tramping all over the ground. On no account should beaters be allowed to pick up birds ; it is a duty that should be left to the keeper, with his well-trained retriever or spaniel. The man who owns a well-trained spaniel or retriever should never go to a grouse-drive without his dog : its presence adds much to his own enjoyment, and it is a great assistance to the keepers. The man with a wild unsteady dog should leave it at home : besides being a nuisance to everybody, it unsteadies the other dogs. Each gun should be able to tell the keeper how many birds he has down.

(2) Dead birds should never be put in panniers and carts at once, but should be allowed to cool.

(3) The packing into the panniers or carts should be carefully and systematically carried out, the birds, with feathers smoothed, being put in singly.

Hints to Young Guns

On entering a butt the first thing the sportsman should do is to look through the barrels of his gun, then measure mentally the distance in front, to know where to pull on his bird. Most men have a tendency to let the birds come too close.

Always take your birds well in front, and do not wait

till they have passed. Take your distance and mark a spot half-way between the next butt on either side, so as to know which birds are yours and which your neighbours. Never fire at your neighbour's birds until he has done with them. Never shoot down the line. Mark mentally a spot in front of the butts, on reaching which you pull off if you miss, lift your gun, and take the bird well behind. Never follow your bird over the heads of the other guns.

When the drive is over, unload your gun, leave it in the butt, being careful not to allow any dirt to enter the muzzle of the gun, and go out to assist in the collecting of the birds—picking up all you can by hand, then using your dog on the difficult ones. Walk as little as possible over the ground—it spoils the scent for the dogs. Start to work the dog upwind on a bird.

Markers

Every gun should count the number of birds he kills in each drive, and try to mark where they fell: this effects a great saving of time in picking them up. It is, however, a matter of training, and a "marker," as on next page, will be found of great assistance. Any tinsmith can make the holder, and as a new card can be used at each change of butts, a record of every drive is thus kept. The spoke is stuck into the butt, either in front or at the side, and all the gun has to do is to mark with a dot where his bird has fallen.

METAL MARKERS

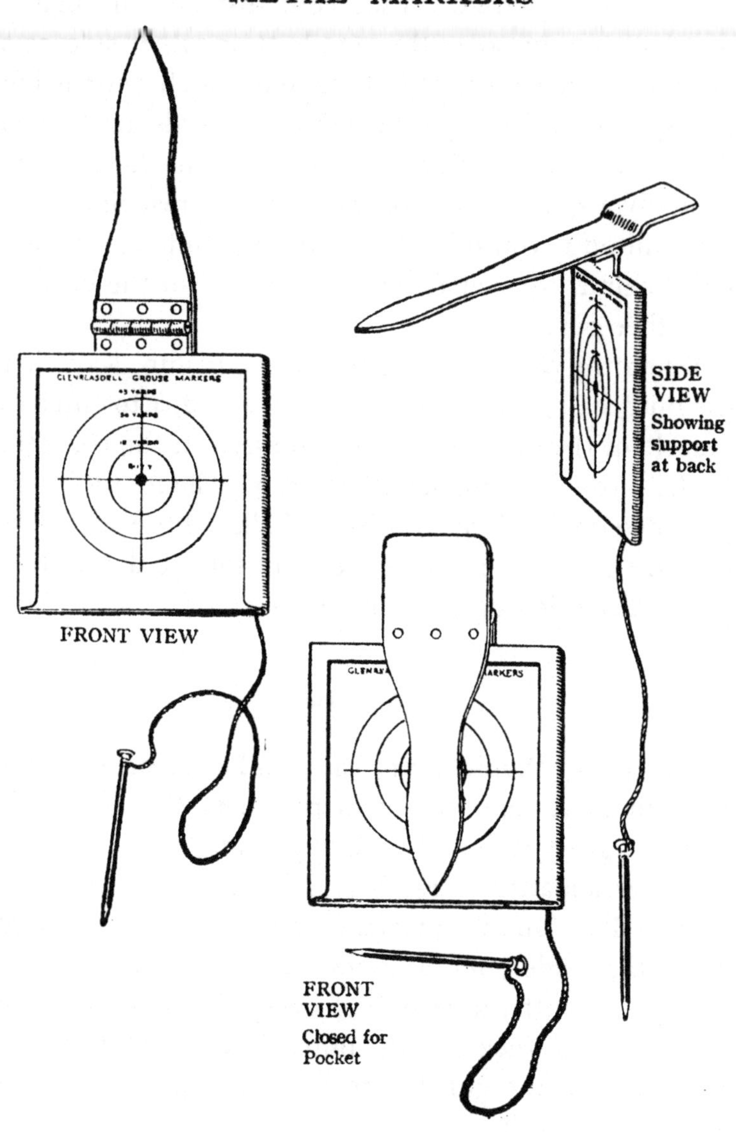

Hill Ponies

In selecting ponies for hill work, whether for carrying panniers, deer, or men, it must be insisted upon as a truism that the main point to observe is to select ponies that can climb. They should never be Lowland born or bred, and their chief qualifications should be strength and good feet. They should possess these qualifications along with that of being good climbers, at the expense of speed, paces, and style, which should never be looked for. They should not be too small : size and substance are what is needed. The shoulders should have a moderate slope—this ensures sureness of foot ; and breadth of loin and substance of bone should be demanded. In working the ponies, they should be allowed as much as possible to have their own way, and to pick out their own stepping-ground. They should also be allowed to go slowly. How often have we seen a pony fall, simply because the rider or the leader would persist in jerking its head backwards !

Black Game

There are a few facts and pieces of advice as to black game which may be recalled

(*a*) Delay killing till the birds are in full plumage and capable of good flight—i.e. black game, except old cocks, should never be shot till the beginning of September.

(*b*) Absence of vermin and plenty of rough ground.

(*c*) Judicious burning of heather and gorse on the fringe of the moor.

(*d*) The neighbourhood of corn and turnip crop to the black-game ground.

(*e*) Killing of old cocks, as discussed when dealing with grouse.

(*f*) Limitation of the number of grey hens to be killed.

With regard to the time for killing black game, the keeper is perfectly justified in indicating to the ignorant or the very young sportsman the fact that it is a recognised rule, despite the present unsatisfactory state of the official close time, to leave young black game entirely alone in August. If a young blackcock gets up in August and trundles slowly away in front of the guns, the keeper should call out, " 'Ware blackcock ! " or simply, " Blackcock, sir." In the latter case, the tone of the voice indicates the fact, which *of course* the " guns " understand, that the bird is not to be killed.

As to the killing of old cocks, the keeper should recall what has been said about grouse. The old blackcock is equally as tyrannical and disturbing as the old cock grouse. As black game are polygamous, no chance should be missed of killing the old cock at any time : you cannot be too severe on him. In attempting to rid the ground of these pests, the keeper has not however, the same difficulty, as in the case of the grouse. Black game are very conservative in their habitats, and generally select a particular spot for their fighting-matches and carousals. The keeper will soon discover some place on the fringe of the moor where the birds congregate in the early morning. It will probably be an open space in some old wood, and, by getting up early and planting himself in cover, he will have an excellent opportunity of " potting " the old cocks. When the blackcock is being stalked as he sits on the top of a dyke on the moor, it is to be recommended that, if the keeper is accompanying one of the " guns " for the purpose, he should take a different route from his companion, keeping far away from him and yet in sight of the birds, the " gun " in the meantime creeping up unobserved from an opposite direction. This practice distracts the attention of the victim from the main danger.

Black-game Driving

In driving black game there are several very important points to be observed :

(1) The drivers must be absolutely silent. This is even more important than in driving grouse.

(2) Like partridges, black game cannot be forced to fly contrary to their customary line of flight. On this account they are difficult to turn, and flank men are not of so much value as in driving grouse. However, the rule indicated when speaking of grouse-driving, as to the drivers first stooping and then gradually rising as the birds come near, sometimes meets with success in turning the birds.

(3) The line of flight of black game is very constant. On this account, in driving a wood, the keeper is soon

able to discover at what parts of the cover the birds usually pass out, and should place the "guns" accordingly. It is useless, as a rule, to line the guns at equal distances, as in grouse-driving. They should be kept fairly close together at the places indicated by the keeper.

(4) Black game will not drive well under the following conditions :

(*a*) When all the corn is not cut.

(*b*) When the weather is wild and blustering.

The best day on which to shoot black game is a dull, misty one when there is little wind. The mist hides the "guns" from the fine, long-ranged sight of the birds. High wind is apt to scatter the packs.

(5) The keeper should not hesitate, unless he is dealing with experienced black-game shooters, to remind the "guns" of two or three very important practices in black-game driving :

(*a*) On no account should a hare, breaking away at the opening of the drive, be fired at; nor should the first birds, which generally come singly and are in all likelihood grey hens, be shot. This is an unvarying rule. To fire at these "scouts" is simply to set the whole pack flying away in all directions, while, if the single birds are left alone, the rest of the blackcock will follow grandly over the guns.

(*b*) "Guns" must keep absolutely silent, well hidden, and as immovable as is compatible with nature.

(*c*) The keeper should warn "guns" that grey hens must not be fired at, unless the stock is so great that it is desirable to reduce it by shooting them. The opening day for black-game shooting should be delayed till 1st September, and the season extended to 1st January.

Poaching Black Game

In addition to the general principles recognised for the suppression of poachers, long stakes, with a nail driven into the top at right angles, may be planted at intervals over the black-game ground, when poaching by netting is common.

Ptarmigan

Every gamekeeper is aware of the fact that ptarmigan are like woodcock in one respect. They always lie in accordance with the wind. They are therefore to be found on the lee-side of hills. This fact is to be carefully recalled when they are being looked for. If, unfortunately, the march stretches along the summit of a hill and the wind is blowing from your side, the birds will be on the other side of the march, and there is not much use undertaking a mountaineering expedition to find them, unless the wise course is followed of arranging with the neighbouring owner or tenant to shoot ptarmigan on the same day. By so doing, the recognised method of killing ptarmigan will be followed, that is, by shooting in two parties. When the "tops" are on the keeper's own ground, the two-party principle enables him to get over the great difficulty of ptarmigan-shooting, which lies in the fact that the coveys fly from one "top" to another. If there is a single party, the guns will have only one chance at the broods, unless they descend again to the "plains" and make another ascent to the other "top," which procedure is apt to become monotonous, even to the most vigorous sportsman.

It goes without saying, that there is no use taking out the guns on a misty day. In all forms of sport, where there is thick mist there should be no firing, and when on a fine day, the guns being on the "tops," mist begins to collect, shooting should cease. On this account it is to be recommended that in ptarmigan-shooting the keeper and each of the guns should possess a pocket-compass. This, together with the fact that in all cases of difficulty one should follow the course of streams, will do much to counteract the disagreeable probability of being lost in the mist, as I once experienced when shooting ptarmigan in Newfoundland.

It may be necessary for the keeper to remind the young sportsman of the possible danger of not having his gun at "safe" while in the act of climbing or in groping his way over boulders and rocks.

The keeper should neither take with him pointers nor setters; they are inclined to be much put out by the presence of blue hares. But an old retriever is of the greatest possible value.

The "Heather Beetle"

The "Heather Beetle," which caused a few years ago so much havoc to the heather, is in reality a caterpillar,

and is one of the plagues that occur periodically and disappear as mysteriously as they come. A Commission sat and reported, and the information they obtained is summarised by J. B. Fergusson, Esq., of Balgarth, Chairman of the Commission, as follows :

" At first the trouble was put down to frost or some sort of blight. The heather turned red and then dry and dead, and the young heather suffered most. The offending caterpillar turns into a grub ; the grub then develops into a small brown beetle. The caterpillar eats the heart out of the young shoots, and it is believed that the beetle bores into the roots.

" Burning is the only remedy, and the greater the heat developed the better ; so the burning must be upwind, and should be carried out at the earliest possible moment after the heather is seen to be affected. If not attended to, the plant will be destroyed and will not spring again. Ordinary winter cold seems to have little effect, and the pest is increasing rapidly. It is therefore of vital importance that owners of moors should deal with the matter promptly."

We have heard nothing of the Heather Beetle for some years.

NOTES.

CHAPTER XI

THE PARTRIDGE

By Sir P. J. Mackie, Bart.

Of the many services rendered to sport by Mr. Stuart Wortley, none should be valued more highly than the emphasis he has consistently laid upon the neglect that has been the general attitude alike of owner, tenant, and keeper, in regard to the rearing and the preservation of partridges. Mr. Wortley, in discussing this important question, finds the explanation of the fact in the recognition of the pheasant as having the primary, often the only, claim to attention. Where pheasants are reared to any great extent, this is notoriously true, but there are other conditions, especially in Scotland, which have acted to the detriment of the breeding and protection of partridges.

In the Highlands of Scotland the partridge has become almost a negligible quantity, not from any choice on the part of landlord or sporting tenant, but from the circumstance that the stock is so comparatively small that it is almost disregarded. The wet climate of the Highlands and West of Scotland, it must be admitted, is against the partridge doing well. The soil is too barren, and in many cases too wet and heavy. A warm, sunny exposure, with a small rain-fall and light soil, is ideal for partridges, so that for a first-class partridge-shoot we must look to England or the fertile parts of south-east Scotland. They require arable land ; and arable land before the War was fast going out of cultivation. Now that we are learning to grow more of our own food, and to keep more people on the land, the partridge will find more agreeable surroundings, especially where there is a certain amount of rough waste ground on the fringes of the arable.

A new danger seems to have developed, which some say accounts for the scarcity of partridges in districts where they were once plentiful—that is, the higher cultivation of land, and the great increase in the use of artificial manures. As against increased fertility of the land, partridges, as a sport, must take their chance and come second. In many districts of England it has been noticed that dead birds have been found to contain arsenic in their crops. How do we account for this ? It looks as if the only source of the mortality must be the artificial manures which are used for keeping up the fertility of the land. If this be the case, there is no remedy. Another contributory cause, on some estates, is the number of rats, a kind of vermin that are undoubtedly severe on eggs. May it not be that the destruction, with the best intentions, of hawks, stoats, and weasels by the keeper, has allowed the balance of nature to increase in favour of the rats, which are usually kept down by those other vermin?

Another serious factor in this connection is the trapping of rabbits in the open by farmers in summer around the young corn. A large number of pheasants and partridges are undoubtedly killed in this way, so that—the eggs and young being left without a protector—a large shortage in stock is bound to take place. It is illegal to set traps in the open, and the law should be firmly put in force without any fear of incurring the displeasure of the farmer. He is in the wrong, and to overlook this is to buy his goodwill at too high a price. The more you give in, the more, as a rule, the farmer will take advantage of you, but if he is a decent man at all, and you have gained his goodwill, he will, on his attention being drawn to the matter, at once stop the practice. If he does not, such goodwill as he has to give is not worth having, and you had better have all the rabbits killed down in winter.

In the Highland area, it is not the pheasant that serves as the involuntary cause of the neglect of the partridge, but the grouse. As in the case of large covert shoots in the South, so in the case of moors in the North, the keeper has betrayed in the past, and seems likely to go on betraying, a kind of snobbery. The pheasant and the grouse he regards as exalted in the social world of bird-life and worthy of pampering, whilst the poor vagabond partridges, which require no hand-feeding like the pheasant, is left more or less to grub for himself.

Much of the blame for this may, of course, be traced to the owners or tenants themselves, but keepers are not entirely released from the responsibility. Many sportsmen only stay at their shooting boxes so long as they are able to get sport on the moors, and return south practically indifferent to the possibilities of good bags of partridges from the cultivated land that stretches down from the strath in front of their very lodge doors. And even when this indifference is not so marked, there can be no doubt that the general run of sportsmen would prefer to bag their ten or eleven, or even their four or five, brace of grouse in the late season, with the joy of a tramp on the hill, to spending a weary day dragging muddy boots through wet turnips and potatoes, even with the prospect of a larger bag of the autumn bird.

This is only one side of the question. There is a more important reverse of the picture. Many sportsmen in the Highlands of Scotland are indifferent to partridge-shooting, not because of the more absorbing claims of the moor, but because of the general poorness of the partridge stock. Such being the case, and granting, of course, the necessary ground conditions, the blame is to be laid largely at the door of the gamekeeper. Readers, whose sporting imaginations have been stimulated by a fine picture of well-cultivated agricultural land stretching from the edge of the moor, in richly variegated tints, down to the edge of a river wending its sinuous way through the strath, may, on interrogating the head-keeper as to the prospects of partridges, have often had their enthusiasm damped by being told, in an indifferent tone, that there may be a few coveys, but nothing to speak of. And such information has been conveyed to them as if the fact finally settled the responsibility of the keeper. Let us emphasise the point that it has only established the existence of wilful neglect of opportunity on the part of the sportsman, and the absence of a due sense of responsibility on the part of the keeper. If there be good partridge ground, the partridges ought to be there. If they are not there, or if there be only a poor stock, it indicates an indifferent sportsman or a casual keeper.

Of course these remarks are made with a full recognition of the fact that the keeper's department may be undermanned. But that has to be taken into account in all that has been said as to the keeper's duties. Those rare cases are intentionally left out of account where one keeper has in his charge, perhaps, a fairly extensive moor, a rabbit-warren, and several stretches of good cover, and whose time is fully taken up on these preserves —trapping, draining, and watching. Such conditions, being rare, need not trouble us. It cannot be said, as a rule, that keepers are overworked. Their duties and responsibilities are great, and there is no greater popular fallacy than that which pictures their occupation as only a very pleasant form of an idle country life. The care and protection of a stock of partridges, although requiring considerable time, patience, and skill, need not prove irksome to any keeper who is at all interested in his work.

In the majority of cases the partridge ground is at his very door, and more easy of control than the moor which may stretch miles beyond his home. And although such be the case, it is a notorious fact that on many shootings the information one can obtain as to the number, position, and condition of partridge nests and eggs is lamentably poor, and quest for specific information is dismissed by a few inconsequent and often misleading general statements. It is curious to observe how glibly the indifferent keeper will, season after season, talk of the drowning of the young birds and of the smallness of the coveys, apparently oblivious to the existence of ways and means to counteract these evil conditions. In the case of Highland shootings, the keeper is perhaps not so much to blame as is the case with the man whose care is chiefly with a semi-wild bird of the hand-reared pheasant type. The imagination of the former may be stunted by the fact that his work is chiefly with birds which, to a marked extent, look after themselves, or at least receive but slight artificial assistance compared with the hand-reared pheasant. But although this may be the case, it ought not to serve as an excuse, and it should be the first duty of the sportsman who realises the possibilities that have been missed, to remind the keeper of the artificial processes that are necessary for the proper rearing and care of a good partridge stock.

Having said so much in regard to the partridge ground attached to shootings where the moor is the first consideration, we return to the conditions to which Mr. Stuart

Wortley has specially directed his remarks. " Most English manors," says that great authority, " have not anything like the stock of partridges which they ought to produce. This I attribute to three causes. First, the keeper's work is not, as far as partridges are concerned, well understood, or properly carried out. Second, which is a result in part of the first, there is a good deal more egg-stealing and poaching than there should be. Third, the stock, being low, is too much reduced by hard shooting." In dwelling on these facts this writer selects a particular shooting—" The Grange "—to illustrate how the partridge stock may be improved, and dwells at length on some of the means employed. " The high average maintained at ' The Grange ' is due to a combination of . . . (favourable) conditions, and the system on which the keeper's work is conducted ; and it is here that I think a lesson may be learned by other owners and keepers. First and foremost, the latter are taught to treat partridges, and not pheasants, as the first consideration. Partridges require a better and more watchful keeper than pheasants. The old-fashioned system of leaving partridges to take care of themselves in the nesting season, while your keepers are devoting themselves exclusively to the pheasantry and the coops, must be abandoned. Everything must be done to watch and thwart egg-stealers and poachers. *To arrive at this, it follows that the whereabouts of every, or nearly every, nest must be known, and these must be watched and visited practically every day.*"

The rule which I have printed in italics must serve as the basis of the keeper's conduct. In no other way will he be able to attain to satisfactory results. To those keepers who have become accustomed to the go-as-you-please philosophy, this may seem at first an irksome addition to their day's work, but we are concerned not with the likes and dislikes of keepers, but with their duties.

As in dealing with the question of moors, we may categorically enumerate the various points that must be regarded by the keeper for the proper preservation and improvement of his general partridge stock :

(1) The supply or improvement of cover.
(2) The careful watching and protection of eggs and nests, and
(3) Artificial rearing.
(4) The improvement of the stock by the introduction of eggs from other districts, and the importation of foreign partridges.
(5) The destruction of vermin.
(6) The suppression, or the frustration, of poachers and poaching.
(7) Tactful understanding and sympathy with the farmers.
(8) The killing of old cocks.

1. *Cover*

Many estates are fortunate enough to possess so much well-distributed cover as to call for little change of a radical nature. Some are ideal in this respect, the various fields of potatoes and corn being flanked and intersected by rough ground of broom and gorse ("whin") with here and there additional growths of birch, juniper, and other trees and bushes. How freely this kind of cover is used by partridges can be proved by the fact that, on the 1st of September, in Scotland, long before the crops are cut, small bags of partridges are to be obtained by simply walking through the patches. As a rule such strips of "rough ground" are elevated considerably above the cultivated land, and in preparing artificial cover the question of elevation must not be lost sight of. In proceeding to lay out this nesting-cover, common sense must be used in distributing the patches of ground about the estate, avoiding, if possible, too close proximity to the pheasant coverts, which must naturally be kept as quiet as possible till the day of the first shoot.

In preparing the strips of cover, or banks, it is well that considerable care should be taken with regard to judicious sowing. If the banks be sown with young broom and left unwired, there is a likelihood of the young growths being eaten by rabbits and hares; but if the wiring be too high, there is a danger of the hen partridge not being able to get her young brood on to the slopes of the banks on those occasions when stormy, wet weather urges her to seek protection for her young. This remark only applies, of course, to the very early days in the life of the covey; but it is nevertheless important—for it is at this very stage that young birds are apt to be washed away by driving storms, or to be drowned in ruts and furrows. With regard to the depredations of foxes, Mr. Wortley rightly points out that "they will not be entirely kept out by wire-netting after it has been up a year or two, but they will always be loath to trust themselves much inside it, and any little alteration, such as an extra strand of wire along the top, will make them suspicious of a trap, and, in all likelihood, keep them out altogether."

It is necessary to emphasise here a point which seems to have been omitted by most authorities—that the cover must no more be allowed to take care of itself than heather on a moor. It will require from time to time judicious pruning, supplanting, and replanting, so as to maintain its value as a feeding- and rearing-ground. It is not necessary to add, after the observations already made, that, in this connection at least, rabbits and hares must come under the category of vermin and be treated accordingly.

The question of expense will naturally arise in dealing with the question of sufficient cover for partridges. In many cases the owner will be satisfied with a considerable improvement of the existing cover: in fewer cases will he be prepared to meet the outlay necessary for the planting of new ground, and—where expense is no object—he may advocate the laying out of sanctuaries or preserves. These may be as elaborate as the covers at Sandringham, or they may simply consist of stretches of corn or rye plantation, preserved in the midst of other cover for the special use of the partridge.

2 and 3. *The Careful Watching of Eggs and Nests, and Artificial Rearing—*

I have already laid down the ideal principle for the protection of nests and eggs from the depredations of poachers. Any slacker method can only lead to disastrous results in so far as the size of the coveys is concerned. Egg-stealing is a very profitable business, and is conducted with ease, owing either to the carelessness or the dishonesty of the keeper or his underlings. This carelessness is a form of neglect of duty that, when called to notice, should bring any self-respecting keeper to his senses, or, if not, should send him to the rightabout. Of course, as in other matters, the criminal neglect of duty by the keeper is often merely a reflex of the casualness or indifference of the master. Here, again, we come on a subject of explanation, not of excuse.

In the matter of the depredation of nests and eggs the keeper has to deal with six types of enemy, each of whom must be watched closely, and frustrated. These are: (1) vermin—including foxes, (2) farmers and farm labourers, (3) casual poachers from neighbouring villages, (4) professional poachers, (5) stray dogs, and (6) mowing-machines. These enemies are dealt with in separate chapters treating of the specific subject concerned. In accordance with the general habits of a great number of keepers, all that is done to prevent the stealing of eggs, and the poaching of young coveys, seems to be an occasional sleepy stroll, diagonally across a field that may contain six or seven nests or young broods, and the occasional slipshod "bushing" in the grass-fields. Every corner of every field should, instead, be gone over carefully at the beginning of the season, until a thorough knowledge is obtained of the whereabouts of nests, and the number of eggs, and then the rule followed as to watching which has already been printed in italics. Any diminution of the number of eggs must be carefully noted, and the cause traced to its source.

With regard to the protection of partridges and their nests, it must be observed, in addition to what is said in the chapter on vermin, that the destruction of vermin is naturally easier in cover which is not too redundant. Accordingly, the rough ground, the whins, the banks, and the fences must be loosely planted. If already thick, they must be thinned out. Trees and shrubs must not be too closely planted together. In other words, shelter, or, as it is termed, "cover," must be sparse and well distributed, full of young vegetation, and well protected from vermin. Where nests are found in the open, it is recommended that "a single strand of wire, about ten inches above the ground, be stretched from stout pegs." This will prevent any fox from crossing the field. Bushing must be carefully attended to—the bushes being liberally distributed and well planted, and careful observation should be made of any tampering with the position in which they were first placed. The factor or land steward should be called upon to see that the farmers keep their ditches cleaned, as otherwise, in times of flood or spate, water does not get away, and is apt to flood out the nests. Keepers should prevent the birds from nesting in ditches so foul with undergrowth that water cannot get free flow.

After any rainstorm, or during it, if necessary, the keepers should be out making observations as to the safety of the nests and small coveys. Some artificial help is often necessary to protect the eggs from destruction, and a wise keeper will often discern a chance to interfere for the benefit of his broods, although it must be remembered that human interference is soon detected by ground vermin, especially stoats, whereupon the future safety of the eggs may be in peril. "If a sad mishap," says Mr. Macpherson, "has befallen a clutch of eggs, and some of the number have actually come to grief, the misfortune can best be redeemed by such eggs as happen to have escaped destruction being placed under the charge of a domestic fowl. When the little fellows emerge into the world, they soon learn to take care of themselves, but the pupæ of ants are requisite for their successful rearing." For it is notorious that the hen bird hesitates to return to her duties if her nest has been partially destroyed or interfered with.

That distinguished observer—"A Son of the Marshes," has described[1] the methods of procuring the pupæ. "Two very different kinds of ant-hills supply the eggs or ant-pupæ to the young of game birds, and of

[1] *Pall Mall Magazine*, 1893, p. 737.

partridges in particular. First, there are the common emmet-heaps or ant-hills, which are scattered all over the land ; go where you will you will find them. These the birds scratch and break up, picking out the eggs as they fall from the light soil of the heaps ; the partridges work them easily. But the ant-eggs proper—I am writing now from the game-preserving point of view—come from the nests or heaps of the great wood ants, either the black or the red ant. These are mounds of fir-needles, being in many instances as large at the bottom in circumference as a waggon-wheel, and from 2 to 3 ft. in height—even larger where they are very old ones. They are found in fir woods, on the warm, sunny slopes under the trees, as a rule pretty close to the stems of the trees.

"The partridges and their chicks do not visit these heaps, for they would get bitten to death by the ferocious creatures. The keepers and their lads procure the eggs of these, and a nice job it is ! A wood-pick, a sack, and a shovel are the implements required for the work. Round the men's gaiters or trousers leather straps are tightly buckled, to prevent, if possible, the great ants from fixing on them, as they will try to do, like bulldogs, when the heaps are harried. The top of the heap is shovelled off, laying open the domestic arrangements of the ant-heap, and showing also the alarmed and curious ants trying to carry off their large eggs to a place of safety. But it is in vain ! Eggs and all, they go into the sack. In spite of every precaution, the ant-egg

getters do get bitten severely, for the ants would fix on anything. They spit, as the men term it, their strong acid venomously. . . . These heaps are harried for the home-bred birds—that is, home and hand-fed ones, both pheasants and partridges hatched by small game-hens—game-fowl kept specially for that purpose—from the eggs that have been taken from the outlying nests." Or, as we have shown, from the destroyed or partially destroyed nests. "Other strains of the domestic fowl are used, but the game-hens are the favourite foster-parents. When the birds are fed with the eggs, as many of the ants as it is possible to get rid of are kept out; but some are sure to be mixed up with the eggs, and these fix on the birds, making them jump off the ground. The common emmets, the creatures that the wild birds feed on—their young broods particularly—are harmless, but the large wood ants are not."

But it is strongly to be recommended that the chicks which have been placed under the care of the game-hen should be transferred as soon as possible to a brood of partridges of much the same age as the chicks. Artificial rearing and feeding present many difficulties and risks, and there is no difficulty in the way of a parent partridge receiving the little strangers into her own home, granted that the domestic hearth is not already too crowded.

For the guidance of the keeper, it might be useful here to summarise the circumstances under which he is entitled to lift eggs and transfer them to the game-fowl:

(1) In those cases where a nest has been disturbed by a dog or a casual intruder, and there is thus a reasonable fear that the parent partridge may desert.

(2) Where the parent birds have been killed or frightened away, either by mowing-machines or by other intruders.

(3) In cases where the eggs are found nested in positions of danger, or where, in the judgment of the keeper, they are lying in too exposed a position.

(4) In cases where two hens have laid in the same nest, and quarrel as to the right of taking sole control of the eggs.

There are circumstances in which a very careful and observant keeper may be able to say definitely that certain eggs have just been laid. If he can trust to the accuracy of his knowledge in such cases, and if he be faced with any of the four conditions mentioned above, he may transfer the eggs to the nests of other birds which have not begun to brood, and have not already their full supply of eggs—that is to say, not more than eighteen or twenty.

The eggs for artificial rearing may either be collected from the nests of partridges on the estate, or they may be bought from recognised English game-farms. In the former case it is sometimes necessary—in the latter always so—to test if an egg be still fertile. This is done by putting the egg into water. If still fertile it will sink to the bottom of the vessel used ; if addled it will float. It may be observed that, occasionally, the larger end of the egg tends to point upwards and does not lie quite flat at the bottom. This indicates that the egg is rather stale. The old adage may be quoted—*The fresher the flatter*.

When the eggs have begun to chip they should, with the exception of two or three—never less than two—be removed to the incubator. When hatching has taken place, the chicks are put into the drying-box for a *short* time before removal to the game-hen who is acting as foster-mother. It is wise to see that the hen is well fed before she receives her hatched brood. Chicks should be carefully turned into the coops at night-time. After six weeks of artificial feeding they are turned into the cornfields.

Attention must be drawn here to the practices which have proved so successful at Sketchworth Park. These were described in detail by Mr. Argus Olive in *Country Life* of 14th November 1903: "The partridges are allowed to go on laying until they have started to incubate their eggs; then, about the third day of sitting, their treasures are removed from them and sham eggs are given in their places, so that the birds continue to sit until their own eggs that have been put under hens are chipped. The process is not completed until twenty-five of these chipped eggs are brought to the sitting partridge, whereas probably only fifteen or fewer were taken from her. She is easy enough to deal with, and if she objects to the hand that introduces the real eggs and takes away the sham ones, she will not move more than a yard or two, and will come back directly she is allowed to do so.

"It is not supposed that she would, from the start, incubate twenty-five eggs, but it is a different thing when the young are so far self-sustaining as to be able to chip the shell; and it has been known, even before the period of the process of incubation, that a desertion and absence of outside heat for twenty-four hours has not killed the embryo. At any rate, without arguing the case, the hen partridge does hatch off these twenty-five chipped eggs. It will therefore happen that three old birds will care for all the eggs of five, so that two birds out of five are not kept sitting upon sham eggs, but have their nests destroyed. The object of this is that they should start laying again, and in order that this should be certain, these two are robbed before incubation begins, for it is a questionable point if partridges that have once become broody very often lay again; and, if they do, how early or rather how late they do it. Personally, I do not believe many ever lay again the same season if they have once started to sit. At any rate, the risk is not worth running, and as these two birds will each be good for about eight second-nest eggs, if the first are taken in time, the moral is obvious. In practice, this seems to be the utmost improvement that has proved successful. Its gross result for the five birds may be stated thus—Safety from thunderstorms and from vermin for the incubating eggs, and besides, ninety-one eggs instead of seventy-five for every five birds."

Feeding of the Young Birds.—I have spoken in former paragraphs as to the feeding of the young chicks which have been placed under the care of a foster-mother. It is only necessary to add a few remarks here on the general feeding of the young partridges when they are reared artificially.

It is essential that the young partridges should have a good supply of the pupæ of ants during the first fortnight after hatching. When these are not obtainable, Mr. Carnegie recommends bruised wheat, soaked and then fried. "About the third or fourth day, some custard may be given mixed with lettuce, chickweed, plantain (the unripe flower), groundsel, rice, broken small and boiled, and small quantities of any small bird-seed. The best way is to make a thinnish custard, and mix some of the other food material with it, always giving preponderance to the green food. Any insects which may be obtainable may also be given, in addition to the ants' eggs, which, it is necessary to remark, ought not to be offered to the chicks till the other food has satisfied their appetites." "Boiled rice, custard, or hard-boiled eggs," says Lord Walsingham, "well crushed, will certainly ensure the saving of a fair proportion of the chicks; but these alone are by no means equal to the same with the addition of ants' eggs. It is a good plan to sweep the rough herbage on the borders of some neighbouring field or wood with a coarse bag-net made of canvas or calico on a stiff iron hoop fixed on a strong handle. By this means a large number of insects of various kinds are easily collected, and can be conveyed in a bag to the coops, and thrown down there for the birds. When the birds are three weeks or a month old, the same food that is given to young pheasants may be provided for them, but grain should in no case be given, unless it be first soaked and crushed."

The coops for artificially-fed partridges are best placed in fields where the grass has been cut. The young chicks are then able to take advantage of the new grass as it grows. The coops should be moved daily, so as to ensure a new feeding-ground, with its potentialities of grass and insect-life. A supply of water is necessary for all partridges, whether artificially reared or in a wild state ; and it is advisable, in a great drought, to distribute small drinking-troughs over the estate. In this way the lives of many young, or even of old, partridges have been saved.

In making these remarks on the artificial rearing of partridges, it is only necessary to add that it is much more important that the keeper should give his time and sense to the careful watching and protecting of the wild birds in the nesting season, than that he should be concerned in the processes above described. Very few sportsmen go in for artificial rearing, and it is practically unknown in Scotland.

It is not intended in this volume to attempt to describe the various methods of rearing of partridges by hand. The French, or Continental, is the principal method, the others being modifications to suit the surroundings and climate. The advantage of more natural surroundings, and the use of the parent birds, are undoubtedly of great value. The Euston system also has been a success, and deserves a trial. This subject is one which requires a small book to itself, and I would advise those intending to take up the French system to buy one or more of the pamphlets devoted entirely to such details.

4. *The Improvement of the Stock by the Introduction of Eggs from other Breeding-grounds, and the Importation of Foreign Partridges.*

In many instances nowadays, it is to be feared, sportsmen expect too large a bag of game—they are not content with the bags of half a century ago. The constant attempts to make ground carry a larger stock of birds than nature intended it to do is creating an artificial situation. This has many risks, and must tend to disappointments. If these are to be avoided, the sportsman should try to gauge the stock of game which his land will reasonably carry with fair attention and feeding.

Enough has been written with regard to the criminal abuse of the practice of buying eggs for the purpose of improving stock, and it is again referred to in another chapter. Far and away the best method is to obtain the eggs from a friendly sportsman. Rather than buy eggs from strangers, it is better to lay down Hungarian partridges or buy Hungarian eggs. This remark, of course, is made with the object of counteracting the dishonesty that is apt to be associated with the trade in eggs. It is most necessary to state that eggs obtained for the purpose of being placed in the nests of parent partridges must be freshly laid ; if incubation has commenced, they are best dealt with under foster-parents. For the improvement of the breed of stock, recourse is had to an interchange of eggs, either simply by transferring eggs from brood to brood on one's own ground (where this is extensive), or by dealing with a friendly neighbour. A similar interchange or transference of birds may be recommended. On one's own property birds may be captured, while at feed, by coops. Two out of three cocks should be killed and the remainder removed to the ground indicated. Here they are kept under coop for a few days, fed sparingly and then turned out. The same process is followed when exchange with birds from neighbouring properties or from a distance is determined on.

With regard to the introduction of Hungarian partridges a few remarks are necessary. They should be turned down sparingly—a few every year. On this point Messrs. Tudway and Hall write : "The earlier they are turned down the better. Birds should always be turned down at night, in the neighbourhood of their water and food supply. If this does not exist, provide both. On the night that the keeper turns them down, let him first separate the sexes, and then place about four hens in one spot, and the same number of cocks at a distance, repeating the process while the birds last. This will give them the chance of mating with English birds the same season."

The practice which is followed by the present writer, who has for years dealt with Hungarian partridges, is as follows: He erects enclosures—each 8 ft. by 5 ft.—at various parts of his partridge-ground. The enclosures are about 3 ft. high, and are made of wire netting fixed on stout poles, covered at the top with packsheet to prevent the birds hurting themselves in their attempts at flight. One end of each enclosure is movable, and is virtually a wired gate. Inside and all around each enclosure are placed fir branches, which act as excellent cover. From six to eight birds are placed in each, and fed on barley and hay seeds for eight days. At the end of that time they are settled down. Food is then scattered outside of the enclosures, and on a dark night the "gate" end is opened. Lord Walsingham's modification of this plan, so far as it affects the letting out of a few birds at a time, is probably an improvement.

But whatever method be adopted, on no account should the practice—observed on more than one occasion—be followed of letting the birds out on the night of their arrival and after being hustled about for days in the process of travelling. Where such a procedure is followed, the birds immediately take flight, and, flying hard, fall exhausted many miles from where they were laid down.

The questions of (5) The Destruction of Vermin, (6) Poachers and Poaching, and (7) The Good Understanding with Farmers and their Employees, have been dealt with elsewhere. It is only necessary to conclude this part of the subject by referring to the question of the killing of some of the cock birds, which are nearly always in excess of the hens in each covey. The keeper should get the consent of the master to kill a few cock birds at the pairing season.[1]

Shooting the Partridge

Walking up.—In shooting partridges by walking them up, pointers and setters are used in those cases where there is not too large a stock of birds and where economy of time and energy is desired. In the majority of cases, however, these agencies are dispensed with. Some of the main points to be remembered by the keeper in the shooting of partridges by the walking-up method may be enumerated :

(1) It is very advisable, before the shooting begins, that the stubble and lea fields be well beaten in the early morning, for the purpose of driving the birds into the covers of potatoes and turnips—the former for preference. The keeper should send out boys for this purpose, or he may gallop on a pony over the fields, driving the birds in, and noting their destination.

(2) A good deal of time will be saved, and a large amount of important information gathered, if a marker, or markers, be posted on high vantage grounds to note and indicate the flight of coveys. Any piece of high

1—It has been recommended by some authorities that at the pairing season the keeper should scour the grass-fields and drive the birds into the cornfields, thus urging them to make their nests there, instead of in the more exposed grass or lea fields.

ground near to the scene of action may be used for this purpose, or the marker may even use a tree from which to "look out." Even when hands are scarce, it is better to utilise a marker, although it imply reduction of the number of beaters and attendants, rather than dispense with him altogether, unless the lie of the land be such that his services would be either useless or superfluous. This will be found, however, a very exceptional condition of affairs. There must be no "hallooing" between keeper and marker. A code of signals may be arranged, a whistle being used for preference. It is well for the keeper or one of his underlings to interview the marker from time to time and thus obtain accurate information.

(3) Guns should not enter a turnip-field unless birds have been seen to go, or are known to have gone, into the same.

(4) Before the guns and beaters begin to cross a field, the keeper should see that the hedgerows at the beginning of the beat are thoroughly searched ; and before the field is finally abandoned, he should be satisfied that all the fences have been explored.

(5) The keeper should be particularly careful to warn the "guns" to keep a sharp look out at the end of every beat. Guns are apt to slacken their attention as they approach a hedgerow or the corner of a field. It is at such places that birds which have run ahead in front of the guns are apt to rise.

(6) If it be left to the keeper to decide how the guns and the beaters are to advance, he may choose one of

several methods, the most usual being the advance in line and the "half-moon." The former plan is the more common, especially when the field is at all extensive, but it is as well to recommend, when this practice is followed, that, if the end guns are close to a hedge, one or two of them should be flanked—that is, a little in advance of the others. When a strong wind is blowing across the field, it would be better that the line be flanked in every beat. The keeper's attention must be constantly kept to the formation and evenness of the line of guns and beaters. If the "half-moon" pattern be used, it is necessary to drop a polite hint as to the danger involved. To do this judiciously, it will be well to address the whole party, and thus avoid giving offence.

For an elaborate description of the "half-moon" form of advance, and for information as to other less-used methods, such as the advance by echelon, the keeper is referred to Lord Walsingham's excellent account in the volume on *Shooting* in the Badminton Library.

It is hardly necessary to add that in approaching a covey in a stubble or a lea field, the guns should never by any chance be advised to advance directly on the birds. They must be flanked, and approached on a wide horseshoe pattern, which tends to become a circle as the guns proceed.

(7) If in beating a field there be no desire to drive birds in one particular direction, then the guns and beaters should wheel; but if it be desired to force the

birds ahead, the line should come back to the original starting-point.

(8) When a single bird is killed, the place should be carefully marked by the keeper or by one of the beaters, and the line should continue to advance till the place is reached. Where several birds have fallen, sticks should be planted at the nearest points possible to the places where they are likely to be found. When a bird towers, or falls at a great distance, an attempt should be made to mark the spot by selecting some object in the field of vision that will give the line of the bird—for instance, a tree at the end of the field, some outstanding piece of growth in the field, or a gap in a hedge.

(9) In working the retrievers for picking up birds, the following instructions should be carefully remembered: (*a*) First pick up the birds that have fallen behind the guns. (*b*) Leave alone all consideration of runners till the dead are picked up. (*c*) Never allow a dog to go on to fresh ground. Runners or birds that have dropped far out may be picked up in later beats, care being taken to remember their line. If, in the later beats, there be any difficulty in finding, a man with a retriever may be left behind, while the guns proceed to new ground. (*d*) Send a dog forward immediately to a killed bird only if you can absolutely trust him. (*e*) In picking up a bird, let the dog have the wind of it. Dogs work better alone, and not with men near them to spoil their scent. Men carrying hares or rabbits are especially to be warned off.

(10) The keeper should remember the unvarying law —the line must move slowly, evenly, and silently.[1]

Driving Partridges

There are several important points in connection with a partridge-drive that the keeper should keep in his mind:

(1) The question of fences is of importance where partridge-driving is regularly practised year by year. The keeper should, along with his employer, try to persuade the farmers not to cut their fences too low. If the good relationships referred to in Chapter IV be maintained, this should be easy. Shooting from behind a good high hedge is quite a different matter from shooting from behind a low-clipped one, or from behind an artificial "butt" in the shape of an improvised hurdle.

(2) In the majority of cases the keeper will find that the guns, guided by their own knowledge of the sport, will themselves take up their positions for shooting, but he may be called upon to indicate to the less experienced the best positions to assume. He will keep in mind the necessity for good cover, and remember the rule of experience—that guns should stand near to the hedge in upwind drives, and well out from the hedge in downwind drives. From a high fence in the latter case, the guns should stand far out.

1—It is in every way to be recommended that, where partridges are habitually killed by the walking-up principle, an occasional drive should be arranged. In this way the coveys are dispersed, there is an interchange of blood, and old barren birds are killed off.

(3) The rule of making experimental drives, as laid down in the chapter on Grouse, must be followed. In this way the line of the general flight of the birds will be learnt, and it must be carefully remembered that partridges will not be driven the way they are not accustomed to go.

(4) It is best to preface a drive by ordering the beaters, in the morning, to drive the birds from off any outlying ground.

(5) It is advisable to have the first drive with the birds driven downwind.

(6) The beaters, on moving forward to a drive, should pass along a boundary fence.

(7) In bringing back the birds for another drive, the knowledge of their flight is important. It is useless to attempt to bring back birds from directly behind the guns, if the birds have not flown there. This seems a truism, but it is necessary to record that such foolishness is often practised. Remember the seemingly simple but oft-forgotten rule—Bring back the birds from where they have flown with the wind.

It is advisable, in bringing back birds against the wind, that some of the guns should walk with the beaters, as a great many birds, in this case, break back.

(8) The head-keeper should form the centre of the line of beaters, to guide and warn the flanks ; and he should, for preference, be mounted.

(9) The law of flanking is the same as in the case of grouse-driving. A screen, well thrown forward, should

always be formed on the downwind side. Flanks should be enlarged and increased according to the wind, and it is as well that good guns be placed along with the flanks who are on the downwind side. When there are no guns on the flanked side, or when their presence is discounted, there should be a good deal of shouting and waving of flags on that side.

(10) In addition to the keepers who stand with their retrievers behind the stationary guns, there should be a keeper or two at the other end of the field in which the guns are standing, to mark and pick up towering birds and those that have dropped far out.

(11) All birds should be picked up on the day of the drive. Scouring the fields on the day following disturbs the birds too much. Partridges should always be allowed a day of rest after a drive.

Poaching the Partridge

Where it is possible, there should always be extra hands engaged in the nesting season, and every care should be taken to systematically watch the fields where there are nests. Bushing must be carefully carried out. " An excellent plan " (writes Sir R. Payne Gallwey) " to check the operation of poachers who net partridges is to procure three sticks of thorn, each 2 ft. long, tie them across in the centre with wire or tarred string in the form of a cross or star, sharpen their ends, and place one of the points lightly in the ground. This arrangement cannot be seen at night, and on being touched by a net rolls up in it, end over end like a wheel. The sticks can be kept from year to year ready for use, and may be quickly placed in position in the fields."

Another plan is to drive oak posts, about an inch square and 2 to 3 ft. long, into the ground at various points over the fields. It will add to their usefulness if a few nails be driven into the posts near the top.

But whether bushing, poling, or other method be carried out, such practice must not supersede careful day and night watching.

NOTES.

CHAPTER XII

THE DEERSTALKER

By Captain Henry Shaw Kennedy

To my mind, for an outdoor servant, there is no more delightful occupation than that of a deerstalker. His life is generally spent in wild and magnificent scenery, and though the house or lodge he lives in may be isolated —perhaps twenty miles from the nearest town or village —yet there is a charm in the isolation, and there is romance in living out of the world, far from human ken. What can be more delightful than to feel that the " wild red deer " are your only neighbours for miles and miles ? Well, if these neighbours are not to the stalker's liking, I should advise his taking to some other trade.

But now to business. Every man is not fitted to be a deerstalker—in fact, very few men are. No man need expect to take on this job with success unless he be sound in heart, lung, and limb, with eyesight of the very best. The stalker must be a first-class walker—never knowing what it is to be tired ; and, above all things, his soul must be in his work.

It is no easy task to outwit a large herd of deer, over ground they have lived on for years, with tricky winds blowing up the corries, and take your "gentleman" safely up to shooting distance.

My experience of the deerstalkers I have met and crawled with, and they are a goodly few, I look back upon with the greatest pleasure. I have invariably found them most delightful companions and keen—in fact, sometimes too keen—sportsmen, and I may say that some of the happiest days of my life have been spent on the hillside in their company. I don't think I am wrong in calling them Nature's gentlemen.

Now and again one comes across lazy and indifferent stalkers—men who, in many cases, have become degenerate by the too frequent use of the black bottle; but as a rule, these are few and far between; for them I have no use; about them I have nothing to say.

These few little hints I am now writing are not meant in the least to serve as advice to the old deerstalker. He has little to learn, and is as wise and cute as the red deer himself, or as an old cock grouse on a mountain-side. It is for the *young* stalker who is learning the practices of his trade that I write these lines of simple advice, which may possibly be of use to him. For, looking back on old stalking days, how well do I remember many a long and difficult stalk and crawl, magnificently planned and carried out by the stalkers, but marred at the last moment by some trifling error arising from want of experience. Instead of the stalk being a red-letter day in the forest—a day crowned by the prize of a goodly stag—it has ended in a long, dreary walk home in the dark, with your "gentleman" in depressed spirits, and fully aware that he will be well chaffed over his *miss* when he returns to the lodge.

We shall now imagine ourselves in front of a forest lodge, time 9 a.m. (I am all for stalkers being "early astir," as the sporting papers term it, for late autumn days are short). Stalkers, gillies, and ponies with deer saddles—the number of the latter varying with the number of rifles to take the hill—are all preparing for the start.

Now, young stalker, the first thing, we presume, is that you are suitably dressed. Nothing to my mind can be better than *Lovat* mixture, but there are one hundred and one different patterns of cloth equally good, and in several forests they have their own particular brand that they swear by, which is worn by stalkers, gillies, and the "gentlemen" themselves. However, these are matters of detail. Of course, the nature of the ground makes some mixtures much more suitable than others.

Of one thing I am certain: it is always best to have the whole of your suit and your cap made of the same material. I have often watched a line of grouse-drivers on a hillside through a glass from a distance, and have always found that the most conspicuous were those who wore mixed suits—that is, coat of one material and knickers of another.

As regards boots or shoes, I prefer the former, as they give more support to the ankles; and spats when wet are apt to make cold feet; but this is entirely a matter of taste.

As each " gentleman " is told off to his beat by his host, this is the time—stalker, young or old—to be observant. Make certain you have got your " gentleman's " rifle and *cartridges.* I have known the discovery made, when nearing the end of a stalk, that " the bullets " had been left behind. If you are to take the hill with a sportsman with whom you have been out before, you have little to learn ; but if he be a *newcomer*, you must try to find out for yourself, unobserved, what he is made of, before getting him up to deer. In all probability you will have a mile or two to walk up the valley, or up the hill, before you come to the first spying-ground. As a rule, your " gentleman " will walk with and talk to you. Now is your chance. He may be an old *shikari* and know every card of the game, and be able to walk as well as, perhaps better than, yourself, and may be able to teach you a wrinkle or two. But this you will not be long in finding out, and vice versa.

Should your " gentleman " be elderly, or you find that he is not a good walker, you must at once suit your step to his pace as much as possible. Many a good day has been marred and many a good stag missed through young stalkers not keeping this fact particularly in mind. They bring their " gentleman " up to shooting distance faultlessly, having made a magnificent stalk in treacherous wind over most difficult ground. But too fast ! too fast ! they have never turned to look at the panting object behind them ; the rifle is pulled out of its cover shoved into the sportsman's hand, and the whisper

" Tak' 'im noo, tak' 'im noo, Captain—the big black ane." But alas ! the sportsman's sides are heaving, his heart is throbbing, his hand is shaking from excitement and fatigue, and, getting up, he draws an unsteady bead, which results in a miss, and in remorse for the rest of the day.

Now all this might have been different had you adapted your pace to that of your " gentleman," which, if deer are *settled*, is just as easy as going at your own pace. Of course there are times, when deer are on the move, that you *must* go fast—in fact, race—for a shot ; but the stalker should always remember that there is not the slightest advantage in his being one hundred or two hundred yards in front of his " gentleman "—a condition of affairs I have seen. The two should be in close touch with each other.

But let us hark back to the spying-point. Now, young stalker, we will presume that you are thoroughly acquainted with a *glass ;* before you have sat down two minutes to spy you will know if your " gentleman " is at *home* with it or not. He may be a first-class man with the glass, but you must not think you are a better man than he, if and because you pick out deer first, as this results from the fact that you know the ground and exactly where to find them. The sportsman, on the other hand, is heavily handicapped, being a stranger and not knowing the likely spots to put his glass on ; but in two minutes, as I said before, you can tell if he is at home and of any use with the glass. The *novice* you will detect at once ; he is quite at sea with it, and has not the slightest idea of putting himself into a spying position, nor of keeping the glass steady—one minute he gazes at the sky, the next he plunges into the heather.

Now, having discovered that your " gentleman " is a *duffer* (you need not tell him so), but seems anxious to learn, do everything you can to show him the best spying positions—off your knee, or off a stick, etc ; and above all things be patient—suit yourself to the occasion. Of course, it is a thousand times better and far less trouble for you to find your " gentleman " an accomplished stalker. You may then very often pick up little hints from him if you are attentive and observant, and you can both work so much better together and consult one another as to the stalk.

But let us suppose that you have found deer from your first spying-point, and a stag among them fit to shoot, and that your " gentleman " is a novice—then take plenty of time to explain matters to him ; make him have a good look at the deer through his glass, point out to him the way the wind is blowing, and how you intend making the stalk. This procedure will be far more interesting to him than if you shut up your glass, telling him nothing, as some do, and simply let him follow you like a shadow as you crawl and creep over rocks and wade through burns.

It is far more exciting for him to know the spot you are making for than to be treated as a nonentity. Therefore explain to him that when you are crawling he must crawl, and when you are slithering he must slither, and when you lie flat he must lie flat, and should you *suddenly stop* (an action prompted perhaps by an old hind looking up), he must also stop at once, in however disagreeable a position he may be, and not move a muscle till he gets the "office" from you. Sometimes you are caught with one knee in a green spring and the other on a sharp rock, which is anything but pleasant; but such are the ups and downs of deerstalking. When you are crawling with an inexperienced "gentleman," it is always best to look round every now and then, to see whether he is acting in conformity with you or not, for sometimes a stalker cannot conceive what has put deer off the ground till he looks round to find his "gentleman's" head buried in the ground, but his heels in the air, or some other part of his body showing.

At last, when, having walked, run, crawled, wriggled and slithered over fearful ground, sometimes in sight of deer and sometimes not, you have arrived safely within a few yards of where you expect to get your shot—now is the time, of all others, for you to keep *perfectly calm.* Nervousness and excitement are very infectious, and you are very apt to infect your "gentleman," especially if he be a novice, even very often if he is not. I cannot imagine any more exciting moments than those spent as you are just crawling up to the last little hillock or rock, knowing that there is one of the finest harts of the forest within one hundred yards.

Have the cover of your rifle unbuckled and all ready to be pulled out in a second ; see that it is loaded and the safety-bolt properly adjusted and in working order. It is never desirable to crawl farther with a loaded rifle than is necessary ; and, above all things, do not take for yourself the best and perhaps the only good spot to shoot from. Make your " gentleman " creep alongside of you, or even a few inches in advance ; let him have the front seat now, and whatever position he likes best to shoot from. I have often seen a good, experienced stalker take the front and only possible place to fire from himself, pull the rifle out of the cover, thrust it into his " gentleman's " hand, and leave him to shoot as best he could.

There are a hundred and one little trivial circumstances that cause *a miss* at the last moment, all of which might have been easily avoided.

Crawl close up alongside your " gentleman." Do not let him fire till the stag is offering a good broadside chance. If the deer have not " taken you up," there is no hurry whatever, unless the light is failing, when the sooner you shoot the better. Now, having given your " gentleman " the hint—" Tak' him noo, Captain "—he will at once place his forefinger round the trigger in the shape of an " 'ook " (as our old drill sergeant used to teach us), " and, without moving the ' 'ead, 'and, or heye,' press it gently until the 'ammer falls." I think, if he follow out these instructions to the letter, the stag also will fall—and thus conclude a successful stalk.

But other little trifles, such as blades of waving grass or heather in front of the foresight, very often cause a miss. Now, to avoid these, the rifle must be raised to clear them, with the result that it is then found difficult to secure a good rest. To overcome this difficulty, if the ground be suitable, lie face downwards in front of your "gentleman," and give him your shoulders as an excellent rest to shoot from. It will, of course, be necessary gradually to raise or lower yourself until he gets the right height. A short stick also is very handy to shoot from, if used carefully, but, of course, you run the risk of its being "taken up" by the deer.

Another point that I would advise all stalkers to be most careful about is that, having got their "gentleman" safely up to the last shooting-point, they make sure he takes the *right* stag. I have often seen terrible disappointment from his taking the *wrong* one. Nor is it always the sportsman's fault. Perhaps for over an hour he has been crawling behind the stalker, his nose glued to the latter's boots, and has never had a chance of looking at the deer he is stalking till the last hurried moment before firing; and it is not always so easy to pick out the *best stag* amongst a big lot, wildly scattered, unless there is something very distinctive about his head or body.

Now, the "gentleman" having taken his shot, and you having seen that the stag has got it in the right place, and is lying dead on the hillside, it is better to remain still for a minute or so, as the herd of deer are much more likely to settle again soon, and not go over the march, than if you rushed in before they were out of sight.

It is safer after the stalk is over to unload the rifle.

Having "gralloched" your stag, put him on the pony, and started him for the lodge, take your lunch, after which, the day being still young, you can commence again, spying fresh corries and finding fresh deer, and you may, possibly, have one or two more successful stalks before night. But on no account should you be bloodthirsty—it is much better, to my mind, to have a blank day than to bring in an *unshootable* stag; it spoils the average weight of the year, and, if many of that sort are shot, it spoils the reputation of a forest. A stalker should know exactly his master's wishes as to how many stags one individual "rifle" may bring in on one day. I have known a "rifle" go out and, being carried away by his own excitement and his stalker's encouragement, bring in five, or even six, stags in a day, none of which were worthy to hang by their heels in the larder.

Now, to my mind, that "gentleman" need not think himself hardly used if he is not asked to shoot in that forest again, and the stalker need not think himself a martyr if he gets the "Royal Order of the Boot." Those "Waterloo" days—when several indifferent stags are killed—spoil the sport for others, as, later in the season, when real good stags come on the ground, they cannot be shot, the *limit* having been reached—which, to put it mildly, is most annoying.

I am going now to tread on very dangerous ground. A stalker cannot be too careful how he acts with regard to the forests that march with him. I don't think I am exaggerating when I say that, as a rule, there is more jealousy, more rivalry, and more cool feelings (may I use the phrase ?) among neighbours on deer forests than in any other locality. I find that these feelings exist not only among the owners, but among the stalkers and the gillies, for they are as infectious as the grouse disease itself. Again, Mr. Stalker, I offer my humble advice. Do all in your power to keep friendly with neighbouring forests and foresters. I am sure it will pay you best in the long-run, for, in many ways and particularly in adverse winds, your neighbour can do incalculable damage to your sport.

Now we will jump from the neighbouring forests to your glass—not to the glass of *Glenlivet*, but to your telescope—to my mind by far the best friend a deer stalker has got ; as, when it fails, he may as well " put up the shutters." It is the one great pull you have over the deer, as it enables you to pick them up long before they, even with their keen eyes, can detect your presence. Now, you cannot be too careful of this glass. In very bad weather it is liable to get fogged and become quite useless until taken to pieces and dried. Remember, then, when your glass is " bunged up," you are badly handicapped, and, to my mind, you lose half the pleasure of stalking. If it be a very wet day, use your glass as little as possible. A good plan is for you and your

" gentleman " to take it in turns to spy, so that, if one glass gets out of order, you have the other to fall back upon. Always take the telescope to pieces every night, and have the sets well dried in front of the fire. This rule applies also to the case, which, if damp, is apt to fog the glass. A waterproof cover to slip on when the glass is not in use will be found a great protection.

I will not go into all the " pros and cons " of different rifles—volumes might be written on this subject ; but every man knows the rifle he prefers. The great thing, to my mind, is to hold straight. I have often heard the very best of rifles abused for inaccurate shooting, when the real cause was " stag fever "—a very common complaint. As a stalker, you will most likely be provided with a rifle of some sort to shoot hinds with in the winter, and, with a little practice, you can soon suit yourself to any rifle. Remember always that, like your *glass*, you cannot be too careful of your rifle or that of your " gentleman." They should be cleaned immediately after you return from stalking, and hung up. Some sportsmen of my acquaintance clean their rifles themselves, and do not trust anyone else to touch them. Of course this is the safest plan, for no blame can then be attached to the stalker if anything goes wrong. I should advise having a rifle sighted—not too finely—to shoot point-blank at a known distance, say 100 yds., and then you can work up or down, i.e. now higher now lower for longer or shorter distances, which as a rule vary from 80 to 200 yards.

Seek to avoid getting too near your deer, and do not encourage the novice to try long shots.

The stalking season being over, and the sportsmen having all gone south, you are left a good deal to your own devices. You have the long winter to get through, which, of course, must be more or less monotonous in your isolated lodge, but if you are a good man, you will find plenty to keep you occupied—watching your deer in the heavy snowdrifts, and doing what you can for them. You will also very often have hinds to kill,[1] and, next to stalking the stag himself, what better sport could you wish for ? Then, when the New Year comes round, you can spend many an hour watching for good stags to shed their horns, for these, and many other little items, such as skins, etc., are looked upon as the stalker's perquisites.[2]

On the Deterioration of Heads

Before concluding, I would like to make a few remarks on a subject that hardly comes under the heading of

1 This question of hind-shooting is of primary importance as applied to the improvement of stock. We leave out of account altogether the question of good venison, which ought to be secondary to the desire to assist the general welfare of the forest. In keeping this in view, the main point to be attended to is the destruction of old hinds, whose calves are in 90 per cent. of cases feeble and unhealthy, and—in the opinion of many authorities—chiefly females. The stalking-gillie is too apt to lose sight of the primary object of his work, and to select well-conditioned hinds, instead of the decrepit females before-mentioned. " It has been proved," says one writer, " that 90 per cent. of yeld-hinds killed would have had stag calves in the ensuing season. Thus, every ten yeld-hinds killed mean a loss of nine prospective stags to the forest." On this account yeld-hinds should be left alone.—P. J. M.

2 Every young stalker should procure, if possible, a *small* copy of Mr. Grimble's excellent book on *Deerstalking*. In it he will get a fund of information.

" The Duties of a Stalker," but yet must be a most interesting and useful study for him. This is—the growth and development of the deer's horn, from the time it commences to sprout (covered with velvet) on the stag's skull, till it develops into what I consider to be one of the most picturesque and most prized and valued trophies a good sportsman can possess—a finely matured stag's head. I feel that I am treading on dangerous ground when I write on this subject, so many abler and more experienced men than myself having made a life-long study of deer's horns, and a great many most interesting and instructive articles having been written regarding them.

In spite of all this writing, and in spite of all this study of animal life, there is no disputing the fact that of late years the heads of Scottish red deer have been deteriorating greatly, and " all the king's stalkers and all the king's men " cannot put a stop to this and make them pick up again. I think I am correct in saying that this deterioration is going on in almost every forest in Scotland, and I am sure all old stalkers will corroborate and tell you the same tale—" Heads are going back, back, back ! " What is to be done ? Money will not stop it, artificial feeding in winter will not stop it, and the introduction of fresh blood and park deer seems of no avail, though I do think that good wintering helps, in a small way, deer to grow better heads. But in my humble opinion—and I trust I will not bring a hornet's nest of deerstalkers about me for what I am going to say—the key to this recent deterioration lies in the wholesale killing year after year of the very stags that should be left to reach maturity and produce good stock.

Now, how is this to be prevented? Prevention is next door to impossible. The majority of forests are let to yearly tenants who pay high prices for them, and, naturally, wish to make the most they can out of them, which, of course, means killing off the finest heads in the forests. As this continues year after year, a good forest goes from bad to worse, till at last it becomes a wilderness of wretched, miserable stags, with heads that no good sportsman would care to hang on his walls.

Now, to be brief, the best possible cure for this deterioration is, of course, to spare as much as possible all six, seven, or eight-year-old stags with promising, well-shaped heads, and so give them a chance, when they are ten or twelve years old, of carrying magnificent heads such as one sees in old drawings by Landseer and Crealocke.

There is one great drawback to this attempted preservation of young stags with promising heads, and that is, that although you do everything in your power and skill to save them, your neighbours may kill anything or everything that comes within reach of their rifles and thus undo most of the good you are trying to effect.

Now, Mr. Stalker, it is very often in your power (though not always) to prevent the class of stag of which I have been writing from being shot, and when you save one of these you contribute your mite to the improvement of Scottish red deer's heads.

Deerstalking Notes

In addition to what has been said in the body of this chapter, the following points should be observed by the young stalker :

(*a*) Never attempt a *downwind* stalk.

(*b*) Always try to stalk *down hill*, as deer seldom look up the hill ; and always try to have the sun at your back and shining in the eyes of the deer.

(*c*) Remember the general rule—that deer move upwind when they are feeding.

(*d*) In fine weather the biggest stags are on the highest hills ; in wet and stormy weather they are on lower ground.

(*e*) Do not stalk, or be very careful, on days when there is a very high wind, as the deer are apt to dash about from place to place without any obvious reason.

(*f*) Remember that whatever wind may be blowing across the hills, there is always a current moving *up and down* the narrow glens. It is therefore wise to carefully spy out the ground near to where the deer are grazing, notice the movements of the grass in their vicinity, and then make your stalk accordingly.

Mist is the bugbear of the stalker, but the times of enforced inaction resulting from its presence are not wasted if you watch carefully, and note the drift of the mist as showing the different currents of air, many of them contrary to the general direction of the wind. Constant observation is the making of a good stalker. Never try to stalk in thick mist. You will do much harm and no good.

(*g*) The distance one may approach near to a herd varies. When there is a strong wind it is not safe to pass within a mile of the herd.

(*h*) In making a stalk, be particularly careful to avoid any outlying herds of deer ; if these see you they may scamper over the forest and upset all your calculations.

> " The best laid schemes o' mice and men
> Gang aft a-gley."

NOTES

CHAPTER XIII

THE RABBIT

By Sir Peter J. Mackie, Bart.

Generally speaking, rabbits are a nuisance on a property, and should be kept down to the lowest limits. They are a constant source of annoyance to the farmer, and a cause of expense to the proprietor who plants. They do great damage to young trees, and unless the keepers are very energetic in trapping them, a few rabbits in hard weather will soon spoil a plantation. The only sure method is netting, but this is an expensive means of limitation, so that it is questionable whether bunny is worth his meat. Some farmers are curiously inconsistent : for instance, it has come within my notice that on an arable farm, where orders had been given to kill down all the rabbits, the grumbling farmer complained that they were being killed down too quickly, and that he could not get as much as a rabbit for his house. Farmers were not content till the law was altered to give them compensation for damage by game, and now that they have got the rabbit kept down, they complain of its scarcity. Another strong objection urged against the rabbit is that it draws poachers.

The gamekeeper is called upon to regard the rabbit in a variety of aspects. These may be thus enumerated—(1) As vermin; (2) as a comparatively unprotected and unpreserved occupant of a shooting estate; and (3) as a member of a carefully preserved and systematically protected warren. In dealing with him in this third capacity the keeper has to view him either as part of a farm—that is, when the rabbit is preserved mainly for market purposes; or as part of a sporting property—that is, when he is preserved for the purposes of shooting.

He will most likely be called upon to view the rabbit as vermin in the following cases: (1) On a good moor, generally; (2) proximate to good partridge-cover; (3) near to special cultivated ground—as, for instance, farms, gardens, lawns, and the like.

Many owners have no objection to a stock of rabbits existing on their moors, but in every way they should be regarded as a pest, especially in those cases where shooting is practised over dogs, or by simply walking-up the birds. Many a brace of birds has been missed owing to the fact that the barrels of the shooter have been loosed on a rabbit. On this account it is as well that the rabbit should be exterminated on a moor, and not on this account only, but also because of the voracious habits of the animal, and more particularly because of the fouling of the ground by its excretions. There are cases, however, on small and badly stocked properties, where the chance of an occasional rabbit affords some consolation to the weary shooter, who, after tramping for hours without a shot, regards the furtive bunny almost in the light of "game." The presence of rabbits at least ensures his return with something in the bag.

(1) To the keen and experienced rabbit shot, nothing affords better sport than rabbits in heather. Where such is desired it is better that a certain part of the moorland be reserved for the rabbit stock. On most shootings there is a considerable acreage of ground near to the lodge where rabbits are plentiful enough for such purposes, and where birds do not generally breed. But these facts do not upset the general rule, that on a moor the rabbit is to be regarded primarily as vermin.

(2) In regard to good partridge cover the same remark has to be made, although in this case the main objection to the rabbits' existence is in relation to the feeding capacity of the ground. As a rule, there is not so great an objection to its presence here as in the case of the moor, especially when the cover is extensive and is used as shooting ground. A day among the "whins" would lose half its attractions were it not for the rabbits, which afford such excellent practice as they dart between the bushes, and the escape of a covey of partridges means merely, as a rule, a flight into turnips or potatoes, the best and natural cover in which to kill them. But if the cover referred to is required for a good stock of partridges, if its food possibilities are limited, and especially if the birds are not to be disturbed till the first drive, it is better to get rid of the rabbits.

(3) The destructiveness of rabbits is so notorious that the keeper will often be called upon by his master to protect the garden and the flower-bedded lawn from their encroachments; and a farmer has a right to protest in those cases where rabbits are laid down to such an extent that they overrun and materially damage his crops.

So much for the rabbit as vermin. In considering him as a comparatively unprotected and unpreserved occupant of a shooting estate, we are regarding him in his most popular and most general aspect. We use the word "comparatively" advisedly, for, in nearly every case, some protection is necessary both for the sake of the rabbit and for the sake of proper shooting. However little effort is being made to develop a small rabbit shoot into the proportions of a warren, it is still necessary, if rabbits are to be at all healthy or numerous, that the rule as to the addition of new blood be observed carefully.

The unvarying rule is—that new blood should be introduced every year. This is a rule, however, that is almost invariably neglected. The law of inter-marriage, be it remembered, is the same throughout the whole animal world. Intermarriage amongst peoples tends to the deterioration of the race. An uncrossed grouse stock tends to disease and death. A rabbit stock which is left to itself accumulates diseases of the most virulent description. The danger is far greater in the case of rabbits than in that of birds, owing to the migratory habits of the latter. Many people refuse to eat rabbits owing to a suspicion that disease is likely to be prevalent. This may be an extreme and an unnecessary caution, but the mere fact that the suspicion exists may be taken as indicating an impression gathered from common experience.

It is difficult, when dealing, not with a warren, but merely with scattered rabbit burrows, to lay down a general law as to the number of rabbits to be put down each year; but about three or four to every hundred acres of ground would seem sufficient. The best time is when the shooting is over, in any case not later than the middle of January. This is late enough to permit of the Christmas shootings. When there is sufficient evidence to prove that the rabbit stock is diminishing from any cause, apart from the destruction by gun and trap, the whole stock should be exterminated and an entirely new one laid down. Great care should be exercised in the selection of the ground from which the new blood is taken. It should come from districts at as great a distance away as is consistent with convenience, and should be from ground where the laying down of new blood is consistently and habitually practised, and, if possible, where rabbits are not too numerous. In selecting the rabbits, bucks should preponderate. In the majority of cases it is easy enough to arrange an interchange of blood. For this, it is, of course, necessary that the health of one's own stock should be above suspicion.

The unenclosed burrows with which we are now

dealing are, in the main, used for the purposes of ferreting, and it will be the duty of the keeper to see that there are convenient arrangements made for the purposes of the guns. It is often necessary to do a little clearing in the vicinity of rabbit-burrows, especially when there is much undergrowth. When the burrows are in thickly wooded cover, rides may be made—not only the wide-open rides as used in pheasant coverts, but smaller ones not open to the sky. Rides should also be made on bracken ground, and on the heather land that is used for rabbit-shooting. In the latter case the rides are most useful, for where the heather is thick, old, and long, there is little or no chance for the gun to spot his rabbit, until perhaps he sees it disappearing over the edge of a knoll, or into a hole, a hundred yards away. If the heather has been well attended to—and this is very exceptional on land that is near to the lodge, and is used primarily as rabbit ground—rides are not so absolutely necessary, and sporting shots might prefer to take their chances without such aid.

It is often desired to lay down stock on ground that is at present untenanted by rabbits. When this is done outside a warren, and chiefly for the purposes of ferreting, suitable ground will of course be chosen; that is to say, ground which combines the necessities of food and good opportunities for shooting. This ground should be temporarily closed in by wire fencing, and should be scraped out here and there to assist the rabbit in the process of burrowing.

The Warren

A warren may be an extensive stretch of ground a quarter of a mile or more in length, or may simply be a three-acre field. In the former case, no change of venue is necessary ; in the latter, it is usual to change it from time to time, say once every five or six years. The ideal warren must be well drained, well supplied with food, and properly enclosed. The soil should be sandy, porous, and free from the possibilities of flooding. Good natural warrens stretch along the banks of rivers, but have a considerable elevation above flood-mark, and slope gently upwards towards the pheasant covert, which stretches in almost parallel lines with the windings of the river : they are enclosed at each end, either by natural fences, protected by wire-netting, or simply by this netting erected on "stobs." A good warren of this type has varieties of cover—bracken, broom, and gorse, heather and hassocks of grass, with here and there small juniper trees and varieties of shrubbery. But although such is described as a "natural" warren, it is subject to the same laws as those which we term "artificial." The extinction of vermin must be thoroughly looked to, the cover must be regularly supervised, wiring must be carefully examined, draining thoroughly carried out, and, if necessary, lime occasionally scattered to counteract the fouling of the ground. Overcrowding must be avoided, and evidences of disease carefully noted.

Where no such natural warren exists, and it is proposed

to construct one, it would be to the advantage of a keeper if he visited some well-known warren and took into view the natural conditions he proposes to imitate. In selecting his ground, he should keep in view the following points : (1) The lie of the land ; (2) the condition of the soil ; and (3) the capacity for cover. The land chosen should in no case be on clay soil, or be rocky ground. Sandy soil is the best, although peaty ground is not to be sneered at. The place chosen should be fairly high and of an undulating nature. Great trouble will be saved if ground can be found which has been already well burrowed, so that the new stock laid down may soon find a home. Where these burrows do not exist, the keeper and his underlings must assist nature by some preliminary digging, such as we have before described.

An excellent form of warren can be made by simply enclosing a piece of moorland of southern exposure where the heather is not too rank, and which already contains rabbit-burrows, a certain number of isolated trees, and some shrubbery. This land, if well cut with rides, is both excellent feeding and shooting ground. It is important that the burrows be distributed pretty evenly and generally in the warren. Where it is found that rabbits have collected in one area to the exclusion of others, and there is a danger of an insufficient food supply, it might be as well to construct temporary enclosures within the warren, in which the rabbits may be placed, and have these enclosures kept up till such time as burrowing is complete. Great care is necessary in regard to the cover available. It may be necessary to scatter fern or gorse seed, or even to plant or transplant trees and bushes. Most good warrens have, here and there, large flat heaps of the branches of trees. These afford excellent cover, and are especially to be recommended when the warren is used for shooting purposes.

Where the warren is a permanent one, or where there is a suspicion that temporary ground has become stale and tainted, some addition to the natural food must be made. That great authority, Mr. Lloyd Price, recommends that portions of the ground should be fenced with wire netting, and crops of clover, oats, or beans grown within the enclosures. When these have been wholly or partly carried, the wire netting may be removed and the rabbits allowed access to this reserved ground. By changing the position of the plots, the rabbits get access periodically to fresh, untainted ground, and thrive accordingly. During the winter it is always wise to give the rabbits artificial food by scattering corn and good hay here and there over the warren. Some authorities recommend swedes, but these are better avoided, for although they agree with some rabbits when they are associated with corn and hay, they are likely to produce intestinal and other troubles.

It may be as well to quote a more elaborate, yet simple enough, method mentioned by Mr. Lloyd Price for constructing a warren (*Encyclopædia of Sport*):

" Find a field or rough open space, either partially or wholly surrounded by woods, in which rabbits live and breed. Let this be walled round, and let holes be made in the wall at regular intervals, and closed by wooden or iron shutters at will. Encourage the rabbits to feed in your walled-in ground. Of course the beasts soon get quite at home in your enclosure. A night or two before you shoot, shut down the shutters and the thing is done. An improvement would be to make the shutters of light iron bars, to swing outwards from the cover into the preserve shambles, or whatever we choose to designate the field of slaughter ; the rabbits would soon learn to use these, and as the gratings would swing back of themselves, preventing the return of the tenants, your enclosure would soon fill itself without any particular attention on the part of the keeper. Care must be taken, however, not to leave the huge trap too long without emptying, or else to supply plenty of food inside, or the rabbits would starve."

It is perhaps as well to impress upon the keeper that great care must be taken with the fencing. This must be thoroughly carried out at the beginning, and examined carefully afterwards, in case any destruction may have been made by sheep or other animals pasturing in ground approximate to the warren. A single or a double strand of barbed wire outside of the warren fence is useful to prevent such inroads. Wire-netting must, of course, be " turned over " both top and bottom, for rabbits are good climbers. It might be as well that a single barbed wire be stretched across the curve at the top. The points at which the wire netting is turned over must be strengthened by fairly thick wire, to prevent bending.

In summarising the facts to be remembered by the keeper for the prosperity of his warren, we might tabulate the following as deserving his earnest attention :

(1) The proper food-supply of the warren. Where cut hay is supplied, care must be taken that it is kept dry and healthy by some form of covering.

(2) The careful and habitual restocking of the ground. This must be done annually with healthy rabbits from other warrens, as rabbits breed rapidly. Kill down stock quickly in winter, especially the rabbits that lie out, these being generally the weaklings expelled from the burrow by the stronger does and bucks, who keep possession of the stronghold, and are useful for breeding healthy, big stock. As rabbits are addicted to interbreeding and remaining about the same burrow, ferreting is useful in order to change the habitat and encourage interchange of blood.

(3) Proper fencing.

(4) The elimination of vermin.

(5) Draining, when necessary.

(6) The occasional scattering of lime and salt to prevent fouling.

(7) Avoidance of overstocking. In a case where a warren is used for profit, about one hundred rabbits to the acre is a good average ; but only

about ten to the acre is enough where it is used for shooting purposes.

Where a warren is small, great pains must be taken with the care of the ground. If the venue of the warren be not changed, careful liming and artificial feeding must be had recourse to. It may even be dressed with some phosphatic and lime mixture, of which, perhaps, dissolved bones are the best. But it is strongly to be recommended in the case of small warrens that the venue should be changed every five or six years, so as to secure new feeding-ground and to give the old ground a chance of recovering its food capacity and its healthy condition.

Shooting the Warren

The main point to be observed in this connection is —and it may be asserted once and for all—that on no account must ferreting be used for making the rabbits lie out. Gas-tar is the best thing to use. Let every hole be blocked about five days before the shoot, and let the thrown-up earth be sprinkled with the tar. Next day go round the holes again, and block as before. Do this every day till the time of the shoot, and the process is complete. Your whole stock is then in the warren, eating in the open, or lying among the bracken or round the base of trees, or under the heaps of faggots. Let this method be tested once, and such processes as ferreting, smoking, and the like, will vanish into the limbo of archaic ignorance.

With regard to a warren shoot, it is only necessary to

remind the beaters that they must prod, and not beat out the rabbits. Every foot of ground must be carefully probed, faggots must be thoroughly overturned and explored, dogs must be kept well leashed and brought up to the line. There must be no stragglers. The whole party of guns and beaters should move across the warren like a battalion of infantry advancing in line. There must be no dangerous rushes forward by beaters or dogs.

Never suggest that rabbits be driven to the guns. It is simply slaughter and not sport, as the wretched creatures come crawling up to the guns, and the shooter soon tires, or his guns get so hot that he has to lay them down. Walking in line over a rough grass-field after rabbits have been bolted is sport, but driving to the guns is not.

Ferrets and Ferreting

The main point to be remembered by the keeper is that ferrets are as liable to disease from bad hygienic surroundings as he is himself. Accordingly, the ferret should be assured of cleanliness, fresh air, and good food. The days of dirty, badly-ventilated boxes ought to be past, and as much care should be taken of the ferret-runs and hutches as of the kennels. Ferrets must therefore be allowed plenty of pure air and sunshine. To secure this, there must be connected to their sleeping-places a sufficient open-air run, which should be on dry, porous, well-drained soil. It is best that these runs should be tiled over, so that they may be well sluiced with permanganate of potash solution, Sanitas, or other antiseptic fluid. It is easy to arrange these tiles so as to secure sufficient drainage. The sides of the run should be high enough to prevent the ferrets escaping, yet not too high to interfere with the easy entrance of the keeper for cleaning and other purposes.

The hutch, which is pierced with holes for the proper exit and entrance of the ferrets to and from the runs, may be a box, the top and sides of which lift bodily from the ground. In many cases the box consists of but one compartment, but recent improvements are much more elaborate, and even go so far as to secure three compartments—one for sleeping purposes, one for feeding, and the other for the other calls of nature. Where such an arrangement exists it is as well that each compartment should have an easily removable "tray," so that it is not necessary to disturb the whole flooring for the purposes of cleaning, and that the ferrets may thus be confined in one compartment whilst the other two are being cleaned. This cleaning must be carried out once in every twenty-four hours, and must be thorough. The runs need not be cleaned so often, but should have careful inspection. Either sand or sawdust may be used for the floors of the trays.

"The food of the adult ferret consists in the main of bread and milk, or porridge and rice, but on no account should it be too sloppy. Meat is given occasionally. This must be fresh, and may consist of liver of deer, mice, rats, birds, or a piece of freshly-killed and warm rabbit. This should be tied to a staple with a bit of string to prevent the ferrets from dragging it into their sleeping-place, and thus soiling the bedding" (Harting[1]).

Ferrets should not be fed too often ; once in twenty-four hours is all that is necessary.

Working.—Ferrets should never be carried in a bag, but always in a ferret-box, and on being brought home should invariably have their feet washed. It is advisable, where possible, to have at least two keepers out while ferreting. If one ferret sticks, the guns may proceed to the next burrow, while the second keeper waits till the "stuck" ferret comes to the surface. If this does not happen after some time has passed, a dead rabbit should be laid at the mouth of one of the holes ; if this does not succeed, the rabbit should be disembowelled and the entrails laid at the mouth of the hole, or a cartridge may be emptied of its shot and fired into the burrow. If all these plans fail, the ferret may be dug out, or nets or harmless traps may be set at several of the holes.

Neither the "guns" nor the keepers should be seen by the working ferret. They should, if possible, stand downwind and out of sight. We hold firmly that a ferret should never be muzzled, and but seldom coped. A rabbit is driven to the surface better by a ferret that is free, and a coped ferret is only capable of worrying, not killing.

[1] *Encyclopædia of Sport*. See also his volume on *Rabbits*, in Fur, Feather, and Fin Series.

Diseases of Ferrets.—The commonest complaint is *sweats*, with symptoms of abnormal temperature, thirst, running from eyes and nose, loss of appetite, and dullness. The affected ferret should be isolated and bathed in some antiseptic fluid, such as mild boracic acid and water, or permanganate of potash. It should be well dried and placed in a clean, fresh, dry, and warm hutch. The invalid should be fed on slops—fresh warm milk, arrowroot, soup, and similar foods. Whatever is used, there should be a very gradual addition of solid food to the diet as the ferret improves. A good thing is a newly-killed sparrow or other small bird, given one piece at a time, sprinkled with a pinch of sulphur, once in twenty-four hours. All discharges should be carefully washed from eyes and nose, and the latter anointed with vaseline.

Foot-rot—Therapeutics.—Creosote or nitrate of mercury ointment applied once a day.

Worms.—Areca-nut or Filix-mas, followed by castor-oil.

Eczema.—Cleanliness and change of hutch, washing with antiseptic fluid, careful drying, and the use of nitrate of zinc lotion.

Itch.—Some form of mild sulphur ointment.

Keeping Down the Rabbit

The rabbit may be kept down by—(1) Shooting, (2) ferreting and shooting, (3) catching by pitfall, (4) trapping, (5) snaring, and (6) netting. Of the last four methods there are endless modifications, and it will be found that most keepers have their own pet methods from which they are very loath to depart. So long as the method is legal, effective, comparatively painless, and economic, nothing need be said in its disparagement. The legality is of importance, for no one may use a spring-trap to catch rabbits except (*a*) in the mouth of a burrow, and (*b*) when the rabbits are taken by an owner occupying his own land. Many methods employed to take rabbits are completely ineffective, and should be at once discarded. Failure often results from the keeper leaving the traps exposed to view. Unless soil is sprinkled over them to hide them from the keen sight of the rabbit, they will be as useless as a piece of dead iron.

Another cause of the ineffectiveness of a snare or trap is the taint of anything that has come from human contact. The smell of man, dog, powder, rabbit, or game, hanging about a trap is a handicap that can only produce failure : therefore the keeper must see that his hands are perfectly clean before he sets his trap, and that it does not come in contact with his clothes. Mr. Harting recommends that after the hands have been well washed in soap and water, they should be rubbed with mould scraped up near the place where the snare is to be set. "When it is time to put the wire into shape, and smooth out any bends or kinks in it, this should be done, not with the bare finger and thumb, but with a bit of wash-leather between them. It is easily carried in the waist-coat pocket, and a snare rubbed down with this will be found to run as smoothly as possible when touched by a rabbit. Moreover, this intercepts any scent from the bare hand. To secure the effectiveness of snares, they should be set in the morning. The evening dews are apt to preserve the scents of the keeper."

The " humanitarian " side of the question must not be neglected. Any trap or snare that catches a rabbit and causes it needless suffering and a long and painful death must be avoided.

It will be to the advantage of the keeper to be cognisant of the best traps and snares that have been recommended by authorities on the subject. Their modifications are endless. From a description of some twenty or thirty, we select three or four which appear to us to meet the requirements of the keeper in the most effective, the most painless, and the most economic way :

(1) *Burgess's Spring-trap.*—This is recommended by Mr. Carnegie in his volume on *Trapping ;* he appends to his recommendation this clear description of its qualities : " The spring is the most important part of the trap, is thoroughly well tempered and strong, but nevertheless easily pressed down when the trap is set. The flap and catch and other important parts in which most makers fail are of copper, and do not wear away like iron, nor do they rust, which would clog the trap and prevent it from acting. The plate is square, with the four corners taken off, and is of zinc, being so fitted as to be level with the jaws when set. These latter are

thick and rounded, the teeth fitting one into another, though not closely, a space of one-eighth of an inch being left between. The teeth should on no account be sharp or pointed, as their being so tends to break the leg and cut the sinews, thus liberating the rabbit; nor should the teeth be continued round the turn of the jaw. . . . In order to prevent the rabbit, when caught, drawing the trap away, the back piece of the gin is furnished with a hole at the end, through which a chain about a foot long is attached by means of an S hook. The chain should have about eight links, with a swivel in the middle, and a ring of one-and-a-quarter-inch diameter at the end. It is purchasable apart from the trap, and should be well tested, as the weakness will be found where least looked for, viz. in the swivel, and this should always be examined. The ring is for a stake which is driven to hold the trap. The best wood for this is ash, which should be cut in lengths of eighteen inches, and split, then rounded off to the required size, fitted tightly to the ring, driven on to within one-and-a-half inches from the top, and should be overlapped by this part, which ought to be left unrounded as far as the ring comes."

(2) *Brailsford Trap.*—This is a trap to catch rabbits alive, and is manufactured by Messrs. Arlingstall & Co., Warrington. The following description is taken from *The Field*, being an extract from a letter from Colonel Butler, of Brekenham Park, Suffolk: "It consists of a wire cage, very strongly made and open at both ends,

the door being kept up by a simple method of setting. There is a treadle made, and as soon as that is touched the doors close and the victim is imprisoned. . . . In setting them in runs, under shelving banks, or by the side of wire netting, I usually make wings at each end of fir boughs, or something of that kind, to guide the animal in ; but when set at drains or holes, it is only necessary to make a wing at the end farthest from the hole, the trap at the other end fitting close up to the entrance of the drain." This trap, it may be added, is extremely useful for catching, not only rabbits, but all forms of vermin.

(3) *Mr. Lloyd Price's Snare.*[1]—" Select the narrowest part of a frequented run, one well covered with herbage, if possible, to conceal the apparatus, either on the flat, or, better still, on the side of a hill. Drive the big peg firmly into the ground at the side of the run, let this be well hidden by the grass, heather, or what not ; then give a hitch or bend to the centre of the wire to hold the same in a loop just four inches in diameter. Next, stick the carrying peg in the ground to hold the loop (which should just easily go round your closed fist) at an acute angle to the run, also in the grass at the side, or otherwise concealed, four inches from the ground, and with the runner of the noose on the low side, so that the loop may run easily along the wire. Properly set, the catchloop should stand up at right angles, or nearly so, from the supported peg, elevated above the surplus

[1] *Encyclopædia of Sport.*

wire. If the latter be at the top, the noose will not run so freely ; this can advantageously be hidden with bits of cut grass, leaves, etc., as also may the string which connects the wire with the holding peg."

Netting may be practised either by the small bag-net, attached outside a rabbit-hole, or by the long net. The first is used, of course, with a ferret. The long net is familiar and needs no description. It is used outside covers and is worked at night.

Poaching the Rabbit

The planting of thorns near to rabbit-runs is of value in counteracting net-poaching. Where the long net is used by poachers or farmers, it is as well for the keepers to forestall them by arranging a shoot in this method : Have a shoot with the long net and let the rabbits away, then a second shoot on the same principle, and it will be found that fewer rabbits appear. The third shoot can be safely left to the poachers or farmers, for they will get nothing.

The fewer rabbits on a property the better ; they are a source of continual trouble.

Note.—The keeper should never forget that it is inadvisable to put fur and feather into the same game-bag or pannier. He should also remember to empty the bladder of the rabbit immediately after it is picked up. How many keepers do this ?

NOTES.

CHAPTER XIV

THE PHEASANT

PRIOR to the war the rearing of pheasants had been overdone. It had become artificial. In many cases a larger number of birds were reared than the land would carry. Complaints by farmers, and agitation, started by cranks, against all forms of rearing and game-preserving were the result. It is to be hoped that in the future this over-rearing will cease, and that sportsmen will be content with smaller bags of wild pheasants, and only rear a supply sufficient to maintain a good stock—shooting few hens, and, after the first shoot, only cocks, and these only high birds.

The science of rearing and " showing " pheasants has produced so extensive a literature, and has become such an elaborate affair, that it is absolutely impossible in a book like this to attempt to deal with the question in any but a summary way. We can only repeat what was said when dealing with grouse-driving—that every man who desires to reach to any measure of perfection in the art and science of the matter must have recourse to the books of the great authorities. In the rearing, showing, and shooting of pheasants, more than in any other branch of sport, it is advisable that a small reference library be at the command of the head-keeper, and it is for the master to see that advantage is taken of the privileges afforded by this literature. Although we have more than once indicated the leading writers on sport, it may not be out of place here to enumerate those books of reference which have been found most useful in the study of pheasants :

(1) Experience—by far the best book.
(2) *The Encyclopædia of Sport.*
(3) *Shooting*, by Lord Walsingham and Sir R. W. Frankland Payne Gallwey (Badminton Library).
(4) *The Pheasant*, by A. Stuart Wortley, and others (Fur, Feather, and Fin Series).
(5) *Practical Game Preserving*, by W. Carnegie.
(6) *Sport*, by W. Bromley Davenport.
(7) *The Gamekeeper at Home*, by Richard Jefferies.
(8) *Pheasants*, by W. B. Tegetmeier.
(9) *Letters to Young Shooters*, by Sir R. W. Frankland Payne Gallwey.
(10) *Shooting*, by Horace Hutchinson, and others.
(11) *The Forester*, by Brown and Nisbet.
(12) *Sport in the Highlands and Lowlands of Scotland*, by Tom Speedy.
(13) *Birds of Norfolk*, by Henry Stevenson.

With these at his command, a keeper cannot say that he has not heard the best on the subject, and he will hardly require the more or less superficial study now proposed to be made.

On no subject of sport is there less room for being dogmatic than on the rearing of pheasants. Experience is the best teacher, and methods must vary according to the climate, position, particular breed of birds, and the many other circumstances affecting them in different localities. The one condition which must be insisted upon, and on which there can be no difference of opinion, is cleanliness. This implies pure water, pure food, and, above all, that the ground on which the pheasants are reared should be clean, and not overstocked with chicks. Coops should be moved daily, and the same field should never be used for rearing two years in succession.

The keeper's duties in relation to the pheasant differ enormously. They may be connected with a shooting in which the pheasant is only regarded as part of a mixed bag, or they may be concerned with rearing and " showing " on an elaborate scale. It is in the latter case that the keeper's knowledge of the literature of the subject will be of importance. In the former case, where he is possibly concerned with only a few head of wild birds, he will have little to learn, and there will be small need of elaborate studies in rearing and " showing." His beating will be simpler than the beating of partridges, and he will only have to bear in mind the general rule affecting flanks and stops. But it is altogether a different matter when covert shooting is conducted on a scale of great elaboration.

The number of birds to be reared should be strictly limited by the number of acres of covers reserved by the proprietor. Nothing looks more like a farmyard than covers overcrowded with pheasants.

Bearing in mind what has already been said as to the impossibility of dealing with the question at any length, let us take a view of the main points that have to be brought into consideration :

(1) There are several ways advocated for dealing with the question of the proper supply of eggs for the next year's sport : (*a*) On some estates the procedure is simply to attract the hens that are left after the shooting is over by a little judicious feeding, and to allow breeding to take place in a semi-wild condition, and then simply to collect the eggs that are laid. (*b*) Another plan is to utilise a particular covert as the breeding-ground ; this covert being protected only in the sense that a certain amount of wire fencing surrounds it, beyond which there is no penning nor other form of artificial enclosure. (*c*) A third and more general plan is to collect a certain number of hens before the shooting begins, so as to avoid getting pricked birds, and enclose them either in the kind of covert just mentioned, or in enclosed pens, after clipping their wings. (*d*) A modification of this is to leave the collection of the hens till the shooting is over. The great objection to the last-named practice is that some of the hens may have been " peppered " by shot,

and may have received injuries to the maternal organs. There is another point in favour of taking hens before the shooting begins. By so doing, one gets rid of the incessant fear that too many hens will be killed, and that there will not be enough left for the mews.

Whether there is a requirement to secure hens for the mews or not, every keeper should ascertain the condition of this stock as soon as the shooting season is over. This is easily done by a little regular feeding. If there be too many cocks, he may exchange them for hens with a neighbouring keeper, and vice versa. If this practice be not convenient or possible, the keeper should indicate to his master the fact of the superabundance, and if a large number of hens cannot be procured to counteract the disproportion, some more cocks should be killed.

But whether there be disproportion or not, the general game law as to the value of fresh blood must be kept in mind, and as much care taken in procuring pure breeds as in the case of rabbits or partridges. Crossed breeds of weaklings should on no account be introduced. Lord Walsingham supports the contention that "there is no better breed than the true *Phaseanus Colchicus*, commonly known as the old-fashioned dark variety without a white ring on the neck. These are free layers and good mothers—straying less from home than the paler-plumaged varieties more recently introduced. They are quite as hardy, and fly at least equally as well. There are few places in England now where some traces of a cross with

P. Torquatas, the ring-necked Chinese bird, are not to be met with ; but, in the opinion of the writer, the cross-bred bird is not so worthy to be encouraged and propagated as are those of the old, dark, pure breed." The exchange of birds and eggs should be frequent—an annual occurrence, if possible.

If the hen birds are to be kept in mews instead of being allowed to breed in coverts, more cocks should be supplied than in the natural state. There should never be more than six hens to each cock in the mews, and there should be every facility for the wild cocks to get to the enclosed hens. The mews, therefore, should not be shut in at the top. In constructing the mews, the main point to be remembered is that it should be absolutely closed in for at least 3 ft. from the ground, so that the pheasants may be free from disturbance and annoyance from without. The birds should have plenty of space, air, and light, and the ground on which the mews is constructed should have a light, porous soil. If the latter condition be not obtainable, the ground should be dusted with sand and lime. Pens are constructed either as separate domestic establishments, containing one cock to several hens, or are made to hold as many birds as one may require, the proportion of cocks and hens being maintained as in the small pen. Half an acre of ground accommodates about forty hens. If the pens are constructed in covert, the place chosen should have plenty of good undergrowth ; if they are placed in the open, the ground should be planted with

shrubs of various kinds. Spruce and privet are generally recommended.

In feeding the birds in the mews, care should be taken that this is always done by the same person, who should on each occasion be dressed in the same type of clothing. No strangers should be admitted, and whether feeding the hens in mews or covert, or the young broods at a later period, there must be no attempt to call the birds by whistling to them when about to distribute the food. This bad habit tends to domesticate the birds to a marked degree. It is to be remembered at this point that, if open coverts are used, on no account should birds be put into coverts in which they will not naturally stay. Select a covert to which they naturally draw and stray. The general law—that it is the duty of the keeper to assist and not to thwart the instinct of the bird—must be observed. It will be found that pheasants naturally select coverts which have plenty of light and plenty of shelter; which are dry and warm, and have well-drained, porous soil, and which face to the south or south-west. This fact will lead the keeper to understand that he must on no account select ground that is cold or damp, which is exposed to the north or the east, and which is dark and dreary. The law that applies to pheasantries applies also to the ground on which the coops are placed.

The food of the penned hens should be of soft consistency—the ordinary poultry-food (barley-meal and biscuit-meal) in the morning, and dry mixed grain in the afternoon. Some green food should be given occasionally. All food, whether for old birds or for young, should be mixed in the morning. On no account should the keeper perform this duty at night-time. Stale food is a marked cause of disease. Too much maize should not be used : it makes the birds heavy, yellow-fleshed, and not agreeable to eat. Feeding should be varied with light barley and oats and a very little maize.

Great care should be taken that the ground of the pheasantries (and likewise the ground on which the coops are placed) is free from vermin, and is not allowed to stale. In the case of the pens and mews, these should be purified by a sprinkling of lime and sand, and, if feasible, the ground should be changed every few years. Stale ground is an important cause of mortality. Some authorities recommend that powdered oyster-shells be placed in every pen.

About the beginning of April the keeper begins to collect his eggs. He will continue to do so for about a month, and can then turn out his penned birds by the middle of June, dig over the ground of the mews, and sow with grass. By that time he will have his foster-mothers ready. Game-hens are the best, and of these the black-red game-hen is to be preferred before others. If such are not to be obtained, small hens should be selected, of which Buff Orpingtons and Rhode Island Reds are probably the best mothers. They should all be strong birds, absolutely free from disease. The keeper should carefully retain the eggs of these hens for some eight or ten weeks before the pheasant-hatching season, as food for the pheasant chicks. The roosting of the game-hens is of importance; care should be taken of them as consistently as of the pheasants. The sitting hens must be allowed an early morning run on the wet grass, so that they may damp their breast-feathers, and keep themselves healthy. This markedly assists in the hatching process. Some authorities recommend that where the hens are kept in closed yards the eggs should be sprinkled with tepid water at the time of the morning meal.

In collecting the eggs it is wise for the keeper to mix some "wild" eggs, and some purchased or exchanged eggs, with those collected in the pens. All nests that have been built in exposed or dangerous places should be denuded of their eggs, except one or two. Leaving these is a stimulus to the wild bird to go on laying. Otherwise she would, as a rule, desert her nest. Of course, when the nests are left, they should be carefully watched.

Suitable ground for the coops having been selected, the eggs are put under the game-hens, whose nests should consist of a square of dry sod or turf. On no account must the ground have been used the previous year. *Ground for coops should be changed every season.* Lime, gravel, and sand should be freely scattered about, and a liberal supply of cover in the way of fir branches be placed at intervals, to afford temporary protection to the chicks from the inroads of their enemies. The presence of the "cuckoo-spittle" should be noted. It contains the larvæ of an insect which is deadly poison to the young chick.

One acre is sufficient for a hundred birds. The sitting hen should not be confined to the coop. This method of confinement, being a severe tax upon the physique of the bird, is unnecessarily cruel. Not only is this so, but the method deprives the chicks of their natural protector, and prevents the hen from cleaning and dusting herself, with the result that she becomes infested with vermin, which are conveyed to the chicks. The hen should be tethered with a cord about a yard and a half long. This allows sufficient room for her to move about and to perch on the top of the coop. When rats or other predatory vermin approach, the hen is able to warn the chicks by her cackle, and they have a chance of running under her wings for protection. The hen must, of course, be shut into the coop at night-time.

When an incubator is used, the eggs are removed from the game-hen as soon as they begin to chip and are placed in the incubator. When hatched the chicks are removed to the tray above. The eggs must never be all removed from the nest at the same time In putting back the chicks there is no need to select special ones for special hens. Chicks must never be let out very early if there is frost or heavy dew on the grass. Make sure that covers are kept quiet, or birds will leave them ; allow no stray dogs, or rabbit-shooting round covers at evening ; and have no broken fences to permit of cattle straying into them. Keepers on their rounds need not leave the rides ; their doing so is apt to disturb the game.

Encourage plenty of undergrowth, wild berries, and hazel for natural food in coverts. Where there are none, transplant in autumn or spring. How many keepers trouble about this ?

For Mr. Carnegie's Table of Food for Young Pheasants, see next page.

Other authorities recommend hard-boiled eggs, passed through a sieve with a little specially prepared biscuit-meal or oatmeal, as the food of the young birds. No water should be given at any time. The moist food supplies enough. No food should be given to the chicks for the first twelve hours after hatching. A good supply of insect-food, as in the case of young partridges, is of great benefit. When this is not obtainable, maggots may be given. These may be obtained from the bodies of dead crows.

Whatever plan of feeding may be adopted—and the variations are too elaborate for us to dwell upon them in detail—war should be severely waged against the habitual extravagance associated with pheasant-feeding. Overfeeding and waste are generally rampant in places where pheasants are reared. Most birds get 40 per cent. more food than is necessary; and the keeper should combine a sense of responsibility with his judgment in discovering the right mean. No encouragement ought to be given to the practice of habitually buying " patent "

Age of Pheasant.	Morning Feed.	Midday Feed.	Evening Feed.	Remarks.
Up to 3 days.	Custard.	Custard.	Custard.	A slight sprinkling of oatmeal may be added if thought desirable.
3 to 7 days.	Custard and meal.	Custard and meal.	Custard and meal.	The meal to be gradually increased.
7 days to 3 or 4 weeks.	Custard, crushed wheat, millet seed, chopped lettuce, burned hemp, chopped potatoes.	Custard, barley-meal, boiled rice, onion, Dari seed, chopped artichoke.	Custard, oatmeal, groats, buck-wheat, rapeseed, dry dough.	Only two of these ingredients need be added to the custard, or the separate diets can be altered day by day or every three or four days
1 month to 2.	Wheat and (or) barley.	Custard and meal.	Wheat and (or) barley.	....
2 months to 6.	Maize, barley, beans, green food.	Custard and meal, Dari oats, maize, green food.	Maize, peas, wheat, green food.	These can be given on alternate days or changed week by week.

foods. The keeper should be able to make and prepare his own supply of food.

When the young pheasants are old enough, the coops and chicks are then removed to the covers.

Poaching the Pheasant

Watching must be carefully carried out by night as well as by day, and the possible depredations by foxes and poachers dealt with. If trespassers or night poachers are suspected in any covert, threads should be stretched in the evening across any likely paths of approach, twelve inches or so from the ground. Their condition in the morning will warn the keeper as to the presence of poachers, and a careful look out must then be kept for the next few nights.

Alarm-guns, bells, etc., may also be used. Artificial pheasants nailed to the branches of trees afford a good plan for thwarting the poacher. In the various camouflage devices employed against the enemy in the War the keeper might get some useful hints, not only for out-reaching poachers but for other departments of his work.

A strict look-out should be kept for any suspicious carts that may be loitering in the vicinity. It is advisable that the keeper should gallop on horseback round the roads and over the estate every evening.

Depredations by foxes or dogs during pheasant-rearing can be frustrated by stretching several lengths of string, with small bells hung on to them at intervals, about nine inches from the ground, all round the approaches to the coops. The fox is sure to scent a trap and clear off. If the string be soaked in carbolic, renardine, tar, or some other high-smelling liquid, so much the better. In hunting districts, where foxes are plentiful, this plan is very necessary, and is thoroughly efficacious.

An excellent plan to trip up poachers is to have wire instead of string stretched across all approaches to the rearing ground. Another practice is to surround the coops with a stout wire, and to attach to it one or more dogs, so that each dog has a free range over a considerable stretch of ground.

On some estates one of the night watchers carries a horn, and blows it every quarter of an hour or so, for the purpose of driving off foxes.

It is very wise of the keeper to go occasionally round the hedgerows with a spaniel and drive in strayed birds.

Shooting the Pheasant

The most important duty of the keeper on the morning of a shoot is to have his beaters out early, and d[illegible]n all the surrounding country so as to have the bir[illegible] the coverts. As he does this, he should have a sufficient number of boys or men carrying yellow flags to act as stops. These boys should be provided with a good lunch, as they may have a long wait, and cannot be expected to remain at their posts unless they are fed. Stops should be left at all the places where the birds are likely to leave the covert. They should carry yellow flags so that their position may be known, and they may join the line of beaters when these come up. Without this, the day's shoot will be an absolute failure, for the birds cannot be expected to be found in the coverts. It is better that the stops should be instructed to keep absolutely quiet. A very occasional tap with the stick when the birds are making for the open should suffice to keep them back. If the coverts are small, it will be sufficient if the stops show themselves and make no noise whatever. All outlying woods should be driven in to the main coverts, where the birds are to be flushed. For this a large number of stops are necessary, and this should in no way be grudged, as they are the most important essential to a successful day's shooting. In a well-known detached covert in Lincolnshire, after the birds are driven in, the wood is practically stopped all round; it takes two hours to drive the maze and surrounding coverts into this wood. Besides the guns over which the birds are to be driven there should always be two placed behind the beaters to get those that go back.

There are four cardinal principles in the beating of pheasants to the guns which must be carefully imprinted on the memory of every keeper:

(*a*) Push pheasants as far as possible on their feet and bring them back on their wings;

(*b*) Drive pheasants on their feet away from home and then flush them homewards;

(*c*) Flush pheasants at a considerable distance from the guns;

(*d*) Flush pheasants from a higher ground than that on which the guns are placed. The keeper who attempts to drive the birds against a gale of wind is fit for the nearest lunatic asylum.

Now these cardinal principles are enumerated on the understanding that the keeper is expected to "show" his pheasants in the best way possible. That is—he is to bring them to the guns flying high and fast; he is not to present a number of "flapdoodlers" and low-flying birds. The latter may please certain people who are quite satisfied if they bring the thing they aim at to the ground, but it is not sport. The great boast of every keeper should be that his birds fly higher than most, and require some "stopping." Accordingly let him remember that, to produce such a result, he must do something more elaborate than sending his beaters in at one end of a covert and marching them in a straight line to the other. He must, in fact, push his pheasants on their feet to a flushing-point, and then allow "the trouble" to begin. In saying so much, it will of course be at once recognised that this can only be done by careful arrangement of covert, beaters, stops, and guns, and that it requires considerable study and patience.

Now, to obtain the desired result on the cardinal and classical principles just summarised, the keeper must first think of the flushing-point: this may be:

(*a*) A detached piece of covert like the famous Scarborough clump at Holkham;

(*b*) A specially planted piece of covert at one of the corners of the main coverts ; or

(*c*) A turnip-field some distance from the main covert.

The Scarborough clump at Holkham produces such excellent results that the practice followed there is to be recommended to the consideration of all keepers. In following the Holkham methods the following important rules should be remembered :

(*a*) The detached covert must not be larger than the main covert ;

(*b*) The end of the main covert must be thinly planted and must not be fenced in ; if it is fenced there must be an open space immediately in front of it.

(*c*) The undergrowth in the detached clump must be substantial, and not hollow at the bottom. Birds are thus prevented from running and crowding together, and rising all at once, or in great numbers.

Having these conditions, the beaters must enter the main covert at the end farthest away from the detached covert ; flankers must be placed, both men and guns, and the beaters must advance. As the birds are pushed forward on their feet, the beaters must not get too close to them. Pheasants can be driven anywhere if kept on their feet. If there is a danger of too much squashing together, or a threatened flush, the beaters must be halted. As the beaters advance, all thick cover must be properly beaten, especially bramble-bushes. Beaters have a habit of neglecting these from fear of injuring their clothes. Every beater should therefore wear a smock and gaiters.

In driving the birds from the main covert, the beaters should stop about one hundred and fifty yards from the end of the covert, which ought to be quite open, and begin to make a great noise; this drives the birds across the open space to the detached covert, and they are now ready to be flushed. Stops are placed around the detached covert, each man being ordered to beat two sticks together to prevent birds collecting in his vicinity, and for his own safety. Guns are placed in single or double rows, as desired, in the space between the two coverts—not nearer than eighty yards to the detached covert—and the flushing begins by a keeper entering the clump and putting up birds one by one, or two or three at a time. After this has gone on for some time, all the beaters enter, and, moving slowly across the covert, drive out the birds, which, passing over the guns, take their height pretty much at the level of the trees of the home covert, from which they had been beaten. A modification of this plan is for some of the beaters, after leaving the main covert, to cross the open space and be lined facing the detached clump, that is, some distance in front of the guns. This will ensure the birds passing over their heads, and it gives the guns a better chance of high and strong-going birds.

(2) Where it is proposed to follow the method of

driving the birds into a corner of the main covert, this should be worked in a series of beats, until the whole of the birds are at the flushing-point. The cover of the flushing-point must be attended to as carefully as in the detached clump. From it there should run a narrow strip of similar cover along the whole face of the wood. In this case there must be a drive or open space made inside the cover, where most of the guns are placed. The birds, on being flushed, will fly homewards, as in the first case. Stops should be placed as before.

(3) The third method consists in driving birds into a turnip- or potato-field some hundred yards in front of the main covert, stops being placed at the end and sides of the field. The guns stand in the open between the main covert and the field, and a few beaters advance into the field some sixty or seventy yards and then halt. The rest of the beaters now go round and bring the field back in the homeward direction. The birds rise, pass over the heads of the stationary beaters, and make for the covert, passing over the guns in their flight.

If a keeper be obliged, from unforeseen circumstances, to place the guns, instead of this duty being left to the host, he ought to post them at a good distance from the covert, in order to give them a chance of getting respectable birds instead of the nasty " skinners " which they are sure to get if they are stationed close to the covert side.

These three methods of " showing " the birds may serve to illustrate the cardinal principles which we have enumerated, and to suggest to the keeper who is ignorant of the matter the wisdom of abandoning methods now regarded as prehistoric. He will find the details of each method described, with some slight modifications, in Mr. Stuart Wortley's monumental volume on *The Pheasant*. Even where there is no artificially arranged flushing-point, the birds may be so driven as to secure their being flushed from a higher plane than that on which the guns stand. For instance, where the covert is lying on the side of a hill or gentle slope, the birds should be flushed from the highest point, never from the lowest. In those cases where coverts are very much on the same plane, and no particular flushing-point is used, it might be suggested that a stretch of wire netting, say twenty-five yards from the end of the covert, will make the birds rise, and give them time to get well over the tree-tops before they reach the guns.

When it is absolutely impossible to conduct pheasant-shooting on such scientific principles from want of suitable coverts or for other reasons, it might be well that, near to the end of the coverts, three parallel rows of wire netting be arranged, with an opening in the centre of the two posterior rows. As the pheasants are pushed forward, some will collect behind the first netting, some behind the second, and some behind the third. Each division can then be flushed separately.

In some places where there are small pheasant shoots, matters are improved, and pheasants are shown better, by prefacing the first covert shoot by a dummy—a sort of dress rehearsal, a few days before. Keepers are placed with blank cartridges, and the birds are sent over the guns once. By this method the head-keeper is able to note the flight of the birds and deduce therefrom the proper position of the guns. In addition to this, the birds fly higher when the real shoot begins.

Supplementary to what has been said, the following practical points may be indicated :

(1) Sewin may be used as an excellent form of stop, both for hares and pheasants.

Sewin is made by fastening white feathers and scarlet tape at intervals of a yard, and ferret bells at intervals of five yards, on to white or yellow cord, which is placed on sticks some two and a half feet high, firmly planted in the ground. The sewin is continually jerked by a beater, specially told off for the purpose. It may be used both inside and outside of the coverts. The sewin is kept on a reel, and is wound round an iron frame. The reel, the frame, and the sewin are supplied by well-known firms, and by the Army and Navy Stores.

(2) Late in the season stoppers are even of more importance than beaters. All stops should, of course, get into position in the early morning, long before beaters start and guns begin to fire ; as the boys may have a long wait, see that they have a " piece " with them.

(3) First shoot the covert that has the most birds in it. Do not keep to a stereotyped habit of shooting coverts.

(4) Always shoot the exposed coverts early, as birds stray to warmer quarters on the fall of the leaf.

(5) All things being equal, outlying coverts proximate to other shooting-ground should be shot early, to prevent the loss of birds by straying.

(6) No wild or untrained dog should ever be allowed in the coverts.

(7) All birds should be picked up as they fall. One or two keepers with dogs following a mixed line of guns and beaters are useful. A keeper or keepers, in fact, should always be behind guns In the clump or detached covert system, they should be just inside the main covert.

(8) The coverts should be carefully searched with dogs, preferably on the same day as, or on the day after, the shooting, with the view of finding any wounded or dead bird that may not have been picked up. The keeper should be allowed to take a gun and shoot any birds that show signs of being wounded.

(9) All birds should be counted at the end of each beat. This will counteract any tendency to thieving on the part of the beaters.

In walking up rough ground, should there be any covert therein which it is intended to drive, be sure and take the woods first, otherwise the shooting in the open will disturb the coverts, and they will probably be found empty when visited.

NOTES.

NOTES.

CHAPTER XV

WILD DUCK

By LORD MALISE GRAHAM

DURING the past few years we have noted the large bags of wild duck which may be obtained by careful rearing and good management. Although the number of wild fowl can hardly be said to have decreased, yet there is little doubt that in some marshes where, many years ago, large flocks of wild duck used to collect, there is now scarcely one to be seen. The reasons for this are numerous. The most important probably is that, as our population increases, wealthy sportsmen and landowners are tempted to seek seclusion, and build their mansions in far-away spots which have always been the haunt of the wild duck. These birds, being of a shy disposition, seek other pastures. The only way to lure them back is to breed and rear by hand others which will act as decoys to their more nomadic brethren. At Netherby and other places, enormous bags have been realised, the size of which would hardly have been credited ten or twelve years ago. Moreover, the trouble taken is well repaid by the excellent sport which these birds afford; and the difficulty involved in killing a really high duck is sufficient to satisfy even the most exacting sportsman.

The common wild duck is fairly plentiful all over the British Isles ; it is generally to be found in lakes, ponds, rivers, or other watery places. The male, commonly known as the mallard, is a singularly beautiful bird. The head and upper part of the neck are of a dark green hue ; the lower part of the neck, which is separated from the upper part by a white ring, is of a greyish-brown colour ; the breast above is of a deep chestnut, below of a greyish-white ; the back is greyish, brown. The wings, which extend to nearly 3 ft., are of a rich purple colour merging into black ; the greater wing coverts have tips of a velvet-black, with a bar of white near the end, and the lesser wing coverts are of a greyish-brown. From the end of May till the beginning of August the male adopts the dress of the female, and does not completely assume his own brilliant plumage till the beginning of October. The female is smaller than the male and is of a brownish hue, the back being blackish-brown and the breast pale yellowish-brown ; the wings brown, with a little green. The male bird has a tail of twenty feathers, the four centre feathers of which are curled up : they are of a greenish-black colour, the others being greyish-white. The female has a tail of brown, the feathers margined with reddish white. The young birds, male and female, known as flappers, resemble each other till after the first moult.

The young wild duck is easier to rear than the young pheasant, and the expense is small ; but certain precautions have to be observed, or the result will be failure. The eggs can be bought nowadays at comparatively low prices, and, having once been bought, there is no necessity to purchase more for the next season, as the females reserved for laying will lay quite sufficient. But supposing, as will probably be the case, that the eggs are to be collected on the estate and along the marshes, it is not necessary to consider the question of purchase. The eggs are usually to be found in the rushes along a river bank or in an open field. The nests have even been found in thick trees. This is not such an uncommon place for a wild duck to build in as might at first be supposed, especially if the trees are situated near a river bank. I have found a nest two years in succession in the same tree in which a jackdaw had built hers. To secure the eggs in such a case is, however, rather a severe test of the agility of a keeper. The eggs, by the way, are of a pale green colour, and are usually eleven in number.

Having procured the eggs, the treatment is much the same as it is for pheasants, but ducks' eggs require to be damped with water more frequently, which is natural, considering that the female duck would always return to her nest with her breast feathers wet. They take twenty-eight days to hatch, and on hatching, the hens, ducklings, and coops should be placed on some sheltered grass-field. The ground selected should be dry, and should be wired in, as the ducklings are inclined to wander. After a fortnight or three weeks the hens may be removed, but the coops should remain, and the young birds should be regularly cooped up at night, and also during the day, if the weather be very wet. It is important to ensure that they have plenty of ventilation when in the coops. It is also essential at this time that the ducklings should not get into any water for swimming, as they will be found to develop cramp and rheumatism: large pans for their drinking-water should also be eschewed, in case the birds get into them. When the water is done with, the pans should at once be emptied. As regards feeding, it is important that the young duck should have plenty, but it must be of the right sort; they must be fed regularly when very young—five times a day, three times in the morning and twice in the afternoon.

The food which is most highly recommended is a meal specially prepared by Messrs. Gilbertson & Page, Hertford. It should be mixed with a little water and given to the birds warm for the first fortnight; after that they may have it cold. No other form of nourishment is required, and, if given regularly, the birds will be found to thrive on it and grow rapidly. After a fortnight, three times a day is sufficiently often to feed them, and this may in turn be decreased to twice a day.

When eight weeks old, the birds may be taken to the stream or water which is intended for their permanent home, and fed twice a day as before. After a time they will become accustomed to their new surroundings, and then they need only to be fed once a day—in the morning. The soft food should, however, be continued for some time after removal to the water, and a few coops should be taken to the water's edge. It should be borne in mind that everything possible must be done at this time to accustom the ducks to their new surroundings, to give the place a home-like appearance, and to ensure their remaining in it. A few pinioned ducks and good food will do more to attain these objects than anything else. Moreover, other birds will be attracted by their calls, and later on in the season, about evening feeding-time, many may be shot when coming in to join their companions.

After the ducks are a month old, oatmeal may be added to the prepared food, to make up a more substantial meal. The birds should always be let out of their coops early in the morning before the dew is off the ground, as they will then amuse themselves by catching the worms and slugs. When it is desired to give up the soft food, Indian corn or maize will be found to be the most suitable diet. This should be supplied regularly once a day—in the morning, and thrown near the water's edge. There are many other kinds of food, however, such as acorns and the dried insides of rabbits, which if chopped up, will be found most appetising and a pleasant change of diet. The great enemy of the duckling is the rat, and these voracious animals are sure to be found wherever there is maize ; great pains should, therefore, be taken to exterminate the rats before putting down the ducks. About the time of the harvest the ducklings will be able to take care of themselves, and will fly away in the evening to feed on the corn. If the keeper blow a horn when he feeds them, they will get into the habit of returning to their old feeding-ground when they hear the sound ; and this custom may be of use later on, when the horn will summon them to sterner realities than those of their morning meal.

It is about sunset that some of the best sport with these birds may be obtained. The wild duck will congregate at dusk in some pond, and if the right place be found the air will be thick with them flying to and fro for about twenty minutes. This period of flighting, as it is called, rarely lasts for more than half an hour. The best way to find out the haunts of the duck at night is to walk round the leeward side of the ponds by day, and observe if there be any feathers lying on the edges. A field of stubble in flood is a certain place for the duck to feed in. As wild duck always settle in the water against the wind, it is generally found best to stand with one's back to it, as a good shot is then afforded as the bird comes down to alight. Excellent sport may also be obtained in the same way at dawn. The duck all fly back to the lake or water where they live, from the fields or marshes where they have spent the night in feeding.

It is necessary, therefore, to find a spot where they all cross over, to select a good place behind a stump or some other natural cover, and to be there about twenty minutes before sunrise. They will fly over the ambushed sportsman in twos and threes, and even in large flocks, and give him plenty of shooting for about a quarter of an hour. For this sport a quick eye and good hearing are essential, as the first indication of the wild ducks' approach is usually the whistling of their wings, especially on a still day. The mouth of a river, where it runs into a lake, is an ideal place for "flight-shooting." Every variety of wild fowl can be shot in this way, as, during stormy weather, widgeon and teal will often come inland to feed; the widgeon can readily be distinguished by their shrill whistle. The more stormy the night and morning, the better chance one has, as the birds then fly lower, and are not so easily frightened away by a shot.

Nowadays, when duck are so much reared by hand, it is possible, as has been explained above, to keep them near the streams or ponds where they have been brought up. One rule, however, should be observed with regard to shooting wild duck, if one expects them to remain. It is not to shoot them in or near the places where they have been reared. Let these be sanctuary, as it were, for them, and then they will be found to return to the same spots again in the evening, as if being shot at were the most natural and harmless thing in the world. Supposing that there are two or three of these sanctuaries (which there should be, if there be a large number of birds), let a man be stationed near each, to frighten the birds away as they try to settle; then they will fly round and round, gradually rising higher in the air, and will give the guns plenty of shooting for two hours or so. The guns should stand in good high butts, circular in shape made up from fir branches, or some other such natural cover, lined alongside a wood for preference, so that the birds may be shot as they top the trees. Of course a great quantity of duck are required for this form of shooting. There are few places in England, at present, where it is possible to enjoy the luxury of a duck drive ; though, probably, in a few years it will become a much more common pastime. As was mentioned above, a horn is a very useful instrument for calling in wild duck, and it is astonishing with what readiness they answer the call when they become accustomed to it.

Another method of killing wildfowl is to stalk them over a river bank and shoot them as they rise. They afford easy shots if successfully stalked, but half the pleasure lies in approaching them without giving the alarm, as they are wary birds, and their sense of hearing, on a still day, is little short of marvellous. A useful thing to remember is to approach them, if possible, from the side from which the wind blows, as they rise against the wind and their breasts afford a good and vital mark. A young wild duck, bred in the river, has a great enemy in the pike. It is extraordinary how many birds these voracious fish account for, and keepers can very well spend any spare time they may have in the summer in catching them. Even in innocent-looking ponds pike may be found. I have known the young duck disappear from a pond in a seemingly inexplicable manner, and yet the cause was not very far to seek, for eventually several large pike were taken out of it. The only way to catch these fish in a pond is with a rod and float.

Now, a word as to the best kind of dog to use for wild-duck shooting. An ordinary retriever, if it take kindly to the water, is as good as could be desired, but this species requires most careful teaching. Nothing is more annoying than for a retriever to take the duck to the opposite bank of the river, drop it, and, on being called, to swim back without it ; yet I have often seen this happen. A day spent in the early part of the season by the river bank, shooting an occasional flapper, is excellent for teaching the young and inexperienced retriever ; the water is warm, and the bird is not so likely to dive just as the dog reaches it. On no account should a dog be forced to take to the water by being thrown into it. Nothing gives him a keener or more lasting distaste for the business. He should also be prevented from getting into the habit of dropping his duck on reaching the bank, for the purpose of shaking himself, as he may leave the bird in some inaccessible spot. He should, on the contrary, be trained to bring the bird up to his master's hand.

The Newfoundland and the water-spaniel are really the best dogs for this work, the former being a very strong swimmer. The spaniel requires to be taught to take no notice of water-rats, as these infest the river banks, and this species is very much inclined to hunt them. All water-dogs must be taught to range to hand. As their radius of vision is very small when they are in the water, it is of material advantage to them if they can be guided and directed by the hand. It is very important, also, that all water-dogs should be very quiet, for the slightest bark or whine is fatal, and is sufficient to spoil a whole day's sport. The constant exposure of these dogs to cold and wet is liable to bring on rheumatic fever, especially if they are accustomed to sit most of the day before a roaring fire. The symptoms are : the dog will resent being touched, will snarl if you attempt to pat him, and will, as a rule, cower in a corner. The best cure is to give him a hot bath, dry him well before the fire, and then apply, by hard rubbing, a mixture of equal parts of spirit of turpentine, ammonia, and laudanum.

The directions which may assist the keeper in bringing up and shooting wild duck must, perforce, be of a general nature, as the method in each case will vary, depending largely on the conformation of the ground, and the nature of the surroundings But it should be observed that wild duck are very capable of looking after themselves ; and that the keeper's chief difficulty lies in keeping the birds from straying, and his chief care in feeding them regularly when very young.

Note.—When the lie of the land is favourable, it is often possible to drive duck up a burn, from their feeding-ground, into an enclosure at a higher elevation. The guns being posted below, the birds are let out in twos and threes. The principle is very much the same as in the case of pheasant "showing."—P. J. M.

NOTES.

NOTES.

CHAPTER XVI

NOTES ON WILDFOWLING IN SCOTLAND

By J. S. Henderson

It is impossible to do justice to a subject so wide in an abridged treatise of this nature, and of necessity the writer must merely touch the fringe, but in so doing an endeavour will be made to bring forward those points with which, strictly speaking, it is every gamekeeper's duty to be conversant.

Flighting

This form of sport, which is annually becoming more popular, is, in the writer's opinion, before all other forms of shoulder gun-shooting. Every keeper, upon whose beat it is possible to indulge in flighting, should make it his duty to be thoroughly acquainted with the feeding-grounds, and the lines of flight in different winds, and so be able to place the guns to the best advantage. One of the chief points to be observed in flighting is to remain perfectly still and keep well out of sight. The keepers should see that, at the various stands, satisfactory cover is available. The " gun " should always face downwind, as it will be found that most duck beat their way upwind, and in stormy weather fly very close to the ground. If no shelter is available, he should try to have his back to a peat stack, peat bank, or any dark object, and if that be impossible, his next best course is to kneel on the ground and remain perfectly still. Duck, when flying to the feeding-ground, shy much more readily on seeing a dog or a man moving about than they do at the sound of the shots. In flighting one requires to keep very much on the alert with both ears and eyes. In uncertain twilight the birds are often heard before they are seen. They should never be allowed to pass the guns, but should be taken immediately they come up.

This applies especially to morning, evening, and moonlight flighting, when the light is uncertain, and the birds are within shot—almost always as soon, and sometimes sooner than they are within sight. Some advocate heavy shot for flighting, but the writer is of opinion that Nos. 5 and 6 are the most useful for this form of sport at all times, except during the day, when No. 4 in the right and No. 3 in the left barrel will be found the most effective. The reason why the smaller shot is preferred for morning, evening, and moonlight flighting is that a far shot is rarely available in the uncertain light, as the birds cannot be seen at a long distance. The flighter should get to his ground early and be comfortably settled before the flight begins. He should be careful to take the warmest of clothing and the strongest of boots.

On fine nights flighting need hardly be attempted. The best sport can be got on stormy nights and in frost. On a fine night the birds will fly too high, and will very probably not start for their feeding-ground till consider-

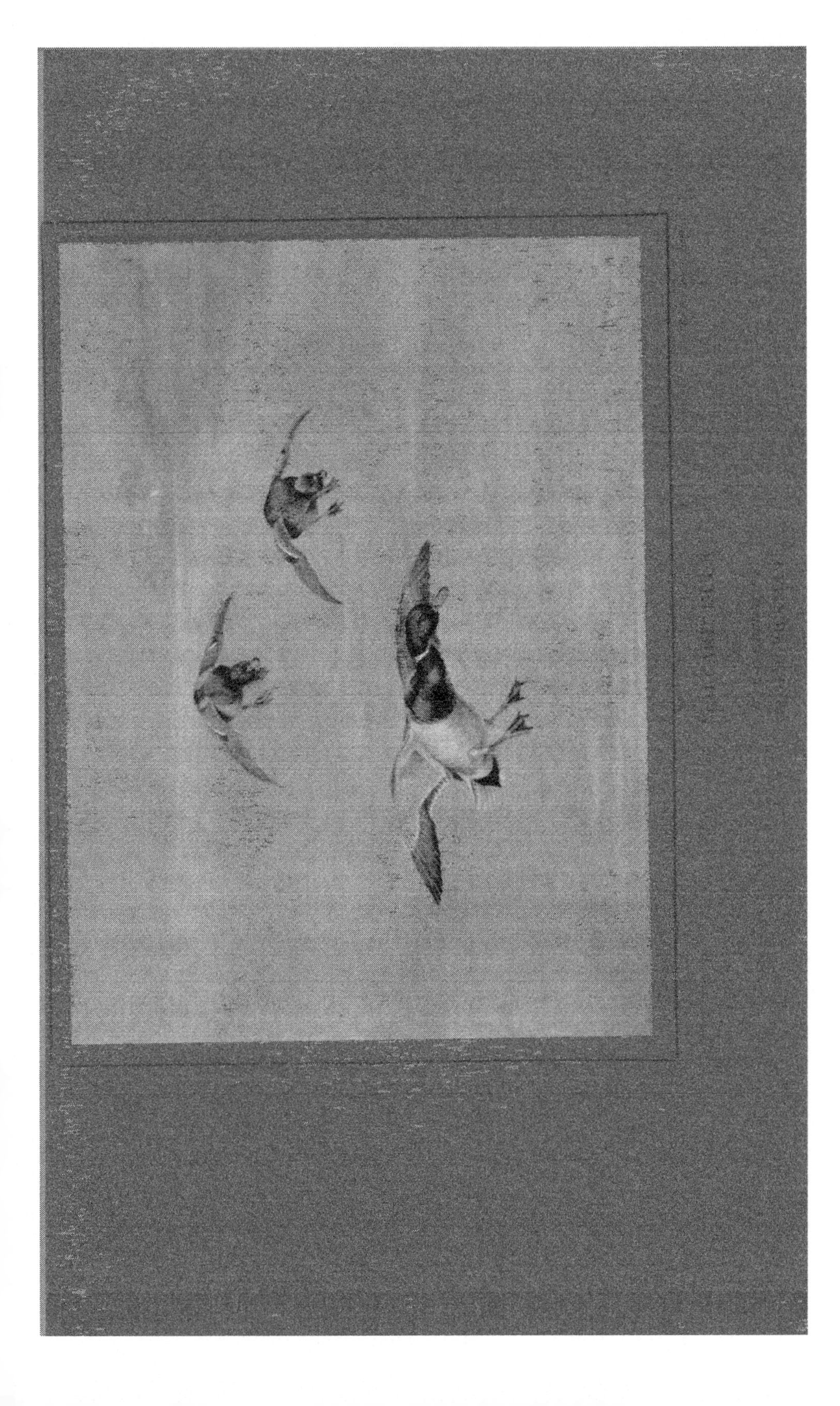

ably after sundown, at which time it is impossible to see them except against a white cloud. The flighter should never be without a reliable dog, but he should not allow the dog to range for every bird that drops. Runners and birds which have dropped into the water should be retrieved at once, as also birds dropped in soft mud, for the latter are frequently so deeply embedded that, if not picked up at once, they can rarely be found. Except in day flighting, when one can mark his birds down, it is wise always to listen for the result of a passing shot, as frequently a fast bird will drop with a considerable thud far behind the gun. A flighter should always be most careful to see that his dog is thoroughly dried on returning home, for the cold and the effect of the sea-water invariably, sooner or later, bring on rheumatism and deafness.

Times of Flighting

Evening—The evening, for about half an hour just at twilight, is the most suitable time, when the birds pass from their resting-ground at sea to their feeding-ground on some inland loch, burn, or estuary.

Moonlight Flighting—It is a mistaken idea that a clear, cloudless sky is best adapted for this form of shooting. A good moon and lots of white, fleecy clouds are by far the best conditions for showing up the birds to advantage. In autumn, about harvest-time, excellent moonlight shooting may be got when the birds are passing to feed on crop, stubble, or potato ground. Barley and potato fields are their favourite attractions, and the best situation for the gun in a field of grain will be at any "laid" spot near the centre of the field.

Morning—At dawn, for about the same space of time, the birds may be intercepted returning from their feeding-grounds to their resting-grounds for the day. This is rarely so satisfactory as evening flighting, as the birds do not conform to the same regular line of flight, and usually return to their resting-ground in large packs. Good sport, however, can sometimes be got by an alert "gun" posted by a creek or channel leading from the sea to the feeding-ground. The birds will nearly always follow this line of flight when returning at dawn to the sea.

Day Flighting—Very good day flighting may sometimes be got in rough weather, when the birds are driven from the open sea or lochs and are making for more sheltered quarters.

Feeding

As so much good sport can be got without the trouble of artificial feeding, the practice is not often followed; but those who care to try it will find that barley and potato-refuse make the most appetising meals for wild duck, although oats, or, indeed, grain of any sort, will serve the purpose. If feeding be resorted to, the ground should be "fed" for three or four nights before a shot is fired, so as to allow the birds to become accustomed to it. Care should be taken not to place the food in hollows where the duck, if they alight unseen, cannot be shot. The most likely spot for natural feeding is just where a burn empties into a loch, and artificial feeding in the near neighbourhood may be often conducive to good results.

The Best Season

The best months for duck-flighting will usually be found to be November, December, and January, although the season varies a little in some districts. One of the chief interests and excitements in this class of sport is the variety of birds that may be killed before the " flighter " realises at what he has " loosed off." Of course, such visitors (and they are frequent) as teal, widgeon, and plover herald their approach long before one can give them the welcome " hail ! "

Shore Shooting

There is little to be said on the subject of shore shooting from a gamekeeper's point of view, but from a sportsman's aspect it is impossible to overestimate the advantages to be gained from this class of sport. One's knowledge for judging distance and pace can be brought to the highest standard by observing the results of the shots on the water, and varied indeed is the bag that may be got by a wary " shore shooter."

Bog Shooting

The chief point to observe here is to mark down the birds carefully. The guns should never loiter about—hunting for dead birds, but should move steadily on from the moment they enter the bog ; for duck, so soon as they become suspicious, will take to the wing if they observe the line standing or hunting about, whereas they will nearly always sit close enough to give a reasonably near shot, if the guns keep steadily on. Some bogs afford better and surer sport by being driven. To execute a successful drive, the wind is the supreme factor to be reckoned with.

Decoy Duck-shooting

Exceedingly good sport may be obtained, especially on a very stormy day, by placing a few decoy ducks within good range of a gun stationed near the bank of a sheltered bay or eddy. The decoy can also be used with success when ducks are flighting to crop or roots.

Shooting Afloat

When shooting from a small boat, especially with an 8-bore, the keeper must be most careful to keep the head of the boat well up to the waves. The recoil of an 8-bore is sufficient to rock the boat and topple the sportsman into the water, unless the boat's head be kept well up. In approaching from the sea towards duck feeding ashore, you should always manœuvre towards them along the shore, and never by direct frontal attack.

Punting

This subject is a study in itself, and only a few practical points may be noted. The rest must be gleaned from experience. First of all—beware of strong tides and southerly winds. A discreet punter will never leave the poling-ground with an uncertain wind, especially if this be from the south. When approaching a flock of duck, always give due heed to the sentinels that will be seen dotted here and there apart from the flock. Upon their conduct the punter should base his scheme of operations. An outlook should also be kept for black-backed gulls : these are a frequent source of disturbance, and often mar what would have been ideal chances. Never attempt punting in rough weather, but watch and take advantage of the first lull after a storm. A punter should be particular in making as fast as he can for the scene of the shot, to secure the wounded. This is especially essential if one be after ducks of the diving species, since they, though wounded, may give much trouble and often escape altogether. It will be found, however, that a wounded duck has considerable reluctance to go under water at first, and, if reached without loss of time, can be finished off with a 12-bore ere it makes up its mind to dive.

The vermin which are most disastrous to wildfowl and their eggs in Scotland are the grey crow and the black-backed gull. The larger species of hawks do a certain amount of damage, but they are becoming so few and far between, and wildfowl are so plentiful, that the sportsman is only too glad to accord to them ungrudgingly their toll of birds. Every effort should, however, be made to destroy the two arch-enemies I have just mentioned. On some of the rocks in the Outer Hebrides where wildfowl nest in large numbers, one may readily see that it is impossible to magnify the damage and depredation caused by such vermin as the grey crow and black-backed gull. The shells of countless eggs—not to speak of the bones of young wildfowl—can be seen on almost every rock or prominence in the nesting-quarters of the wildfowl.

Wild Goose Shooting

To attempt this class of sport with any degree of success, one must first procure a double 8-bore gun, although at times, with great luck, a considerable bag may be made with a 12-bore and heavy shot. There are three recognised means whereby the sportsman may get to the windward of the wily goose—*Stalking*, *Driving*, and *Flighting*. I have stated these processes in their order of merit, as I think that everyone who has had experience of wild goose shooting will admit that *Stalking* is by far the most interesting, although at the same time the most difficult, means of attack. Further, a successful stalk usually means a considerable slaughter.

The wild goose, when feeding or at rest, always has his position guarded by alert sentries. To stalk him with success one must approach him upwind and take advantage of every available piece of cover, having first carefully surveyed the ground with a telescope. The grey lag goose is undoubtedly the most difficult to approach. He usually adds to his security by taking up his position in the centre of a flat, where it is next to impossible to approach him under cover. Sometimes, however, he will allow a horse and cart to get within easy shooting-distance of him, provided a circular manœuvre is adopted, and not a direct approach. Barnacle geese are much easier to stalk, and they will usually be found on a piece of good green pasture.

Driving.—There are various methods adopted with more or less success in driving. One is by the usual process of taking cover. Another is by digging pits, both in the probable line of flight, which one should be able to gauge with considerable accuracy. Thereafter the geese should be driven towards the guns in as quiet a manner as possible, without causing undue alarm. A method of driving usually successful is, where the geese are found on a small island, for the guns to take " post " in some narrow creek or channel which the geese are known usually to follow on leaving the feeding-ground. In such a course they will nearly always be got flying low and well within shot.

Flighting.—This is always an uncertain form of sport, and requires the exercise of much patience. A great deal of the matter bearing upon duck-flighting is applicable to geese-flighting, but the geese—at least the grey lag and barnacle—are best found flighting to corn- and potato-fields. By an examination of the ground, the keeper will find ample indication as to where the guns should be placed, and, if sufficient patience be exercised, success, to a more or less degree, is practically certain. The flighting hours of geese correspond with those of duck.

Note.—As wildfowling is a sport practised only by a privileged few, it was thought inadvisable that it should be dealt with at any length. The reader is accordingly advised to seek further information from *The Encyclopædia of Sport*, from the volumes on *Shooting* in the Badminton Library, and from the works of Mr. J. G. Millais, Mr. H. G. Folkard, Mr. Abel Chapman, Mr. L. Upcott Gill, Mr. Horace Cox, and Colonel Hawker. Those who are interested in the question of shooting with swivel and other forms of guns will find full information in the works of several of these writers.

NOTES.

CHAPTER XVII

MISCELLANEOUS SPORT

By Various Authorities

Golden and Green Plover

THERE is very little to be said with regard to the keeper's duties as these affect plover. He may be called upon to direct the guns how to proceed. There are no very definite laws to be laid down. Golden plover should no more than partridges be approached in an open field, for they are even more wary than partridge or green plover. They should be approached by the outflanking tactics described in our chapter on the Partridge. The best chances, however, are obtained by attempting to drive them downwind, the drivers approaching the birds in a circle, slowly and noiselessly ; imitating their call with special wooden whistles attract them.

The following is recommended by the *Fowler in Ireland* : "Another method of getting within range of Plover congregated in a field is to tie a dog to a short stick and peg it down into the ground, leaving the animal a tether of five or six yards. Secure him a couple of hundred yards away from the 'stand,' to windward, and every bird's eye will be turned in his direction as he moves or struggles. You may then steal up to them on their other flank against the wind, and will always get within fair, often easy, shot."

This is truly Irish.

Pigeons

Pigeon-shooting from traps hardly comes within the scope of a keeper's duties, but a few remarks may be made as to the killing of wild wood-pigeons. A few head may be obtained by simply beating a wood. When this is done, great care must be taken that the guns are placed a considerable time before the beaters enter the wood, for on the first crackle of a broken stick the pigeons will begin to leave the covert. The keeper should take care to note the customary flight of the birds, and place the guns accordingly. Pigeons generally fly from covert to covert, and as a rule take the shortest line to get out of a wood. The question of wind is, of course, important. In leaving covert pigeons seldom fly against the wind, but almost invariably do so when returning to it. But to obtain any large bag of pigeons in a short space of time, decoys must be used. These may either be stuffed pigeons or birds just shot. In the former case the decoys should have copper wire passing from within the bodies of the birds down the legs, with, say, some sixteen inches projecting from each foot.

In the latter case, pieces of wire netting are cut so as to fix the fresh-killed birds with their wings clasped to the sides, and their heads erect, on to branches of trees.

But, whatever the form of decoy, it must always be placed with its head facing the wind, and the gun or guns should stand some fifty yards away, facing it. "It will be found useful," says Lord Walsingham, "to be prepared beforehand with several short sticks, pointed at both ends, and when ten or twelve birds are down, to gather them quickly and set them up on open spaces beneath the trees as assistant decoys. With wings closed to their sides, resting on their breast-bones, they can be fixed with heads erect or craning forward, as if in search of food, by passing the upper end of the stick through the lower portion of the beak, the opposite end being stuck into the ground beneath the crop of the bird."

Great care should be taken by the keeper in selecting the cover for the "guns," and he should also warn the latter as to the necessity of their clothing being as nearly as possible akin in colour to that of the cover in which they are standing, and to remain quiet; patience is a virtue in pigeon shooting.

Capercailzie

In placing the guns for capercailzie-driving, knowledge of the usual flight of these birds is of value. In our experience capercailzie generally come out of covert, take a wide sweep round and close to it, and then fly in again. They seldom fly out into the open. Guns should be placed quite near the covert. In preserving the stock, care must be taken, as in all other cases, to eliminate vermin.

Woodcock

The movements of these migratory birds are very uncertain. They come to-day and are gone to-morrow; and nothing can be done to increase or encourage them. Soft feeding-ground is, however, a great attraction. A certain number remain in this country and breed, but the most of them come in with the first severe weather. When a thaw comes they move away, and they seldom return, but it has been noticed that when they cannot be found in the coverts they are very often got on the moors and open ground, not having left the countryside, as some have supposed. In the event of woodcock not being in coverts, it is well worth trying the open moor for them, especially when the moor lies to the sun. As soon as the cock are in, the keeper should advise his master, and as their stay is very uncertain, get at them at once. Young larch covers are favourite places for cock.

Woodcock as a rule, during the time they remain on the ground, are loath to leave any favourite shelter they may have chosen, and will even fly back to the place from which they have been flushed in a beat. Accordingly, it is often wise to go over the same ground a second time. Markers outside the coverts will be able to give important information as to whether cock have left a covert or not, although it is often very difficult to accurately mark the place where a bird has alighted. Woodcock that have been marked down should be followed up at once, as they have a habit of rapidly changing their quarters when they know that guns are about. They often fly into the hedges or under the dykes at the outside of the covert. It is very desirable that these should be well beaten. The covert ought to be beaten thoroughly, and if the beat is specially for cock, the holly bushes and laurels should be well shaken. The best days to shoot woodcock are after clear moonlight nights, or days on which the sun is not too bright. Then the keeper may be certain that the woodcock, which is entirely (except under very pressing circumstances) a night feeder, has fed well and that he will lie well, being inclined to be sleepy and lazy. Cock, of course, vary their habitat according to the weather. After a frost they will be found where water can best be obtained. Accordingly the ditches and drains in the covert should be carefully explored.

The first days after a severe frost are the best for single or two or three guns. All likely places should be worked first, then the ground the birds have flown to, and the guns should finally return to the beat which they first worked, but not sooner than two or three hours after the time they first shot over it.

When the birds are lying well—that is, after a bright night in which they have fed amply—it is better to walk them up ; if they are lying badly—that is, after a night in which they have not fed well—it is better to have the birds beaten to the guns. In such weather, an outside gun, walking with the beaters, or a little in advance of them, is of great importance, and he should be warned to keep a sharp look out in passing any openings in the covert.

In looking for woodcock in the open, it must be remembered that they generally feed on the lee-side of a hill, and may be found where they feed. It is better to remember this rule than to trouble one's memory by north, south, east, or west. When there is no wind, they choose the brightest or sunniest side.

The keeper should remember to draw the leg sinew immediately on picking up; it enhances the eating quality of the leg of the bird. The question, Do woodcock carry their young? is no longer in doubt, the author and others have seen them in the act.

The migration of birds is a most interesting study; for other reasons, as showing the long flight taken by some small birds. Mr. Mason Mitchell, American Consul at Malta, wrote lately, "The common quail are now returning in their migratory flight from Europe to Africa *via* Malta. I went out this morning, but only flushed one bird; a south-east wind is needed to bring them over from Sicily or Italy to Malta where they remain but twenty-four hours to rest up before renewing their flight of 100 miles to Tripoli or Tunis. It is marvellous how this little bird can sustain so long a flight without rest." (See on this subject Dr. Gätke's *Birds in Heligoland*.)

Roe-shooting

In shooting roe-deer by driving, the main point to be remembered by the keeper is the tendency for the roe to break back through the line of beaters. He should, therefore, advise, if necessary, that some of the guns should walk with the beaters. The other guns should be kept absolutely out of sight.

Hares

In considering how to maintain a good stock of brown hares, it is necessary for the keeper to remember that they require a lot of cover.

In driving hares, the drive should be downwind, there should be plenty of flanks, and the beaters should advance slowly and quietly.

For the improvement of stock, a few bucks and does should be turned down yearly. They are easily obtainable from certain game farms, at a moderate price. It is better, however, to secure them from a more intimate source. Owing to the size of the hare, which makes it an easy mark, the stock needs to be constantly renewed; otherwise it would soon disappear altogether. A strict limit should be fixed every season to the number of hares to be shot.

Poaching Hares

Hare-poaching is generally carried out by driving the hares towards a gate, on the outside of which a net is fastened. On this account the bottom bars of gates should be so close together that a hare cannot bolt through.

Snipe

Snipe are migratory birds, but increasing numbers are year by year nesting in this country. They rather upset one's usual methods of shooting, but make good sporting shots. Where the ground is of little value, it should be arranged, while making plans for draining, that a little wet land be left on a shoot here and there, to be the home of snipe and wild duck. Why some grounds should be more suitable than others for snipe it is hard to determine, but it is more than likely that the feeding is the attraction ; rich, soft land, with lots of worms, is the most likely haunt of the woodcock and the snipe.

The observant keeper should have a very definite idea as to the haunts of the snipe on the ground under his charge. He should remember the important fact that snipe are very conservative in their habits, and that, once they have selected a habitat, there will they always be found. From the many facts known as to the habits, habitats, and shooting of snipe, we select the following as worthy of being memorised by the keeper :

(1) Snipe are markedly affected by the moon. Choose, therefore, for shooting, a day after a clear night. Then they will have fed well, and will lie well to the guns. Like woodcock, snipe feed chiefly at night-time ; but after dark nights they feed during the day, and are very much on the alert.

(2) The best time to shoot snipe is during the thaw after a frost. At such time they get a plentiful supply of worms, which always come very near to the surface of the earth after frost.

(3) Snipe lie best in muggy weather, with a gentle breeze and a barometer which shows a tendency to fall, and after a moonlight night.

(4) Snipe lie worst in bright, fresh weather, with a high breeze, and after a dark, cloudy night.

(5) In the generality of cases, for finding the birds, the guns should walk *downwind*—this is unusual with other game—

(*a*) In a thaw—when the birds will be lying well;

(*b*) When the birds are lying badly during a strong wind.

On the other hand, the guns should walk *upwind*—

(*a*) During a sharp frost, when the birds will be lying badly ;

(*b*) When there is only a light breeze (but not during a thaw) after a dark night ;

(*c*) In approaching a bird for the second time after flushing.

(6) The best hours to shoot snipe are those immediately following daybreak, and the hours just before dark.

(7) Snipe-shooting should not be commenced on 1st August, as is commonly done. The end of September is the earliest time that they are likely to be found in good condition.

(8) Better shooting is obtained in big grass-fields soaked with water, or in bogs that have only shallow pools, than in large flooded bogs and extensive marshes. In the latter case, a single shot may cause a whole flock to rise in "wisps," and thus offer poor sport. In these cases it is perhaps better to drive the birds. If suitable arrangements can be made, a rope may be drawn across the bog or "moss." In most cases where mallard and teal are also present, capital sport can be obtained with good guns.

(9) It is wise to remember that, after being shot at, snipe may fly, or be blown, long distances, and then fall dead.

(10) The best dogs for snipe-shooting are Irish water spaniels and red Irish setters, the latter being used for shooting over bogs or large marshes, and the former for smaller and drained marshes.

NOTES.

NOTES.

CHAPTER XVIII

DISEASES OF GAME

By Sir P. J. Mackie, Bart.

Grouse Disease

There is not much that a keeper can do in the way of directly attacking disease in grouse, but, as prevention is better than cure, he should take care that the directions in Chapter X, for the improvement of ground and stock are carefully carried out. We may in this place recall the principal causes that are known to be favourable to disease in grouse :

(1) The presence on the moor of " peppered " birds.
(2) Want of draining ; much old and rank heather.
(3) The presence of decayed or decaying matter, such as the carcasses of sheep, grouse, etc.
(4) Inefficient water supply in dry seasons.
(5) Absence of grit and lime.
(6) Interbreeding and overstocking.

These conditions may not actually be the direct cause of disease, but they are recognised ***predisposing*** causes, and as such always ought to be taken into account in the study of the disease.

When a dead bird is found, the keeper should endeavour to discover the cause of death. If he become satisfied that it has been killed by wire fencing or telegraph wires the fact should serve to remind him that there are remedies for such possible sources of disaster. If no such cause is discovered, he should cut the bird open and look for disease. All grouse found dead on the moor should be burnt.

The Grouse Commission, under the able Chairmanship of Lord Lovat, has published the results of its investigations, which form most interesting reading for sportsmen. We advise all who are interested in the subject to study this publication carefully.

Internal parasites, it would seem, are the immediate cause of the disease, or, strictly speaking, the two principal diseases, for grouse, like human beings, are subject to many diseases.

Of the two diseases, we shall treat first that which is caused by the nematoid worm.

Nearly every grouse is more or less infested by these worms, which inhabit the intestines. So long as the bird is in good bodily health, and has plenty of good food and water, they do not injure him ; but if he is suffering from overstocking or other causes, or from want of food, or otherwise gets below par, then these threadlike worms get the upper hand and destroy their host.

Diseased grouse contain thousands of those worms, and each worm lays thousands of eggs. Every grouse-dropping contains hundreds of fully-segmented eggs. It will, therefore, be seen that a moor will very soon become covered with this supply of infection. The eggs turn into larvæ in two or three days. The larvæ become transformed into cysts, in which they remain for some weeks. After that they again change into active larval forms, which live and crawl among the leaves of the heather, where the grouse swallow them, and thus the round of mischief proceeds.

It has been suggested that liming dissolves the cysts or spores, but it is impossible to lime a whole moor. Besides, in time this would destroy the heather, which would be very much worse than admitting the disease. Our belief is that burning is the most effectual remedy when a moor is infected.

The cause of the second disease is a coccidium, the identity of which Dr. Fantham of Cambridge has determined. This attacks the young birds badly in summer. It is an oval cyst, and is generally picked up in the food and water. It multiplies very rapidly and disappears as quickly. Heather and tarns hold the mischief, in the form of droppings loaded with these cysts. When dry and powdery, the substance blows and contaminates the other ground. These cysts have been known to retain life for twelve months. Flies, such as the dung-fly and the grouse-fly also carry this disease. These flies lay their eggs in the fæces of grouse, hatch them out, and leave the larvæ to feed on the fæces, which may be infected with coccidium cysts. Blow-flies also contains these cysts. Lowering of temperature delays development of these sporo-cysts—also wet and cold weather. The spring and early summer is the worst time, but of course one cannot burn heather then. There is no doubt that these coccidia are carried from moor to moor by the agency of flies. Dr. Klein originally thought the grouse disease was pneumonia. Doubt is now cast on his theories. Dr. Shipley says that a considerable fauna lives both in and on the grouse—that there are eight species of insects or fleas on their skin and feathers, and that there are fifteen different species of parasites in their intestines. Undue development of any of these, in the case of a bird in impaired health, may soon cause disaster. Dr. Shipley adds :

" It is difficult for the layman to grasp what is going on in and on the soil, and on the plants which it supports. Suppose we could, by means of a gigantic lens, magnify a square yard of a grouse moor one hundred times. The heather plants would be as tall as lofty elms, their flowers as big as cabbages ; the grouse would be six or seven times the size of ' Chantecler ' at the Porte St. Martin. Creeping and wriggling up the stem and over the leaves, and gradually yet surely making their way towards the flowers, would be seen hundreds and thousands of silvery white worms about the size of young earthworms. Lying on the leaves, and on the plant generally, would be seen thousands of spherical bodies the size of grains of wheat, the cysts of the coccidium ; and on the ground and on the plants, as large as split peas, would be seen the tapeworm eggs patiently awaiting the advent of their second host. This is perhaps a picture that will not appeal to all, but yet it represents what, unseen and unsuspected, is always going on on a grouse moor."

The last-quoted paragraph contains valuable information which quite a number of people, although interested in this subject, would never think of considering ; such information is well worth serious attention.

In a previous chapter we mentioned that Dr. Shipley, F.R.S., who is investigating the subject, has not yet been able to find the host of the tapeworm. The theories are many, but before any can be accepted abundant proof will require to be brought forward. Some keepers think that the dog will be found to be the cause of the tapeworm in grouse. Dr. Shipley has been giving mites and ticks careful attention. In Ross-shire ticks are numerous in certain woods, and keepers say that they kill a large number of black game ; but the tick has never been found in the crop of the grouse. He says that the tapeworms which live in the alimentary canal of the grouse pass their younger or larval stages in the body of some lower animal. This lower animal—presumably an insect, or mollusc, or spider—must be eaten by a grouse, whereupon the larval tapeworm is set free. This process of transference from one host to another must take place before the parasite can grow up into the adult tapeworm which we find in the intestine of the grouse. In searching for the primary host, it was natural to begin with the ectoparasites, which one would imagine were being continually snapped up by the bird. We have, however, up till now, completely failed to find any cestoid larvæ in the grouse-fly or in the numerous "biting lice" which abound on the skin and amongst the feathers

AA

of the grouse ; and, what is still more significant and remarkable, we have never, in the hundreds of crop contents which we have examined, found one of these insects among the grouse's food.

Dr. Shipley also describes the different parasites, commencing with ground-lice, which do so much harm to the grouse in the bad years when they are feeble and unhealthy. This louse is the commonest of the insects which infest the skin of the grouse, and appears to some extent in numbers that are in inverse ratio to the bird's health. Careful search will discover only two or three on a healthy grouse, but on a "piner" hundreds may be met with. No doubt we shall yet discover the host of the tapeworm and the cause of the grouse disease.

I made the following note some years ago, on a moor, where attention had been given to burning, draining, vermin-killing, etc., with the hope of bringing the bag up to a given limit. A larger stock of grouse than usual was left in 1907, and one hundred and fifty brace, that might have been shot, were spared in the hopes of a record year in 1908. One fact, however, was omitted from the calculations. The season had been a very bad heather year, so that there was no feeding during the winter for a large stock of grouse ; and, in consequence, the grouse got into poor condition, pined, and suffered much from disease. The result was that instead of being a record year, as was expected, the season of 1908 was a complete failure, and no shooting took place at all. Next season new blood was introduced from Yorkshire, and the birds have again increased in number and are healthy. There can be no doubt that neither land or water will support more than a certain amount of life, regulated mainly according to the food supply. Overstock, and you are certain to bring disease and death. How often do we forget that Nature's laws cannot be set at naught with impunity?

Prevention is the best cure. A good road or path through a moor is excellent, as it allows the birds to gather grit and dust themselves. Grit or quartz is most essential to the health of the birds, and where a large stock of grouse is wanted, grit should be artificially supplied, if it does not exist naturally.

Pheasant Disease

Overcrowding and interbreeding are the main causes of disease in pheasants. When disease breaks out, all affected birds should be killed, the rest of the stock moved to fresh ground, and a careful examination made into the dietary and hygienic surroundings of the birds. The bodies of all pheasants killed by disease, or killed on account of disease, should be burned. Disease is often caught from the domestic fowls. The condition of the fowls should be carefully inquired into, and the same procedure taken with the affected fowls as with the affected pheasants. It is wise, as soon as disease shows itself, to give lime freely to all the birds. Lime should constitute an essential part of the food of pheasants and also of the ground upon which they live.

When worms appear, isolation of the affected birds

becomes imperative, and likewise the removal of the unaffected birds to healthier soil. The affected pheasants in these cases may be sprinkled with a weak solution of salicylic acid or salicylate of soda, and a little of the solution should be added to the drinking-water.

Mr. Shipley says: "In individual cases the worms may be removed by dipping a feather stripped of its barbules, except at the tip, into a mixture of one part of oil of turpentine with two of olive oil, or into oil of cloves, and then inserting it into the trachea; on its withdrawal it will probably bring with it the worms. This operation requires a little care, or asphyxiation may result. Garlic mixed into the food and rue mixed with the water have also proved successful."

Putting birds into boxes containing two parts, by weight, of powdered chalk to one of camphor is recommended by some authorities, while Mr. Tegetmeier recommends that the birds should be fumigated by volatilised carbolic acid. This can be done by putting the affected birds into a box in which a hot brick has been placed, and pouring a solution of carbolic acid on the brick.

Gapes.—Lime dust sprinkled in the coops in the morning is useful in this disease. At a later stage garlic should be given once a day with the food.

Cramp.—Change of soil is the treatment recommended for this.

Ophthalmia and other Eye Affections.—The birds should be removed from their present rearing-ground.

Diarrhœa.—A little starch mixed with food soon corrects this. Food should also be changed, and giving water to the birds discontinued.

Scurfy Legs.—The coops should be thoroughly cleaned and whitewashed, the legs of the affected birds well soaked in hot water, the scales peeled off, and the legs then washed with some antiseptic soap. All affected fowls should be removed, and all affected pheasants isolated.

PARTRIDGES

The remarks made above in regard to overcrowding, interbreeding, change of ground and food, cleanliness, and the burning of all dead birds, apply as much to partridges as to pheasants. What has been said about supplying partridges with drinking-fountains in very dry weather must be remembered in considering the question of gapes. Mr. Horace Hutchinson practically cured his estate at Newmarket of this disease by putting down numerous drinking-fountains as soon as dry weather set in after hatching-time.

RABBITS

The constant change of blood, attention to the feeding capacities of the ground, and the avoidance of turnips as a food, are the best preventives of disease in rabbits. If disease has spread to any large extent, the whole stock should be killed off. This applies also to partridges and to pheasants. The ground should be thoroughly dressed with salt and lime.

NOTES.

CHAPTER XIX

LOADERS AND GUN-CLEANING

It is only by practice that the loader can learn to come into sympathetic practice with the shooter. The harmony between the two must be complete, if success is to be looked for—a harmony so perfect as to make the practice of exchanging guns almost as automatic as the action of a machine. The first point for the loader to remember, and never to forget, is that the gun is an enemy to life, and that no weapon, whether it be a 12-bore gun, fowling-piece, rifle, air-gun, or penny pistol, should ever be held, loaded or unloaded, with the barrels pointing at any living thing, except for the purpose of killing. The muzzle of a gun should always be *inclined* to the earth or to the sky, clear from every creature whose life is of value.

If these rules are impressed on the mind, they will assist the loader in carrying out his duties with success. In loading he must remember to keep the point of the barrels clear of everyone, " to depress the muzzle while turning away from the shooter, and in shutting the gun always to raise the stock to the barrels, and not the barrels to the stock, so that if by any accident the charge explodes, it can only make a hole in the ground." The gun should never be closed, if loaded, while the loader is turned towards the shooter. Guns should never be loaded until the shooter takes his place at his stand, and should always be unloaded as soon as the drive is over.

It is highly desirable that a little rehearsal should take place between the shooter and the loader, if they are strangers to each other. When the loader is the shooter's own servant, five minutes' practice in the gun-room on "off" days should be indulged in, and also now and again during the summer. This will save a lot of bother, wasteful movements, and irritation when "the trouble" begins. The loader must always be keen and watchful, not of the birds, but of the man who is using the guns. He is not intended to spot the birds and call "left," "right," or "over"; he is only there to see that his shooter gets a loaded gun with the least amount of trouble. He must be on the alert to get out of the way, as the shooter varies his position so as to get a suitable angle to loose on his bird. The position varies most in partridge-driving, at which practice the capacity of the loader will be tried to the utmost. Coolness is a most valuable quality, and is demanded most when rapidity of loading is essential. All guns should be loaded as if they were wanted quickly, even though the loader be aware that there is no particular hurry. He errs then only on the safe side, and the practice of quick loading at all times will perfect his art in general. To assist in the

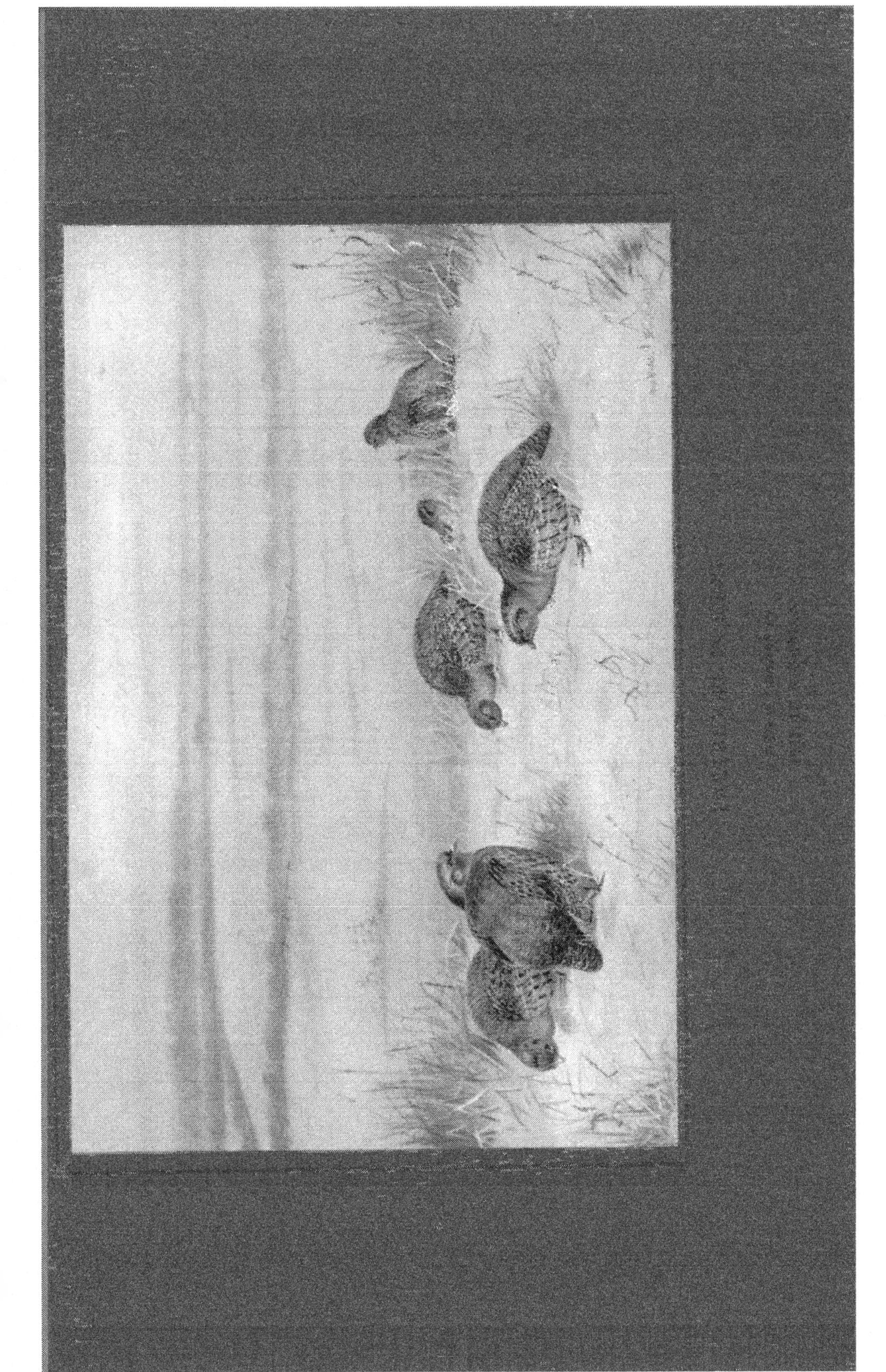

perfecting of his practice, the loader should rehearse the loading and unloading of guns—at other times, of course, than shooting-times.

The position of the loader is varied by the preference of the shooter and by the game to be shot. Some shooters like to have their loaders immediately behind them, some on the right, and others on the left. On this point Lord Suffolk and Mr. Craven write: "When rocketing pheasants are the sole objects, the loader may stand right half-forward without in the least interfering with his master, who, indeed, will be rather helped than hindered; but if hares and rabbits are also coming out of covert, the man must be well half-back. In grouse-driving a position on the immediate right is obviously to be recommended, for, thus placed, the loader will only interfere with a shot which would pepper the occupant of the adjoining butt on that side. For partridge-driving over high fences or belts, the rule is the same as with tail pheasants."

In changing guns, the shooter throws up the barrel and grasps the gun by the neck, then turns slightly to the loader, who takes it with his left hand and passes the second loaded gun smartly forward with his right. While holding the unused loaded gun, it should be grasped just below the triggers with the right hand, and the right arm should be leant slightly across the chest, so as to rest the barrels on the left arm. The barrels will then be pointing in the air to the left and behind.

Hints to Loaders

(*a*) The loader should never touch the " safe " slide, and when loading should turn his back to the shooter. After loading, in closing the breech, raise the butt and not the barrels. This is most essential to the safety of the gun and the loader. Of course it is understood that the point of the weapon will be pointing to the ground when loading.

(*b*) The loader should never talk, and should never smoke on duty. Such are considered very bad manners, and can only be excused on the score of ignorance.

(*c*) The loader in wet weather should protect the mechanism part of the gun as much as possible, and should wipe it from time to time with an oiled rag.

(*d*) Should any difficulty be experienced in working the lever, the gun should be carefully examined for dirt or any remains of cartridge-paper.

(*e*) Damp cartridges should never be used.

(*f*) If mud or sand or other foreign substances get into the barrels, they should be well run through with the lead cylinder and the pocket cleaner.

(*g*) Always inspect the gun thoroughly after any accident of the nature of tripping or of dropping the gun. No gun should ever be used that has the barrels badly indented.

If a third gun be employed, it should be held by a keeper or a second loader, who stands behind the shooter and the first loader. It is this man who may keep his eyes on the birds—never the loader.

Look through the barrels of the gun occasionally in the course of a day's shoot.

Cleaning of Guns and Rifles

In addition to the regular cleaning of the guns at the end of the day's sport, there is something to be said for cleaning them at intervals in the shooting. When there is much heavy firing, as in a big grouse or partridge drive, or a big covert shoot, it is in every way desirable that the barrels should be at least " run through " some time during the day. Clean barrels minimise any tendency to " rebound," or to create such recoil where it does not naturally exist. The procedure to be recommended in cleaning a gun in the gunroom is :

(1) Take the gun to pieces, and place the barrels on a cloth.

(2) First clean the barrels with hot water, and run over and through with tow.

(3) Put finest paraffin or Rangoon oil on clean tow at the end of a rod, and run the barrels well through.

(4) Run through the barrels again with clean soft tow.

(5) Coat the inside and outside of the barrels with vaseline.

(6) Remove all grease from barrels and chambers before the gun is used.

In addition, the breech action should be carefully inspected and wiped over with vaseline. The ribs and the sides of the ejector part should be gone over with a soft mop dipped in the same. A similar practice should be followed in the cleaning of a rifle. With the introduction of cordite and other new powders, it is often found necessary, especially in the cleaning of rifles, to use some special preparation like *Nitroclene*, or *Webley's* 303, or *Semper Idem*.

When a gun or rifle is put away and not inspected daily, the barrels should be covered with a mixture of paraffin and neatsfoot, and the inside of the barrels rubbed with the same mixture.

If there are signs of lead, this may be removed by corking the bore at one end and filling it with spirits of turpentine.

If a gun or rifle be very rusty, boiling water and then paraffin may be used, care being taken to remove the paraffin before the weapon is put away.

In addition to what has been said, the following points may be noted: (*a*) No keeper or loader should interfere with springs, screws, etc. If the gun or rifle goes out of order, he should inform the owner as to its condition, who will, unless he is himself an experienced mechanic, which is unlikely, send his weapon to the maker; (*b*) gun-locks should never be cleaned with thick oil: this is apt to collect dirt and become sticky, which causes clogging ; (*c*) no paraffin should be left wet on a gun, as it evaporates rapidly and causes rust. Refined paraffin should be used. Instead of paraffin, chronometer oil, or refined neatsfoot has been recommended. Care must be taken never to lay a gun flat on the ground ; it should always lean against something solid and firm—muzzle upwards.

Every gunroom should have a card, hung or pasted up, giving directions for the cleaning and the keeping of guns and rifles. These cards should be supplied by the gunmaker, and should record the following points in large print :

(1) All guns to be thoroughly wiped immediately after the shooting is over. (If the shooting is some distance away from the gunroom, the guns should be wiped in the open.)

(2) All guns and rifles to be thoroughly cleaned and freed from rust and lead, as soon as possible after they are brought to the gunroom.

(3) Wet guns should never be put in a warm place, as this is apt to cause swelling and steaming and rusting of locks.

(4) All injuries or inefficient working of any part of guns or rifles should be reported at once to the owners of the same.

(5) Great care should be taken that when a gun or rifle is in the possession either of keeper or loader, it be not injured by falling or knocking against anything that may damage it in any way.

(6) If by any carelessness—for instance, by loading with a cartridge that has fallen on the ground—sand or grit gets into the breech or lock, special care must be taken in cleaning, so as not to scratch the mechanism.

(7) After cleaning a gun, always look through the barrels to see no obstruction is left in them.

Ammunition

Note.—Cartridges are private property, as much as a man's horse, dog, gun, or money. The practice of robbing a magazine is therefore criminal, apart from its being beneath the dignity of a sportsman.

NOTES

NOTES.

CHAPTER XX

THE GAMEKEEPER AS A FISHING GILLIE

By P. D. Malloch

With the limited space at my disposal, it will be impossible for me to exhaust this subject, or do much more than mention the principal duties of the fishing gillie.

River Salmon-fishing from the Bank.—The first duty of the gillie is to see that the river is properly protected from poachers. Should there be no net shots on the beat, the places which could be netted ought to be protected. This can usually be done, and at little expense, by putting large boulders, anchors, or stakes in the river. When pools are thus protected, sweep-netting will, as a rule, be prevented, and trammel-netting also, in part. The latter method of netting is, however, difficult to put a stop to.

A careful look-out should be kept for any signs of trammel-netting. If it be suspected that this method of poaching is being carried on from a boat, the gillie should observe whether any scales of fish have been left in the boat or on the bank.

A sharp look-out should be kept in the morning, to see that the pools are not fished before the owner comes down to the water. There is nothing more annoying to the angler than to find, from marks on the sand or grass, that the pools have been fished by a poacher an hour or two before.

If the gillie be unable to keep watch in the morning, he should stretch a few threads across the paths where the poachers are likely to pass ; he will thus at once be able to detect if anyone has been on the paths since he was last there. Should he find the threads broken, he can then set a watch for the intruders.

The gillie should have a knowledge of the time when the fish begin to run up ; where and when they begin to rest at different seasons ; the effects of snow water, frost, and fresh water on their running ; and the time the river will take in coming into ply after a flood, so that he can advise the angler when his water is ready to be fished.

The temperature of the water should be taken daily. Much can be learned by doing this. When a daily record of this temperature is kept, the gillie will have some idea of what size of fly to recommend, and whether bait-fishing should be resorted to or not.

A gillie who has an interest in his work will take every opportunity of watching the river, the fish, and the direction of the wind. He should also have a knowledge of all the pools and streams—their depth, the lie of the fish, and the state of the river which suits the fish best. This knowledge is most important, for by the possession thereof much of the angler's time can be saved. To acquire such knowledge requires years of careful observation on the part of the gillie, although much valuable information may be got from older fishermen who know the beats.

The gillie should discover the effect of the sun upon the pools, the direction of the wind that catches certain of them, and the most advantageous side from which the pool should be fished.

When the river is low and out of ply, the whole beat should be carefully inspected, and all dangerous roots and sticks on which a fish might foul should be removed.

The croys, if any, should be repaired, the paths along the banks put in order, and the banks of pools looked to after a flood. As a rule, far too little attention is given to these matters, with the result that many fine pools become worthless. The clever gillie does not need to be told this ; he is always considering how he can improve his fishing by, for example, erecting a croy at one point, and another on the opposite side, so as to contract a wide part of the stream into a narrow part, and thus form new pools and improve others, or, by rolling a stone into a pool, to make a rest for the fish. On one occasion (20th October) I killed three salmon behind a stone which a keeper had rolled into a pool on the river Earn two years earlier, where probably no fish had rested before.

Now I shall suppose that the gillie or keeper has instructions to telegraph to his employer, or to the angler who is to fish the water, whether he ought to come or not on the opening day. The angler has never fished the water, or seen the keeper before. The river is in order, and plenty of fish are showing, and the keeper accordingly wires advice to come down.

If arrangements have not been made as to the terms on which the gillie is engaged, the angler ought to make it his first duty on arriving at his beat to rectify the omission. The wages should be fixed at so much per week, to be paid fortnightly or monthly, as may be arranged. When lunch is not provided, a money payment is usually given instead. The arrangements come to should be perfectly clear and definite, so as to save any possible annoyance afterwards to either party.

Before going to the river, the gillie should see the tackle, rods, reels, lines, flies, casts, and baits which have been provided for the fishing ; he will then be able to advise as to the best length of rod, the most suitable reel and line, cast, line, and fly in the stock, and what will be sufficient to take out for the day. He should not fail to see that there is a gaff, a suitable landing-net, a bag to carry the fish, and a basket or bag for the luncheon. *It is the gillie's duty to see that nothing is left behind.* He should run all the items over in his mind before starting for the river. Perhaps by repeating the following well-known rhyme, he might assist his memory :

> " Rods, reels, baskets,
> Hooks, worms, flaskets." [1]

[1] To modernise this old rhyme and make it so complete that it will include gaff, baton, landing-nets, fly-books and cases, waterproofs and luncheon, we would suggest the following as being fairly comprehensive :

> " Rods, reels, and hooks,
> Nets, bait, and baskets,
> Gaff, baton, books,
> Coats, lunch, and flaskets."

With regard to the last-mentioned article, and for his own refreshment, the gillie would do well to see that it contained no more spirits than he could safely carry home. The gillie or keeper who takes a drop more than he should do, lowers himself more in the estimation of his employer than by almost anything else.

Having got to the river, the first thing to do is to put up the rod, and then see that the reel fits tight, and that the line is put through all the rings without being twisted round the rod. The gut cast should be carefully soaked, and then fitted neatly to the main line before the fly is attached. The cast and fly should then be tested, and the rod handed to the angler, who may thereupon begin fishing.

The following remarks might be overheard at such a time, if one were within earshot of a well-trained gillie : " Cast a short line to begin with, but when you get down to that ripple, let out a few yards more ; that is where they usually come. From that part fish carefully down for another twenty yards ; we shall then go on to the next pool."

The angler begins to cast, and during the first half-dozen casts there are anxious moments for the gillie. He knows by this time whether his employer is an experienced angler or not. He sees that his employer is casting straight across, and politely requests him to " Cast a little straighter down, sir."

After a few more casts, something pulls down the rod and the line begins to run out. After a run or two, the fish shows itself to be a kelt. "Do not be particular with him, sir," the gillie remarks. The fish is brought backwards as quickly as possible. Instead of the gaff, the net is put under it and pulled ashore. The hook is carefully extracted, and the kelt returned to the river with as much care as possible. On no account should the gaff be used. The fly is examined to see that the tinsel has not been torn by the kelt's long teeth.

Another start is made at the same place; there is another pull, and the reel sings out again. A livelier fish this time, and he jumps into the air. "A spring fish, sir; be more careful." After a little time the fish nears the shore. The gillie remains quiet, gaff, instead of net, in hand this time. Several times the fish comes within a few feet of the gaff, and as often rushes out into the stream again. The next time it comes within reach of the gillie, who puts the gaff quietly over the fish's back and pulls. The moment he does this he stands erect, with the end of the gaff-handle pointing upwards, and the fish hanging on the gaff hook. He then walks quietly to a safe place, seizes the fish by the tail, takes out the gaff, lays the fish on the ground, gives it three or four sharp knocks with his little baton, extracts the fly, weighs the fish, carefully washes it, and puts it away in the bag provided for the purpose. A note of the weight is then recorded in his book. The whole of this procedure should not take more than three minutes, at the end of which time the angler is again ready to resume.

He fishes down the pool ; sees nothing more ; walks on to the next pool, and is directed in the same way as at the last. This pool is fished down without a rise, so the gillie begins to think that the fly is either too large or too small, or not of the right kind ; and advises that a more sombre-coloured fly two sizes smaller should be put on and the pool fished over again. This is done, with the result that two other spring fish are added to the basket. The angler by this time sees that the gillie understands his work, and is accordingly willing to place every confidence in him. The two become friends, and the fishing turns out a success, being a source of pleasure to the angler, and of profit to the gillie.

When the fishing is over the rod is taken down, everything is carefully packed up and taken home. The gillie unwinds the wet portion of the line on to a line-drier, so that it may be thoroughly dried and ready for use the next day. The flies which have been used should be dried before being put away. The waders should be turned inside out and hung up to dry. The wading-boots and worsted stockings should also be thoroughly dried. Sometimes, before looking after these details, the fish have to be carefully packed, labelled, and sent away.

Before leaving, the time is arranged for starting next day. Day after day passes in the same pleasant way until the season is over.

What a contrast to the gillie who does not understand

his work! He goes out in the morning with his flasket filled to the top. When he gets to the riverside he finds he has forgotten the reel, and has to walk or run back a couple of miles to secure it, leaving the angler on the river bank wasting the best hour of the day. The gillie knows that a certain pool is a good one, but does not know the exact spot where the fish rise. He tells the angler to begin at the top and fish to the bottom. Instead of fishing only fifteen yards, he fishes three times that distance, with no real chance of hooking a fish.

When a fish is hooked, this inexperienced gillie tells the angler, in an offhand way, to hold up his rod, or to hold it, as the case may be, down. If the fish does come to land, he rushes up and down the side of the river frightening it, and takes double the time he ought to in bringing it to the gaff. When a chance of gaffing is offered him, he misses it.

This stamp of gillie causes, to put it mildly, much annoyance and displeasure to the angler.

River-Salmon Fishing from a Boat.—In river-salmon fishing from a boat, the gillie's duty is to see that before the anglers come out in the morning the boat is brought up to its proper place, the water baled out, and everything made clean and tidy, so that when the anglers appear no time is lost before starting. There should always be suitable landing-places for the boat, whatever the state of the river. Where the boat has to be pulled up on to the riverside, the bushes should be cut every year and the footpaths kept in order.

The boat should be taken quietly to the side of the stream, sufficiently near for the angler to command it. The more quietly the boat is worked the better the sport will be; a boat always disturbs the water, although many gillies think the contrary. I have many times proved my point. After a good angler has fished over the water in a boat, I have often quietly waded in and killed many fish; so, Mr. Gillie, never go splashing over the water, and on no account cross over a good pool, if it can be avoided. The boat should be held as steady as possible. After every cast it should be let down a yard, and no part of a good stream should be missed.

If the stream be so broad that the angler cannot command it from one side, both sides can be fished; but if too wide to be fished from both sides, the boat should be worked quietly first out and then in. When a rise is got, the boat should be pulled up a yard, so that the fish may get another chance of taking the fly: this is easier said than done, as it is difficult to keep a boat in the same place in a stream. A sharp look out should be kept for some bush, tree, or stone on the bank that may serve as a guide to keep the boat in the exact spot required. When a fish is hooked, never be in too great a hurry to get to the shore. As a rule the fish will follow the boat. The angler will find that the best way to get the fish out of the stream is to hold his rod steady and not to wind in the reel. Should a fish make a run, the boat should be stopped until it settles down, then the gillie should pull towards the shore, selecting a spot where the water is deepest as the best place to land a fish.

If possible, try to get the fish up into the fished water, so that it will not disturb the unfished water. When the shore is reached, do not bump against it. If you do so, there is a danger of your upsetting the angler. When sufficient line has been taken in, and the fish is under command, the seat should be taken away and the angler allowed to land. He should be told, if inexperienced in angling, to keep well away from the bank, as he will thereby run less risk of losing the fish. The fish can be either worked towards the stern of the boat and then gaffed, or worked towards the land and gaffed from the shore. The gaff, by the by, should be kept as sharp as a needle.

An expert will usually take the first chance of gaffing the fish, as it comes within reach many times before it is played out. Some gaff the fish under, others over, the back, while others again gaff the fish in whatever way opportunity presents. When gaffing over the back, the gaff should be reached out, laid quietly over the back fin, and pulled. The moment the fish is gaffed the handle should be held perpendicularly and the fish lifted into the boat. Before the gaff is removed, the fish should get three or four sharp knocks on the head with the baton. The gaff can then be removed, the hook extracted, the fish weighed, a note being taken of the weight, and then washed and laid in the bow of the boat. Any blood in the boat should be carefully wiped up. All this should not take more than three minutes. A fish should never be gaffed near the head, as there is the risk of gaffing the line instead of the fish.

In gaffing, the gillie should try to get within reach of a fish as quickly as possible, but should never be in a hurry in striking. When the right moment arrives he must do the stroke quietly and deliberately, not by raking at the fish three or four times in quick succession. If he does so he will be sure to make a mistake. The number of fish which are lost at the gaffing is enormous. I usually tell a man who has never used a gaff before to put it over the fish's back and pull, and as a rule he does it all right. The great thing is to keep perfectly cool.

Fish which are caught with minnow or prawn should always be gaffed. If landing-nets are used, the hooks usually stick in the meshes and the weight of the fish breaks them. The fish should always be killed before being laid down in the boat, otherwise the hooks may stick in the bottom of the boat and get broken. Grilse of small size are difficult to gaff; they are much more easily netted. Salmon up to 40 lb. can be netted, but over this weight it is safer to use the gaff.

In netting, the net should be quietly put under the fish, lifted up, and then pulled towards the shore. This is infinitely better than lifting it clear of the water and bringing the whole weight of the fish on the net. The great thing to remember is—get the head of the fish away from the side of the net before lifting. If this be not done the hooks are apt to catch in the net, the head does not get down, the tail part falls over the ring ; the fish is outside, the hooks are attached to the net ; there are one or two wriggles, and the fish is gone. A gillie should never attempt to net or gaff a fish while he is wearing white sleeves, nor should he run up and down after a fish ; he should rather wait quietly in one place and reach out the gaff when the fish passes him. Many a time when alone I have dirtied the water by stirring up the mud at the side with my feet ; when the fish has been guided into the muddy water, it cannot see, and the gillie is therefore quite safe in then walking in and gaffing it.

Another opportunity of gaffing a fish may be obtained when the fish's head is out of the water, for in that position also it cannot see. If both the gaff and net have been accidentally left behind, the best way of landing a fish is by first tiring it out and getting it to turn on its side. It can then be pulled up into shallow water. A very large fish can be pulled up in this fashion. Every time it moves, a little pressure is put on, and in this way it can be brought on to the gravel, and gradually landed high and dry. The gillie may then go forward and catch it by the tail, and push it farther up, or lift it on to the bank.

Harling a River from a Boat.—This method of fishing is only resorted to on large rivers, where the pools cannot be conveniently fished from either bank. It is done by placing two or three rods in the stern of the boat ; if three, one at each side, and the third in the centre. A fly is attached to each rod, a minnow sometimes being substituted for one of the flies. From twenty to forty yards of line are let out from each reel. Two gillies row the boat from one side to the other, dropping down a yard or two at a time.

To be successful, the gillie must have a knowledge of the river in its different heights. He must also be able to tell the angler the proper length of line to put out, the bait line always being a yard or two shorter than those with flies ; and the proper kind and size of flies to use. The gillie must, besides, know the proper angle at which to keep the boat, so that the lines and flies may be kept in correct position. In turning, the boat should be brought slowly round so as to give the flies also plenty of time to turn. Observant gillies who take an interest in their work always excel in this style of fishing.

Trolling or Salmon Minnow-Fishing from a Boat in a Loch.—In this method of fishing the gillie's duty is to find out which parts of the loch the fish frequent ; the different depths of the loch, so as to avoid fouling in the bottom, or coming against hidden rocks ; the kinds of bait to use (and to see that it spins properly) ; the proper length of line to put out ; the correct weight of lead to put on the trace ; and the direction of wind which affects certain parts of the loch. He must also know how to drop the bait over a fish which has been seen to rise, without taking the boat over the place and disturbing the fish. Care should be taken to row sufficiently fast, so as to make the bait spin. When a fish is hooked, the boat should not be pulled all over the loch. Many gillies are never content unless they are following that bad practice, and they sometimes kill a fish a mile away from the place where it was hooked, thereby wasting valuable time, and, by disturbing the water, spoiling the chance of getting other fish.

Trout Fishing from a Boat in a Loch.—In Scotland more gillies and keepers are employed in this style of fishing than in any other. The angler depends on them for his sport and pleasure. As a rule, the sport is proportionate to the knowledge of the gillie. The gillie's duty is to obtain a perfect knowledge of every part of the loch, its deeps, shallows, and bays, and the places which trout frequent at different seasons. He should know at all times where he is, the depth of water he is fishing, the nature of the bottom—whether gravel, rocks, mud, etc.—the places and time of day the flies hatch out, the direction of winds that suit the different places, the effects of cold and heat, sunshine and shade, the different kinds of flies, and whether strong or fine tackle should be used, how to keep the boat to the wave in drifting, whether the bow or stern should point in a certain direction, and whether the boat is drifting too fast or too slow.

If there be only one angler in the boat, the gillie should be able to advise which end he should fish from, and whether it would be better to row the boat instead of allowing it to drift. All these points must be carefully studied and mastered before the gillie can be said to be an experienced hand. When a trout is hooked, the net should be quietly put under it and then lifted out, the fish being caught with one hand and the hook extracted with the other. The fish should then be knocked on the head, for nothing is more disgusting than to have a trout, half-dead, wriggling about in the basket.

There is a great art in taking out a hook ; those who know how to do it can extract the hook very quickly without bending the iron, or breaking the barb, or destroying the fly. The cast and hooks will often get entangled, but the experienced gillie, with one or two shakes, will usually be able to set them free. These are some of the principal points which the experienced angler depends on for filling his basket.

The "Compleat Angler's Gillie."—A clever gillie is always in request. He is usually an agreeable and pleasant companion. I know of such a gillie. The one I have in mind I have known for upwards of thirty years. I reckoned that he was the means of adding 10 lb. daily to my basket. He is far and away the cleverest gillie I have ever had. The manner in which he lands a trout, extracts the hook, and unravels the cast is simply marvellous ; the time he takes is little longer than it takes to make a cast. The way he will row to the centre of a loch, and turn round the boat within thirty yards of a sunken island, requires to be seen to be believed. This gillie is worth double the usual wage, and I am quite sure he gets it.

The worst enemy the gillie has to contend with is

drink. It is most unkind of an angler to give his gillie more than is good for him. I dare say I employ more gillies than any man in Scotland. I always impress upon them never to grumble or make complaints to the anglers they are attending upon and who come for sport and pleasure. The more the gillies are encouraged in habits of temperance, the better for all concerned.

Note on the Improvement of Loch Fishings

It is in every way desirable, for the improvement of loch fishings, to attend to the following points :

Throughout the autumn and winter, keepers and gillies usually have abundance of spare time, and are at a loss to know how best to employ it. To such I would strongly advise turning their attention to the stocking and improving of any lochs that may be found on their employer's estate. All over Scotland there are lochs and streams containing far too many trout, and others again with few or none. To remedy these defects is, to the intelligent gillie, a most interesting and fascinating work, and a source of pleasure and profit to his employer. How pleasant to tell your master that you introduced forty or fifty tiny trout into a small lake of his, not more than two acres in extent, four years previously, and now he can see them for himself, rising of a summer evening like miniature salmon. Excitement takes possession of him, and he is not content until an opportunity presents itself of casting over them. Then what joy when a dozen lusty fellows from 3 to 5 lb. grace his basket! The puny little loch, once his pet aversion, is now a delight to all, and to none more than to the gillie who had taken the trouble to stock it.

The gillie must not, however, lose sight of the fact that, where there is no spawning-ground, he cannot expect to maintain a stock unless he keep on making up the numbers by introducing more trout. If none be added to make up the deficiency, in a short space of time most of the stock will have disappeared, for the life of a trout does not extend over more than from seven to eight years.

When trout are introduced into a loch for the first time, the feeding is generally so rich that they grow very rapidly. Most lochs, if not too deep, can sustain from 100 to 200 trout per acre, so that when only 20 to the acre are introduced, they have more than sufficient food, and quickly increase in size.

Every gillie should have a large landing net and pail to carry trout from one place to another. By netting the small streams, 1,000 trout can often be caught in a day, and then distributed over several small lochs and allowed to grow at their own sweet will. On reaching from 1½ lb. upwards, these trout will give capital sport to several rods for a whole season. Similarly, lochs containing too many trout, and too small to give sport, may be netted and the fish transported elsewhere; or the spawning-ground can be curtailed, when numbers will soon be lessened.

On many occasions I have known anglers capture, in an overstocked loch, a score of small trout with rod and line, and carry them to another, and troutless, loch, and in after years recapture those that had reached a takeable size. This is a slow process, but it answers the purpose quite well, and it serves to show what can be done in this modest way.

Lochs that are too shallow can be deepened by raising the level of the outlet by means of a few stones. An hour or two spent at this is often rewarded by the opening up of many acres of fishing-ground, formerly covered with weeds. Other lochs of too deep a nature for producing food can be made shallower by deepening the outlet ; and little falls can often be blasted, thus allowing trout to enter a loch. Many other points will occur to the observant gillie as things he should bring to the notice of his employer. I know of no other contributory to sport that is so much neglected as the care and improvement of trout-fishing.

Proprietors often put themselves to no end of trouble to obtain an extra brace of grouse, but pay no attention whatever to trout, which are equally valuable.

Hotel-keepers come under the same reproach ; they will take every trout they possibly can out of their lochs, without ever giving a single thought to the restocking of them.

Notes by Editor

The size of trout in a loch depends on the feeding. If feeding is naturally deficient, the supply can be augmented with little expense, and a sanctuary made for shrimps, mollusca, and other fish food.

Take a slight inlet in the loch where a small stream runs into it ; dig out, say, 18 inches deep. Suppose it is 25 by 30 ft., bank up the end near the loch to the level of ground for 20 ft., leaving 10 ft. open, which you will close with ⅜-in. wire netting or perforated zinc to prevent fish, rats, etc., entering. Cover all over with wire netting, 1 in., to keep out birds, etc ; manure well, and lay turf in the bottom—insects like rich soil—and then plant the usual water plants. Watercress at the inlet is good. Lay in also some moss-covered stones from a burn which has good feeding ; then get, from a fish hatchery, shrimps, cadis worms, snails, and other usual food of fish which are valuable colourers and give a pink flesh ; and place these in the sanctuary. The fish will then breed, and, as they get crowded up, will move off into the loch of their own accord ; or you can move them by catching them in a net. You will then get pink-fleshed and big-game trout.

NOTES.

CHAPTER XXI

SOME BROAD FACTS IN ANGLING LAW

By Henry Lamond

(Secretary of the Loch Lomond Angling Improvement Association)

It would be absurd to attempt to comprise within a single brief chapter a compendium of the law of fishing in Scotland, if at the same time one were expected to advance reasons and authority for each proposition stated. Proprietors and their keepers, or fish-watchers need never, however, be at a loss on any given point if the country-house library contain, as it ought to do, Stewart's *Treatise on the Law of Scotland Relating to Rights of Fishing*, and Tait's useful book on *The Law of Scotland on the Game Laws, Trout, and Salmon-fishing*. In both of these, care must be taken to distinguish between what has actually, in recently decided cases, been found to be the law and what is merely the author's opinion. A useful feature of these books is that they give as appendices the Salmon Fishery Acts from 1828 to 1868 as well as the Trout Acts of 1845 and 1860, but not the latest Trout Act of 1902. With these Acts every fish-watcher should be familiar, because it will add much to the value of his services, if he has made an intelligent study of them. Not only so, but besides giving him, or indeed any keeper, confidence in his work, it is safe to say that friction and misunderstanding will be absent from a neighbourhood where rights are clearly understood and equitably insisted on. The aid of his legal adviser must of course be invoked by a proprietor before actions of interdict regarding fishing, pollution, or rights of way are thought of, or even before poaching prosecutions are contemplated: but the following brief notes may be of guidance in an emergency, or may help to support an argument.

I. Salmon

Legal Definition

By statute the word "salmon" means and includes "salmon, grilse, sea-trout, bull-trout, smolts, parr, and other migratory fish of the salmon kind" (1862 Act, Section 2). In this comprehensive sense the word is here used.

Public Rights

There is no public right of salmon-fishing in Scotland, either in salt water round the shores, or in fresh water. Where the right is not in the hands of a private proprietor, it is vested in the Crown, and administered by the Department of the Commissioners of Woods and Forests. Hence any person fishing for salmon, whether by net, or by rod and line, without a title, or without express written permission from one who has a title, is, in the eye of the law, a poacher and as such liable to be prosecuted. (1844 Act, Section 1.)

Private Rights

These are too involved to permit of any useful summary being given. The basis of right must be some written title, perhaps interpreted and modified by the Courts, but often the exercise and extent of rights depend upon friendly agreements.

Close Times

These vary in different localities. The foundation for them is Schedule C annexed to the 1868 Act : but many alterations have since been made, under powers contained in that Act, on petition by District Fishery Boards to the Secretary for Scotland. The appended Table (see p. 411) gives a compendium of the close times for the whole of Scotland, as in force at January, 1924.

Exercise of the Right

Apart from some few survivals of an ancient time, the result of special Border legislation, the only legal means of netting salmon within rivers and estuaries, is by " net and coble," and also, of course, by a landing-net used as an adjunct to rod and line. The limits of all estuaries are laid down in Schedule B annexed to the 1868 Act. The legal mesh of a salmon-net is not less than " 1¾ in. in extension from knot to knot, measured on each side of the square, or 7 in. measured round each mesh when wet"; while any device, such as placing two nets together, intended to diminish the mesh, is illegal. (Schedule E, 1868 Act.) The centre of each knot, it has been decided, may be taken as the basis of measurement.

Poaching and Illegal Practices and Tackle

The following may serve as a rough guide to the numerous offences specified in the various Salmon Acts. It is illegal under:

1. *The Salmon Fisheries (Scotland) Act*, 1828—

   (1) To trespass in any ground, enclosed or unenclosed, or any river or estuary, with intent to kill salmon. (Section 3.)

   (2) To break the law regarding cruives laid down in the 1877 Act; i.e. to let the hecks remain shut during Saturday's slop, or to have them measure less than 3 in. wide. (Section 7.)

2. *The Salmon Fisheries (Scotland) Act*, 1844.—To take, fish for, or attempt to take salmon in all inland waters which salmon frequent, or in any estuary, firth, sea-loch, creek, bay, or shore of the sea, or any part of the sea within one mile of low-water mark; or to assist others in doing so, without having a legal right or permission from the proprietor of the salmon fishery to do so. (Section 1.)

Note.—It is under this Act that proceedings are generally taken in simple cases of unauthorised angling. Possession of "salmon" (1868 Act, Section 25) is *prima facie* evidence of intended contravention, which charge respondent can only refute by production of previous written authority.

3. *The Salmon Fisheries* (*Scotland*) *Act*, 1862

(1) To put into a salmon river any poisonous or deleterious liquid or solid matter, to an extent injurious to the fishery, failing proof (open only to persons having a prescriptive right to pollute) of having used beforehand the best practical means, within a reasonable cost, to dispose of or render such matter harmless. (Section 13.)

(2) For three or more persons acting in concert, at any time between one hour after sunset and one hour before sunrise, to enter or be found upon any ground near a river, estuary, or the sea, or actually upon these waters, with intent to kill salmon, or to have in possession any net, rod, spear, light, or other instrument for that purpose, or to engage in, attempt, or aid in doing so. (Section 27.)

4. *The Salmon Fisheries* (*Scotland*) *Act*, 1863.—To export unclean or unseasonable salmon, or salmon caught in a district during the time at which the sale of salmon is prohibited within the district. (Section 3, and 1868 Act, Sections 21 and 22.)

5. *The Salmon Fisheries* (*Scotland*) *Act*, 1868—

(1) (*a*) To catch salmon otherwise than by rod and line during the annual close time for nets.

(*b*) To catch salmon (except during Saturday *or* Monday by rod and line) during the weekly close time, or to contravene any bye-law in force regarding its observance.
Note.—This makes *Sunday* rod-fishing for salmon illegal in Scotland. It is legal in England.

(*c*) To catch salmon by rod and line during the annual close time, at a period not authorised by bye-law. (Schedule C.)

(*d*) To fish for salmon with a net of illegal mesh. (Schedule E.)

(*e*) To intercept salmon when leaping at an obstruction, or when falling back after leaping.

(*f*) To prevent salmon passing through a fish pass or to take them in the passage through.

(*g*) To put sawdust, chaff, or shelling of corn into a river.

(*h*) To contravene any bye-law. (Section 25.)
Note.—In each of the above offences, attempting, or assisting, is also punishable as an offence.

(2) To use any light or fire of any kind, or any spear, leister, gaff, or other like instrument, or otter, to catch salmon, or to have such articles in possession, under suspicious circumstances; *excepting* a gaff used in angling with rod and line. (Section 17.)

(3) To fish with any fish roe; or to buy, sell, or expose salmon roe for sale; or to have it in possession; *excepting* its use for artificial propagation or other reason satisfactory to the Court. (Section 18.)

(4) To take smolts or salmon fry: or to buy, sell or expose them for sale; or to have them in possession; or to place any device or engine to obstruct their passage; or wilfully to injure them; or to injure or disturb salmon spawn; or to disturb any spawning-bed in which spawn may be; or, during the annual close time, to obstruct salmon in their passage to the spawning-beds; *excepting* for artificial propagation or scientific purposes, cleansing or repairing a dam or mill lade, or exercising a right of property in the bed of the stream. (Section 19.)

(5) To take, fish for, or attempt to take, unclean or unseasonable salmon, or to assist in doing so; or to buy, sell, or expose them for sale; or to have them in possession; *excepting* such as may be accidentally taken when fishing, if the same be forthwith returned to the water with the least possible injury; and excepting those taken for artificial propagation or for scientific purposes. (Section 20.)

Note.—There is no statutory definition of the words "unclean or unseasonable" as descriptive of "kelt" fish. The Sheriff will doubtless convict if it be clearly proved that the fish taken was "on the eve of spawning, in the act of spawning, or had not fully recovered from the effects of spawning."

(6) To buy, sell, or expose for sale, or have in possession salmon taken between the commencement of the latest, and the termination of the earliest, annual close time in force for any district. (Sections 21 and 22, and 1863 Act, Section 3.)

(7) For proprietor or occupier of a fishery, within thirty-six hours after the commencement of the annual close time, to fail to remove, and effectually secure against being used, all boats, oars, nets, engines, and tackle; *excepting* angling boats and oars, family boats and ferry boats, identified by owner's name, and kept under lock and key when not in use; and for the proprietor or occupier of a cruive, within the same time, to fail to remove and secure all hecks, rails, and inscales, and all temporary obstructions. (Section 23.)

(8) For a proprietor or tacksman of fixed nets to evade the bye-laws regarding the observance of a weekly close time. (Section 24.)

Powers of Keepers and Water-bailiffs.—To be dignified when courtesy is out of place, to be angry without loss of temper, and to use force without violence is, with a first-class keeper, instinctive. He must read the Acts to understand the extent of his powers. In these, it will be observed, there are three classes of guardians of the law referred to, viz: (1) private individuals, the "any persons" of the Acts, (2) officers and authorised employees of District Fishery Boards, and (3) police officers.

1. Unless he be in service of a District Board, the keeper or fish-watcher has no higher powers than any man in the street, and must comport himself accordingly. The Acts make some exceptions, however. Section 11 of the 1828 Act makes it lawful for any person, without other authority than the Act itself, *brevi manu* to seize and detain an offender—the offence under Section 3 being apparently contemplated. Having seized him, he may carry the offender before a Justice of the Peace or other magistrate, or hand him over to a police constable to do so, when he will be further dealt with as the Act prescribes.[1] Section 1 of the 1844 Act gives similar powers to any person, who may further seize the fish, boat, tackle, and nets of the poacher. The watcher has no right of search, unless he be an employee of a District Board, or a police officer. Finally, Section 29 of the 1868 Act gives similar powers to the private watcher, to seize offenders against

[1] *Brevi manu*, though it may mean coming to grips, does not excuse a violent attack.

the first six sub-divisions of Section 15, and Sections 17, 18, 19, 20, 21, and 22 of the Act.

2. Employees of District Boards are statutory officers and have statutory powers which the Acts make clear.
3. Police officers, although specially authorised by the Acts to take certain steps in certain cases, will, as a general rule, be found willing to extend a helping hand to maintain law and order when occasion arises. They are not bound to originate plans of campaign against poachers, but ought to act when flagrant cases come under their notice.

The Fishmongers' Company of London.—No other organisation has done so much to conserve our Scottish salmon fisheries. In general, but specially in cases where there is no District Fishery Board, this Company, or its local solicitor, being " any person " in the sense of the Acts, will prosecute offenders. It is requested that information as to offenders may be sent in confidence to the Clerk, Sir J. Wrench Towse, 24 Charlotte Square, Edinburgh, or Fishmongers' Hall, London Bridge, London, E.C. 4.

II. Trout

Legal Definition

In the latest statute the legal expression used is " the common trout, *salmo fario* " (1902 Act, Section 1), but the definition has been held to include Loch Leven trout, *salmo levenensis*, in a Sheriff Court case.

Public and Private Rights

1. *The Public.*—There is no public right of trout-fishing in Scotland, except in navigable rivers so far up only as the tide ebbs and flows, and in those few fresh-water lochs which are at once tidal and navigable. This right belongs exclusively to proprietors of lands adjoining the fishing, and neither the custom of fishing for any length of time, nor lawful access to the water by boat, bridge, ford, ferry, right of way, or otherwise, shall give to the public a right to fish for trout.

2. *Tenants.*—Apart from agreement, an agricultural tenant has no right to fish for trout, in respect of his lease. On the other hand, the lessee of the salmon fishings, if any, has an implied right to fish for trout.

3. *Private Proprietors.*—As between proprietors, the following broad rules obtain according to Scottish law, and an intelligent keeper, or fish-watcher, will keep them in view in order to protect his employer's interests, or at least to escape causing needless friction between neighbours.

(1) *Private Rivers.*—A private river, as regards trout-fishing, is one from which the proprietors may exclude the public from fishing. That is, all rivers except such as are at once tidal and navigable, and only in so far as they are so. Where a river intersects one proprietor's lands, he alone

has the right to fish in it for trout. Where the river is the boundary of opposite proprietors' lands the law declares (apart from title, which may rule otherwise) that the centre of the stream is the boundary. Each proprietor may wade to the centre, fishing from his own bank, but the Court has expressed an opinion that, from the practical difficulty of doing otherwise, he need not confine his casting radius to his own side of the water. In a river there is an interest in the trout, as in the water itself, common to upper and lower proprietors. The exclusive right of property mentioned is in the right to fish, not in the trout itself, which is a *fera natura* and belongs to the catcher, unless (1) it be taken from a pond, stank, or artificially stocked reservoir, when it is theft to take it, or (2) it is forfeited by statute.

(2) *Private Lochs.*—A loch is private where the proprietor or proprietors may vindicate their right to fish for trout as against the public, that is, every loch which is not both navigable and tidal. If a loch be situated wholly within the lands of one proprietor, he alone has the right of trout-fishing in it. If the loch verges upon the lands of two or more proprietors, they have an equal right of fishing over the whole surface irrespective of the extent of their foreshores. Unless restricted by the Court—no instance of which has yet occurred—each proprietor may communicate his right of

fishing to an indefinite number of persons, and put upon it an indefinite number of boats. The right to land, however, is confined, as regards proprietors and those to whom they have given permission to fish, each to his own shores.

(3) *Public Rivers.*—A river is only public as regards trout-fishing to the extent that the public may fish in it for trout, flounders, and other floating fish, except salmon, so far up as it is both tidal and navigable. In this sense it is not public where it is only tidal, or where it is only navigable, and in these cases the rules of fishing applicable to private rivers apply. The "publicity" of a non-tidal river consists in a mere right of passage by boat on the surface of the water, and gives no public right to the water, or its inhabitants, or the *solum*. Where a river is tidal and navigable, it, and its *solum* (broadly speaking), is vested in the Crown, for behoof of the public's right of free navigation and white fishing, which is the sole basis of any right of trout-fishing which the public may possess.

(4) *Public Lochs.*—On legal principle alone, no lochs in Scotland, except such as are both tidal and navigable, can be held to be public as regards trout-fishing. Where they are not at the same time tidal, access to them either by a navigable river, or by a canal will not confer a right of trout-fishing on the public, whose right is no higher than in the case

of a non-tidal navigable river. It is right here to warn inquirers that Stewart, in his book, makes some very misleading observations on this subject, through a failure on his part to make clear the exact extent of the rights of the public in a navigable river.

Close Time.—This extends from the 15th day of October to the 28th day of February, both dates inclusive. (1902 Act, Section 1.)

Poaching and Illegal Practices and Tackle

1. *Act of Scots Parliament, James VI,* 1607.—It is theft under this old Act to take trout from a stank or pond.

Note.—A prosecution under said Act was upheld by the Court of Justiciary, in the case of a reservoir artificially stocked with trout, in 1909, and since then other prosecutions have been successful.

2. *The Trout (Scotland) Act,* 1845.—It is illegal under this Act for any person (other than proprietors or those having their written permission)—

(1) To net trout or other fresh-water fish in any river, water, or loch, or to attempt to do so, or to aid or assist in doing so, or attempting to do so. (Section 1.)

(2) To trespass upon any ground, enclosed or unenclosed, or any river, water, or loch, with intent to net trout or other fresh-water fish. (Section 2.)

3. *The Trout (Scotland) Act,* 1860.—It is illegal under

:his Act for any person (other than the proprietor or those ıaving permission)—

(1) To net trout or other fresh-water fish, or to fish for them by double-rod fishing, or cross-line fishing, or set lines, or otter-fishing, or burning the water, or by striking the fish with any instrument, or by pointing, or to put into the water lime, or any other substance destructive to them, with intent to destroy them, or to attempt to do so, or aid in doing so, or attempting to do so. (Section 1.)

Note.—It has been held in several Sheriff Court cases that a rod, mounted with worm tackle, fixed to the bank of a loch, is a set line in the sense of the Act.

(2) To trespass upon any ground enclosed or unenclosed, or any river, water, or loch, with intent to commit any of the above offences. (Section 2.)

4. *The Fresh-water Fish* (*Scotland*) *Act*, 1902, makes it illegal :

(1) (*a*) To fish for or take trout in any river, water, or loch in Scotland by net, rod, line, or otherwise ; or (*b*) have possession of trout ; or (*c*) expose trout for sale during the close time. The section excepts operations for artificial rearing and sale for restocking ; but sale of dead trout, or live trout from waters where they are reared or kept in captivity for food during the close time is prohibited. (Section 1.)

(2) For proprietors, or those having written permission to fish, to do any of the acts made illegal for

other persons by the 1860 Act; except (*a*) tha all the proprietors of a pond or loch may agre to net "trout," and (*b*) that a net may be use for scientific breeding, or restocking purposes (Section 3.)

Powers of Keepers and Water-bailiffs

Keeping in view previous general remarks when con sidering the Salmon Acts, it may suffice to say, generally that one may take any lawful steps to protect one's pro perty. The 1845 Act (Section 4), however, gives to an person, without other authority than the Act, a right *brev manu* to seize offenders against the Act, and carry then before a Sheriff or Justice of the Peace, or hand then over to the police to be summarily dealt with. Power t seize boat, net, and fish is also given. The 1860 Ac (Section 3) gives power only to proprietors, and to an persons authorised by them, to seize boats, nets, 'anc other tackle used in contravening that Act, and any fisl taken. Both these Acts are to be read along with th 1902 Act, in all matters not inconsistent with the latter It is usually the Procurator-Fiscal who prosecutes unde the 1902 Act; but any person "having an interest" may do so.

III. Coarse Fish

There are no special legal restrictions in Scotland a to the capture of coarse fish, and it is doubtful whethe the prohibitions as to their capture by net or otherwise s in the case of common trout, apply to them. There eems to be no direct decision on the point. The 1902 ᴧct, however, makes it illegal to kill them with exploives.

There is no close time for such fish in Scotland.

As in the case of common trout, the right to fish for hem belongs to the proprietors adjoining the waters in vhich they exist, except where the tide ebbs and flows n a navigable river or loch, in which case the public may ish for them without challenge.

Note.—By the Salmon and Freshwater Fisheries Act, 923, which came into force on 1st January 1924, the aws of England and Wales regarding salmon, trout, and :oarse fish have been consolidated and amended. Similar egislation for Scotland is long overdue, and probably, ılthough in many respects English and Scottish conlitions vary in fundamentals, any fresh legislation for Scotland may be expected to follow, where appropriate, he lines of this statute. In particular, it is more than ikely that any new Scottish consolidating and amending ;tatute will deal with all species of fresh-water fish, and loubtless some method will be suggested whereby the oublic, under reasonable conditions, may obtain greater acilities for angling in what have hitherto been practi:ally—though not legally—" open " waters, through he medium of angling associations. Proprietors—and, ndeed, all interested in our fisheries—will be well ıdvised to study carefully present conditions in order hat intelligent criticism may be directed to any New

Freshwater Fisheries Bill which may be tabled in Parliament.

An " Index " of the English statute, with the Act itself as an appendix, prepared by the National Association of Fishery Boards (England and Wales) can be obtained, price 1*s*. 6*d*., or 2*s*. post free, from the Hon. Secretary, Mr. J. T. Sanderson, 67 Church Street, Lancaster, or from the publishers, Messrs. Sherrall and Hughes, 34 Cross Street, Manchester.

TABLE SHOWING ANNUAL CLOSE TIMES FOR NETTING AND ROD-FISHING IN SCOTTISH [illegible]

(*From information supplied by the Fishery Board for Scotland, pending publication of the 42nd Annual Report. All dates are inclusive.*)

NAME OF RIVER.	ANNUAL CLOSE TIME. For Nets.	ANNUAL CLOSE TIME. For Rods.
Tay (except Earn)	From August 21 to February 4	From October 16 to January 14
Earn	,, ,, 21 ,, ,, 4	,, November 1 ,, ,, 31
Forth	,, ,, 27 ,, ,, 10	,, ,, 1 ,, ,, 31
Forss	,, ,, 27 ,, ,, 10	,, ,, 1 ,, February 10
Helmsdale, Brora, Kyle of Sutherland	,, ,, 27 ,, ,, 10	,, October 1 ,, January 10
Thurso	,, ,, 27 ,, ,, 10	,, ,, 6 ,, ,, 10
Hope, Polla or Strathbeg, Halladale, Strathy, Naver, Borgie	,, ,, 27 ,, ,, 10	,, ,, 1 ,, ,, 11
Findhorn	,, ,, 27 ,, ,, 10	,, ,, 11 ,, February 10
Ness	,, ,, 27 ,, ,, 10	,, ,, 16 ,, January 14
Conon	,, ,, 27 ,, ,, 10	,, ,, 16 ,, ,, 25
Cave, Beauly, Dunbeath, Lossie, Spey	,, ,, 27 ,, ,, 10	,, ,, 16 ,, February 10
Drummachloy or Glenmore (Bute)	,, September 1 ,, ,, 15	,, ,, 16 ,, ,, 15
Add, Eckaig, North Esk, South Esk, Fyne, Shira, and Aray (Loch Fyne), Ruel	,, ,, 1 ,, ,, 15	,, November 1 ,, ,, 15
Ythan	,, ,, 10 ,, ,, 24	,, ,, 1 ,, ,, 10
Bervie, Carradale, East Harris Waters, West Harris Waters, Fleet (Sutherland), Fleet (Kirkcudbright), Girvan, Howmore, Inver (Jura), Iorsa (Arran) Irvine, Garnock, Laggan and Sorn (Islay), Luce, North Uist Waters, Orkney Islands	,, ,, 10 ,, ,, 24	,, ,, 1 ,, ,, 24
Stinchar	,, ,, 10 ,, ,, 24	,, ,, 1 ,, ,, 24
Annan, Ugie	,, ,, 10 ,, ,, 24	,, ,, 15 ,, ,, 24
Urr	,, ,, 10 ,, ,, 24	,, ,, 30 ,, ,, 24
Shetland Islands	,, ,, 10 ,, ,, 24	,, ,, 16 ,, January 31
Nith	,, ,, 10 ,, ,, 24	,, December 1 ,, February 24
Tweed	,, ,, 15 ,, ,, 14	,, ,, 1 ,, January 31
Other waters (the great majority)	,, August 27 ,, ,, 10	,, November 1 ,, February 10

NOTES.

CHAPTER XXII

FISH-HATCHING ON A MODEST SCALE

By Henry Lamond

In these days of intensive cultivation, it is more than probable that a gamekeeper or fishing-gillie will find it of advantage to be more or less familiar with the art of pisciculture. Given that knowledge of nature solidly based upon a study of the ways and wiles of bird, beast, and fish, which this class of employee already possesses, little more in addition is required except care, scrupulous cleanliness, and sound common sense, to turn even an ordinary gillie into a competent hatchery manager. It is proposed to indicate in this chapter " the little more " that is required.

It is possible that even the employer's attention may be actively turned to the subject when he learns that there is no particular mystery about the business ; that, given suitable conditions, a small hatchery is neither a troublesome nor a costly undertaking either to construct or to maintain ; and that—again given suitable conditions—some real return may be expected from the outlay incurred. It may, therefore, be of service to give a description of a hatchery which has been in active operation for fifteen years, and which has had an annual output of nearly 300,000 healthy fry of trout, sea-trout, and salmon. To assist the practical man as far as possible, a sketch-plan of the hatchery, with specification and estimate of cost, and other particulars are appended. It is, of course, obvious that a financial estimate based upon prices which ruled during the halcyon days before the war cannot now be of actual utility, except in so far as the reader may judge from it that the construction of a practicable hatchery involves no very great expenditure.

There is no occasion at this time of day to refer to the practical benefits which may be obtained from artificial trout-hatching. Nor am I concerned to defend the practice of salmon- and sea-trout-hatching, the necessity for which, in my opinion, depends solely upon local conditions. At Luss—on Loch Lomond—it has been found from practical experience, that the available natural spawning-ground is so deficient and the streams themselves so obstructed, that a hatchery forms a valuable supplement of nature. There is really nothing artificial involved in the process. The ova collected are simply placed in security. There are many small sea-trout streams in the Highlands, especially on the west coast, where similar conditions prevail. For these a hatchery would be similarly valuable. Proprietors, moreover, need have less hesitation in hatching sea-trout for this reason—that the sea-trout does not roam far afield, as the salmon does, but is essentially an estuary fish. A large proportion of Loch Lomond fish--marked when spawning in the tributaries, have been recaptured the following season, spawning again in the same tributaries. In two instances the same fish were actually found spawning in three consecutive seasons. To the hatching of sea-trout, then, as well as trout, attention may be usefully directed.

Now, what are the essential requisites of a hatchery? Obviously land and water—the first, if possible, conveniently close to the dwelling of the prospective hatchery-manager, and the second—ample. There are few estates, I believe, where a combination of such circumstances will not be found. For the site itself, any gently sloping plot of ground upon which a wooden house, 20 ft. square, can be erected will do. If the subsoil be porous so much the better, but, if not, a gravel foundation can easily be provided. The water-supply is a more important consideration. This must be ample, pure, and not liable to the slightest risk of interruption—for any cessation of the flow at a critical juncture would be disastrous. For these reasons, the water-supply available will determine the site.

If it be impossible to secure, as has been managed at Luss, with the kind permission of the proprietor of the estate, connection with an existing domestic water-supply, then a stream must be looked for where a sufficient head of water can be obtained. At Luss, delivery is made by a ½-in. lead pipe. But the head of water in each case will determine the diameter of the pipe necessary to deliver the quantity of water requisite. This, roughly speaking, must be sufficient to give to each hatching-box a complete interchange of water every three minutes. In a convenient stream, then, a natural pool must be looked for, giving a fall of at least 30 ft. to the proposed hatchery. If, however, no such pool can be found, a small dam may easily and cheaply be engineered to form one. In the pool so found, or formed, a small covered chamber should be constructed—guarded at the intake by an iron grating to exclude flotsam. From within this chamber, the main water-pipe, further protected by a rose, will be led to the hatchery. If the water can first be filtered through an outer chamber of gravel, additional security will be given against danger from the deposited sediment of "spate" water. The pipe will terminate within the hatchery itself, which we are now in a position to describe.

The hatchery, then, is a simple wooden structure, 20 ft. long by 17 ft. broad, standing on a sloping gravel foundation. The back wall is 7 ft. and the front wall 11 ft. 4 in. in height, giving the lean-to roof, which is covered with patent roofing-felt, with sufficient slope from front to rear to throw off the rainfall. The whole structure is thoroughly tarred over. Instead of the roofing-felt, corrugated iron sheeting, superimposed upon rough serking, will be found equally serviceable and possibly in the long run more economical. As direct sunlight, or indeed a strong light, is detrimental to the ova, the house faces away from the south. In this front wall alone are the door and three small fixed windows, one being over the door and one on each side. These windows are obscured by green cloth roller-blinds.

PLAN OF LUSS HATCHERY
SHEWING ARRANGEMENT
OF HATCHING BOXES AND WATER SUPPLY

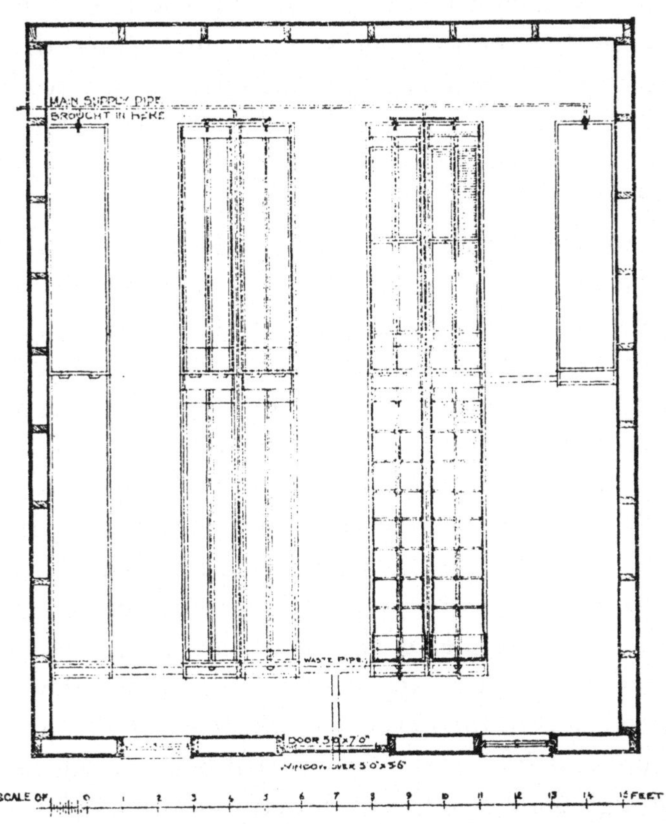

The walls, of ordinary white pine, are built double. The spaces between the standards need not be filled in with sawdust or other material. The double walls maintain sufficiently an even temperature.

The floor space—sloping towards the front door—is occupied by eleven hatching boxes, which, as the plan shows, are arranged to allow of convenient working. Against the left wall are two boxes—end to end. Two groups of four boxes each, arranged end to end in pairs, occupy the central floor space, while against the right wall, away from the door, is one box. The space left on this side near the door is useful for tackle. The boxes stand on frames at a convenient height from the floor; and, as at Luss, the water-supply enters from the rear, the tier of six boxes farthest from the door is on a higher level, by the depth of a box, than the tier of five nearest it, each upper box draining into the one set beneath. At Luss the six higher-level boxes are fitted with glass grilles for carrying the ova, while the four central boxes of the lower tier are fitted with perforated zinc baskets.

To trace the water-system more precisely—the supply is delivered from a continuation of the main ½-in. lead pipe within the hatchery to each of the six upper boxes. Separate connections with this pipe are made for each box, the taps being finished with ⅝-in. nose-cocks. After serving the upper boxes, the water flows over lipped slots to the lower tier, whence each box drains to a common lead waste-pipe carried beneath the flooring through the doorway to a fire-clay drain-pipe, leading to the river a few paces away. The supply of the lower tier of central boxes is, by a separate connection with the main inside the hatchery, supplemented by block tin tubes fixed inside the boxes, perforated with needle points about ½ in. apart. The tubes are carried round the upper inner edges of each box, and stop-cocks control the supply for each box. When the water is turned on, it is thrown from each pipe to the opposite row of baskets in the box, for its whole length, practically like a spray bath. This supplemental supply ensures to the ova massed in the baskets a sufficiency of oxygen, of which the water flowing over the eggs of the upper tier has already been partially depleted. The whole water-supply system permits of each box being worked as an independent unit. At Luss a cistern and filter within the hatchery were installed and abandoned, as sufficient pressure from these could not be obtained from the delivery pipe to give the requisite flow of water.

It will be sufficient now to describe one of the hatching-boxes, arranged for the glass-grille system of hatching, and one fitted with the perforated zinc baskets. To take the former first. The glass-grille system is here most effective for hatching out ova. It shows a slightly lower percentage of loss than the basket system, but its practical drawback is that it requires more space in proportion to the number of ova hatched. The hatching-box is made of 1⅛ in. dressed deal carefully charred inside. It is 6 ft. 9 in. in length, 1 ft. 7 in. broad, and 7¼ in. deep, outside measurements. It has wooden ledges on each side of the bottom, and a removable wooden runner in the centre, placed longitudinally. On these rest the four frames carrying the glass grilles.

The grille upon which the ova rest is a series of glass tubes, each tube being 6⅝ in. long and ¼ in. in diameter. The tubes are set in a row close together—but not touching—across each frame, and are kept in position by serrated wood, or zinc strips fixed to the inside edges of the frame. The level of the frames in the box is so adjusted that the eggs, when placed upon the grille, are 3 in. from the bottom of the box, giving that depth of water beneath them, while the water-level is maintained at ½ in. over them. As it is important to strain the water of all sediment, the nose-cock at the upper end of the box discharges first into a perforated zinc strainer, which, with a further inch or two of space before the trays are reached, distributes the inrush of water to the box in a uniform gentle flow. At the lower end of the box, a removable perforated zinc screen prevents any egg lapping over into the lower box, and, later, prevents the escape of the alevins and fry when the eggs hatch out.

Between the system of glass grilles and the perforated zinc baskets, the only difference in principle is that the eggs on the grilles are laid in uniform rows, while in the baskets they are deposited in mass, perhaps two, perhaps three, layers deep. At Luss, two layers deep has been found to produce results equal to the grilles, while hatching double the quantity of ova, that is, the proportion of loss is no greater, the total loss being in both cases from 2 to 3 per cent. only. The baskets are carefully made of finely and closely perforated zinc sheets, and are 8 in. square and 3 in. deep. Two rows of eight baskets occupy the space in the hatching-box—a number sufficient for convenience of working. The whole sixteen baskets rest upon the longitudinal side-ledges and central runner already described, at such a level that at least three-quarters of an inch of water will flow freely over three layers of eggs. When it is added that, as in the upper boxes, a strainer is placed at the intake, and a screen at the outflow, and that these boxes are fed in addition by the spray water-piping already described, enough has been said to give an idea of both systems. There is only this to be added—that all woodwork must be carefully charred ; that every separate piece must be carefully smoothed and exactly fitting, without the least projection or crevice ; and, further, that all zinc should be varnished by a special varnish, which can be obtained from any of our commercial hatcheries.

Let us assume now that everything in the hatchery is prepared for the reception of the ova. All the taps are in working order, ready to be turned on or off as occasion requires ; a steady flow is left running ; the escape pipes are clear of obstruction, and the glass grilles (or the baskets) are all in their places submerged to the proper depth. If the weather is specially severe, we have provided a small oil stove, to keep the temperature of the house above freezing-point. Candles or stable lamps are also at hand, as the winter day gives brief light to work by.

It had been reported (I shall suppose) that the fish

would likely be on the redds that afternoon, and now the dogcart, or, better still, the motor-car, is awaiting orders ready to start at a moment's notice, for we have some little distance to travel. Our head man has meantime been putting aboard the vehicle four white-enamelled tin basins of 15 in. diameter, a couple of white-enamelled tin pails with lids, and two or three kitchen towels, the use of which will immediately appear. Our man has donned his salmon-waders, as likewise have his four or five assistants, who are already on the ground. They have with them the nets, which have been kept all day in readiness near the waterside, and they have also a couple of stout poles 6 ft. long, not only to beat the water and prod the banks but to help them to keep their balance in the icy stream.

Arrived at our destination, we are told that several pairs of salmon, or sea-trout, or trout, as the case may be, are on the redds. We see for ourselves the females flashing their sides occasionally in the brown water, and the attendant males dashing every now and then almost ashore on the shallows. The river (we may suppose) is some fifteen or twenty paces wide, gravelly runs alternating with slacker places, scarcely pools, of from 2 to 4 ft. in depth. We select a stretch of water where there are several pairs of fish, and at the lower end of this, at a point where the river narrows, we fix our principal net.

This is a large bag-net of a 4-in. mesh, neither floated with corks nor leaded, but simply reeved to a circle of rope, the diameter of the mouth being 20 ft., and the bag extending 40 ft., tapering to a point where, by means of a slip-knot, we can take out any of the enclosed fish that are required. Besides this large net, four smaller bag-nets, 10 ft. diameter at the mouth and 10 ft. in depth, are useful for catching trout in small burns, and for retaining large fish temporarily till wanted. The large bag-net is now fastened by two guys at the water-level, one on each side of the stream, and kept open by two others fixed higher up on opposite banks. The flow of water keeps the bag distended. Meantime the men have entered the water at the head of the spawning-stretch, 200 yds. or so upstream, and begin to beat the fish down to the bag-net. Two men follow with a sweep-net stretched across the river, to prevent fish breaking back, while a third wades behind the centre of this net to lift it over obstacles. Both banks are poked and prodded with the poles to prevent fish taking cover. All the fish in the " drive " fall back in some little excitement, till at last they find themselves within the bag-net.

A ripe female is selected, taken from the tail of the net, and handed to the chief operator, who—all his appliances ready, is waiting to strip her. He takes the fish, wraps one of the towels round her to prevent her slipping, leaving the vent clear. Then, sitting down, with a clean, dry basin between his feet, he holds the fish, head towards him, tail outwards, and belly down, with the vent over the basin. If the fish is perfectly " ripe," a slight pressure will cause the ova to fall into the basin. If not, a repeated gentle pressure from the throat towards the vent will bring it away. When all the ova are extracted, the fish, if carefully handled, will swim off little the worse for her adventure.

One of the males in the bag-net has meantime been selected to perform his part of the ceremony. He is taken, then wrapped in the towel, and held exactly as was the female, while his milt is allowed to run over the eggs in the basin. A slight pressure near the vent is necessary to start the flow of milt. A very few drops is sufficient to fertilise the mass, and one male will fertilise the ova of several females. But it is poor economy to be niggardly if males are plentiful, or, on the other hand, to be extravagant if males are few. In any case it is good policy to retain all superfluous males until the day's work is over. Hence the practical utility of the small bag-nets. After depositing the milt on the eggs, which at this stage are all separate, the operator stirs them gently with the tail of the male fish. He in turn is then liberated, or kept captive for further service, if required. The eggs are then covered with water 1 in. deep over them, and in a few minutes another ¼ in. of water is added. The eggs meantime have coagulated in mass. Then the basin must be left perfectly still for a time, which may be anything from twenty minutes to two hours—according to temperature. During this time the mass will be disintegrating, so any disturbance must be avoided. Now and again the operator may look carefully to see if the eggs are separated, when, if they are, the process of fertilisation is over, and they may be washed clean of milt by gently pouring water over them. When they are quite clean, the eggs will be found to have changed their former rich salmon-pink to an opalescent hue, which indicates that fertilisation is complete. The same procedure is gone through with other fish. As each lot of ova is fertilised and cleaned, it is placed in water in the covered pails, not mixing the ova of sea-trout and trout, say, indiscriminately, but using separate pails for the ova of each species of fish stripped. When sufficient ova has been collected, or all we can get on this occasion, we re-enter our conveyance and make for the hatchery with our precious property.

While this system of capturing the spawners in bag-nets, of a size adapted to the various streams, has hitherto been in operation at Luss, the question of constructing a series of fixed traps in the channels of some of the streams is receiving serious consideration. It is quite plain that only those fish can be caught by the bag-nets which happen at the time to be in the section of stream where the drive occurs. No doubt the psychological moment for the visit is selected with care ; but, on the one hand, perhaps during the night, some fish may have reached and abandoned the ground, while, on the other hand, some late-comers may not yet have arrived. Always, too, some fish are taken in the nets which are not ripe for stripping. To meet these contingencies, Mr. W. H. Armistead, the well-known pisciculturist, devised a very practical type of fish-trap into which the ascending fish can enter easily but from which it is almost impossible for them to escape. In his interesting book, entitled *Trout Waters: Management and Angling*, Mr. Armistead describes this trap as follows:

"At a suitable place a trap should be built which will catch every spawning fish as it runs up. Usually the best site for such a trap is just where the stream enters the lake. Its construction is not very difficult; but the method must be modified to suit the particular conditions. I have always used a large wooden tank, built into the stream, taking care that the bottom is so laid that the current cannot, in flood-time, work its way underneath and make a hole up which the spawning fish can run. This is a most important point. The tank is composed of a wooden floor and two wooden sides, with screens at each end through which the stream flows. The screen at the upstream end may be a fixture; but it is better to have it so arranged that it may be removed when the spawning season is over. The screen at the lower end should be made in halves and hung on hinges, so that it may open inwards.

"When the trap is set, the two lower screens are slightly opened upstream, so that there is an opening of about a foot between them. To this opening and inside the trap is fixed a net funnel extending from top to bottom, and about two feet into the trap, reducing the aperture to about three inches. Through this the trout will find their way when running upstream; but once inside, they will be stopped by the upper screen—their return through the narrow opening of the net funnel is a very remote contingency. Should an odd one happen to find its way out, it would be back again in an hour or two, so strong is the instinct to travel upstream. There are several ways of keeping the net funnel extended ; but I found the most satisfactory was to have an iron rod hinged to the screen reaching from top to bottom, with one or two arms projecting horizontally up stream, to which the net was laced. One of these on each screen made a very satisfactory framework for the net, and they enabled one to widen or diminish the entrance to the trap at will.

" Unless the tank is built sufficiently high out of the water to prevent the fish from jumping out, it is well to have movable lids. The screens are best made of wooden bars well supported by cross horizontal pieces behind. For all ordinary conditions these bars may be cut ⅝ by 1 in., and fixed with the narrow edge upstream. The distance apart will, of course, depend upon the size of fish which will be caught ; but as spawning trout are usually a fair size, it will seldom be necessary to place them closer together than 1 in., and in many waters 1¼ in. will not be too wide. Screens of this kind do not block readily, and if any rubbish should collect, they are easily cleaned with a rake. A screen with a square mesh made of wire is very bad for blocking, and extremely difficult to clean, as leaves and grass cling tightly to it under the pressure of the current." The advantages of such a trap as Mr. Armistead thus describes are plainly apparent. It will suggest itself that the trap should be frequently examined, and very little ingenuity seems to be required to utilise one to the best advantage in any district.

It may be said at this point that the whole operation of spawning is, in principle, the same for salmon, sea-trout, and trout ; but as salmon spawn when the weather is, as a rule, very cold, their eggs take longer to fertilise than do those of trout or sea-trout. In most books, a female salmon is credited with providing one thousand eggs for each pound of her weight. This is probably an overestimate, but the figure gives a rough indication of the total quantity of ova obtained. An average sea-trout or trout provides about eight hundred eggs for each pound of weight. In the operations of netting above described there is not the slightest difficulty, except that it is sometimes not easy to get a ripe male at the same time as a ripe female, and so a male may require to be floated with the party down or upstream in the small bag-net. Sometimes, too, darkness descends on the scene and the work has to be done by lantern-light, while frost always protracts it. In cold, wet weather trout and other fish can stand a good deal of handling and can remain out of water for a considerable time without apparent injury. But the important thing is to have one person in sole command, whose duty it will be to see that everything is done systematically and rapidly—not in a flurry and hurry. A trap would eliminate some inconveniences.

Arrived safely at the hatchery, the ova have now to be deposited on the grilles, or in the zinc baskets. This requires some neatness and care. An enamelled cup may be used to ladle out the eggs from the pails. If we are working with glass grilles, no more ova must be placed on each frame than will occupy exactly the available space. Each little rack must contain its exact quota of eggs, so that when the frames are filled all the eggs will be uniform in rows, and all the rows uniform in the box, with half an inch of water passing gently over them. If we are using the perforated zinc baskets, each may safely be filled with two or three layers deep of ova in mass ; but at least three-quarters of an inch of water in this case must flow over the eggs. In these boxes, too, the auxiliary sprays will now be carefully turned on, so that each jet falls into the centre of the opposite basket in the box. Everything being now in order, water-taps all flowing freely and all tackle put away, the house may safely be locked up for the night, for the labours of the day are satisfactorily ended.

In water with a temperature varying from 40° to 45° F., about the thirtieth day the eyes of the embryo fish may be seen, two little dark specks in the substance of the egg.

Eggs may safely be handled within, say, three days of fertilisation, but after that time and until they are "eyed," they should be left alone and not subjected to handling or shock of any kind. This is important.

Trout may be expected to hatch out in about seventy days altogether, with water at the above temperature, sea-trout in about ninety days, and salmon in about one hundred and twenty days. All these periods will be protracted in proportion as the weather is colder, so that no anxiety need be felt at delay in hatching. Throughout this period of incubation nothing requires to be done but to keep the water constantly flowing, and to maintain a careful watch upon the ova, for which purpose the hatchery should be visited daily.

A few matters of some practical importance may now be referred to, as applicable to the present stage.

Stress has been laid upon the advisability of keeping the eggs in exact uniformity on the glass grilles. The reason is that, so arranged, any speck of foreign matter, and any dead or barren or diseased eggs, will be detected at a glance, just as a defect of uniform in a soldier will be detected in a regiment drawn up in line. A small glass syphon tube, one end closed with indiarubber, will suck up, after a pressure of the thumb, any egg for closer examination. If the slightest trace of white fungus is observed upon it, the egg should be at once destroyed, for the fungus growth develops very rapidly if not checked. Careful charring of all wood used in the construction of the boxes, cleanliness of all utensils, and careful examination of the eggs, are the best preventives.

A thermometer, several syphon tubes, two or three clear-glass wineglasses, a tiny gauze landing-net, and a bunch of seagull wing-feathers should be always at hand.

The eggs are almost as easily examined in the baskets as on the grilles. All that one has to do is to take each basket in turn, raise it an inch or so in the water, and press it down again firmly. The water, rushing in through the perforations, will cause the eggs to boil and simmer, and any dead or barren egg, being lighter, will come to the top. It can then be picked out with the syphon tube. So, too, any foreign substance will show up at once in the mass. But even so much disturbance as this is dangerous before the eggs are "eyed."

The only occasion for real anxiety is during a spate, when a large proportion of matter held in suspension in the water may be expected to be deposited, if not on the eggs, yet in the boxes. Of course, the best means to prevent this is careful filtration, first at the source of supply, and then, if convenient, within the hatchery. But, notwithstanding, the boxes will still require occasionally to be cleaned. This can be done without injury to the eggs after they are "eyed," but, as great care is necessary in the moving, cleaning with clear water, and replacing them, not to mention the cleaning of the boxes, it is a troublesome enough business. The danger of a deposit on the eggs is that it prevents the free absorption of oxygen from the water through the shell of the eggs, and the free giving off of the carbonic acid gas generated by the growth within, resulting in suffocation and death of the embryo.

Periodical inspection should also be made, at this time, of the intake chamber of the water-supply, and the rose of the main pipe examined, to see that no floating matter has got in to foul it. Decayed leaves are often troublesome in this respect.

With ordinary care, all the eggs will duly hatch out at the appointed time, when our young fish will have reached the alevin stage.

When the eggs have all hatched into alevins, some little rearrangement of the hatching-boxes falls to be made. A few points of management appropriate to the period before the fish becomes a "fry" may also be referred to. When the embryo fish bursts its shell, it is not in the least like a fish. To the blunt head, with its staring black eyes and the thin transparent body, is added an elongated bag larger than the fish, containing sufficient nourishment to last it for a further space of fifty days. The fish is not perfect until this bag, or umbilical sac, is wholly absorbed. During the period of absorption the instinct of the little creature, which can only wriggle spasmodically on its sides, drives it to hide in any minute crevice that it can find. Now it is that previous careful smoothing of all angles, and exact fitting of all fixed and movable parts of the box, will prove to be of the utmost importance. For into every corner and crevice the alevin will attempt to wriggle, and success, or partial success, will almost certainly have fatal results. The best protection for them at this time, beyond careful construction of the boxes, will be found to be absolute darkness in the hatchery.

In those boxes containing grilles it will be observed that, as the eggs hatch out, the alevins drop through between the glass tubes to the bottom of the box, and the syphon tube will now be in constant use removing the empty eggshells. When the eggs are all hatched, the glass grilles and the frames which carry them are removed, thoroughly cleaned, and carefully put away. The hatching-box has now become a small rearing pond, in which the alevins live comfortably until they are perfect little fry of 1 in. or 1¼ in. in length, capable of fending for themselves in the great world of water out of doors. Before they have left the hatching-box—even before the sac is wholly absorbed, they may be seen, all lying head upstream to the inflowing water, and " rising " now and then inquisitively to some tiny floating speck.

As in the grille boxes so with the baskets. When all the eggs are hatched, the baskets and supporting ledges are taken out, cleaned, and put carefully away. It is convenient to keep all the alevins of one mass of ova in their own basket till the whole box has hatched out.

Not much need be said by way of hint or warning now. Care and cleanliness are still essential. Risks of spate water must still be run and guarded against. But the main thing is to see that the alevins do not find out some new and original method of committing suicide. Every joint and junction must, therefore, be examined in the boxes, and no flaw in the intake or outflow perforated zinc screens must be permitted. So, too, any dead or injured alevins should be removed at once, as should also all " deformities," of which there are always a few. Double-headed and double-tailed fish are perhaps most common, but often two are found joined together at the belly, or actually crossed through each other, like the sign of multiplication.

As I have not contemplated the construction of rearing-ponds in connection with our supposed hatchery—a somewhat costly business—things have now reached a stage when two matters of importance have to be considered. The first is, Where are the fry to be put? And the second, How are they to be conveyed to the spot? The first of these will, of course, depend upon what kind of waters one has it in mind to stock, and also whether we have been preparing to stock them with sea-trout and salmon, or with trout only. If with salmon or sea-trout, or both, we may safely put the fry into any clear, running stream. Wherever there is gravel, running water, and marginal growth, the fry will find both security and food and may safely be left to themselves. Should our stock be trout, the same principles will apply to the restocking of a river. If, however, one is restocking a reservoir or natural loch, local conditions require to be studied. Any small feeders, if such exist which promise to afford both food and shelter are the places in which to put the fry. They will very soon fall back to the main sheet, when they require a wider space to range in. But if no feeders are available, the fry must be placed in the loch itself. When this has to be done, a shallow, sheltered side of the water should be selected, and instinct will teach the young fish how to protect themselves. Undoubtedly many will fall victims to numerous enemies of all kinds, but their numbers allow considerable margin for casualties. In any event the brood should be from 3 to 4 in. in length after one year, and from 6 to 8 in. in length in two years, if trout and sea-trout. Salmon do not often exceed 6 or 6¼ in. in length prior to migration.

As to the carriage of the fry, we have found that they carry most easily and conveniently in large glass wicker-covered carboys, such as are used in chemical works. The carboys should be full of water to prevent jarring in transit, and not crowded to excess with fish. Should there be any risk of delay, or the journey be long, fresh water should occasionally be added. With ordinary luck, the whole consignment will safely reach its destination. If only a short distance has to be covered, the fry can be quite safely carried in ordinary zinc pails. But ordinary lidded white enamel pails stow easily in the motor-car.

I have not overlooked that the hatchery may be stocked with eyed ova purchased from one or other of our well-known hatchery companies. Eyed ova, if carefully packed, stand well the vicissitudes of a long journey. The main points to be observed are—that the consigner thoroughly understands the route and the various means of transit between the point of departure and the end of the journey. Van, train, steamer, cart—all may have to be requisitioned before the hatchery is reached, and all should be accurately timed before the consignment begins its travels. There should also be complete understanding by the consignee as to the time of the arrival of the ova, so that arrangements may be made for the final stage of the journey, and everything be in readiness at the hatchery. Telegrams ought to pass between the parties, intimating and confirming the dispatch of the ova. The further career of the purchased eyed ova, from that stage onwards, will follow the lines already described in the foregoing pages.

It may be of interest to add that at Luss the only difficulty of collecting ova from salmon, sea-trout, and *fario* has been caused by untimely floods. In very few of the fifteen seasons during which the hatchery has been in operation, the ova treated have been supplemented by consignments of eyed ova from Howietoun and the Solway Fisheries Co., at Dumfries.

The whole hatchery arrangements were designed by the late Mr. Thomas Duff, I.M., Glasgow, a member of the Loch Lomond Angling Improvement Association. Its practical management is now in the hands of the watching staff of the Association.

Notes by Editor

The Royal Commission on Pollution of Rivers have made some interesting experiments with distillery effluent at Craigellachie, Banffshire. The operations were conducted under the direction of Mr. Littlefield, with the view of avoiding pollution of the River Spey.

Complete success has crowned the efforts of the experimenter, for salmon ova not only hatched out in the effluent three days earlier than in the Spey water, but the fry grew faster in it than in the ordinary water.

Another discovery worthy of notice is a cheap way to supply feeding to lochs before stocking them with trout. To encourage food, place large bundles of bracken, weighted down by heavy stones, all round the margin of the loch in two feet of water, and allow it to decompose ; this will prove at one and the same time a hatchery and a sanctuary for mollusca and all sorts of fresh-water shrimps ; and a large increase in size of trout will soon be observable.

Where American weed is bad in lochs, Mr. H. Gordon Burn-Murdoch has found that covering the bottom of those places where the weed is worst with large stones curtails the area where the pest can grow, while the stones afford shelter for feeding and for small fish. Of course, if the weed covers an extensive area this is rather an expensive business.

P.J.M.

COST OF ARTIFICER'S WORK OF HATCHERY AT LUSS

I. *The Hatchery*

		£	s.	d.
1.	Removing turf and preparing site @ 9*s*.	0	9	0
2.	5″ × 2″ Sawn standards and runners of walls (red pine), 440 lin. ft. @ 2*d*.	3	13	4
3.	21 Do. stakes in ground under sole runner each 24″ long, to be charred and well tarred, and the runner spiked to do. @ 5*d*.	0	8	9
	Forward . .	£4	11	1

		£	s.	d.
	Forward	[illegible]	[illegible]	[illegible]
4.	1⅛″ White pine tongued and grooved flooring in 6½″ breadths, on outside of walls well tarred on outside, 76 sq. yds. @ 1*s*. 9*d*.	6	13	0
5.	1⅛″ Beads at angles, 37 lin. ft. @ 2*d*.	0	6	2
6.	⅝″ White pine half-checked serking on inside, 68 sq. yds. @ 1*s*.	3	8	0
7.	6½″ × 2½″ White pine spars of roof, checked to runners at top and bottom, 162 lin. ft. @ 2*d*.	1	7	0
8.	6″ × 2″ Do. dwangs betwixt do., 34 lin. ft. @ 2*d*.	0	5	8
9.	⅝″ White pine half-checked serking on do., include doubling fillets at sides, 40 sq. yds. @ 1*s*.	2	0	0
10.	Tarred felt on serking in two thicknesses, 40 sq. yds. @ 1*s*.	2	0	0
11.	Packing with sawdust space between flooring and serking of walls 5″ thick, 69 sq. yds. @ 3*d*.	0	17	3
12.	1⅝″ Fixed sashes with astragals glazed with sheet glass, and primed and painted, 2 coats (red pine), 26 sq. feet. @ 8*d*.	0	17	4
13.	⅝″ Chamfered checks to do. (—do.—), 34 lin. ft. @ 2*d*.	0	5	8
14.	⅝″ Bevelled weather plate over sashes (—do.—), 8 lin. ft. @ 3*d*.	0	2	0
15.	1¾″ Frames and lined door (—do.—), 20 sq. ft. @ 1*s*.	1	0	0
16.	⅝″ Chamfered checks (—do.—), 16 lin. ft. @ 2*d*.	0	2	8
17.	Do. facings (—do.—), 17 lin. ft. @ 2*d*.	0	2	10
18.	1 Pair 6″ d. j. hinges and screws @ 6*d*.	0	0	6
19.	1 Galvanised iron 6″ rim lock with brass mounting and four keys @ 5*s*.	0	5	0
20.	Fitting and hanging and onputting mounting of 1 door @ 2*s*.	0	2	0
	II. *Hatching-boxes*.—All dovetailed at corners and raggled and jointed with white lead			
21.	1⅛″ Dressed deal bottoms of boxes in boards, 6′ 9″ × 1′ 7″, 64 sq. ft. @ 8*d*.	2	2	8
22.	Do. sides and ends of do., 6″ deep, 50 sq. ft. @ 8*d*.	1	13	4
23.	2″ × 2″ Double checked teak framing of grille sliders, scalloped on under edge, 40 lin. ft. 6 in. @ 8*d*.	1	7	0
24.	¾″ × 1″ Plain do. do., 81 lin. ft. @ 1*d*.	0	6	9
25.	1⅛″ × 1″ Checked teak frame of grilles, 160 lin. ft. @ 2*d*.	1	6	8
26.	2⅛″ × ½″ Bevelled (pine) fillet at end of box, 9 lin. ft. 6 in. @ 1*d*.	0	0	9
27.	Fine wire gauze 6″ broad tacked on to box, 9 lin. ft. 6 in. @ 1*s*. *Note*.—Superseded by perforated zinc screen.	0	9	6
28.	3″ × 2″ Mill dressed framing under boxes, 162 lin. ft. @ 1¼*d*.	0	16	10
29.	⅞″ Deal boxes for overflow, 14 sq. ft. 6 in. @ 6*d*.	0	7	3
	Forward	£32	16	11

		£	s.	d.
	Forward . .	32	16	11

III. *Water-supply*

No.	Item	£	s.	d.
30.	½″ Lead 7 lb. supply pipe and laying in track where required, 66 lin. ft. @ 7*d*.	1	18	6
31.	8 Solder joins of branch supplies @ 1*s*.	0	8	0
32.	1 Brass ½″ screw down stop-cock @ 5*s*.	0	5	0
33.	10 do. ⅝″ do. nose-cocks @ 5*s*. 6*d*.	2	15	0
34.	Forming connection of lead pipe to 3″ iron pipe, include boring and tapping and brass ferrule, @ 17*s*. 6*d*.	0	17	6
35.	2″ Lead 5 lb. waste pipe, include laying in track where required, 60 lin. ft. @ 1*s*.	3	0	0
36.	4 Lead flanges in bottom of boxes @ 9*d*.	0	3	0
37.	4″ Fireclay drain-pipe, include digging track and filling up, 12 lin. yds. @ 2*s*.	1	4	0
38.	2 Bends on do. @ 2*s*.	0	4	0
39.	2 Eyes on do. @ 2*s*.	0	4	0
40.	1 Y junction piece @ 2*s*.	0	2	0
41.	Connecting drain with lead waste @ 2*s*. 6*d*.	0	2	6
42.	Charring timber of boxes	0	5	0
43.	Executing all jobbings and removing rubbish at completion @ 10*s*.	0	10	0
	Total Contract Price .	£44	15	5

IV. *Glass-grille System*

No.	Item	£	s.	d.
44.	2,500 Glass tubes 6⅝″ × ½″ (carriage 2*s*. 6*d*.) per 100 @ 4*s*.	5	2	6
45.	1,200 do. do. (carriage 2*s*.) per 100 @ 3*s*. 8*d*.	2	6	0

V. *Basket System*

No.	Item	£	s.	d.
46.	Cost of perforated zinc baskets .	6	6	4
	Total Original Cost .	£58	10	3

Note.—Attendant's wage for the period from October to May is fixed at £16, and men's wages for the special work of collecting ova vary from £6 to £8 a season. The cost of upkeep and repairs amounts to a negligible sum.

These prices were pre-war. It will be interesting to compare present prices, which may be roughly doubled.

NOTES

CHAPTER XXIII

THE ROD IN SALT WATER

By F. G. Aflalo

The following notes on sea-angling for sport are intended to be helpful to the gillie. The result will depend more on the gillie than on the notes. His general duties have been admirably summarised in the earlier chapter written by Mr. Malloch. But the case of sea-fishing is somewhat different from the duties which that writer had under review. Sea-fishing is a comparatively new sport —it is not much more than a quarter of a century old— and has not yet been reduced to the same exact science as some other kinds of angling. Among many advantages, it is at its best in those weeks of July which precede activity on the moors. Now, gillies who take sportsmen after salmon or trout know their work more or less (occasionally less), and he is a bold man who tells them their own business. I have had gillies in both hemispheres and in five continents : garrulous Greeks, imperturbable Moslems, lazy Spaniards, independent Yankees, merry Basques, blasphemous French-Canadians, but only one Scot. He was really a gamekeeper, and he once as good as told me that I was a fool. I have rather cherished the memory of his red beard and beady eyes ever since. As a seeker after truth, he had not his equal in the whole boiling of them.

If the sportsman on whom the gillie is in attendance knows what he is about, then the gillie's job is simple: he has merely to do as he is told, handling the boat or gaffing the fish as directed. There are, of course, gillies who do not find doing as they are told very easy. They always think they know better than their employer. Sometimes they are right; but even then, I always make it clear, in a quite friendly manner, that I am fishing for my pleasure, not for theirs.

For convenience of division, the subject will be dealt with under the heads of fish, tackle, bait, and general hints, with such incidental notes on various matters as may suggest themselves.

(1) *The Fish.*[1]—The colder seas of Europe are not the best in the world for fishing, since, unlike the salmon and trout, the most sporting salt-water fishes grow to the largest size in warm latitudes. I have caught bass of 17 lb. in Turkish waters, and tarpon upwards of 100 lb. off Florida, but nothing in British seas of more than 30 lb., with the exception of a shark. Even within the limits of these islands this difference is appreciable, and the bass

[1] Having only fished in that region off Taynuilt and elsewhere in Loch Etive, I have been guided, as regards the west coast of Scotland, by the admirable *Fauna of the Outer Hebrides*, by J. A. Harvie-Brown and T. E. Buckley (David Douglas, 1898), a work which is now out of print, like some others of the same excellent series.

and grey mullet, two of the gamest of sea-fish, are finer and more plentiful in the English Channel than in Scottish waters, where the best of the fishing is for lythe and saithe, or, as they are called in England, pollack and coalfish. Indeed, in these colder seas, the fishes of the cod family are the most conspicuous, including the aforesaid lythe and saithe, the cod, haddock, whiting, and torsk. The last four are ground-feeding fish, and must be caught from piers or anchored boats, with the bait on or near the bottom.

The cod and whiting are widely distributed, but the haddock (like the hake—a larger cousin) is " uncertain, coy, and hard to please," and comes and goes without why or wherefore. These fishes are almost too familiar to need description. There are the heavy-looking cod, brown on the back and white beneath, with a little beard on the lower jaw ; the haddock, with the black mark on its shoulders and the family beard ; the whiting, smaller and more silvery, and beardless ; and, in all, the line along the sides showing plainly, white on the cod, black on the others, and very marked in the haddock. The lythe and saithe (*English*, as above : pollack and coalfish) are predatory fish : they stand in relation to the more ponderous cod and torsk as the eagle does to the buzzard. They readily seize a moving bait near the surface (even a large fly or bright spinner will attract them), so that they are best caught by casting from the rocks, or by trailing the baits behind a boat. They bear some resemblance, but the saithe is blue rather than green, and has a small beard, which is missing in the other. Both these fish abound on all rocky ground around these islands, but the saithe is most plentiful in Scottish waters, and it dwindles in numbers as we go south, whereas the pollack is as plentiful in the English Channel as anywhere.

Three other members of the cod family call for passing mention. Of these, the hake and ling grow to a great size, while the pout, or " rock whiting," rarely exceeds 5 lb. The hake is a long grey fish, with formidable teeth and no beard. It grows to a weight of 25 lb., and is found in pursuit of the herring. The ling, which is still more elongated, and not unlike a conger with a beard, grows to a 100 lb. weight, and has probably the heartiest and most accommodating appetite of all our British fishes : it even swallows such dainty morsels as halibuts and sharks. Nor is there any immediate fear of the species dying out, for a full-grown female has been found to contain 100,000,000 eggs !

The mackerel is one of the gamest fish in our seas. Only its small size is against it. If it grew as big as ling or lythe, there would be no need to go to California for tuna. But as it rarely exceeds 4 lb., only the lightest of rods and tackle should be used when mackerel are to be caught for sport. Catching them for the market is another matter, and either drift-nets or handlines must be employed. It is for sport that the use of light tackle is advocated, and not, as for bass and grey mullet, because it is more likely to deceive the fish, for mackerel will take almost any bait, and—when in the mood to feed—almost any tackle. As they do not like the temperature of the water to fall much below 45° F., they are more plentiful in the English Channel than farther north, but they are to be found all round the Scottish coasts, and the absence of a fishery on the west side is not their fault, but that of the fishermen.

There are several kinds of flatfish which give the angler sport—plaice, dabs, and flounders are the chief. The plaice is known by its red spots, the dab by its rough scales, and the flounder by its dark markings and a few rough scales along the curved "lateral line." All three feed on the sand, where they may be caught with fine tackle and small hooks, baited with sandworms or mussel. Two of the larger flatfish—turbot and halibut—are also occasionally caught by amateur fishermen. Turbot occur in the more southern waters of Britain, and rarely exceed 25 lb. They have rough scales on the dark or upper side, and feed on small fish or shellfish. Halibut (which in many parts of Scotland are known also as "turbot") grow to a weight of 200 or 300 lb., and are caught by sportsmen at several places on the Irish coast, notably at Ballycotton.

The gurnards, also ground-feeders, are easily recognised by their grotesque heads, as well as, in some of the kinds, by their brilliant colouring, containing various combinations of blue and scarlet that make them, with the wrasses, the smartest fish of our seas, which, as a rule, do not favour such gay attire as the seas of the tropics. Properly cooked, the gurnards are good table fish, but he is an emotional sportsman who can find much pleasure in catching them. The best sport I ever had with these fish was in a little backwater of the Gulf of Ismidt, in Asia Minor. The water was so still and clear that, even in three or four fathoms, one could see the great scarlet gurnards crawling slowly over the bottom, and a bait dropped in front of their nose on a single gut line, with a light rod, was instantly seized, when a few moments of fair sport would result. So, later in the day, would a dish of baked gurnard.

Both bass and grey mullet—I bracket them merely as our most sporting marine fish, and not for any family connection—occur on the West Coast of Scotland, and are of large size, but the English Channel is their true home in these islands, as they are Mediterranean forms. The bass is a handsome, silvery, perchlike fish, with a big head and prickly fins. The mullet—also silvery and less like a perch—has a small head and mouth, and softer fins.

They differ much in their habits, except that both are fond of the mouths of rivers and of haunting piers and docks, for the food they find there. The bass, however, is a predatory fish, chasing the sand-eels and other fry, and therefore seizing moving baits near the surface. The grey mullet (which must be distinguished from the totally different red mullet) is in great part a vegetarian, though it will take ragworms, and occasionally—particularly about sunset—a white fly. In our seas, neither are taken on the rod of weights much over 10 lb., though bass of 15 lb. are occasionally recorded; but in warmer seas such weights are frequently exceeded. I have taken bass in Turkey of 17 lb., and in the Persian Gulf sportsmen catch mullet of 18 lb.

The John Dory is another warm-water fish and is at its best on our south-west coast—in Cornwall, where it reaches a weight of 18 lb. In fact, I never heard of large dory being much caught north of a line drawn across the estuaries of the Thames and Severn. The fish has as ugly a face as any in our seas, but this does not prevent its being excellent eating. No one goes fishing specially for it, but a John Dory is occasionally taken when swallowing a smaller fish already on the hook, and then, being probably over-heavy for the tackle, it must be played cautiously to the landing-net or gaff.

The only other big sea-fish caught on the rod in this country are congers, skates, and sharks. The conger is a great eel that lives in the rocks, and is caught on very strong tackle, chiefly at night. The skates, or rays, are those great, kite-shaped, flattened fishes with the long, whiplike tails, which in some cases are furnished with sharp spines. Like their relatives the sharks, the rays have their eyes above the head and their mouth underneath. The upper surface is usually dark brown or grey, and the lower white. They live on the sand, and will take any large bait that lies there, and they show about as much fight as one would expect from a billiard-table. For this reason I have always had difficulty in believing that there are men who deliberately set out to catch skate for their own amusement: but it is a fact that some do so.

The sharks and dogfish are also only caught accidentally, save at a few spots on the coast, like Herne Bay, in Kent, and Filey, in Yorkshire, where dogfish up to 50 lb. are made a special object of sport. Otherwise, they are caught only when they seize a hook meant for pollack or some other large fish. I have taken both sharks and porbeagles in Cornwall up to 20 lb. or 30 lb., and both these species occur in Scotland. At times, the smaller spotted and rough dogfish occur in such swarms that fishing is impossible—the only thing to do is to get up sail and go back to the harbour. The same plague used to inflict itself on us in Australia: but we used to go snapper-fishing in steam-tugs, and it was easy to steam away to fresh grounds and outdistance the greedy vermin that give better fish no chance.

Among other large sea-fish, the rarest catch in the amateurs' diaries is an angler-fish. It is not that this curious creature is scarce, for on the West Coast of Scotland, at any rate, it is plentiful. But its manner of catching its food does not expose it to much risk from the angler's hooks. The fish simply lurks in the shade of a rock or in an ambush of weed, and dangles a silvery bait on a kind of fishing-rod that grows on the top of its head. Little fishes, which are as curious as little women, gather round to see what the strange object is. Perhaps they nibble at it, but, whether they do or not, the enormous mouth beneath suddenly opens, and they are carried inside by the rush of water. Nor is the angler-fish satisfied with such modest fare, for large skate and conger have been found in its stomach. It will be seen, however, that only by the merest chance would a baited hook dangle within reach of its jaws. Still, it does occasionally happen that one is caught on a rod or line, and then it is a case of Greek meeting Greek. But if anyone will show me the man who would deliberately go forth to catch an angler-fish, I will show him a man ripe for the asylum.

(2) *The Tackle.*—I cannot attempt, within the limits of this chapter, any exhaustive treatise on all the fishing-tackle used in salt water, but I think I can lay down the general principles on which it has been adapted from that used in our rivers and lakes. The great feature of recent years has been the popularising of the rod, in preference to the older handline, the method adopted (and rightly so, since it often saves both time and fish) by those who fish not for sport, but for silver. And as a still further advance in the artistic style, lighter rods are gradually superseding the unnecessarily heavy patterns that were in favour ten or fifteen years ago, when sea-angling began to come into its own in the public favour.

The golden rule is—never use a heavier rod than is necessary. The lighter weapon may take twice as long to do its work, but it may give thrice the pleasure. I am not advocating a cat-and-mouse policy. Each fish should be got into the boat as soon as it is tired out: to prolong the agony is not only unnecessarily cruel, but it also entails the risk of the hook coming away. There is, I believe, a recognised time-schedule for the killing of salmon, so many minutes to the pound ; and the same sort of principle should rule in the capture of sea-fish. But a rod should be a rod—not a billiard-cue or clothes-prop. Even tarpon are being caught now on light Japanese rods, such as I used in California, though when I caught tarpon in Florida, some years ago, only very stout rods were in favour. The kind of rod usually sold for catching sea-trout, about 11 ft. long and fairly whippy, serves me for bass and other fish up to 20 lb. For bigger fish than these, something heavier should be used. Treat the rod well ; not perhaps as tenderly as a corn, but do not tread on it. It will not, as sometimes advertised, last a lifetime (unless its owner drown himself before using it), but, with fair play, it may last for years.

In float-fishing, which is a deadly method from piers and rocks, and in a few cases (as for grey mullet alongside piers) from boats, a rod is absolutely necessary, as also for any kind of fly or bait casting. There are a few cases, however, in which I would still advocate the hand-line, even for sport. One of these is undoubtedly the case of conger-fishing at night, an amusement in which a rod is out of place and will probably be smashed, if the conger run large. Then, again, when fishing for lythe or even mackerel, from a boat going fast under sail, the strain is too great for a rod, and a handline—or two, one used in either hand, with wooden toggles to prevent the line cutting the fingers—is far more workman-like. But whatever sort of rod be used, do not expect more of it than it is prepared to give, and do not use it as a boathook to punt with, or to push off from the pier.

Much the same advice applies to the line. Use it as fine as is compatible with saving the fish. It is wonderful how fine a line will save a big fish if the line be properly used.

The link between rod and line is the reel. A reel may cost anything from five shillings to as many pounds. Indeed, I have given nine pounds for an American sea-reel before now ; but in America you have to pay on the grand scale for everything. A good, useful reel for sea-fishing, of the so-called Nottingham pattern, with optional check action, may be had for a sovereign in wood, or about twice as much in vulcanite. The latter material has the advantage of lightness ; nor does it, like wood, swell after immersion in salt water. On the other hand, it is brittle stuff, and apt to smash if dropped on a hard surface.

The check, or, as Americans call it, " click," action is designed to put a greater strain on the fish. The same effect may be obtained with a silent brake, which takes longer to wear out ; but many fishermen love the sound of the check, and will have it on the reel at all costs. All the same, the angler with no soul for any music but the scream of a winch is a poor creature. The great thing about the sea-reel is that it shall carry plenty of line. Here is no question of thirty or forty yards of fine line for brook-trout, but a good hundred or hundred and fifty yards, to hold fish which may tear off half that length, before their first rush can be checked. A multiplying gear is also a labour-saving improvement ; that is to say, for every turn given to the handle, the barrel revolves twice or oftener. Lastly, some sort of line-guard, like that devised by " John Bickerdyke," is a desirable preventive of over-running—that most fruitful cause of disaster at critical moments.

The rest of the tackle, the various combinations of gut, hooks, and lead, must be regulated by a common-sense consideration of the habits of the fish and the kind of ground on which you are fishing. By this I mean that there are obviously some tackles which, though safe to use on a smooth, sandy bottom, would be certain to get foul on rocks. When fishing near the surface for lythe, saithe, or bass, little or no lead is wanted. In bottom-fishing a heavy weight is sometimes required. When the tides run very strong, and this lead has to be of 1 lb. or 2 lb. weight, a handline is preferable to the rod. At the same time it should be borne in mind that the finer the line, the less the lead required to take it to the bottom.

Gut, single or otherwise, is much used in sea-fishing in the new style. In Turkey, where the water is very clear and the sunshine exceedingly bright, one has to use twenty or thirty feet of single salmon gut, for the bass will not look at anything stouter ; but in our thicker water and duller weather at home, I usually find nine or ten feet ample. An occasional brass swivel—particularly where the gut is attached to the reel-line—will be found useful, and is absolutely necessary when the bait is being towed astern of the boat, as the gut would otherwise get irretrievably twisted up. When after small fish, such as pout or whiting, three or four hooks may be used; but for bass and pollack, a single large hook gives the best results, for not only are the big fish more wary, and more likely to be scared by a second hook, but success might be as disastrous as failure, since two lusty pollack on the rod at the same time would be a bad job for the rod.

The "sundries" which make up the angler's furniture have been well memorised in Mr. Malloch's chapter. Tackle and bait (particularly *liquid* bait for master and men) are not likely to be forgotten, but a dozen odds and ends suggest themselves as obvious adjuncts to comfort and safety. The special case of fishing in small boats some distance from land demands a few items that were outside Mr. Malloch's scope. The weather or temperature may change with suddenness, so waterproofs, or other protection against wet and cold, should not be overlooked. A change of wind may necessitate a long beat back to port, and, as darkness or fog may in the meantime fall over sea and land, a lamp should be carried. Some means of signalling in case of distress is also desirable where there is any chance of being run down, either coloured lights (Roman candles serve admirably), or a heavy revolver with blank ammunition.

Personally, I never go afloat without a little court-plaster and boracic lint, as weevers and other fish, if carelessly handled, can inflict very painful wounds, and much pain and subsequent mischief may be saved by prompt washing and dressing. In summer-time, too, it should be borne in mind that, even in these latitudes, the sea-fisherman is continuously exposed to the sun, so a broad-brimmed hat, with protection for the back of the neck, is a precaution that should not be neglected, while tinted spectacles will be found a welcome protection for the eyes against the glare of the water.

(3) *The Bait.*—The right bait is even more important than the right tackle, though the best promise of success lies in a combination of the two. A few fish, like pollack and mackerel, will occasionally seize almost any bait that is drawn across their noses. As a rule, however, not only has every fish its own particular fancy, but a bait which is deadly for, say, a bass, at one seaside resort, would not necessarily tempt the same kind of fish a dozen miles farther up or down the coast. Grey mullet resemble the bass in this curious variety of their appetite in different localities. Thus these fish are caught on paste at Margate, but at Littlehampton, in the neighbouring county, they must have ragworms. As a matter of fact, the list of baits used in the sea is a very long one, and something suitable is generally to be had, because, we must remember, the right bait is, after all, only what the fish you are after feeds on in the neighbourhood.

Occasionally, it is true, the visiting angler springs a surprise on them with success. I remember a man, years ago, while making a great catch of bass and other fish at Littlehampton, wading out in the surf and casting his bait, of which no one learnt the secret, just beyond the waves. Speaking generally, however, it is the local bait which answers best. Thus, to take the case of the bass. In estuaries, like that of the Devonshire Teign, beside which I am now writing, where these fish chase the sand-eels over the bar, no other bait is so deadly as a living sand-eel. In Cornwall, on the other hand, where the big bass are scavengers, nosing among the weed for refuse from the pilchard boats, a dead pilchard is the best bait, and they do not object if it is a few days old. Elsewhere, again, the baits differ : at Felixstowe, ragworms or artificial bait ; at Ramsgate, mackerel ; at Aldeburgh, a phantom minnow ; at Barmouth, a bait made with plaice skin ; at Padstow, green crab ; at Tenby, ray's liver. Such are a few of the chief temptations which lure this fish on different parts of the coast.

It must be admitted that the bass is an exception. Most other fish have one universal bait which is best, wherever they are caught.

Mussels or sandworms are good bait for cod, flatfish, and whiting, and for mackerel, when the last-named are feeding at the bottom.

Pieces of fresh herring or mackerel will catch cod, whiting, mackerel, and gurnard.

Squid and cuttlefish are perhaps the best bait for conger.

Ragworms (which are distinct from lugworms, being found in the soft mud of harbours and estuaries, whereas lugworms bury in the hard sand along open coasts) or paste are the best baits for grey mullet.

Soft crab (i.e. shore crabs that have cast their shell) will lure bass, cod, and other kinds of fish.

By way of experiment, mussels or sandworms may always be tried in a locality where you are not certain of what will be caught. If fish-baits be used, herring, pilchard, or mackerel, should be cut up in preference to others, as they are oily and silvery—both attractive features in a bait. Whiting and flatfish are next to useless, though I have known a bait of gurnard, with the skin left on, successful at times. Shrimps and prawns, used alive, are also deadly baits for bass and pollock.

Next to knowing the right kind of bait comes a knowledge of how to use it. Here we find some latitude, though there is in most cases a way that is better than others.

Mussels, one of the best of all-round sea-baits, are not easily kept on the hook. The difficulty is sometimes got over by scalding them, but this process, though it hardens them, undoubtedly makes them unnatural and less attractive. With a little practice, moreover, first passing the hook through the small piece of gristle, and then, after a turn or two through the soft parts, bringing it out at the " tongue," mussels may be made to stick on the hook, though few baits are more easy for the fish to remove without getting caught.

Baiting with worms is too familiar to need description.

Herrings and mackerel should be cut in strips diagonally, the bone removed, and the hook passed twice through the flesh.

Squid and cuttlefish must be washed and hammered until soft.

Living sand-eels are hooked through the lower lip, the point of the hook being then lightly passed through the skin of the throat. Live shrimps and prawns may be hooked through the tail. Turkish and Greek fishermen use a very attractive bunch of five or six.

(4) *Hints on Catching and Playing Fish.*—Here, again, severe condensation is necessary, and all that can be attempted is the enunciation of broad principles. The ordinary process of holding the rod and either watching a float, or the top of the rod, and striking at the right moment, is a question of knowledge and practice. When using light tackle with large fish, due regard must be had to their behaviour when hooked. Thus bass often make a last rush, as spirited as any that went before, on catching sight of the gaff or landing-net, and if the angler does not know this, he is very apt to lose many a good fish just alongside the boat.

Pollack make a determined rush for the bottom, where they hope to cut the line against their native rocks. Short of exceeding the breaking strain of the tackle, every effort must be made to keep them clear of the rocks, or you may come to the parting of the ways. Mackerel sheer wildly to right and left, frequently dashing under the boat's keel, and—if played on fine gut—need much humouring. The right time to lift the mackerel into the net or over the side of the boat is at the moment when its head points towards you. Any attempt to coerce it when it has its shoulder to the line will more probably than not end in escape. Conger must be bullied into submission. On them the arts of give-and-take are thrown away, and the " new diplomacy " answers best. Should a John Dory be hooked on a smaller fish, as previously described, it ought to be coaxed very carefully over the landing-net or gaff, for it has probably not taken very firm hold, and sometimes it relinquishes its grip just when victory seems certain. Grey mullet are tender in the mouth, and, unless played very cautiously, are apt to get away with a torn lip.

As in fresh water, some fish are more apt to hook themselves, without the angler troubling to strike, than others. This is true of skate, flatfish, and gurnards : but, on the other hand, whiting, pout, and bream need prompt striking the moment a bite is felt. For the gillie's information it may be mentioned that gaffing a lively bass or conger from a small boat, in a dancing sea, is not quite the same thing as gaffing a salmon from the banks of the Tweed, and even my friend Bob Muckle, of Tweedside fame, might make a mistake in a yacht's dinghy. If the angler knows what he wants, the gillie must do just as he is told. Then, if a good fish is lost, the gillie is not to blame. (He will probably be blamed all the same, but that need not upset him.)

To revert for a moment to playing the fish, much

depends on the extent to which the fisherman can trust his rod and tackle. If he be confident of every inch of it (always remembering that it is the weakest spot that lets him down), then he may play the fish firmly to the gaff. I have played a tarpon of nearly 150 lb. to the gaff with more confidence, and in less time, than a bass of 17 lb., because in the first case I knew perfectly well that I could take liberties, since it would have needed a suffragette on polling day to break away from tarpon tackle.

As has already been indicated, the fish should be brought to the gaff as soon as possible, short of hauling it as if the rod were a derrick. I have known fishermen so addicted to the music of the reel that, as soon as a fish is hooked, they swing back the top of the rod, so as to pull more line off the reel. Sometimes, owing to difficulty in winding up the slack, the fish is lost, and then I rejoice to see such folly pay the price. With heavy fish and stout tackle, the most effective way of reeling in the fish is by what the Americans call "pumping," the top of the rod being lowered and raised alternately, and the slack reeled in as often as possible. The novice should keep the top of the rod well up, always (particularly when a big fish is hooked in deep water) with due regard to the strain it will bear and the curve it will take without snapping. The quick gaffing of a fish depends not only on the skill of the gillie, but also on the manner in which the fisherman brings his fish to the gaff. Should he get excited at the critical moment, and either slack the line or lift the fish out of the water—an error which is sure to goad it to another dash for liberty—then the gaff, however expertly handled, is likely to be baulked of its prey. Needless to say, it is easier to play a big fish when the boat is not anchored, for it then follows the fish, and the strain on the rod is much reduced.

The most difficult case of all is when fishing from a high pier, fifteen or twenty feet above the water. Unless the fish can be gaffed or netted by a gillie in a boat, or on a lower step, or unless, as an alternative, the fish can be coaxed to the beach (this depends on the architecture of the pier), practically the only way of saving it is first to tire it out, and then to lay the rod down and warily haul it in by the line, hand over hand. A single kick while a heavy fish is in the air will probably break the line. The difficulty of playing a big fish from piers is aggravated by the posts and chains round which, in its struggles, it may wind the line. Nor is it lessened by the crowd of idlers who usually gather about in the summer season, not caring whether they give the fishermen elbow-room, but imbued with the one idea of getting as good a view as possible of the proceedings. Indeed, luck counts for more in pier-fishing than in any other branch of angling.

The gillie will be held responsible for the boat, and, whether it be a dinghy or a cutter, everything should be shipshape. There is, or should be, a place for all things, and they should not be put just anywhere, but in the one particular place. Nothing is more irritating than to find the bait—possibly a box of writhing worms—where the lunch ought to be, nor is there any comfort in sitting on a heap of loose hooks. The bait-knife should be kept in one spot when not in use, and so placed that the fisherman, reaching out for it, encounters the handle, *not* the open blade. All ropes and sails should be piled neatly out of the way when fishing at anchor, for if the sportsman should trip over a footboard or a bit of ballast just as he is playing a good lythe, there is no telling what he might say or do next.

The boat should be kept as dry as possible, for it is no pleasure to sit in a puddle or to fall over slippery boards. The fish, large and small alike, should be kept in a basket, if the boat is unprovided with a well for the purpose. Dead fish floating about the bottom of a boat between one's boots are simply disgusting, and enough to make a man sea-sick on the spot. Each fish should be knocked on the head when removed from the hook. I am not one of those who telegraph to the editor of *The Times* whenever they suspect an eel in a fishmonger's shop to be suffering from a headache; but needless cruelty is always reprehensible. Incidentally, too, this improves the fish for the table, for, if allowed to die slowly, they are apt to injure and bruise themselves.

Sport at Various Resorts.—Local knowledge is of prime importance in all fishing. This is illustrated time and again by the small village urchins, who catch more trout with a withy and bent pin than the visitor, armed with all the latest temptations from the tackle shop. So, too, in the sea; you may be using the right tackle and the right bait, but, without some acquaintance, on your own part or your gillie's, with local conditions, such success as you may have will be a mere matter of luck. There are places, indeed, where, without the exact bearings of the fishing-grounds, you might as well hang your baits from the cross of St. Paul's Cathedral, for all the fish you are likely to catch.

There are, it will be realised, two kinds of local knowledge : the broader knowledge of what fish are taken in the neighbourhood and what bait they like best ; and the more specific, but equally necessary, acquaintance with the marks or bearings of the different fishing-grounds. These have to be taken with reference to sundry conspicuous objects on land : a tree on a hilltop, a chine, a coastguard-station, a church steeple, are all favourite marks because sufficiently permanent to serve. They have come into use by oral tradition. In prehistoric times some old fisherman of the place anchored by chance on a spot where he had a great catch of pollack or whiting, and he immediately took his bearings so that he could come again next day. In course of time he would make his son free of the secret, or it would leak out somehow.

New grounds are continually being discovered, and the greatest pains taken to keep the knowledge. I have been fishing on such a mark, which may be known only to my own fisherman, and as soon as another boat, already perhaps a mile away, came in sight, my man would quietly get up the anchor and let the boat drift about anyhow, while we pretended to be having all the sport we wanted. The trick was of course apparent to the practised eye of the spies, who would take their defeat in good part and presently sail away to other grounds.

I cannot, for obvious reasons, set down in this chapter any of the hundreds of marks round the coast, with which thirty years of sea-fishing have made me familiar : but I can at least indicate a few of the resorts, chiefly along the English coast, where the best fish of each kind are to be taken.

Bass, which occur all round Britain, are at their best along the south coast of England, from Land's End to the Forelands. Plymouth, Teignmouth, Sidmouth, Seaton, Weymouth, Selsea, Brighton, Ramsgate, and Margate all give large bass, and at each a different style of fishing is in vogue. On the east coast, Clacton, Felixstowe, and Aldeburgh, and on the west side, Tenby and Barmouth, are also good spots for bass-fishing. For the information of yachtsmen, I may add that there is sheltered anchorage in a harbour or estuary at or near most of them, only Selsea, Sidmouth, Seaton, and Clacton being open roads.

Grey Mullet of good weight are taken at Plymouth, Weymouth, and Margate.

Conger are found on almost any rocky ground in the British Isles ; but Cornwall and the Bristol Channel, as well as the rough ground round Beachy Head, in Sussex, seem to be their headquarters, so far as the south country is concerned.

Pollack and Coalfish are found on the same grounds as conger, but the coalfish is scarcer as we come south. Very fine coalfish are taken on the herring-grounds off the Yorkshire coast.

Cod and Whiting, which are at their best between October and Christmas, are to be caught from boats wherever there is the mixture of the hard and smooth ground to which they are partial. There is, in autumn, good cod-fishing from the piers at Folkestone, Deal, Felixstowe, Clacton, and Great Yarmouth; also from the shore at Lowestoft and among the wykes and scars in the neighbourhood of Scarborough.

Sharks are mostly taken in Cornwall, about ten miles from the land on hot, calm summer days, and the largest dogfish (topes) are found at Herne Bay, in Kent, and Filey, in Yorkshire, where the Brigg, a magnificent natural pier of rocks, offers what is undoubtedly the finest shore-fishing for mackerel and pollack in the British Islands.

These are particular cases. A fuller list, with details, can be found in most of the manuals on the sport. But, by way of general principles, there are certain topographical features associated with particular kinds of fish which may, in the absence of any local information to the contrary, be fairly expected to be found in the neighbourhood.

The broadest distinction is that between a rocky and a sandy coast. Where the foreshore is bold, with cliffs and rocks, the angler may look for lythe and saithe, for conger and cod, bream, wrasse, and probably bass. Where, on the contrary, there are no rocks, but a low, sandy beach, he must expect rather flatfish, whiting, gurnards, with perhaps bass, close inshore.

If there be a harbour or river estuary, bass may certainly be looked for, and probably also grey mullet.

A shingle beach, with deep water close inshore, should supply bass on summer evenings, and cod and whiting in winter.

Artificial conditions are occasionally responsible for the occurrence of some particular fish. Bass will haunt the neighbourhood of a fish-factory, the refuse from which attracts them under unsuitable natural conditions, while the potatoes and other waste thrown over the side of Margate Jetty throughout the crowded summer season of that popular resort must undoubtedly be held accountable for the abnormal abundance there of large grey mullet. On the other hand, the disturbance of engineering operations has of late years been detrimental to the once admirable fishing at Dover and elsewhere.

Having concluded the practical side of the subject, so far as is possible in the limited space, I would say a word about the birds and beasts which are the constant companions of the sea-fisherman in the happy hours he spends on the water. Every angler should be something of a naturalist, not limiting his nature study to the habits of the fish he seeks to catch, or the baits with which he hopes to catch them, but watching also the creatures of the water or waterside which have no direct influence on his sport. When Dr. John Brown wrote of Struan Robertson that, " Like all true sportsmen, he was a naturalist," he enunciated something more than a half-truth. There is, no doubt, something enviable in mechanical perfection, whether in throwing a fly or in pointing a gun, but it is less enviable in the man with no eye or ear for the wonders of nature, and, be he ever so successful as a fisherman, he is no " Complete Angler " in the best sense of the title. The finest passages of Walton's classic—the passages which have lived—are not those which tell how to put a worm on a hook. There is in it something, surely, about the music of the nightingale that is treasured by many who never wetted a line.

For the sea-fisherman, who is visited neither by the gorgeous kingfisher nor the sombre heron, the most friendly birds are the gulls, familiar in every marine scene, whether circling in the eye of the storm or paddling in the tidal harbour. No one should shoot gulls. In the first place, they offer such easy marks that none but a duffer could miss them. Secondly, save in very exceptional circumstances (when too attentive, for instance, to the nurseries of young trout), they do no harm. Indeed, they are useful birds in their way, keeping many a harbour clean that would, but for their services, be a hotbed of typhoid, and, in foggy weather, warning the fishermen off the rocks, just as, in fine weather, they often show them where the fish are.

Thirdly, these birds, so beautiful in life, are useless

when dead. I am aware that there are lassies who stick them in their hats. Why ? If the face underneath the hat be comely, it needs no such advertisement ; and if it be of the other kind, the less attention drawn to it the better !

Occasionally, particularly in northern waters, a large dark bird is seen among the gulls—generally the centre of a commotion. This is the skua, a robber of the air, a pirate of the lochs, which waits till the feebler gulls have picked up a fish, then dashes at them in the air, forcing them to drop their prize, and recovering it before it touches the water. Near Aberdeen the fishermen call them " Dirty Devils," and in Cornwall " Jack Harries," because they harry the gulls.

The shag and cormorant, which do not soar like the gulls, but fly swift and close to the water with outstretched necks, are birds of another feather, and dark as sin. They are greedy fellows—eating only living food, and therefore useless as scavengers. They are silent fowl—making none of the tumult of the gulls at mealtime ; so they are useless as guides to the whereabouts of the shoals. They do not offer easy shots, for they fly fast, dive at the flash of the gun, and carry away almost as much as an elephant. Wherefore, I have no hesitation in saying—shoot them whenever so inclined, for there is no danger of exterminating the species. They are terrible enemies to a trout stream, once they find it out : he who would blame a keeper for shooting them, would blame the man for saying his prayers. Their bright green eye is full of evil. When swimming, they leave only the head exposed, offering a very difficult shot. Shags, I think, nest only in the cliffs, but cormorants at times choose sites in trees or on the ground—especially on lonely islands where they are free from interference.

A first cousin to them—but as different, when seen on the wing, as a bird of paradise from a turkey—is the beautiful gannet, or solan goose, a great white bird with black bars across its wings. The gannet fishes in a manner peculiarly its own. Soaring a couple of hundred feet above the sea, it keeps a sharp look-out for fish. I have watched it through binoculars and seen the bill turn from one side to the other, as the eyes ranged over the preserves far below. Then, catching sight of a gleam of silver, it suddenly folds its wings and drops, literally like a bolt from the blue, doubtless stunning numbers of fish with the impact, and then swallowing them at leisure. The bird is spared the discomfort which such high diving might otherwise cause it by the structure of its nostrils, which are covered up by the skin, so that it breathes only through its mouth.

The other birds with which the observant sea-fisherman grows familiar are of smaller calibre—puffins, guillemots, razorbills, and shearwaters. If not molested, these soon grow so friendly that they paddle round his boat and dive for such small fish or scraps as he may from time to time throw to them. Detailed description of these small fowl—black above and white beneath—may be found in any natural history book. The puffin may be recognised among the others by its parrot-like beak, which, in the courting days, assumes half the colours of the solar spectrum. They are all divers, except the shearwaters, which fly in great curves over the sea and never seem to rest. That these remain so plentiful is remarkable, as each lays only a single egg ; but they are careful to lay it on an inaccessible ledge in the cliffs, and, besides, few people shoot them. The only other little bird in the sea-fisherman's visiting-list is the least of the petrels—the little white fellow, known as Mother Carey's Chicken (who Mother Carey was, I have not the faintest notion), or the Stormy Petrel—generally recognised by sailors as the forerunner of bad weather at sea.

Sooner or later the fisherman with a turn for natural history is sure to be attracted by those marine mammals which we term whales, porpoises, and dolphins. Of seals, which are carnivorous animals of a higher order, he may also get a glimpse, particularly in the sea lochs of the West Coast. I remember watching one basking on a flat rock in Loch Etive. But seals have practically vanished from southern England, and are no longer seen, save at long intervals, even in the wilder scenery of Cornwall and its island satellites, where they once were numerous. Whales and porpoises, on the other hand, are encountered all round these islands. Great herds of the larger whales are uncommon south of Orkney and Shetland, but I have seen the grampus fishing close to land, rushing through a shoal of pilchards or herrings, open-mouthed, with a noise like the blasting of a quarry.

These whales and porpoises are not fish, for they breathe air, with lungs, like ourselves, and have neither the gills nor the scales of fishes. The young are born like calves, and nourished with the mother's milk. These animals have, in fact, nothing in common with fishes beyond their watery home, and a somewhat superficial resemblance. If, however, the fish and the cretacean are closely compared, the differences are immediately apparent. The tail of a fish, for instance, is set vertical. The only fish I ever saw with the tail horizontal (as in whales and porpoises) was a shark, in the museum kept at Yildiz Kiosk by Abdul Hamid, when Sultan of Turkey. Then, again, whales and porpoises have a blowhole on the head not found in fishes. It is through this that the great whales send up that cloud of condensing vapour which, mistaking it for a column of water, folk at sea describe as spouting.

It must at one time or another have occurred to most sea-anglers that, if the smaller porpoises (of, say, 50 lb. or thereabouts) could only be induced to take a bait, they would give exciting sport on tarpon tackle. No doubt they would. The difficulty is to persuade them to oblige. During the last twenty years I must have received scores of inquiries on the subject. But I have not yet succeeded in solving the problem to my own, or to anyone else's, satisfaction. He who does so will confer a boon on a good many human beings, though not perhaps on porpoises.

NOTES.

NOTES.

CHAPTER XXIV

ANGLING AND THE OPEN MIND

By Arthur Mainwaring

One of the most important attributes of a good angler, whether master or gillie, is undoubtedly the preservation of an open mind. In the last quarter of a century our still very limited knowledge of the sea lives of salmonidæ has been turned upside down and inside out, as the result of recent microscopical examination of fish-scales. Who knows what strange surprises in the matter of their food-supply and feeding, or non-feeding, in fresh water may be awaiting us in the near future? In no other sport is there so much ignorance, doubt, and contention. The wisest have to admit that the more we know, the more we know we don't know, and so we eagerly assimilate every scrap of knowledge that we can pick up either by our own close personal observation, or from the tips which we obtain while watching other men with other manners, these being the results of life-long experience on other waters.

The term gillie covers a multitude of widely differing personalities, ranging from the dignified, long-bearded

Highlander, whose duties lie wholly by river and loch, to the casual lad, picked up to carry for one on the strength of his reputation as an angler, by waters where it is sometimes a little the reverse of easy to understand how such reputation can have been legitimately acquired. No matter ; one and all they are, almost invariably, real good fellows, their sole idea being the improvement of your sport. In over a quarter of a century of salmon-fishing, I have only met with two bad gillies—one sulky, the other dishonest.

As a rule, their knowledge of their own water is excellent, which indeed it should be, since the majority have spent their entire lives in one locality ; and their advice as to the lies of fish, virtues of different pools at different heights of water, and sizes of flies may be followed with confidence, while even the most experienced angler is feeling his way in strange waters. They are generally obsessed with the worth of certain flies to which they pin their entire allegiance. The reason is not far to seek. Someone has struck one of those golden days when every fish takes and has landed half a dozen salmon on one pattern : from which time forth it became the local indispensable.

A friend of mine, who carried about with him the largest and costliest selection of flies I have ever seen out of a shop, was fishing our Cachalot Club water as a guest, our best gillie being deputed to accompany him. After fishing a pool blank in which two or three fish were showing, my friend determined on a change of fly.

Garrett, the gillie, looked through several hundred specimens without seeing what he wanted. " I'll mount ye a shmall little lemon grey," he muttered at length, taking one out of his cap, " and I'll bring ye out a few more to-morrow." Now this notable fly, excellent pattern as it is, had probably been seen by every fish, in every pool it had rested in, throughout its forty-mile swim up the river. If it be true that a salmon can differentiate in colour, it is, humanly speaking, probable that some slight variation would be far more likely to tickle its curiosity, or arouse its passion, than the harmless combination which had already passed over its nose *ad nauseam*. But Garrett had fished the river for over thirty years, and his belief in his beloved pattern was not to be shaken, until it was dispelled for ever by the method of fishing to be explained later on.

Before leaving this part of our subject, let us note the words of two high authorities on this fly question—Sir Herbert Maxwell, and H. T. S. of *The Field*, respectively : " The greater the number of fishing seasons behind me, the less credence can I yield to the supposed preference of salmon for one fly to another " ; and, " As for the local pattern, I have no belief in it as a sort of talisman for a particular district."

In the early days of the Cachalots we had another gillie, known as " Old Tom," by virtue of his being an octogenarian. Poor dear " Old Tom ! " In spite of his years, no weather was ever too bad for him, no day too long, no load too heavy. I have walked home with him after one of the golden days, when he utterly refused to let me help him to carry even one of the three fish he so proudly bore on his brave old back.

" Johnny " and " Mike " are two gillies of another class. Earning their entire livelihood on the banks from early spring to late autumn, and by tying flies during the close season, there is very little they do not know of their art. Instruction and pleasure join hands as one watches their marvellous casting, and speedy is the reward of those who are content to take their advice. From these two brothers, and the great amateur artist who introduced them to me, I have learnt whatever I know of salmon-fishing, and I gladly take this opportunity of expressing my gratitude. More than a couple of decades ago I stood by a friend who had just risen a fish : it came again and again, eight times in all, when " Johnny " arrived on the scene. " One size smaller," was all he said, changing the fly in a twinkling : the fish rose for the ninth and last time, was at once hooked and duly landed—an unforgettable lesson. On another occasion, when four rods had given up after a blank day on a famous water, he urged me to put on waders and fish it down from the opposite side. The reward that time was six grilse. Could anyone ever forget such a tip as that ?

The Shannon cotmen—they call their punt-like boats *cots*—have no superiors in the art of navigation of the heavy rapids of that noble stream and the management of the great fish found there. As a rule they are silent,

watchful men, who know at a glance if their clients can fish, and give all their attention to "holding the boat convenient," occasionally exhibiting marvels of dexterity in the following of wild fish.

On one occasion I rose a salmon which would not come again, nor did a change of fly serve to tempt him. It was an awkward cast—from the bank—but I tried a dozen times to get a spoon over him. "That'll do now," muttered one of my boatmen. But I knew I had not covered him, and tried on, till at last my clumsiness was overcome. "That'll cover," I commenced, when at that moment the fish was hooked. "No thanks to me ye got that fish," said honest Thomas, as he tied up a twenty-three pounder. Then my host arrived with the post and the shrimps, and presently a thirty-five pounder lay alongside the first—a very pleasant afternoon's work for the first day of an exceptional week. Once I saw one of these Shannon men, seventy years of age, literally festooned with fish, a thirty-pounder over each shoulder, and a twenty-pounder in each hand, all tied mouth to tail—a worthy subject for a camera!

Amongst other matters of which a gillie should be careful are the point of the gaff, the taking off of waders without waiting to be called upon, looking out for fish showing, and *not* trying his employer's rods. One of the best and keenest men I ever fished with met me, on arrival at the river-side, with the apologetic remark that he had just been trying a cast with my rod, and had accidentally killed a fish—the only one in the river that day. Never mind, "Jamesy," you made ample amends in a hundred different ways: amongst other things, when you taught me that the art of trolling does not consist in merely rowing a boat round and round a lake with a couple of baits trailing forty yards behind.

The gillie should be impervious to weather and incapable of fatigue, and, above all, an optimist from the first cast to the last. Pessimism was the one weakness of another of the finest gillies—albeit he had only one hand—I ever knew. To see him tie a fly or put on a bunch of worms with one hand and an iron hook was an abiding reproach to my own want of skill in both departments. But to be met with the remark that I might as well go home and fish in the garden, because the river was up or down a foot, or had a bit of colour in it, or because the shape of the clouds was not quite to his liking, was, to say the least of it, the reverse of encouraging.

An instance of the ever-present chance was recounted to me by a Highland gillie quite recently. The day he told of was a dreadful one—the last of the season, the 15th of October. His master and a friend had fished every pool, from breakfast to tea, without stirring a fin, and all three went home in despair. The last day of the season! But his mistress wanted a fish, and, after giving him a cup of tea, bade him go out again for the last half-hour of daylight. He was back well inside the hour with a sixteen- and an eighteen-pounder. Keep that story in mind if you are wise.

Another very important thing for a gillie to remember is—that strange methods are not necessarily bad ones. If the gentleman he is attending wishes to try some mode which the gillie has never seen practised, far from throwing cold water on the proposal, he should encourage him in every way in his power. The dodge, new to him, may have proved eminently successful elsewhere. Not only does his employer wish to try it, which in itself should be enough, but he—the gillie—should ever be on the look-out for the obtaining of new tips. No one ever yet lived who knew everything about anything. " Live and learn " is an excellent motto for an angler.

Ten years ago, on the Boyne, they put me in charge of their head gillie. A good fish rose to a Claret Boyne, but refused all further advances. Hazarding the opinion that he might take a shrimp, " Jimmy " replied that he had not got any. Luckily I had, and mounted one in the Galway manner. " Well, sir, you might fish all the year round that way and you would never kill a fish in this river," was all the encouragement he vouchsafed. Bidding him take the fly-rod and amuse himself casting, I devoted myself to the fish, a very handsome seventeen-pounder. " There's lunatics among fish every bit the same as among human bein's," muttered Jimmy, wiping away the blood that welled from the gaff-hole. Next day it poured : suddenly Jimmy spoke. " In one half-hour ye'll have the town mud on ye : better try that way of yours, sir." He was doubly right : in half an hour a yellow torrent obscured everything, but in that time two more lunatics of about ten pounds each had left their asylum, and Jimmy was converted for life.

No self-respecting gillie would leave a line without drying it, or a rod without wiping it down, after a wet day ; or easing the joints should it be left up ; or putting in the stoppers should it be taken down. Flies should not be left to take chills in soaking hats—you may pay eight shillings a piece for some patterns—but should be carefully tended and put to bed.

Thus there is a good deal to be done in one way or another before a gillie can conscientiously feel that he has earned his rest and food.

But before leaving this part of the subject, it is only fair to say that there are various ways in which sportsmen may lighten the labours of their servants. Punctuality is one ; suitable clothing is another ; up-to-date implements—especially those for carrying fish—come close behind, followed by numerous other little matters in consideration of their comfort. For instance, I have never yet seen the perfect fishing-hut, though I have known two that came very near it. Both of these huts, in addition to the room for the sportsmen, contained another for the attendants, with a drying-room behind for clothes, waders, etc. These huts were palatial affairs, and, being picturesquely built, added to the beauty of the scenery.

More often than not, however, such luxury is impossible, and the hut, as its name implies, is generally a tiny one-roomed affair. But, however humble, let it always contain a stove, that master and man may know the cheer of a cup of hot tea before starting for the long walk, or drive, home. It should also admit of rods being left up, than which nothing saves more trouble and time—the latter occasionally an important item. The best of all positions for a rod so left is upright, which merely involves one corner of the edifice being eighteen or nineteen feet high, though one seldom sees such long rods in use nowadays as were in vogue twenty or thirty years ago. Then each rod may stand at ease comfortably, retained in place by a small falling bar, some three feet from the ground ; while a line-drier—clamped to the table opposite—empties the reel, and everything is ready for use at a couple of minutes' notice next day.

If this high corner be not approved of, let the hut be long enough to admit of the rods lying along one of the walls. But in this case be sure there are sufficient supports to prevent any part of the rod sagging, for the position otherwise is inherently bad. The best supports I ever saw were in a house on the Wye. They consisted of an ordinary brass curtain-rail near the ceiling, from which were suspended a number of narrow zinc strips, bent the reverse way at each end, like pot-hooks ; one end of each thus hung over the picture-rail, while the other formed a carrier for the rod. About five or six should be used for each rod. The first lot—perhaps six inches long—would then carry the top rod ; the next lot—about a foot long—the second rod ; and so on for as many rods as were likely to be in use at a time.

An additional improvement would be a series of beds for the butts, made of wood, and attached to the end of the hut, the beds corresponding to the various lengths of the zinc supports. At the other end of the hut might be fixed the line-driers on brackets, the lines being wound on the driers, before putting rod and drier up for the night. These zinc strips might be replaced by brass hangers and rests, joined by cords for convenience of packing and carriage. Small brass chains might do better still, so far as appearances are concerned, without adding very greatly to the expense. The advantage of the pot-hook style is that the rods are held a little away from the wall—thus avoiding any damp that may be about.

A well-cared-for rod will last a lifetime. A neglected one will crack in its second—if not its first—season. Reels, too, last for ever. When not in use, each should live in its own little leather and velvet-lined bungalow. When left up on the rod, a duster should always be thrown over each reel. As an example of how a line can even improve with age, I possess what was, twenty years ago, a double-tapered trout line, from which, owing to constant snippings of ends, both tapers have disappeared; the rest of it is perfect—strong, smooth, and lissome, and is going to be spliced on to backing to make a grilse and sea-trout line.

But it is time to be up and doing on this beautiful morning, if we are to take full advantage of the likeliest time of day in salmon-fishing. A little too beautiful

RACK FOR HANGING RODS

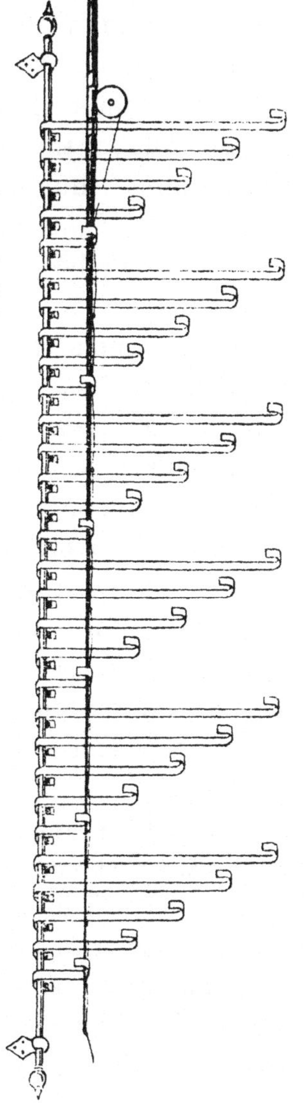

An alternative hanger, made in brass, with red or blue cords or brass chains : rod-beds covered with plush-velvet, in sets of six according to number of rods. Probably more expensive, but certainly more decorative, and easier to carry about, etc.

perhaps, from your point of view, though there is a bite in the fine spring breeze which is blowing,unfortunately, from the wrong direction to enable you to do full justice to your casting. Never heed the sun. Salmon like it as much as you do. As regards the best time of day, fishermen will vary greatly. Some will vote for the early, early morning, some for the late evening. But practically all will have a good word to say for the three hours between ten and one ; while some of my own best sport has been obtained in the afternoons.

So the longed-for pull may come at any moment, and is never more likely to arrive than when you least expect it. Wherefore, in addition to Francis Francis's advice to keep your fly in the water, be prepared for a call at any moment. And if you would add a hundred per cent. to the joy of your sport, and the weight of your authority in the smoking-room, not to mention your welcome in the boudoir, do not fail to keep a careful record of your fishing, with plenty of illustrations, photos, and sketches, together with details of weather, air, and water temperatures, barometer, and, of course, numbers and weights of your fish and the baits that killed them.

This wind from the wrong direction is rather a nuisance. You wanted to show Donald that you were not altogether a novice, and now your fly will insist on curling back with the last two feet of your cast. Suddenly you remember that it is just the day, the wind, and the water to try " tipping the bob." This method was taught to me in the West of Ireland, where it is the custom to fish for salmon with two flies, some four feet apart.

It is impossible to resist the temptation to explain why I gave it up, except when fishing under such circumstances as those which confront us to-day—an up-stream wind and a deep, still water. Its drawback is obvious. While you are playing a fish on one fly, the other is making desperate attempts to hang you up round a rock, or to retrieve some wretched old snag for which it can have no possible use. One evening I hooked a fine springer on the tail-fly. After making two spring-bow jumps he made his way through a bridge, where I was able to follow him in confidence, owing to arrangements which had been made to counteract such tactics. Alas ! the bob-fly, in passing, buried itself deeply in the hide of a large, very dead, white dog that had been caught up against the arch, while the salmon went on his way back to the sea with the other.

Having, to Donald's immense astonishment, attached a second fly to the cast, with about four or five inches of gut some four feet above the tail-fly, cast just as you were doing before, but with a slightly shorter line, and perhaps a trifle more across the stream. Then, as the line sweeps gracefully round, lift the point of the rod a little, so that the bob-fly comes tip-tip-tipping over the crests of the waves, retained in position by your late enemy, but present friend, the up-stream wind. It was once my good fortune to see a salmon, in a deep, clear pool, swim up from the bottom to take a fly fished thus—a never-to-be-forgotten sight. Just one more piece of advice, keep your teeth tightly shut when tipping the bob, for if he does come, the rise you will get will bring your heart straight bang into your mouth, and, whatever else he may do, a fisherman should never lose heart.

We have now arrived at the style of fishing hinted at some pages back in relating the conversion of Garrett and "Jimmy." There is nothing novel about it: it is simply the method practised in Galway, where hundreds, sometimes thousands, of fish are caught by it yearly. But it seems to be very little known, though it is so well worth knowing. The Angling Editor of *The Field*, than whom it would be difficult to find a higher authority, wrote of it: "Subsequent experience has more than confirmed me in my gratitude to you for the best salmon-fishing tip I ever had."

Before going further, let me make it quite clear that I write in no spirit of controversy. "Fishers should not wrangle," said good old Izaak Walton, and this is no place for the discussion of the merits or demerits of this or that method. Fly-fishing is far and away the pleasantest, cleanest, and easiest way of catching salmon. Some people are so constituted that, even when it is clear that fish will not look at the fly, they still prefer to fish with it, even should doing so result in a blank day; while others prefer to try some other bait and go home with a fish or two. "Each on his own strict line we move," and everyone should be permitted to pursue his own sweet fancy without envy, hatred, or malice on the part of anyone else. Yet will such as may be tempted to give a trial to the following branch of their sport discover that shrimping may be as artistic as fly-fishing, and that "admiration grows as knowledge grows"—in which respect it resembles many other scientific attainments.

For the great tip simply consists in a special method of prawn-fishing. To begin with the prawns themselves; if you order a bottle from a tackle-maker, you will almost certainly obtain them about the size that are commonly met with in aspic at a dinner-party—far too large for our purpose. In Ireland, those of the right size are very generally known as shrimps, an error in nomenclature which is not so very misleading after all, as the correct ones are just about the size of really big shrimps. In that country the term prawn is usually applied to the delicious cray-fish of Dublin Bay, a fact which once resulted in my opening a packet of the latter as I sat opposite a fish which showed repeatedly, but which did not require any flies, thank you. They had been sent in response to a telegram, and I had not opened the parcel before starting. So it is as well, when ordering from your fishmonger, to state the purpose for which they are required—culinary or piscatorial.

But if you wish to get the very best sort, you should communicate with Mr. Johnny Lydon, Corrib View, Galway. This may savour of gratuitous advertisement; but he deserves it, as I do not know where else to obtain the correct article. Long use has taught the Galway folk how to prepare them; so that, in addition to getting them of the right size, you will also find that they are of a special colour, while they cook them in such a way as to toughen them, thus making them not only easier to mount, but prolonging their stay on the hook when mounted. Whenever possible, it is best to use fresh ones sent by post daily, or every other day. A sprinkling of salt and exposure to the air overnight will work wonders in their health on the second day ; but it is as well to have a reserve in a bottle of glycerine, for the days when the bait fails to arrive with your letters.

The next point is the hook. Turn up the pages of any of your fishing catalogues, and you will find a variety of mounts for prawns, consisting of some six to twelve hooks, sometimes accompanied by a needle. Such tackles may be very suitable for the huge bottled prawns, though for my part I prefer a single hook such as those on which one mounts a small natural bait, which you desire to spin with a wobble, obtained by the simple expedient of curling its tail round the bend of the hook. But for our purpose no such enormous weapon is necessary, and the hook should be a round bend No. 1°, 1, or 2, tied on a strand of single gut, with a loop at the end for attachment to the trace. Before putting the shrimp on—I have got into the habit of calling them shrimps—it is well to tie the end of about a foot of the finest copper-wire to the shank of the hook, just below where the gut line begins.

And now comes the difficulty, for to get that shrimp on to that hook is undoubtedly a knack, and difficult to explain without a practical demonstration. But it has got to be done, and even if a few baits are destroyed in the process, this is of no very great consequence. Hold the shrimp near the tail by the forefinger and thumb of the left hand, and straighten it out by placing the second finger under its head. Now insert the hook at the very extremity of its body underneath the tail (Fig. I). Push it in, and the shrimp will begin to bend round the curve of the hook (Fig. II). Now let go with the left hand, and seize it again by its head and shoulders with the

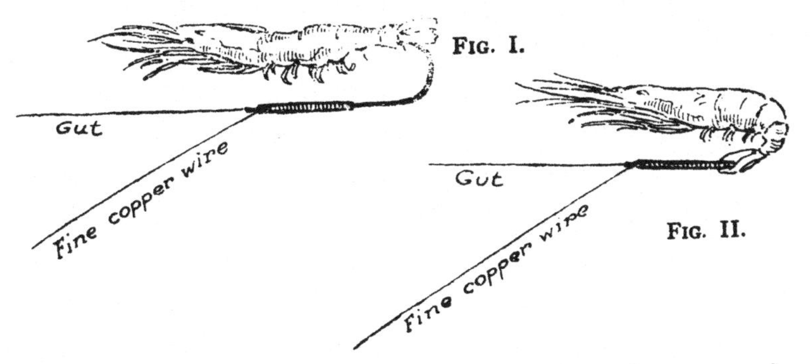

FIG. I.

FIG. II.

thumb and second finger; put the first finger on its back, press, and over it goes. As it begins to slide, encourage it, and it will slip on quite easily and lie out straight along the hook.

The point of the hook should come as far up the head as possible, and there is no harm in the point showing, though one very successful friend of mine has his hooks coloured red. Then wind the copper wire round the bait a few times, especially the head, finishing off with a couple of turns round the hook, which is quite enough to keep it tight, and if there be half an inch or so over, it only looks like an extra whisker whose brightness is likely to prove an additional attraction. Some people tie on with silk; others don't tie on at all, but the use of the copper wire is a distinct advantage in strengthening the bait for its perilous voyage, and is exceedingly easy of manipulation. If any difficulty is met with, it is quite simply overcome by omitting the loop at the end of the gut, when the shrimp can be put on with a baiting-needle.

Two more questions remain before commencing to fish. Firstly, the depth and strength of the water and the amount of lead necessitated thereby. This may vary from some ounces to a single split shot, which in itself is a proof of the varying water in which this bait may be fished. The best weighting material is the ordinary lead wire, which any tackle-maker sells in different sizes. Its advantage consists in the ease with which it can be put on or taken off, as one may frequently be obliged to change the weight three or four times in fishing down a single pool. Just how much to put on can only be learnt by experience. If you continually hitch up in the bottom you are using too much: if you never touch bottom you are not fishing deep enough.

Secondly, and lastly, comes the question of the most suitable rod and line. You need make no change from the favourite you have been using for your fly, unless the water be a very rapid and powerful stream, necessitating the use of extra heavy leads. But, in nine cases out of ten, your fly-rod will do perfectly well, nor need there be any fear of injuring the top joint through swinging out the light lead wire generally in use. Of course, if you have a short top joint and prefer to use it, there is no reason why you should not do so, except that you will command a few feet less water and derive less pleasure from playing your fish with the stiffer top.

If, however, you would rather not use your fly-rod, and have somebody with you to carry another, the ideal rod for shrimping is a sixteen-footer in three pieces, of which the two lower joints are made of hollow East India mottled cane, and the top joint of greenheart, washaba, or split cane, as your fancy chooses and your purse permits, with porcelain or agate rings throughout. Such a rod is very light yet quite powerful enough, and, as it is not necessary or advisable to throw a long line, there is little or no chance of breaking it. Another plan is to have the middle cane joint made to fit the spare top of your fly-rod, when they can all house amicably together by adding a couple of extra compartments to your rod-bag, the change being made from one rod to another by your attendant in the time it takes to fill and light a pipe. Your tapered fly-line will also do excellently; but it is not healthy for it, since it must do a good deal of groping along the bottom, over rocks and other rough surfaces.

If it be considered undesirable to carry a second reel, nothing is easier than to substitute eighty or a hundred yards of dressed spinning line, in place of the backing at the end of your fly-line, and to reverse them when changing from one method of fishing to the other. The thinner spinning line is more suitable for shrimping than the heavier fly-line, and it also enables you to fish more neatly and comfortably.

We are now ready to make a start, and it is only necessary to observe that the water that carries a fly well is the best adapted for the swimming of a shrimp, especially if it has a clean, gravelly bottom. However, one cannot always have everything to one's liking, and practically any water will do, provided it has some current in it. But we will imagine you have risen to the fly a fish which obstinately refuses to come again, for that is the most promising of all times for the shrimp. This being the position, draw off a little more line than the length of the rod, and hold another yard or two in the left hand. Swing the bait well round behind and then swing it—not cast it—out, letting the line in your left hand shoot, and then recover about a foot of it. If the current be rapid, throw opposite you at right angles to the river, or even a little up-stream, so as to give time for the bait to sink. If it be slower, swing the bait more diagonally down-stream, as you would cast a fly. Let it come round of its own sweet will, gradually sinking till it passes the middle of the river, when the straightening of the line will cause it to rise again close under your own bank.

Now lift it very slowly and gradually till the bait is on the very surface, and let it linger there momentarily, for there is no more likely time for a salmon to seize it. If you could only see what has been going on in those mysterious depths ! The little red fellow has swum round, twisting and turning, dancing and gyrating in the current, bouncing off a round boulder close in front of the dark, pointed snout of the fish which has just satisfied itself as to the fraudulent nature of your glittering silver doctor, and resisted the more subdued charm of a Lady Caroline. " Now what the deuce is that ? " he mutters, sliding after it with an easy turn of his broad tail : he watches it rise till it reaches the surface, seemingly on the point of departure, like some gigantic caddis about to burst ; he simply can't resist it—he must see what it is—and all you know is a mighty boil, a heavy pull, and you are on him, with every drop of blood in your body tingling and every pulse throbbing. Easy, easy with him while he lashes on the top : easy, till he sinks and dashes off, making your rod bend and your reel scream, and bringing Donald up with a jerk from his cosy seat under the golden gorse-bush, and you feel yourself slowing with the greatest joy known to a fisherman—the hooking of a fine salmon.

Sometimes the fish will take it in mid-stream, the line coming to a gentle stop if he has taken it quietly, or giving a great jerk if he turned as he snatched at it. Every time the line knocks you must raise your hand, till you learn to differentiate between a rock and a fish : nine times it will be the former, the tenth time—look out for squalls.

As is well-known, fish lie in different sorts of water at different times, occasionally maintaining positions in the swiftest and heaviest currents ; at other times taking their ease in deep, almost motionless, pools. In either case they may be tempted with a shrimp. On the Shannon the boatmen have a way which they call "hanging the shrimp." While the angler fishes fly or spinning-bait with one rod, the other is laid in the bottom of the boat with some twenty yards of line out, at the end of which the prawn—and in this case the boatmen prefer a large prawn—swims and darts about as the current twists and turns it. A stone is laid on the line, near the reel, to strike a fish should he take hold, and no further attention is paid to it. It is regarded as a third hand—as an off-chance, without any great expectations, but all the same not to be despised. If one desires to fish the shrimp oneself, they call it pitching it ; if one produces smaller shrimps they shrug their shoulders ; if one insists on a single hook they admit it is no bad way ; when the single hook hooks a fish they wake up, confess they have learned something, and handle their boat with almost uncanny skill.

But it is when the water is deep and still, with surface like polished glass, lacking all life and motion, till porpoise-like, some old thirty-pounder swirls prodigiously on the top, that the uninitiated really open their eyes and begin to doubt the evidence of their senses. Such a pool lay just above our Cachalot Club boundary. But when approached with a view to trial Garrett smiled derisively. " Man and boy I've fished this river thirty-five years and never knew but two fish to be taken out of it, and that by a man spinning for pike." Over ten feet deep, with a barely perceptible movement in its sluggish waters, the Quarry Pool, especially after such an introduction, would not have tempted many people. But a shrimp, with scarcely any lead to sink it, had hardly commenced a reconnaissance of its depths when it was taken prisoner by a twelve-pounder. When Garrett released it ten minutes later, after knocking its lilac and silver captor on the head, he muttered, " I was full sure ye had him outside." But another fish or two converted him and his " shmall little lemon grey," and a third of my fish—and that the heaviest third—came out of the long-neglected and despised old pool.

Lower down the same river, in an equally still boating-reach, there was an occasional fish to be picked up close to the bank, in the cool of a summer evening, by an angler sitting in the bows of a boat, quietly sinking and drawing a shrimp, while a comrade in the stern-sheets let him down, foot by foot, by hanging on to the grass and rushes growing on the bank. Under the alders, amongst the water-lilies, skirting the weeds, rose and fell the little red bait.

Queer sort of salmon-fishing ! Yes, queer indeed, but it would have been long odds against getting a fish by any other means in that still water. Yet who is so bold as to venture to account for the ways of salmon ? Why should one fish a small pool, no bigger than a billiard-room, three times with flies and three times with shrimp, without stirring a fin, and then meet with one when wading out of the water, and another shortly after the first was lying shining amongst the primroses ? That fish hunt in couples has often been observed, the unhooked following every turn and movement of its hooked mate. But why should it so often happen that the capture of the one induces the other to follow suit ? Can it be that it attributes its friend's fate in some way to the bait it has seen it take, and that it is actuated by a spirit of revenge ?

Can fish smell ? I never doubted it till some time ago. One of our greatest angling authors was wading in fifteen inches of water fishing for trout, while I watched and chatted with him from the bank. The stream was full of kelts, one of which came slowly dropping down and across the river. My friend could not see him, but I told him what was coming. "Wonder if he'd take a trout-fly ? " said he. " Looks much more as if he was going to take you," I answered. Nearer and nearer the kelt came in a manner menacing and sinister, every fin on its lanky body clearly visible from my vantage point. Within a yard, within a foot—I am not sure it did not rub its shoulder in a friendly way against my friend's waders, only sheering slowly off when so near that it was impossible to say whether it was touching him or not. Blind ? Yes : blind, of course : but are fish dependent only on their sight ? I watched this old kelt for days where he had taken up his lie within a few feet of the bank. He had no objection whatever to being tickled with the point of a trout-rod ; but he would give an angry shake or two of resentment if one rubbed his dorsal fin the wrong way.

Can fish hear? Why should they not? I can hear under water; and if you will bury your head in your tub to-morrow morning, and get a friend to speak, you will find you too can hear what is said.

A further comfort in fishing with the shrimp is that, just as any pace and depth of water will suit it, so will any condition. From high, porter-coloured spates, just before and just after floods, down to gin-clear, lowest summer level, you may catch fish with this bait. When there is life in the water, leave it to fish itself: when there is not, an occasional twitch can do no harm, while the sink-and-draw style—as in drop-minnow fishing—may result in much good. Should you actually see your fish nosing round and yet forbearing to lay hold, twitch it and he will have it in a twinkling. But if he steadfastly refuse to take a hand in the game, and you get tired of holding the rod, and endlessly swinging the bait, and long to sit down and rest, don't leave your shrimp in the field, but in the water.

Choose some quiet spot where the current flows deep under your bank; rest the rod over the bough of an ash or alder, so adjusting it that the shrimp waves, tethered a few inches under the surface; sit down and make yourself comfortable, but keep the line in your hand. It may be only an eel that will result, but it has often and often been a salmon. The fish love to lie under the shade of over-hanging bushes; so be chary of too much execution with the bill-hook. Talking of catching eels, I have also caught trout, and good ones, pike, perch, and fresh-water mussels on the shrimp. These last-named occasionally contain pearls. There is no knowing what may turn up ; and in that alone there is a charm, excepting when you catch an eel—there's no charm in those brutes. Should the capture unfortunately prove to be one of these slimy horrors, put your heel on it just below its head, and cut it off on the other side of your boot. Then, if the hook is well down, undo your gut cast from your running line, and pull on the hook, hauling the trace right through its mouth.

There are many old-established maxims in salmon-fishing, on which those who think while they fish are beginning to look askance. Does the sight of a man on the bank frighten a salmon ? A large percentage of anglers would answer hastily in the affirmative. But why should it ? For, consider, the fish has swum up many miles of river and rested in many pools : beside most of them stood men waving sticks, or minding cattle, or strolling with maidens, and none of them have done him any harm. Why should he fear them ? There were none in the silent depths of the sea wherein he has spent so many months, or—as recent investigation shows—years. At all events, it is open to doubt, especially in the minds of those who have captured salmon while standing on high banks, silhouetted in bold relief against clear skies.

Again, does the playing of a fish alarm other fish ; or does it attract them ? What heresy in this last idea !

Ah! But the best of us would have been labelled heretics in a good many countries on a good many accounts, not so many years ago. For, take the innumerable occasions when a fish has been seen following closely on another fish with a hook in its mouth. When a fish rolls on the surface, or jumps three feet into the air, or dashes after an elusive minnow, does it scare other fish? Then why should playing a fish terrify them? Those who have caught fish after fish in one small, deep pool, don't believe that it does.

A question often discussed is—whether the use of a shrimp spoils the water for the fly, as so many fly-fishermen claim? Those who have seen a man hook a fish on the fly, immediately after another man has fished the same pool blank with a shrimp, refuse to believe that shrimp-fishing can have any deleterious effect whatever.

It has occurred to me that an interesting book might be produced, if a collection could be made of the most marvellous experiences of a number of different anglers. Here is my contribution. Pondering on why it should be so difficult to catch fish in hot weather and low water, it came into my mind that they might be asleep, and I ventilated the theory in the columns of *The Field*, only to incur the ridicule of my more orthodox friends. Shortly afterwards, one of these elders stood with me beside the Quarry Pool, which we had both fished for a couple of hours without reward. Then our friends the quarrymen warned us to move away, not without reason, seeing that a fuse was already smoking amongst the rocks. A fine earth-shaking discharge was followed by the ascent of many a riven rock, one of which—after completing a beautiful parabola—fell with a mile-resounding smack plumb into the middle of the pool. " Now is the time to prove your rotten theory," remarked my age-privileged friend. The ripples had barely subsided when I sent in a shrimp and, sure enough, there was a touch. Examining the head of the bait, whereon there was a nick as though one had pressed it with one's nail, " A fish," I said, " as sure as eggs : when you see that little nick——" " Skittles ! " exclaimed the aged and sceptical one. But at the very next cast, I hooked, and presently killed, a fourteen-pounder.

That set me thinking with a vengeance. Desperate cases demand desperate remedies. Although not recommending the starting of a day by heaving a load of bricks into the water, yet it is a sober fact that on two subsequent days, when all else had failed, I bade my gillie throw in a couple of stones the size of a Dutch cheese, and was each time rewarded by a fish. I have also, I must confess, tried this dodge unsuccessfully on a good many occasions.

Few men have written more pleasantly and more wisely on fishing than the late Earl Hodgson. At about page 100 of his book on salmon-fishing this experience of mine is mentioned. He confesses that, when he read it, he feared some angler was stretching the long bow—a lapse too dreadful for contemplation : but shortly afterwards, he continues, he met with the narration of almost exactly the same thing in a book written by a fisherman and a scholar some thirty or forty years previously, clearly proving that Solomon was right, as usual, when he said that there was no new thing under the sun.

Quite recently, when fishing in company with my wife, a salmon showed within four feet of the bank under a bush in the Quarry Pool. For twenty minutes I tried him in every way I knew, sinking and drawing, twitching, hanging on the surface, and resting on the bottom—in which I finally got hitched up. The water was only three or four feet deep and very still, but I could not free the line. I left it loose, drew it tight, twitched it up-stream, jerked it down, splashing meanwhile like a schoolboy in a cold tub. It looked as if the line would have to be broken and the hook and some of the gut lost, when suddenly it came away. "That's settled that place anyway," said my wife. To me it did not seem so certain: nor was it: at the next cast I hooked the fish. Now, who can account for that?

If what has been written contains a moral, it is surely *nil desperandum*. Never, never despair in salmon-fishing.

Having begun with an appeal to all to preserve an open mind, an appropriate conclusion may be found in the words of good old Izaak: "For angling may be said to be so like the mathematics that it can never be fully learnt: at least, not so fully but that there will still be more new experiments left, for the trial of other men that succeed us."

NOTES.

CHAPTER XXV

MISCELLANEOUS DUTIES

As supplementary to the many questions that have been discussed throughout this book, I append a few notes on questions of miscellaneous yet very important interest, which lie within the routine work of the keeper.

(1) The very first duty of a keeper on entering a new situation is to ascertain his boundaries, and walk round his marches. When he is able to obtain the assistance of the outgoing keeper or of an under-keeper, this is simple enough. But there are often instances where he is unable to do so, and there are occasions when a keeper cannot, at the time of his arrival, obtain the advice of his master—who may not appear at the shooting till August or September. When the property is very extensive, he will of course consult any plan or map of the ground that may exist, and should not hesitate to make inquiries of the farmers and shepherds. It often happens, on very large moorland shootings, that the new keeper has some difficulty with the outlying beats, and may inadvertently trespass on ground not under his

charge. He may, under these circumstances, discover his mistake by observing the marks on the sheep, and noting the difference between those that he knows belong to his own ground, and those which are on the ground on to which he has inadvertently trespassed. The difference in the marks may help to put him right.

(2) Some time before the shooting season, the keeper should make a systematic inquiry into the following questions :

(*a*) Any necessary assistance required in the way of under-keepers, gillies, beaters, and drivers.

(*b*) The hiring or buying of hill and other ponies and horses, panniers, game-bags, cartridge-bags, game-carts, coop-carts, etc.

(*c*) Dogs—the number required, and if to be hired or bought ; their condition and capacity for work. Chains and leashes, condition of kennels, food and bedding, etc.

(*d*) Ferrets—number required ; their condition and capacity for work ; presence and condition of living accommodation, food, etc.

(*e*) Tools—the proper supply of spades, flags, and sticks for beaters and drivers, flankers, and stops ; the accessories of the gunroom—oils, tow, etc. ; the keeper's personal tools—e.g. corkscrew, cartridge-extractor, knife, matchbox, watch, flash, whistle, and whip.

(*f*) Baskets, boxes, and labels for game.

(*g*) Arrangements for selling game.

(*h*) The keeper's gun and ammunition; condition of fishing-rods, fly-book, tackle-case, waders, gaffs, landing-nets, fishing-baskets, and bags.

(*i*) Licences.

(*j*) Drugs for horses, dogs, and ferrets.

(*k*) Cleaning and disinfecting material for stables (where there are no coachmen or stable-hands), kennels, ferret-boxes, and runs.

(*l*) Boats—oars. Number and condition of repair—boat-chains, balers, etc.

(3) The keeper and his underlings must always be on the alert to assist in the following courteous actions—(*a*) Giving all assistance in their power at luncheon-time, for instance, by supplying game-bags or other forms of seats for the shooters, by putting soda-water bottles into running streams for the purpose of cooling, by opening wine, beer, or whisky bottles, by laying out the contents of the luncheon-basket, and by carefully stowing away the debris of the luncheon before the guns start shooting again; (*b*) holding guns while the sportsmen get over or through dykes, gates, or hedges; (*c*) procuring waterproofs, or any change of clothing which may have been brought on to the shooting-ground; (*d*) carrying the gun of any sportsman who may desire to be temporarily relieved of it; (*e*) opening gates or otherwise assisting the guns to pass through or over obstacles; (*f*) indicating the proximity to good springs and burns; (*g*) making inquiries from time to time as to any desire

on the sportsmen's part for more cartridges ; (*h*) assisting the guns to make themselves as comfortable as possible in the butts ; and (*i*) the hundred other little attentions that will suggest themselves to the courteous servant.

(4) The keeper must look to his health. This is a duty not only to himself, but also to his master ; he must wear flannels next his skin, and have clothing and boots that will give him suitable protection from the vagaries of climate. He must see that he does not fall back upon the idiotic notion that, by putting whisky in, he can keep cold out, and make this habit an excuse for not changing his wet clothes. The clothes must be serviceable, tidy, and quiet—not of a pattern and colour that will scare game a mile away.

(5) The keeper, when off active shooting duty, should go about with a dog—one to which has been given a reputation for ferocity (even if it be as mild as a toy spaniel). He will thus be a terror in the eyes of mischievous small boys, and other minor depredators.

Of additional miscellaneous duties, the following ought to come under his observation :

Larders.—It seems hardly necessary to say that there should on every shooting-lodge be two larders—one for meat and the other for game. Larders should be large, clean, and airy. On no account should the flooring be too near the ground. An ideal larder should have the flooring 4 ft. from the ground, and so placed as to ensure a free current of air passing beneath it. This ideal larder is built of stone or brick, tiled inside, and contains large windows, " paned " with perforated zinc, which open to the east, west, and north, the south side only being built solid and windowless, for the sake of coolness. A small compartment for the use of the cook should be framed off from the main larder, with a small window opening into it, through which the keeper gives game for the use of the house. The keeper has sole control of his larder, and the cook of hers, by a separate door. This arrangement saves much annoyance. Height is an important point in the consideration of space ; and on no account should a ventilator on the roof be omitted.

An ideal construction, if only wood is employed, is to have both the meat- and the game-larders fairly close together, enclosed in a large wooden framework, which is covered with very finely-perforated zinc or small-meshed wire. This is a second protection and keeps out all flies, while allowing on every side a free draught of air. The roof should be high, and covered with shingles or slates. Entry is by door covered with wire. The floor is of concrete for cleanliness, and on that floor stand the two wooden larders—1 ft. off the ground—their contents thus doubly protected against dust and insects. The covered roof shields the larders inside entirely from the rays of the sun. The inside larders have, of course, the usual perforated zinc windows. The door of the outside framework, as well as each of the larders inside, is furnished with lock and key.

There should be shutters on the outside of the perforated zinc windows, which should be closed in stormy weather, to prevent dust, etc., from being blown into the larder. The shelves inside should be of slate, and there should, of course, be plenty of hooks on which to hang the game. This should be done in regular rotation as to the date of killing. Omission of the latter point is bound to lead to confusion in the mind of the cook. The larder must, of course, be kept thoroughly clean. The best site for a larder is a high mound, shaded, if possible, from the hot sun, and in a position to have the advantage of the prevailing wind and the benefit of any airs that blow. Spots under trees should be avoided, as the drip off the leaves is not favourable to that freedom from damp which is necessary for keeping game.

Disposal of Game.—When game is to be disposed of to dealers, arrangements should be made, before the shooting season, with respectable firms, and a contract-price fixed, if possible, for the whole season, as many dealers are apt to return any price they like—varying the amount according to the character of the sportsman. If the sportsman happens to be an indifferent, easy-going person, the price is likely to be a small one, but if he is a business-like man, he will be able to secure better quotations. The keeper should ask for estimates from several dealers before accepting any particular offer.

In packing game for the dealer, the following rules should be observed : (1) All game should be thoroughly cool before being packed ; (2) Fur and feather should not be packed in the same basket ; (3) Feathers should be carefully brushed and straightened—the head being placed, along with a piece of heather, under one of the wings ; (4) The heaviest birds should be placed at the bottom ; (5) All badly shot birds should be kept for home use ; (6) Baskets should, if possible, be dispatched by train or steamer on the evening of the day on which the game is killed. Many keepers are apt to postpone the dispatch of game till the following day. This often accounts for the bad returns which sportsmen receive from the dealers. (7) A note of the quantity of game dispatched should be given to the sportsman, and a duplicate sent to the game-dealer.

Game Book.—The keeper's game-book should be kept correctly, regularly, and methodically. Details of the day's sport should be filled in every evening, and on no account left over till the following day. The facts entered should include the number of guns, the details of the bag, the number of hours the guns were shooting, the state of the weather, the part of the ground shot over, and any particular and interesting circumstances relating to the day's sport that may have appealed to the keeper. It is as well also that notes be kept referring to the points of interest connected with the breeding season. Careful memoranda as to the stock of birds left on the ground after the shooting season is over will no doubt be afterwards found of considerable value.

NOTES.

CHAPTER XXVI

TIPS

By Sir Peter J. Mackie, Bart.

It is neither easy nor pleasant to speak frankly on the subject of " tips," and as it is a question that essentially concerns the master and his guests, it might seem an irrelevant subject for a keeper's book. But we feel that it will not do any particular harm for the keeper to listen to us " thinking aloud," and whilst we address a few observations to all whom it may concern. What was originally a recognition of good and special service has now, in every branch of life, come to be regarded as a matter of course, apart altogether from fairness or justice. In the cases of certain well-known restaurants—where waiters are not paid, and are even compelled in many instances to pay for the privileges of the position—a tip is in reality no longer a tip ; it is a wage, and a most unfair and mean attempt on behalf of the proprietors to throw upon the pockets of the public the payment of their servants, while they themselves retain sole control and the right of dismissal.

Such tips are, of course, not obligatory in law, but, as things are at present, the claim is irresistible. The sooner the whole system is abolished, however, the better. One does not wish to insult one's friends by placing their servants in the category of the unpaid waiter; yet the conduct of many of these servants seems to be so much regulated by the size of their tips that there is occasionally a suspicion that the establishment in which they serve is run on the restaurant line. The practice of indiscriminate tipping has crept into every department of estate and household life, until the stable, the covert, the moor, the kitchen, and the pantry have all become free-flowing drains upon the pocket of the guest.

And it is not only the guest who suffers. The abhorrent practice of secret commissions, and the high-handed way in which many servants demand these, have compelled even tradespeople to submit to this form of tyranny from sheer sense of self-protection, with the result that the swindling recoils back upon the master. In a large number of cases the tradesman is chosen, not from the quality and comparative cheapness of his goods, but from the liberality of his tipping practices. This line of conduct harms the master in two ways: he does not get the best value for his money, and he has the price of his goods raised so as to recoup the tradesman for the money doled out to his servants in bribes.

Let us take an example relevant to the particular class

of servant we are at present dealing with. Every competent keeper should, of course, be able to prepare his own pheasant food ; if he is not, he does not possess one of the primary qualifications for his post. Yet it will be observed how eager many keepers are to run up large accounts with pheasant-food manufacturers—either from laziness, or more often that they may receive the commission offered by certain firms to induce keepers to buy their commodities. I have been told by a dealer in keeper's requisites that, when he began business, he tried to deal honestly by the employer, by not giving commissions to the servant. But so unusual did he find this to be, and so great was the dissatisfaction of the keeper, that he perceived that his chance of doing business was in danger, and he had—much against his will—to pay the usual " blackmail " to the keeper, the amount of which was no doubt added to the price of the commodity supplied.

Stable requisites from saddlers are increased 25 per cent. to cover the blackmail of coachmen and grooms ; and the same statement applies to the case of the chauffeur and the garage-keeper. A corn-merchant has informed me that the demands for commission are so great that they have become a severe tax upon his profits, " for," said he, with feeling, " there is a limit of price at which even the most careless master will stop." Admitting those indisputable facts, all employers, on engaging their servants, while agreeing to pay them good—even liberal—wages, should make it clear that they will allow no secret commissions. They should indicate these facts to all manufacturers and merchants with whom they are dealing, and intimate that any suggested change in their business relations must be decided by the employer and not by his servants. In the majority of cases, the dealer will be only too well pleased to do business on these lines. No wonder that so many people cannot live on their own places, but have to let them and go abroad, to escape from the thraldom of unscrupulous servants. No employee should have permission to pledge his employer's credit, or to order goods without a written order from himself or his factor or manager.

An Act has been passed prohibiting secret commissions, and is having a good effect. Numbers of dealers in commodities under servants' control have been only too glad to escape from their blackmail. It only wants a little backbone, and a little co-operation on the part of such firms, to successfully resist any movement towards a renewal of this objectionable practice. A hint to the master would speedily put an end to it, and prevent the Act from becoming a dead letter.

From this form of " baksheesh " we pass to the question of tipping as it affects shooting guest and keeper. Needless to say, there are many shootings at which the traditions of moderate tipping are so well maintained that no one, except the meanest or the most cantankerous of mankind, can find reason to object to the common usage of recognising the services of the keeper by a small present of money. While wholly condemning blackmail, secret commission, or baksheesh, the object here is not to advocate the abolition of tipping, but merely to press home the point that it should be kept in moderation. With this all sensible keepers will agree. But if these shootings can be counted by the tens, the other sort can be counted by the twenties. So excessive are the expectations of some keepers, that it is only the man of almost unlimited means who can accept invitations to shoot. The man of moderate means, in fact, has to fall back upon moderate shootings.

The only deduction to be drawn from this fact is that a guest has in reality to pay for his sport. We all know the story of the " Sovs. and Half-Sovs." " Put the Sovereigns at the wood end, Bill, and the Half-sovs. can walk with the beaters and stop back." But nowadays " Sovs. and Half-Sovs." sink small before the two guineas and the five-pound notes which are expected by some keepers, not for rendering any particular individual services, but simply because, being keepers, they expect to be paid by the guests for the birds which they have had sent over the guns. So marked is the disagreeable attitude of certain keepers to men of moderate means, that one is not surprised to hear of the increasing difficulty experienced by some sportsmen in getting guns. Some of the very best shots are comparatively poor men, and certainly not plutocrats. Nothing is more galling to the good sportsman than to challenge him with unsportsmanlike action. But the mere fact that he encourages the pernicious habit of reckless over-tipping proves a man careless of the interests of his brother guns. Such a man is *not* a good sportsman.

The argument is often put thus : " Surely the keeper of a good shoot should be tipped higher than that of a moderate one." Not of necessity. The keeper of the moderate shoot, if the matter is to be taken into consideration at all, may show his birds better than the keeper of the first-class shoot. The same reasoning would apply in the case of a butler who gave the guests Château Lafite, as compared with another who was only able to supply Médoc. " But," our friends may reply, " in the case of the big covert shoot, look at the enormous labour involved." Are the guests, then, to be considered as payers of wages ? Certainly not. Tips are given, not as part of a man's salary, but in recognition of special services rendered, or from desire to recognise the marked efficiency of the keeper. We give from our free will, and not in accordance with any stereotyped tyranny—a tyranny which found its most obnoxious, and altogether unbearable, expression in the case of a keeper who was seen to hold the proffered tip in his hand, to regard it with a look which combined curiosity with disdain, and then to hand it back with the remark that it was not " up to his standard ! "

The following stories, though hardly credible, are vouched for as true. A sportsman was called away to town after the first day's covert-shoot, and, having another shoot a few miles off, asked the keeper to send on his gun and cartridges by train to be waiting him there, at the same time tipping him a sovereign for the day's sport. Arriving at the shoot a few days later, he was surprised to find no sign of his gun, etc. ; he telegraphed for them, and got back a reply from the keeper, " I will send on your gun when you give me my proper and usual tip—two sovereigns." Sending this letter to the keeper's employer, he got the reply, " I can't interfere. Besides, it's the middle of my shooting season, and I can't afford to quarrel or part with my keeper—better pay." Here is another. Scene—Smoke-room. Host informs his guests, " My keeper's tip is a fiver." They all decided to tip low. None were asked back. The only conclusion one can draw from these stories is—that the host was a cad, and looked to his guests to pay his servants.

The *nouveau riche* is, we fear, the sinner who has encouraged heavy tipping, which may be regarded as a species of selfishness prompted by two motives : first, that the tipper may get the best of everything ; and, secondly, to show that he has plenty of money. The first reason is unsportsmanlike, and most inconsiderate towards his fellow-guests ; the second shows him to be vulgar and purse-proud.

In studying the matter of tips, it were as well to get to the foundation of the habit. Etymologically the word means something small, and originally it meant something given secretly or *sub rosa*. Now it has grown to mean something big, and something very much advertised and above the table. We began to tip porters when we found that they had to deal with very heavy luggage, or when they ran for our cabs, or were in any way particularly smart and useful. Now we tip as a matter of course. A tip was—and ought still to be—a recognition of special service. We tip the valet because he looks after our clothes, and we tip the gamekeeper, not for having a fine stock of hand-reared pheasants, but because he cleans our guns, or holds them as we get over fences, or helps us at the luncheon hour. If every man remembered this fact, tipping would soon come back again to that level of moderation which seems not only desirable but necessary.

As has been said, it is no pleasant task to write on this subject. A charge of meanness is abhorrent to every Briton, and especially to every sportsman of the race. In the long-run it may be better to give too much rather than too little. And let not the argument be interpreted as a subtle apology for meanness. There are hundreds of first-class keepers who deserve every farthing they get. There are no payments that are given with greater delight than the tips to the keepers who have shown birds flying high and strong, who have worked their beaters or their dogs to the satisfaction of everybody, and to the advantage of the bag; who combine, in all they do, skill with courtesy and energy with patience; who present our guns every morning as clean as the day they left the gunmaker.

Especially do we rejoice to recognise the keeper who gives us a good day over dogs, who is keen that we should go on, who works his ground for all that it is worth, who is interested in the way we shoot, and ever anxious that he, his underlings, and his dogs should do us more than justice. Such a keeper does not look upon us as the mere carrier for a tip. He performs his duties out of respect to his master's wishes, out of love of the sport itself, and principally from that noble self-respect which is the foundation of all capable labour.

Where such a keeper is in charge, there will not be heard the common complaint that a man cannot go for a week-end's shooting without five pounds for tips in his pocket—two of which are to go into the pocket of the keeper, one to be given to a loader, and the other two to be distributed amongst the rest of the men-servants in the establishment. This is a great hindrance to hospitality, and deprives many a host of the pleasure of entertaining his friends. Often the most amusing and charming of guests are the poorest. One knows of cases where the host has actually had to supply the tips for his guests, in order to facilitate a more pleasant departure. This is an altogether wrong state of affairs, and it is a pity it should exist.

There are a few isolated cases, in houses of wealthy men, where no tips are allowed on any pretext whatever. An arrangement is come to between the master and his servants for a bonus being paid at the end of the season, according to scale, instead of the usual tips. This plan should become more general. It would mean very little extra expenditure to the host, and it would save him many an unpleasant upsetting in his household, by servants choosing the most inconvenient time to give notice. He would get better service, and retain a more complete control. In any case, his servants would wish to be on their best behaviour, and so remain on until the annual distribution. Ladies should be exempt from tipping men-servants in any circumstances ; and head-keepers only should be tipped ; under-keepers should wait promotion before they are recognised. In other houses it is the custom to place a money-box marked " Keeper's Fund " in the gun room. This is advocated by Lord Walsingham, and is an excellent plan.

It is not possible to suggest any absolute scale of tips that might be regarded as a reasonable average. Of course, if a man be very poor his tip must be very small. In certain cases it should not be given at all—for instance, where a keeper has, by bungling and incapacity, shown poor sport. Not only has he put the guests to considerable trouble in coming with the intention of shooting and spending a pleasant day, while it has only turned out a day of annoyance, he has heaped on his master considerable indignity, and made him ashamed of his shoot, as well as of his servants. Many masters, on such an occasion, intimate to their guests that there will be no tips.

For a week's stay at a house where there is, say, three days' shooting over dogs, a fair average tip from each guest would be a pound from a man who was fairly wel off, and ten shillings from the man of moderate means,

POINTERS AT WORK

a few shillings being given to the man or boy who carries the cartridge-bag. For a single day's grouse-shooting, five to ten shillings is a good and moderate fee ; ten shillings should be regarded as a very generous one. For a day's covert-shooting the same applies, although we have generally found that the common tip, especially in England, at the first shoots, is a pound a day. In small or single-day shoots it is a usual and sensible practice for the guests, where they intend to give a tip, to consult together and each give the same. Let the tip be moderate—suitable to the pocket of all, so that no one will feel that he has given more than he wishes to or can afford. It may be laid down as a safe and general law that no tip—unless in those very exceptional cases where a man has made a prolonged visit to a shooting—should exceed a sovereign, and that no man of moderate means should be ashamed of giving half that amount—or nothing at all, if he be so minded. It must be remembered that a tip is purely a mark of good will and a present, that it should in no way be counted upon, and that a sportsman suffers nothing by the supposed loss of esteem of a greedy keeper or servant of any kind. Nor in such a case should he hesitate, even if he wish to accept the hospitality of such a shoot again. Finally, the necessity for heavy tipping does not now exist, as every host who is a real sportsman, and anxious to do each guest justice, places the guns himself, instead of leaving this duty to the keeper.

Secret commissions come in some aspects within the

category of tips, and although they are in reality a species of dishonesty—which tips are not—they have almost grown to be recognised as respectable. Since the passing of the Act to prohibit these commissions, however, the practice has very much declined, and rightly too. There is a society now in existence whose object is to carry out the provisions of this useful Act, and it is to be hoped that all who have it within their power will endeavour to prevent it from becoming a dead letter.

NOTES.

NOTES.

CHAPTER XXVII

A CHRISTMAS TIGER SHOOT

By Bunnie Wyndham-Quin

It is a peaceful day in the camp of an Indian Civilian, in the depths of a forest, a few miles from the foot of the towering Himalayas. The tall trees wave and sigh in the wind. The noon-day sun is hot—hotter than on a summer's day in England—but a cool, fresh breeze causes the skin to tingle if in the shade.

The tents, of various sizes, all face the hills, and so by sitting either in the verandah, or outside, a lovely scene can be lazily contemplated. A few feet away is a steep bank, and below, a sluggishly-moving and winding river —silvery fish, otters, and alligators (*muggers*) being the natural inhabitants of this. Close down to, or actually fringing, the water grow reeds and tall yellow grasses, and above and overhanging is the dense foliage of the forest.

As the eye travels up the winding river's course, beyond can be seen the deep-shadowed mountains towering, range on range, above each other, with perhaps a peep of the ethereal snows beyond. Birds flit about, vultures soar above in the limitless vault of the pure blue heavens, gay butterflies flutter around.

The ladies of the party sit under the trees either writing, sewing, or talking disjointedly. Suddenly the thuds of a cantering pony, on a sandy forest track, break the silence, and the master of the house dashes into camp. The dogs rush out in welcome, servants appear hastily, other ponies whinny from where they are tethered under a tree close by, and the whole camp comes to life. The Civilian—having just ridden many miles out to inspect some villages, and having heard many complaints about stolen cattle, stolen water, a runaway wife, a forged will, an unjust landlord, and a hundred other things—tells the amusing cases, and, being hot and thirsty, demands lunch.

Christmas is drawing near, and that being a time when the civilised world gather together and make merry, the subject of a tiger-shooting party is discussed, and before long plans mature.

The first step is to write to the Forest Officer asking that certain jungles in certain blocks may be reserved for the proposed Christmas fortnight. When a satisfactory reply comes in, letters are written to neighbouring Chiefs, asking if they would care to lend any elephants for the distinguished party's shoot. For without a sufficient number to beat the jungles, and for the guns to shoot from, a large party in the jungles is an entire frost, so far as shooting is concerned.

In due course the kind Rajah friends reply, and state

the number and the quality of the elephants they will be pleased to lend. Elephants, like shooting-dogs, vary tremendously both in quality and steadiness, and also in size. They take some thirty years to mature, and require to be used as tenderly, and with as much consideration, as young horses.

The owner of an elephant should always choose his mahout—the man who drives the elephant—with great care, as it is up to the driver to make or mar a shooting elephant. The fearless mahout teaches his beast to stand immovable—as steady as a rock—in the face of the angriest and fiercest charging tiger, not to mention pig—an old boar never minces matters, and charges also in a manner most alarming to the uninitiated. The feelings and spirit of the mahout communicate themselves to the elephant.

On one occasion a well-known old shikar elephant, of many years' standing, had a new mahout driving her when out on "stop" in a tiger beat. The tiger was wounded and charged down a steep bank, roaring. Just as the "gun" on her back—a lady—was about to fire, the elephant swung round and bolted, with the tiger racing after in full cry. The ensuing moments for the occupants of the howdah—two children and the lady who was shooting—were exceedingly exciting ones. The avoiding of branches of trees, holding on for dear life—there being a possible chance of being swung out—and the pursuit of the tiger combined to keep them very busy. To shoot was literally impossible—not to say dangerous—a leap on to the back of the elephant on the part of the tiger being more than an unpleasant probability.

Three other guns gave chase, each on their respective elephants, but none daring to fire for fear of hitting the runaways.

A little wordy pressure, and the threat of a rifle-butt by the exasperated lady, brought the craven mahout to his senses, and he pulled up to a dead stop. At that moment the lady leant over the back and fired at the tiger in mid-air, as he sprang, shooting him through the eye. Simultaneously another shot rang out. The lady's husband, having raced to their rescue, shot also, getting the tiger through the neck—both shots being fatal ones—and down went the splendid creature. He measured 9 ft. 2 in.

The episode might not have had such a fortunate ending. The two children were in a seventh heaven of delight, and quite unconscious all the time of any danger.

The same elephant, on a previous occasion, had two tigers charging her at the same moment and never flinched a muscle. A week's tutorship by a craven mahout can do terrible mischief to the best elephant.

When getting elephants for a shoot it is most essential that the howdah elephants, on which the guns ride, should be staunch and steady. Each gun will have his howdah elephant allotted to him, probably for the duration of the shoot.

In other parts of India from that of which I speak, tiger-shooting may be, and is, done on foot and out of "machans" (a string and wood bed), in trees, and with lines of beaters on foot. But in big grass and tree jungles, at Christmas in the north of India, elephants are used when they can be procured.

A sufficient number of howdah elephants having been got—say for seventeen guns—the rest would be used as beaters, these being called "pad" elephants, or familiarly the "pads." A mattress of rushes is roped on to the back, like a saddle, with padded quilts laid over—a most comfortable mode of travelling, just sitting on the pad with one's legs dangling over. To every howdah there should be two or three pads, or even a larger allowance. This, however, is not always feasible.

Having secured the jungles, a sufficient number of elephants, and the "guns"—this last being a very easy concern—the host has a vast number of arrangements to make to ensure his shoot being a success. The unstinted energies and efforts of many are set to work to this end.

The catering and such like mundane necessities are left to the capable hostess to arrange. Stores from Calcutta, butter from Bombay, meat from elsewhere—sixty odd miles by train perhaps—and all essentials, each in turn require calculations and some correspondence. Tents, with appropriate furniture, are required for each guest.

Numbers of young male buffaloes, of a few months

old, are collected from neighbouring cattle-owners, these being destined to be enticing baits for the tiger, and to induce him to lie up close by his victim, after eating his fill—unconscious of the eager sportsmen slowly and quietly surrounding his lair and planning his destruction.

The host has many consultations with his native shikaris, to each of whom he gives his separate instructions, appointing them to go and make a thorough investigation of certain beats of the jungles taken for the shoot. These men go out to their beats, days or, when possible, weeks, before the shoot, to examine the condition of the jungle, as each year it varies. Examinations of sandy roads and river-beds will soon show, to some extent, what species of game frequent the particular spot; the probable number of tiger and leopard there may be about, and, from the size and shape of their "pug" marks, their age and sex: also the parts of the jungle dense enough to hold these animals during the day-time. In many cases a tiger will make hunting expeditions many miles from his home, and thereby easily mislead the unwary and ignorant sportsman.

In the winter the cane-breaks and marshes, and such like dense wet places, will not attract the tiger. But when the hot weather comes he will live only in these, on account of the unfailing water-supply and coolness, not to mention the quiet thereof. In winter, therefore, when the grasses are of immense size, and the jungles all green and dense, with quantities of water everywhere, to find the real home of the tiger is a much more difficult matter. The fire lines which are cut and kept clear by the Forest Department, for the prevention of forest-fires in the dryer season, are also generally overgrown.

Every tiger takes possession of a certain beat of forest or grass plain, and maintains his right if any rival attempts to hunt in his preserves. A curious proof of this is that, within a few days after a tiger has been killed, another will come and take up his abode in his predecessor's haunts.

When a tiger, or tiger and tigress, are found to live in a certain forest, the shikari will then tie up "kutras" (the buffalo baits) in places where they will be seen by "hairyback" during his midnight strolls. But "tying up" is an art in which many fail hopelessly; for consideration of what and where the tiger will be likely to carry or drag his victim to, after he has killed him, must be kept in view.

The object, therefore, is so to arrange that the killer should lie up close to his kutra. A good dense piece of grass or jungle, possible to beat with elephants, must be chosen close at hand, into which he can take his kill, and in which he will stay during the day.

Meanwhile, our host will be kept well informed as to progress and the number of tigers his party are likely to bag in their week or ten days. With him lies the decision as to what tigers it would be best to hunt first, according to how they are killing the kutras. Generally some miles separate the different beats, and as elephants can only do a certain amount of work each day, changes of camp have to be planned.

The first, of course, must be within easy reach of the railway. In our particular locality, a queer branch railway brought the expectant guests some forty miles, first through tracks of cultivation, then through forests and grass plains, with ever a wonderful view of those towering Himalayas and their glittering snow-caps beyond. As the train trundles and squeaks nearer and nearer the blue and grey mountains, the snow-caps begin to disappear, the forests and rocky prominences on the lower hills taking more visible shape, and filling the hearts and thoughts of the sportsmen with varying speculations as to what their luck was going to be, and whether they would return the proud possessors of a record tiger. Tiger—the real object of life !—stags, sambur, ghond, cheetah, even panthers don't make the heart thump ; but oh ! for a real charge from a herculean tiger ! With every moment the destination of the hunters draws nearer ; and the shades of night close down.

Meantime the days and weeks of preparation have passed. The first " camp " for the shoot is all prepared. The spot, to the lover of scenery, is a truly glorious one.

The tents are pitched in neat rows, in a large clearing. On the north and east are the ranges of mountains : to the south and west the forests, ever mysterious. The rushing of many waters continually thrums in one's brain, and a walk of twenty yards from the tents to the edge of the clearing, towards the east, opens out a new vista. There below, some forty or fifty feet down a steep cliff, commences a wide, stony river-bed—in all about a mile across to the foot of the hills opposite—the forbidden land, Nepal. To the north and south the eye travels up and down the river's course, the wide sea of boulders and yellow sand being relieved by long islands covered with a sort of larch, their silvery trunks gleaming in the sun, the lower branches blended with the thick green undergrowth and tall yellow grasses, with the darker patches of reeds marking the swamps.

Then the river itself—a great and formidable body of water—divides into two or three different branches; each wending its course in and out among the islands, amalgamating again to flow on together for some miles, and each and all hurrying to their destination—the sea. The blue ribbons glittering away into the distance look easy to ford to the spectator on the top of the cliff; but nothing less than a boat or an elephant would take us to those inviting islands, the happy winter homes or resting-places of deer and tiger, and daily visited by intruding cattle, who swim across from the mainland.

The scene in the camp itself is most attractive. The dining- and sitting-room tents, in the centre of the camp, are naturally the largest. Great trouble is taken to make them as comfortable as possible with easy chairs, tables, and a small portable piano. Decorations of flowers, holly, and mistletoe, greatly brighten up the interiors.

Between these two tents a large bonfire of tree-trunks piled high on each other is prepared, for the guests to sit round each evening after a long day's shooting.

The servants' tents are tucked away at the edge of the clearing, and all are humming with men chatting and working. The horses tethered under the trees are lazily content.

In the distance the many camels, used for transporting the camp equipment, kneel in a ring, heads to the centre, eating from a pile of leaves put there for them. Then trumpetings and squeaks from the depths of the forest cause a stranger to wonder what the disturbance can be. A few minutes' walk will bring him to where the many elephants are encamped, each and all under trees browsing on great piles of branches which their keepers have cut. They are amusing beasts to watch, never being still for a second—an everlasting swing of trunk, tail, or flapping of ears. A thick rope, secured to a tree-trunk and tied to a chain, linked round one or both hind-legs, hobbles them. There are two attendants to each elephant : the driver—the mahout—and a " chaur-cutter," whose chief duties are to wash his charge, bake the daily allowance of flour into cakes, and go into the jungle to cut down the particular kind of green food suitable to the elephant at that season. This fodder the elephant will be taken to, to fetch home after his return from shooting. If a very arduous day's shooting is expected, and there are a sufficient number of elephants to spare, some are left at home to fetch in their absent companions' green food during the day. The neatness with which elephants will strip leaves and bark off a branch, between their trunk and lower lip, and then tuck it into their mouths, is amazing. Some come, dripping and shiny, strolling lazily up from the river where they have been having a luxurious bath, lying in the water squirting and wallowing, while a long-suffering under-keeper—the chaur-cutter—has been scrubbing them clean with a bit of pumice-stone.

The camp also has its livestock—ducks, chickens, turkeys, and pigeons. Dogs sit about waiting their opportunity of biting a scared and cringing native. Cows and goats also wander round and graze till their "gwalla" has leisure to take them further afield. Every camp must provide for its own necessities so far as possible.

At last comes the great day, about the 22nd or 23rd of December. The party are on their way, and are to arrive that evening by the train—not an express! Bullock carts ("peons"), chaprassies, and coolies assemble at the quaint red-brick station.

It is dark: lanterns are lit: all wait expectant. When the train is signalled, a man dashes back to inform our host, who, with his family, walks down to the station; and then follows another wait—the train is not hurrying.

At last she comes; shouting and rushing ensue, heads emerge, cheery greetings are exchanged, and out the sportsmen pour: a great introducing follows, and the party divide up and return to camp. The bonfire roars and crackles a welcome, throwing its illuminating rays on to the ghostly white outlines of the rows of tents. It is nippingly cold and there is frost in the air. All assemble round the bonfire after a merry dinner to warm up before turning in early to bed.

By 5 a.m. our host is up, and, accompanied by two shikaris and his head mahout, he treks out some five odd miles on a pad elephant to a certain jungle, that he may trace the movements during the previous night of a large hairyback and his tigress, who are known to live there. All is misty and damp—the trees and grasses sodden with dew. Every now and then, a deer leaps away into the recesses of the forest, as the pad swings along the track almost silently. Having arrived, the party alight and divide up, each going to examine a different part of the beat. Quite often some miles of jungle have to be tramped round—there being probably two or three smaller beats in which the tiger likes to live during the day—to see if any of the various kutras (buffaloes) that are tied up invitingly have been killed.

Our host, followed by one man with his rifle, goes up a river-bed : a small stream of water wanders about its course. They move along silently, only talking in whispers if necessary. Backs are bent. Ah ! here are " pug " marks in the sand, leading from the grass beat into the forest and high ground on the farther side. There are marks of both animals, the male tiger's being firm and round and the imprints more plainly shown than that of the female the male being much larger and heavier than his mate, the tigress's " pug " making a smaller, narrower, and longer-shaped impression.

The party proceed. The shikari whispers that round the next bend there is a kutra tied, at the mouth of a ravine leading down from the forest—a route much used by the tigers on their midnight excursions. They cautiously peep round the bend and exchange pleased grins. The " buff " has gone! Not a sound reaches them. The sun is gilding the hill-tops, and the grey light is fast disappearing. A careful survey shows that the hairybacks, on returning from their hunting expedition, chanced on the lonely little buff. There were signs of a scuffle in the sand—the buff had shown pluck and fight.

The shikari mentions that he had purposely tied up a large one, for the tiger was big, and that anyhow, even if both the tigers had fed there and then, there would still be enough for them to return to. The frayed and broken rope by which the kutra had been tethered told a sad tale, one end being securely fastened to a peg well hidden by stones. For some yards there was a smooth " drag "—the trail along which the buff was first dragged—blood and hair also marking the way. On coming to the bank below the grass beat, the tiger had evidently swung the kutra across his back, and sprung up into the grass—dislodged stones, sand, and claw marks showing the spot. At the top he had dragged the buff again, bent grass and bloodstains being just visible; the dew had also been brushed off, thus showing that it was towards morning when the kutra was killed.

The sportsmen clamber on to the pad elephant—to go farther on foot would be foolish—which had followed them silently at a distance. From the edge of the grass, the eye could follow the trail some way into the depths of the great expanse of grass. They then retire, for quite possibly the tigers are lying up close by. They continue their investigations up the river to make sure that the tigers are still in the beat.

Some hundreds of yards farther up, a forest " fire-line " joins the river: there another kutra is tied, but is found untouched, gazing out of immense, pathetic, limpid brown eyes. A shikari joins them here, and informs them that the two or three other kutras are all safe. The " pugs " of three panther and footprints of deer are also reported.

Besides the shikari who last joined the party, there are four shivering coolies: these go in couples—being afraid of going alone—and it is their duty to look after the kutras each day. Those that are tied on thoroughfares likely to be disturbed by day are unloosed and conducted to a village or forest-ranger's hut. There they are fed and watered and kept during the day, to be taken back in the late afternoon to their appointed spots—and to their probable end—where they remain all night. Those in secluded and wild places are not removed, but watered, generally at the nearest stream, leaves and grass being given them to eat, morning and evening. The kutras are not attended to till after the shikaris have made their morning rounds in the above manner.

The plan of beating for the tigers is then arranged, the natural escapes being used to drive the tigers to their doom. Any deep nullahs, paths, or depressions are taken into account. Instinctively, if it be possible, tigers will always keep under cover when disturbed. In broken, hilly country they will generally make for the hills, where they can dodge backwards and forwards, ever out of sight of the pursuer, whose efforts and noisy scrambling will be easily audible to the smiling tiger, who is probably lying stretched at the top of a cliff above, his head resting on his paws.

To put the general plan of beating concisely. The densest and most likely lair of the hairybacks being near the kill—the dead buff—the " stops " will be placed to command the river and fire-line, and on the side farthest from the kill. This will also allow of the guns having full sight of any animal trying to escape across the open, as it breaks from the cover ; and it will give the sportsman those few moments in which he must either shoot, or curse himself for many a day after. The danger of anyone shooting a neighbour will likewise be reduced.

Taking the meeting of river and fire-line as the apex, the row of beaters—the pad elephants—will form up in line at the farthest end of the beat, to try and drive everything in the jungle towards the " stops " posted along the river-bed and firing-line, the guns at the apex having probably the greatest chance of the shot.

Meanwhile, a return to the high-road track has been made by the scouting-party. The shikaris will remain and feed at a forest-ranger's hut, and one will see that no cattle or woodcutters—the deadliest enemies of the sportsman—wander in to disturb the tiger beat.

A pony will soon take our host back to camp—to a well-earned bath and breakfast, and generally some office work which has to be done. The other sportsmen are bustling about, getting their paraphernalia together—rifles, guns, hunting-knives, and all their pet additions—as an early start is arranged for, and the kit has to go ahead at 9.30 in the howdahs.

The party stroll out to inspect the elephants, all assembled beyond the tents, the howdah elephants to the front. Every gun is apportioned off with his particular howdah, on to which, each day, his servant will put his rifles and guns, thereby preventing confusion and loss of belongings. A better record can also be kept as to the conduct of the mahout, when the time of reckoning and tipping comes at the end of the shoot. Rugs and coats—most necessary accessories—are not forgotten. Into most of the howdahs would-be sight-seers clamber; and off go the howdahs, "mullan, mullan!" one behind the other, to the appointed beat for the day. The weight of the howdah makes the elephants slow, and as a long day's shooting is tiring, every plan is used to husband their strength and energy, and therefore they are sent on ahead of the rest of the party, to take their own pace.

In due time the sportsmen assemble and clamber up the tails of the pad elephants, going in parties of twos and threes. Everybody is up. The large skin-covered lunch-baskets, full of many luxuries, fill every soul with satisfaction. The surety of a good lunch and a long drink most undoubtedly adds to the enjoyment.

Our host, accompanied by a couple of friends and his shikari, sits perched on a fast pad, who is to lead the van and set the pace to the others. They are waiting for something. A shikari gallops in on a pony, pulls up by his master, throws himself off, and drags the sweating " tat " nearer, by its string bridle. He has brought the " kubber " news, from a distant tiger beat. He tells of how another kutra has been killed there, but most of it having been demolished, he had dragged the kill into the open and given it to the vultures. Another live buff has been put to replace the dead one.

This was the last of the men expected in with the daily report ; and so off go the cavalcade, everyone chatting quietly the first few miles, and admiring the view ; the elephants, with their quaint ways, not being the least absorbing of topics. When nearing the beat, a request for silence is passed down the line, and everyone looks expectant.

The howdahs come in sight and alongside. The sportsmen climb into their own, while our host has a last confab with his shikaris, and then explains, in a few quiet sentences, the plan of the beat. The guns draw for numbers—the fairest way of dividing sport—the idea being that No. 1 should get the best chance that beat, and, having got his tiger, should move down and take the place of the lowest number, thereby moving everyone else up one place.

The guns to be placed in the river-bed will follow one shikari, the lowest number, viz. the gun whose place will be nearest the line of the beaters, to go first, and the highest number last, so that as each gun is placed, the other elephants will pass on quietly, without noise of speaking. The guns appointed to the fire-line will go with another shikari, and be placed in a like manner.

Our host will take his place in the centre of the line of beaters, so as to control the entire line, placing a gun at either end, a few yards ahead, to form flanks. Guns among the beaters give the mahouts extra confidence. Some 50 or 60 yds. ahead of the gun on either flank will be a "flying stop," to move with the line, always keeping ahead. These are to have a sharp eye on any animal trying to sneak out of the beat. When the "flying stops" come into touch with the stationary guns, they drop into line, to replace the "flanks." These latter quickly move a few yards towards the centre of the line, among the beaters, thus presenting a strong front to any wounded and charging tiger. Sometimes the outlying "stops" will also fall into line as the line passes them, though the guns at the apex will not move upon any consideration.

The line of beaters starts from the farthest point of the beat, probably on a track or fire-line, each pad some 20, 30, or 40 ft. apart, according to the character and thickness of the jungle, and also according to the number of elephants available. A whistle will be blown to start the line.

The pace is generally taken from the slowest pad, a unity of motion being required, for a tiger will often canter down the line to find a weak and open space, and any laggard or coward shying to one side will give him the opportunity to break back. He will roar and charge time after time to try and break through. Here the mettle of the mahout's spirit is brought to light. The bold will force his elephant, even if a "funk," to stand firm or move forward. Elephants should be made to converge together, when charged by a tiger or panther.

The line is ready and awaits the return of the two shikaris who have placed the "stops." Eyes are directed to the top of a huge cotton tree, where sit a great number of India's chief scavengers—the great, ugly, black vultures—a sure sign that the tigers are about, and probably near their kill. The guns on "stop" are well hidden behind trees and grass, and all keep as quiet as possible.

The line, on the contrary, with the whistle blast move forward, and begin to kick up a real shindy. The mahouts shout and scream directions to each other, and encourage, abuse, and praise their elephants, making them crash down small trees—anything to scare the hairybacks forward. Scrimshanking mahouts, hesitating to penetrate into dense masses of undergrowth for fear of what may rush out, are watched by the all-seeing shikaris, who shout and rage, and try to keep the pads in line. One or two are given guns to fire if any extra bedlam be required.

Everyone is worked up to a high pitch of excitement. Movements in the grass in front, and a rush to the left, and the left flank swings forward to send the fugitive flying ahead. The heart of a " stop " will pound as he hears the rush through the jungle towards him; up will go his rifle, only to drop, as a sambur stag leaps out into and across the open, its horns laid back, not seeing the elephant in its terror. A crackling of leaves to the right, and a herd of cheetah (spotted deer) creep cautiously to the edge of the jungle, peering out of the undergrowth, their eyes full of fear and wonder, looking over their backs and listening with twitching ears to the advancing bedlam, their tails tucked tight to their bodies. A greater burst of sound, and they dash into the open, and bound away behind. Jungle fowl, with busy and angry chuckings, scuttle into safety. Pig, pea-fowl, porcupine, each and all come and go at different sides of the beat, and ever the line sweeps forward. Moments seem hours. Squeaks and trumpetings, and out of a grass nest rush a "sounder" of pigs, quite unnerving a small pad in the line, as she swerves aside. The pigs break back, and imprecations in showers descend on the mahout.

Suddenly—ahead of our host—the grass trembles and parts. For an instant a mass of yellow and black flashes as the tiger moves quickly forward, but quietly. " Tiger, tiger ! care ! steadiness ! keep together ! " the shouts pass from man to man. Elephants get the scent, trunks thud on the ground—making a curious ring—a peculiar and most welcome warning. The nervous tremble, squeak, and trumpet, and prepare for flight : but thumps and prods on their heads with an iron " ankas " —iron goad—from their mahouts, keep them unwilling partakers in the fray. Excitement is rife—on the right an angry " wuff," simultaneous with the usual shindy, denotes the presence of another tiger. All is well : both are going forward. No thicket is left unbeaten.

A rustling in the grass opposite, on the edge of the river-bank, attracts the second " stop," in the river-bed, nearest the line, and the next moment a tigress's head appears out of the grass. In great excitement the sportsman aims and presses his trigger, but a second too late, for she has swung round with a low grunt, and gone galloping back to the line. Warning voices shout out ! She charges a staunch pad in an unavailing effort to break through ; a gun is fired by a shikari to move her ; she dashes nearer the right flank and charges again ; elephants converge together, but one elephant hesitates an instant—leaving an open space, and in a flash she is through and away. Two more shots ring out from the gun on the right flank, in the forlorn hope of hitting her as she goes at a lightning pace through the long grass.

A disappointment this, that is felt by all—but the tiger is unaccounted for yet. All are anxious. At last! Again he moves slowly ahead, the pace is quickened, and the line gradually close in, the "stops" are in sight and the beat is narrowing to a point; the grass is heavier, requiring an infinite amount of care. The pace is slackened; the tiger has disappeared.

Suddenly a gun on the fire-line sees the massive form canter past opposite him through a sparse piece of jungle. He fires! The tiger starts galloping towards the apex—straight to a "stop." Both the sportsman and the lady with him, in the back seat of the howdah, have a splendid view of him.

In front of them is the river-bed—very narrow at this point, then a sandy patch overgrown with patches of yellow grass some 10 ft. high; beyond this a green, grassy glade, fairly thickly grown over with trees, but with very short grass growing around their trunks.

On, on he goes, head down, tail out—a perfect model of strength and vitality! When some five yards from the edge of the glade, our friend Captain M. fires, hitting him in the middle of the chest, as he gallops towards him. The tiger pulls up, springs, and stands on his hind-legs, then roars. Eyes like fire—full of such hatred and cruelty as it is hard to conceive, as he looks up searching for his aggressor and the dealer of so deadly a hurt. Captain M. fires again, and brings him rolling over with a broken shoulder; but he is up again and springs forward: he falls once more to a third shot, and his roars vibrate through the brain. With fury and desperation he strains to charge, for at last he has seen the enemy. Two more shots follow each other in quick succession, as he rolls towards the elephant—the two last behind the shoulder. His head goes down after one last quivering effort and long sigh, rife with hatred, and with a spirit dauntless and unconquered—though overcome.

No word is spoken: a keen feeling of respect and contrition cannot but be felt for a foe so brave and great.

The line comes up, and the hero and the tiger are surrounded. Having made quite certain that the noble tiger is really dead, everyone hurries down, and a measuring tape is produced—a fine, great tiger, 9 ft. 7 in.

Lunch is called for and unpacked, close under the all-embracing branches of a large and shady tree. Meantime, a strong rope net of some 12 ft. by 6 ft. of a large mesh is unpacked—the tiger-net—and after the shikaris have counted the claws and whiskers, the tiger is enveloped in the net, and many willing hands help to "pad" him. A staunch and big pad elephant is brought up and made to kneel down, tail towards the tiger. After many hoistings and pushings from below, and pullings and draggings from two or three men perched above, at last hairyback is up and secured by ropes to the pad, and the elephant is allowed to stand. A couple of responsible men are told off to take the tiger home, and to superintend skinning operations, for which purpose a " mouchi " (taxidermist) has been engaged for the shoot. The skinning operations are not to be begun till the party return to camp, so that a good photo may be taken in camp. A careful examination proves that the first shot fired at the tiger missed the mark, and that Captain M. was the undisputed owner of the tiger, having drawn " first blood."

While the party satisfy their pangs of hunger, the shikaris—to be joined by our host, after a hurried lunch—have been trying to locate the whereabouts of the escaped tigress. They track her into a sâl-tree forest, where to beat for her would be an endless business. However, as most of the " kill " is still intact, there is every chance of her returning to feed after dark, and also to hunt for her mate. A small string wood bed—a machan, of some 4 ft. square, with an iron ring at all four corners—is roped securely amongst the branches of a tree, from which a " gun " will have a good command of the approaches to the " kill," along any of which the tigress might come. The kutra happened to be near an overhanging bank, and on the edge of a nullah leading direct to the river, only a few yards off. An excellent spot for the sitter-up ! By carefully clearing away branches and grass, an unimpeded view of the " kill " is ensured, with as little trampling of the ground as possible. The tigress will return suspicious ; and will get easily alarmed by the scent of men and elephants, and most of all by cut branches, if left on the ground.

There is no moon, alas ! by which the sitter-up can see to fire at the tiger. Under these circumstances it is almost useless, and rather cruel, to sit up—only to fire at random into the dark towards a crunching of bones, as the tiger feeds. One of the party is, however, the happy possessor of a " Rhodda light "—a neat electric apparatus which will clip on to the barrel of a double-barrelled rifle ; and when the tiger comes, a button can be pressed which will light up the back-sight, and throw a circle of light beyond, dazzling the astonished beast, and allowing the gun to take a steady and fatal aim.

" Sitting up," as done by many, over water-holes, and for weeks on end, is " a mug's game " : it is not the most sporting of methods, and is only excusable if all other ways are unavailing.

One shikari has been sent to remove all live kutras so as to prevent the plans miscarrying by the tigress killing another and remaining away.

The rest of the party, having finished lunch, are ready in their howdahs, awaiting orders.

Our host, returning, picks out those whose turn it is for the next chance of the shot, and they draw to sit up. The " lucky beggar " quickly gets together two rifles, rugs, coats, cushions, a packet of food folded in a piece of linen to avoid any crackling of paper, and a flask containing a good draught of whisky and water. The all-night vigil will be a bitterly cold one, felt all the more after the hot day. Gloves, a whistle, and the " Rhodda light " complete his outfit. The afternoon is well on the wane, and no time is to be lost. The sitter-up departs to his machan under a shower of good wishes, to be left alone in his glory, perched up many feet above the ground. He watches the rest of the party slowly file out of sight and earshot—homeward bound. Having tied and arranged his impedimenta carefully, so as to be easily got at in the dark, taking special care not to drop anything or to make the slightest sound, he then leans back comfortably and surveys the scene.

Below him is the sandy nullah, not more than a couple of feet under the level of the grass plain. The dead buff lies on the edge of this, the limbs distorted. Claw-marks and blood on the head and neck indicate the death strokes from a whack of the tiger's forepaw. One hind leg is missing, the other being partially eaten—not much for two tigers to have made a meal off. A comforting thought this for the silent watcher above, for the tigress is sure to be hungry and to return to feed, if she has not killed elsewhere.

In front the grass beat stretches, the tall grass waving slowly and sighingly in the breeze. The open river-bed to the left winds away round a bend, being hidden by a belt of forest. On the farther side the country is wooded and broken, and cut up by deep nullahs, cliffs, and banks, covered with thick undergrowth and majestic sâl trees, their straight trunks more suggestive of an army of soldiers than of trees. Behind the machan there is a stretch of tree jungle on a higher level than that of the grass beat. The sun's setting rays gild the dark sâl trunks and glorify the whole surroundings. The bubbling of the river breaks the forest's silence pleasantly, and alleviates the feeling of utter loneliness and aloofness from the busy world. The presence of the whistle in the sportsman's pocket, however, brings to his mind the thought that he is not utterly deserted, for a pad elephant with its mahout and a shikari await his summons in the event of the tigress's return—and death—before dark! They are hidden away some distance off, near the fire-line, from whence a whistle would bring them quietly down the river-bed, through the open, to the machan. Then at dark they will return to camp, leaving the watcher alone to an all-night sit-up.

With the lengthening shadows suddenly the forest livens up. The vultures, who have been sitting at the top of a cotton tree, within view of the kill, and longing to descend and demolish it, all fly off to roost elsewhere—well aware that the man in the tree would not allow of their approach. A supply of stones in the machan, ready to be thrown at them, is a useful asset to a sitter-up. The black and common crow is more noisy in his displeasure; he is the gossip of the jungles, and if you would find out the whereabouts of a lost kutra keep a watchful eye on the crow's every movement. He flies around and attracts the vultures' attention, for a dead beast is not much use to him to eat until well torn to pieces by the vultures. Then comes his turn to descend and pick at his leisure. If you would hide a beast from the vulture, first hoodwink your sharp-eyed crow!

Cracklings in the jungle keep the sportsman on tenter-hooks and his senses strained. Pigs file out of the jungle from behind, their beady eyes glittering. They grunt and scuttle along, then, scenting the kill, bristle up, approach nearer, get scared, and dash off, to cross the river-bed presently, where they will drink before disappearing into the forest opposite, heading probably towards a forest-bound village, with a view to a good night's feed on the crops. Next comes an old boar alone in his glory, his whole appearance that of a tyrant. His approach to the kill will be careful but business-like—his great enemy, the tiger, may or may not be near ; nothing daunted, he will go forward with a full intention of eating his fill of the kill, if so willed.

When a tiger and boar meet on a narrow path neither gives way, both advance and fight it out to the death. In instances when these fights have had eye-witnesses, the fight is said to have been an equal match. The boar dashes in, the tiger springs; the one rips the stomach open, and the other tries to break the neck of his fiery opponent. When both are exhausted they slip off, unconquered, but to die of their wounds in dark and silent places. Meantime no such tragedy is wished for, and a well-aimed stone and a wave of the hand from the machan sends the boar off grunting furiously.

Lower down a herd of cheetah creep quietly out into the river-bed to drink, and are sent leaping away by the noisy descent from the sâl forest of a sambur stag, sedate and majestic in its movements. Noisy cackling and fluttering of jungle fowl will amuse the watcher, but the disturber of their peace will follow close behind, a large yellow wild cat—a terrible enemy to the feathered tribes. The piercing cry of pea-fowl, well known to everyone, startles all as they fly to the tree-tops to roost for the night. A happy family of monkeys go jumping from branch to branch, squabbling, squeaking, and playing on their way to the river. No second is really dull for those who love nature and wild life.

A " kaka stag " (barking deer), delicately picking its way across the boulders, suddenly throws back its head, listens intently, sniffs, and is off in a flash up into the sâl forest—its terrified alarm-calls vibrating from cliff to cliff. The alarm is taken up on all sides. The low, mellow notes of the sambur, the " coo-ee "-like call of the cheetah, pea-fowl, and jungle fowl ; on every side warnings ring out. What was the cause of the commotion ? The near proximity of a panther or tiger ? Suddenly, from round a bend of the river on the left, a cat-like form glides nearer and nearer down the river. A fine panther ! Slowly its head moves from side to side, with a swaying of its tail. Every few yards it halts, and inspects its surroundings. In an instant comes a change. The watcher sees the panther stiffen, crouch, with every muscle tense and rigid. He thinks the panther has caught sight of the machan. But no, it is because, having come down the river, the beast had not come on the dead kutra's trail, but the scent has just reached him.

Cautiously the panther moves forward, down the river and along the sandy nullah, drawing nearer the kill at every step, and making no sound. On sighting the kutra he crouches down, listens, breathes deeply, then glides up to the kill to discover whether its rightful owner be a panther or a tiger. If a panther, to satisfy his hunger and settle accounts later will probably be the course taken. On the other hand, to tamper with a tiger's kill would be a more serious affair, and not to be contemplated lightly, for, if caught, the penalty would be almost certain death.

The panther's hesitation does not last many seconds; a slight noise near-by sends him flashing away to melt into the grass beat, not to return.

The shadows lengthen into night; a thick haze enshrouds everything; the breeze turns into a strong wind, locally named the "Dadu"—an icy blast from the snows, sweeping down every valley, very unhealthy and a promoter of fever. A tinkling of the stones, and the shaggy, uneven form of a hyena—an animal hated universally and admired by none—shuffles off into the dark forest.

The jungle seems a place of the dead. The sportsman thinks of the good dinner and the home comforts that he is missing; he is frozen about the hands, feet, and nose; everything has become supremely uncomfortable; he is cramped all over, and blesses himself for a maniac! A panic as to whether the "Rhodda light" will work or not comes over him. Hour after hour creeps by. He wonders if it is midnight, and gingerly glances at his illuminated watch—it is only 10 p.m.! Gloom descends on his damped ardour; he nods with sleep.

All at once, in the distance, in among the foothills the alarm-calls of deer pierce the night. The jungles vibrate as the sounds come nearer, and at last surround him. The tiger must surely have come! The watcher has a fear that she may have come and gone while he dosed. A herd of cheetah come close by his tree, all calling loudly and stamping their feet when standing. Stones rattle in the river, and he hears something moving down it. It passes the nullah mouth, and continues down-stream. Then, with a terrific bellow, a sambur—who apparently was standing in mid-stream—hurtles up to the sâl forest. It must be the tigress; but why did she pass the nullah mouth—what can have occurred to put her off? The experienced would know that, if the disturber of the peace was indeed the tigress, it was a good omen that she had gone on down-stream. The dead kutra—when alive—had been tied round the bend; and so in all likelihood the tigress had returned to the place—to follow up the "drag and trail," stage by stage, until she reached the spot where she and her mate had last left it: also to see if her lost spouse had returned; and in the hope of finding him already replenishing himself.

The minutes pass so slowly that it is impossible to keep count of them. Some twenty minutes later, a low rustling causes the sportsman to raise his rifle and be ready to fire. The deer still continue to warn each other. A sniff under the tree, and the " man " almost stops breathing ; his heart is thumping like a sledge-hammer. He leans over, expectant. A rustle in the grass again and then the sound of licking. Is it the tigress, or a panther, or maybe only a pig ?

Crunch, crunch, and a low purr. The die is cast ! The " man " cannot wait another second. He cautiously raises his rifle—aiming toward the sound, presses the button of the " Rhodda light," and the kill, tiger, and surrounding grass are framed in a dazzling glory of light.

The great beast is so surprised that it crouches rigidly, gazing up into the light—and the muzzle of the rifle—its scared eyes glinting. With great coolness the sportsman aims between the eyes. A re-echoing report follows. The hand was steady and the reward great, for the tigress lies dead in her tracks !

The excitement of such a moment cannot be described. For some minutes the sportsman covered the tigress, in case she were not really dead. Having spotted the hole in her head he felt convinced, and then proceeded to make himself comfortable for the night, and have as much sleep as the small dimensions of the machan would allow.

In camp the party were all gathered round the bonfire, talking over the day's events and the numerous qualifications of the dead tiger.

Into the midst of these discussions the one faint report from a rifle dropped as a bolt from the blue—though not quite unexpectedly. Everyone, all the evening, had really been listening for the welcome sound. All jumped to their feet. Our host looked at his watch, 10.30 p.m. !—too late to go out to the machan that night. But at dawn next morning, our host, with three of the party, three pads, and some natives, hastened to the spot.

On approaching the kill our host whistled softly, then more loudly a second time, to be answered with a cheery greeting from the machan—an obvious sign that the tiger was quite dead and that a silent and cautious approach was unnecessary. In the case of a wounded tiger every precaution has to be taken against getting the elephants mauled by a surprise charge. Before many minutes the tigress of 8 ft. 6 in. was " padded," and away went the cavalcade home to breakfast, having first pulled the kutra into the open for the vultures. The little buff had not given his life in vain.

The happy owner of the tigress regaled his eager listeners on the road home with a detailed account of the events of the night—a tale to be oft repeated during the next few hours. Great jubilation of spirits prevailed. The day was well begun by the bringing in of the tigress. Besides this, it was Christmas morning, and the old-time greetings were exchanged by all, greetings probably coming more from the hearts of those who uttered them than they often do in the Home

Country. Rows of native gentlemen and officials hailed our host and his family after breakfast, bringing them their tokens of good will in kind—rice, fruits, nuts, oranges, and such like offerings—which an English official can accept in good faith, and not in the light of a bribe.

The native staff of the office now present a golden sovereign to be touched by their master. Shoals of fantastic Christmas cards, chosen with the native's love of bright effect, also pour in. The start out is somewhat late, for a great deal has to be done owing to the day. The party send telegrams, write letters, and are generally slow in their movements. There are also many visits to the mouchi's (taxidermists') tent to inspect the skinning of the tigress. The claws are removed—by special request—cleaned and given later to their owners; also the lucky jumping bones—the "suntôake"—corresponding rather to the chicken's "lucky bone."

By some these bones are supposed to have been extra collar-bones, meant to lessen the jar when the tiger jumped, in days when the world was wilder and tiger more active. But as generations passed, the necessity for the bone became a minus quantity, and so it has gradually diminished in size. There are two such bones in each of the cat species, lying in the muscle under the skin on either shoulder, and joined by cartilage to the bones beneath. These bones are much prized by natives as amulets, and so a sharp eye has to be kept on them. Many excuses are given for their disappearance

—a " kite," " dog," or slip of the skinning-knife—none of which are to be believed.

The " kubber " is not of a good enough nature to devote the day to going after any particular tiger ; so it is settled to beat some of the wooded islands in the bed of the great river several miles below the camp, to which spot the party now depart.

The word is passed for " armed shikar " in every beat during the day. A mysterious order this to the new-comer—its meaning being that all the guns, whether on " stop " or in the line, may shoot with impunity at any animals they like—stags, birds, panther, pig, or alligators—does and hinds of course excepted. Meat is wanted badly for the camp, as up till now the early morning stalks have been denied the sportsmen, on account of disturbing the forests with promiscuous firing. But from this time on each successive morning they are sent to certain tracks of forests, taking it in turn to try their luck either at a sambur or cheetah stag, singly or in couples, according to their own inclinations. The allowance of different species of game on the shooting pass has, of course, to be kept in mind. The stalkers please themselves as to whether they go on foot or on pads, and also the length of time they are out, so long as they are ready to start off after breakfast when they are required.

The day on the islands is most enjoyable, the fording of the river being quite an exciting sensation. The whirling by of many waters and the swaying of the elephant make some feel dizzy, or conscious of a sinking feeling internally.

The shooting of birds is barred during the first half of the day. The beats are run on the same system as the tiger beats. Each time a pig or porcupine, wild cat, or such like animal is shot at by a gun in the line, the line of beaters halt till the reason is known, and then the whistle starts them again.

Shooting off an elephant is very hard at first, the angle and footing being so different to shooting from the ground. The secret is to shoot low. The mahout of a howdah elephant stops his beast and keeps it still when an animal breaks—to allow of a steady shot.

A number of stags break during the morning, and one quite good sambur is shot; also a ghond stag (a swamp deer); these have the last offices performed on their throats by eager mahouts. Without this throat-cutting no Mahommedan may eat any animal.

After lunch, a last island is beaten in the hope of getting a panther, whose "pugs" a shikari had discovered. Everyone becomes more serious.

The "stops" are placed and the line starts, the noise causing the panther to stir. The deer get wind of him, and start their alarm-calls all over the island, rushing out past the "stops" as the line advances. The panther canters ahead of the line: through the tree jungle a shikari sees him and shouts the warning. There is a very heavy piece of grass ahead, with the "stops" some 20 yds. beyond. A family of monkeys in the trees above the edge of the heavy grass on the right spot the panther, and immediately hurl such an avalanche of abuse and outrageous splutterings down upon him that the entire line are made acquainted of the whereabouts of the fugitive.

Monkeys are among the greatest friends a sportsman can have. They often follow a panther or tiger for quite a distance, swearing roundly the entire time, as they leap from branch to branch. On this occasion, the right wing of the line swung forward, to keep the panther on the move.

Luckily, the heavy grass was not of large dimensions, and the pads in the line all worked shoulder to shoulder. The panther kept lying close under the bushes and in depressions : and each time the line came on him the pads spoke, and a tremendous rumpus ensued. One gun in the line at last saw him slip into a clump of thorn bushes : the pads concentrated on the clump. Two or three guns were ready for him to break. At the last second, with a low grunt, he shot into a sandy nullah a few feet beyond—giving a very difficult snapshot.

Major H., who was one of the guns in the line, fired, hitting him between the shoulders. A splendid shot ! There were a few low groans and a tossing of the sand in the nullah, and then all became still. The line was steadied, and advanced carefully, the guns ready for a possible charge from the wounded beast. No second shot was, however, needed, the panther had gone over like a rabbit and lay dead with a broken spine ; in its death agony it bit its paw through and through, and the jaws of the animal were tightly locked. Wounded animals will often bite themselves in their pain.

The measuring tape being produced, the guns alighted and measured the panther, over the curves, from the tip of the nose to the end of the tail. A fine beast of 7 ft. 8 in., looking specially well in his thick winter coat. It is always best to measure animals at once, as after stiffening they shrink in length. Besides the above method of measuring over the curves, there is another ; the tape is stretched between two pegs, one at the nose and the other at the end of the tail.

After the padding of the panther, the party returned home. The two tiger skins were well advanced : having been cleaned, they were pegged out on a lair of straw with nails, the skin being stretched a foot more than the original length and breadth. The simple method of the first curing, as done in the camp if no taxidermist is at hand, and one which is absolutely safe, is to thoroughly soak and wash the skin in a tub of water. After removing all fat and fleshy portions from the skins, they are pegged out, then given a good washing over with arsenical soap, followed by a couple of pounds of powdered alum rubbed well in by hand, especially into the ears, eye-splits, pads and lips, inside and out. Then they are left to dry slowly, and if in a very hot sun, a light covering of straw prevents the skin cracking by too quick drying. The best method for preserving the skull, but one not often feasible, is to leave the head for weeks in a tin of water to allow the flesh to rot off gradually; for to boil the teeth causes them to discolour in time. Nevertheless, generally the skull is boiled and cleaned, then filled with alum. The claws are always better out of the skin, as, when set up, they can be put back, and all chance of their causing the paws to rot will thus be avoided.

Good news awaited the party on their return. The tiger had killed, and was to be hunted on the morrow. A second had also killed, but the advent of wild elephants coming into his beat, and trampling down the grass, had put this tiger out to seek another lair.

Wild elephants are always to be avoided, when possible, from the sportsman's point of view.

The Christmas dinner was merry in the extreme. Nothing of the old-time fare had been forgotten—White Horse and soda, mince-pies, and a flaming plum-pudding; and the table was gay with piles of crackers, warming the hearts of all.

And here we must leave them—singing "Auld Lang Syne."

NOTES

CHAPTER XXVIII

GUNS AND RIFLES

By MAJOR HUGH POLLARD

THE choice and selection of proper equipment for shooting is important, for if it is wisely done gear will last a life-time with proper care. The first and most important part of the outfit is the gun. To-day we can take the game gun as a standardised article, whose design has been stabilised and perfected. As things are, it is doubtful if anyone will succeed in producing any very great improvement upon the modern type, for the gun is dependent on the cartridge; and we have to-day reached a point where any material or revolutionary advance in design or efficiency is improbable. The game gun, like the bicycle, has reached a stabilised point where the best designs have become universally adopted.

The standard game gun of to-day is a twelve bore hammerless ejector, and such variations as exist are, when all is said and done, only elaborations or refinements on this particular framework. We attribute a gun to a maker, and speak of "my So-and-So's." Actually any gun is the product of a score or more of craftsmen, and the really good gun is a work of art rather than mechanical engineering. Every gun will shoot, comparatively inexpensive guns may indeed shoot extremely well, but they will not handle well, and they will very seldom shoot anywhere near as effectively as a gun which fits its owner. It is perhaps best to look on this question of guns as very much like tailoring. You can buy fairly cheaply a ready-made suit of good, practical hard-wearing cloth—but it will not fit you. If by some chance you happened to fit a ready-made suit perfectly no tailor could improve on it, but suits and guns have to be fitted to the individual. This is more and more manifest as age advances. A limber youth can shoot fairly well with any moderately straight stocked gun, but once a man's figure has "set" he must be properly fitted. The art of fitting is to produce a gun which so conforms to a man's build *that it shoots where he is looking*.

The perfect refinement of balance and handling is only found in the "best" guns, but the actual difference in practical efficiency between the grades of guns costing £120 apiece and those costing £50 is a very small percentage. A naturally good shot can often do well with even an indifferent gun, but the poor to medium shot requires the very best he can afford.

In every generation certain makers acquire a special pre-eminence, and weapons bearing their name become specially renowned. A century ago Joe Manton, Egg and Nock were the leaders. Their men, in their turn, founded businesses, the names of which were household words until the late Victorian era. Names change, reputations are eclipsed, old workmen die, and though a modern firm may bear an old name, it may have lost just that spark of illuminating connoisseurship, that curious intangible touch of art and genius that originally established the supremacy of the firm's wares. It is as well to buy the most modern designs to-day, as the wares of the progressive modern gun-maker do not suffer the heavy depreciation which is overtaking those of some of the old-established but non-progressive firms.

The tendency of our time is toward shorter barrels. To-day a pair of first-class game guns by a leading maker have if they have thirty-inch barrels far less second-hand value than if they have twenty-eight. Messrs. Churchill, Holland and Holland, the B.S.A., and other makers are now making guns of twenty-five-inch barrel length, and this shorter and more convenient barrel length is typical of the gun of this period, for it kills as far, shoots as hard, and is easier to handle than its longer barrelled predecessors of the black powder era.

Two main types of action exist to-day : the side lock and the Anson and Deeley. The former is the more expensive and the pleasanter handling of the two, and it is uniformly used on "best" guns. The Anson and Deeley is, however, just as good, and a better selection for guns which may be taken overseas. It is simple, robust and, in the unlikely chance of its going wrong, is easily repaired by any gunmaker. The more delicate sidelock usually represents a standard of workmanship only repairable by the maker or by an equally good craftsman. So far as efficiency is concerned, there is little to choose between them. A gunmaker's catalogue will offer a possible choice of half a dozen grades of standard game gun at prices from £120 to £25. The differences may not be easily perceived by the novice. It is perhaps best explained by comparing a gun to a scientific instrument of precision. The better the quality of work and material put into the better it will last. Shoddy work has short life; good work and close fitting is almost everlasting. A cheap gun will wear easily and soon knock to pieces; a well-built one will endure more than a lifetime of hard wear without deteriorating in any way. There is only one rule—buy the very best you can afford and you never need give another thought to them.

The average gun is bored to give a different degree of shot concentration or pattern with the right and left barrels. The left is usually more fully choked than the right. As a result, it shoots a closer pattern and has a rather longer killing range. In a game gun the degree of choke is always moderate. In a special gun for long range use such as wild fowl shooting both barrels are usually given as much choke as possible. This means that such a weapon is of little use for driven game at close ranges, for in place of dispersing its shot charge over a wide killing circle it concentrates them to a degree needing far more accurate shooting at close ranges than is normally possible.

The degree of choke is estimated according to the

percentage of pellets of a standard charge grouped in the thirty-inch circle at forty yards, but it occasionally happens that a gun which gives a very mediocre pattern on the test plate is yet, in practice, a redoubtable killer. The reason is that the shot charges string out and we measure on the plate only in two dimensions in place of three. Some barrels of indifferent performance on the plate seem to have the trick of producing a shorter shot column or one in which a higher percentage of pellets have an efficient killing velocity. These are exceptions, and for ordinary purposes the pattern given by a gun may be taken as a proof of its efficiency. It should, however, be borne in mind that all shotgun ballistics are very different in their standard of accuracy to rifle ballistics. Dealing with a single projectile we can be fairly accurate, but dealing with a multiple charge of pellets is a very different affair, and the margin of error is substantial.

It can be taken that with well made factory loaded cartridges a good gun will always perform well, and that the maximum possible care and precision of loading will not increase its efficiency by more than two or three per cent. Actually our guns and our cartridges shoot a great deal better and more reliably than we do, and it takes a great deal of error in loading to approach the very obvious twenty-five to thirty per cent. variation in efficiency most shooting men will show.

Though the twelve bore is the standard gun, smaller and larger bores are sometimes used. The old four, eight and ten bores are obsolete even for wild fowling, and are replaced by twelve bores firing a three or even three and a half inch cartridge. Eight bores are still occasionally made for goose guns, but, in general, the "long case twelve" has superseded the large bores. The gun, in convenience and manageableness, is considerable, for an eight pound long case twelve bore is far quicker to handle than a fourteen pound double eight.

In the small bores the sixteen is far preferable to the twenty, for the latter introduce a serious element of danger. If a twenty bore cartridge got mixed with ordinary twelve bores it may be accidentally loaded into a twelve bore, when it lodges just in front of the chamber. If a twelve bore cartridge is loaded into the apparently empty chamber and fired a dangerous burst is inevitable. This particular form of accident is unfortunately fairly common, and it is a wise rule entirely to forbid twenty bores. The smaller bores of twenty-eight and .410 are useful for small game up to thirty yards, but cannot be considered seriously effective in comparison to the standard twelve. As a boy's gun, the .410 is excellent, but it possesses marked limitations.

The gun cabinet should hold as well as the guns a rabbit rifle and a deer stalking rifle. To-day the .22 rifle, using the .22 hollow point long rifle ammunition.

is, owing to the high cost of other cartridges, about the only small rifle in general use. Many forms are obtainable : single shot, repeater or automatic. The latter are preferable, and either the F.N. or the Walther are extremely good. The latter is adequate in size and it is a good rule to select a miniature rifle not too reduced in scale, as practice with the larger size more closely corresponds to the bigger rifle.

For deer stalking the .30—'06 U.S. Government (Springfield) is now a popular cartridge, both for Mauser, Mannlicher, Winchester, Savage and Greener-Mauser rifles. It possesses a very flat trajectory, and the 150 grain pointed soft point bullet is extremely effective, having a muzzle velocity of some 2,700 feet per second. The British .303, with pointed Mark VII. ammunition, is very similar, but owing to restrictions on its use abroad, in India and parts of Africa, has limited general value. In general, any small bore high velocity rifle is suitable for deer stalking where all shots are taken at fair sporting ranges under two hundred, preferably under one hundred and fifty yards. The advantages of the higher velocities are not only a simplification of sighting, but an increased shocking and killing effect, which considerably reduces possible disasters with wounded game. In general peep sights are useful, and telescopes and hair triggers are both to be avoided. The latter have both special applications in the hands of experts, but do not simplify matters for the average shot.

The maintenance of arms is almost entirely a matter of scrupulous cleaning, drying and oiling after use. The shotgun cartridge of to-day is not very corrosive, but rifle cartridges leave an acid residue which requires an alkaline oil to neutralise. The .22 cartridge are now made in Klean Bore and Stainless by Remington and Winchester, and are entirely non-corrosive. This abolishes a serious source of trouble, but with these new cartridges, even if the rifle is not cleaned at all, there is no corrosion. With deer stalking rifles a great deal has been done to reduce metallic fouling by the adoption of Lubaloy bullets by the American makers. The British cartridge makers still, however, use cupro-nickel and cleaning both with cordite cleanser and K.N. or one of the metallic fouling removers are essential. For the woodwork of guns and rifles linseed oil alone should be used, but this, or any other vegetable oil, should never be allowed on the metal work. For general cleaning Three-in-One oil is the best for all uses, and when arms are put away a dressing of B.S.A. Safeti-Paste will keep the bores in good condition.

Cleaning can seldom be overdone, but the use of a wire scratch brush is to be deprecated. If it has to be used one with brass, not steel, wire should always be used. Care, too, should be paid to cleaning rods. A. G. Parker's " Country Life " celluloid covered rods and jags are the best, as however carelessly used they can never hurt a barrel.

If in process of time a gun works loose it should be sent to the makers for setting-up, and in any case a seasonal inspection and overhaul is a wise policy. With care and cleanliness a good gun or rifle should last a lifetime, but with neglect they are easily and quickly spoilt for ever.

NOTES.

MEDICAL AND SURGICAL HINTS

CONTENTS OF FIRST-AID CABINET

1. 6 ASSORTED ROLLER BANDAGES.
2. 6 TRIANGULAR BANDAGES.
3. 1 ROLL BORACIC LINT.
4. 1 ROLL COTTON-WOOL.
5. 1 SMALL ROLL OF GOOCHE SPLINTING.
6. 1 ELASTIC TOURNIQUET.
7. 2 OUNCES PURE CARBOLIC ACID, LABELLED "1 TEASPOONFUL TO 2 PINTS WATER TO MAKE ANTISEPTIC LOTION."
8. 2 OUNCES TINCTURE OF IODINE, LABELLED "IODINE FOR WOUNDS."
9. 6 OUNCES METHYLATED SPIRITS.
10. 8 OUNCES OF 1 PER CENT. SOLUTION PICRIC ACID, LABELLED "FOR BURNS, APPLY ON LINT."
11. 2 OUNCES IPECACUANHA WINE, LABELLED "IPECACUANHA WINE TO INDUCE VOMITING." A TABLESPOONFUL FOR AN ADULT.
12. 1 POUND LINSEED MEAL, IN A TIN.
13. 2 OUNCES SAL VOLATILE, LABELLED "HALF TO A TEASPOONFUL IN WATER, FOR FAINTING."
14. ½ OUNCE PERMANGANATE OF POTASH, LABELLED "RUB INTO WOUND FOR SNAKE OR ADDER BITE."
15. ½ OUNCE DILUTE AMMONIA, LABELLED, "APPLY FOR INSECT STINGS."

INDEX

CHAPTER XXIX

MEDICAL AND SURGICAL HINTS

BY ARNOLD JONES, M.B., Ch.B.

(Senior Surgeon, Ayr County Hospital; Consulting Surgeon, Seafield Hospital, Ayr; Consulting Surgeon, Davidson Memorial Hospital, Girvan)

A BOOK such as this would not be complete without a few hints on medical and surgical emergencies, as it frequently happens in connection with sport that accidents and sudden illnesses occur, remote from immediate medical aid.

The chapter has been arranged in paragraph form with separate index. A list of articles suitable for a First-Aid Cabinet is appended. The cabinet should be kept in an easily accessible position.

A knowledge of first-aid is an important asset for a keeper. He should attend first-aid lectures and gain the St. Andrew's Ambulance Certificate. With limited space no attempt can be made to treat the matter systematically, but hints of proved value only can be given. If the directions are properly carried out, the immediate emergency shall be overcome. In all cases which are, or appear to be at all serious, a doctor should be summoned.

1. BLEEDING.—Bleeding from any part of the body surface may be controlled by—

(1) Direct pressure on the bleeding part.

(2) Compression of the vessels going to the part.

Direct pressure in the first instance may be applied by pressing the wound firmly with the thumb, a clean handkerchief or rag folded into a pad intervening. If this is successful, then pressure may be maintained by binding firmly over the pad. This will control bleeding in most instances, but where a large vessel has been severed in a limb, the vessel should be compressed by means of a tourniquet.

Compression of Vessels.—A tourniquet must be applied nearer to the body than the bleeding-point, and should be applied over the ordinary clothing, which will act as a pad and make the tightening process less painful. A large handkerchief, cartridge-bag strap, or even a piece of rope, is tied loosely round the thigh or the upper arm, a stout stick is inserted between it and the limb and used to twist the tourniquet until it is tight enough to stop the bleeding. When the bleeding is under control, the pressure must be maintained, but not for a longer period than two hours, as permanent damage to the blood-supply may result.

2. INTERNAL BLEEDING.—(1) *From Stomach:* The blood is vomited and mixed with particles of food. It is usually dark and may be "coffee-grounds" colour.

(2) *From Lungs:* The blood is bright red and frothy and is coughed up.

Treatment.—Lay the patient on his back, admit plenty of fresh air, give ice to suck, and keep perfectly quiet. Avoid all stimulants, give one teaspoonful of vinegar in water or fifteen drops of turpentine in milk every half-hour.

3. BLEEDING FROM NOSE.—The patient should sit upright and avoid hanging his head over a basin. If he is full-blooded, let bleeding continue for some time, as it is probably acting as a safety-valve. To stop bleeding, grasp the nose firmly between the finger and thumb just below the bony part, and in this way press the two sides of the nose together. This local pressure will control most cases. The effect is increased by previously plugging the nostril with a strip of lint damped in cold water.

4. WOUNDS.—The chief indications in treating wounds are—

(1) Control of bleeding (see Bleeding).

(2) Prevention of infection.

When dressing a wound, the dresser should wash his hands and take every precaution to prevent fresh dirt or infection being conveyed to the wound.

Every accidental wound must be considered infected. If it has gross dirt in it, this should be washed out with clean water to which, if available, a few drops of carbolic acid or other antiseptic should be added. If there is no gross dirt apparent, the application of some form of spirit will be sufficient without any washing. Raw whisky is an excellent antiseptic. Methylated spirit or tincture of iodine painted on the wound is probably the most efficient application to prevent inflammation.

5. Applications of Dressings.—If the wound has been treated by washing, a wet dressing should be applied. A piece of clean linen or, if available, boracic lint damped in the water containing the antiseptic is laid next the wound and retained in position with a bandage. If the wound has been treated with spirit or iodine, it should be kept dry, a piece of dry linen or dry boracic lint laid on and bandaged in position.

The most usual first-aid bandage is a clean handkerchief folded to form a triangle. This in turn may be folded by placing the apex of the triangle on the base. Further folds in the same fashion will make either a broad or a narrow bandage suitable for retaining dressings or splints in position. As a triangle it forms a serviceable sling.

6. Gunshot Wounds.—Wounds caused by an ordinary shotgun vary in severity with the distance from which the shot is fired. If fired at close range, the wound may be very extensive, involving bones and the larger vessels. The chief indication in such cases is to combat the bleeding by local pressure or tourniquet and treat as under Wounds and Fractures.

Shots from some distance usually mean peppering. There may be several small punctured wounds where pellets have entered. They do not as a rule call for any special treatment other than some local pressure to stop bleeding.

7. GUN-BURSTING WOUNDS.—Hand and face injuries are most likely to occur with this accident. The injuries may be very slight, a mere reddening of the skin, or very extensive, involving bones and blood-vessels.

The treatment is mainly directed to control of bleeding and the proper cleansing of the wound. If a fracture is present, treat as under Compound Fractures.

8. BRUISES.—These are really wounds under the skin, and bleeding takes place causing swelling and later "black and blue" discoloration. They should be treated immediately by firm local pressure applied by a pad and bandage; this stops the bleeding and limits the swelling.

9. SPRAINS.—These are injuries which occur at joints and are due to the stretching or tearing of the ligaments and tendons which surround the joint. Bleeding under the skin takes place and causes swelling and dull, sickening pain which is much increased by any attempt to move the part. The application of cold relieves the pain, and firm pressure applied round the joint stops the bleeding under the skin and limits the swelling. The injured joint should not be allowed to hang down, as this increases the swelling and pain. If the ankle or knee-joint is sprained, the patient should lie on his back with the whole limb supported at a higher level than the body. If the wrist or elbow is involved, the arm should be supported in a sling. If an ankle is sprained some distance from home, the boot should not be removed, but a firm strap or bandage should be applied over the

boot. Sprains get well much more quickly when massage is started within the first twenty-four hours.

10. FRACTURES.—Two kinds of fractures are recognised :

(1) Simple, when a bone is broken without any outside wound.

(2) Compound, when an outside wound is present and communicates with the fracture.

TREATMENT OF SIMPLE FRACTURES.—These must be prevented from becoming compound—(1) by careful handling so that the broken ends of bone are not pushed through the skin ; (2) by fixing the part in splints so that this accident is prevented while moving the patient.

11. TO APPLY SPLINTS, one person should grasp the hand or foot, according to which limb is fractured, and exert a steady pull away from the body and in the direction the limb is pointing to. There must be no twisting or pulling of the limb from side to side. This steady traction in one direction is called extension ; the weight of the patient's body forms the counter-extension. The limb may, however, be steadied by an assistant grasping it above the seat of the fracture and in this way reinforcing the counter-extension. The immediate effect of extension is relief of pain. While this is being applied, splints suitably padded should be improvised and fixed on either side of the limb. The bandages should fix the splints above and below the fracture. Four bandages at least should be used for this purpose.

Splints may be formed from a great variety of articles. A gun for the lower limbs ; the barrels or the stock will make splints of different sizes ; branches of trees, walking-sticks, wood from boxes, newspapers folded several times, etc.

12. TREATMENT OF COMPOUND FRACTURES.—The great danger is, that septic poisoning may set in unless the wound is properly dealt with at the beginning. Treat as under Wounds. If the bone is protruding through the skin, do not attempt to replace. If the patient has to be moved, fix in splints without applying extension. If bone is not protruding, having treated wound, apply extension and treat as simple fracture.

13. FRACTURES IN SPECIAL SITUATIONS—COLLAR BONE.—The whole shoulder hangs down and the patient tends to lean to the injured side and attempts to relieve pain by supporting his elbow with his sound arm. Place a large pad in the armpit, support whole forearm in a large sling, arranged to press up and support the elbow, place a firm binder round the chest to bind the upper arm and forearm to the chest wall.

14. FRACTURE OF UPPER ARM.—Apply splints and support wrist with a narrow sling. This allows weight of elbow to hang and exert extension.

15. FRACTURE OF FOREARM.—Bend the elbow to a right-angle across the chest with the thumb pointing upwards, apply splints, one on front, the other on the back, of the forearm and support with a large sling which includes the elbow.

16. FRACTURE OF THE THIGH.—If possible, apply a long splint reaching from the armpit to the feet, apply a short one on the inner side of the thigh and also reaching to the feet, fix with bandages above and below fracture, round chest and round hips, and finally fix sound limb to injured limb. This enables patient to be moved with minimum risk and discomfort.

17. FRACTURE OF LEG BELOW KNEE.—After applying splints, fix sound limb to injured one to facilitate moving.

18. DISLOCATIONS.—A dislocation is the displacement of one or more bones forming a joint.

Treatment.—Do not attempt to reduce it. Keep the part at rest and apply hot fomentations until skilled advice is obtained.

19. BURNS.—Burns are divided into three degrees :

(1) When the skin is merely reddened.

(2) Where blisters have formed.

(3) Where destruction of the deeper parts occurs.

In extensive burns of the second and third degree, shock is always present. Shock shows itself by absence of pain, weak, rapid pulse, the patient feels cold and faint. This should be treated by warmth applied to the body, hot blankets, hot-water bottles, and stimulants.

Local Treatment.—Burns of first degree may be covered liberally with dusting-powder, composed of boracic or zinc or even ordinary flour, and the parts wrapped in cotton-wool.

Burns of second degree may be treated in the same way after the blisters have been punctured with a needle sterilised by passing through a flame.

Burns of third degree are usually treated by some oily preparation such as vaseline, carron-oil, olive-oil, butter, etc.

These are merely suggestions for first-aid. Every house should, however, have the means of treating burns in a more up-to-date way. Ambrine, which is a paraffin-wax, is melted and applied, or the burn is treated with 1 per cent. solution of picric acid applied freely on strips of lint or clean linen. This treatment is suitable for burns of all degrees and stages.

20. DROWNING.—It is necessary first to remove the water from the patient's lungs. This may be done by placing a coat folded into a firm pad at the lower part of the chest, the patient lying on his face with his head slightly to the side and his arms extended in front of him. Kneel astride the patient and place the hands on the small of the patient's back, one on each side. Bend forward, allowing the operator's weight to press firmly downwards. This presses the air or water from the patient's lungs. The time occupied by the downward pressure should be regulated by the operator counting slowly one, two, three. Immediately after, relax the pressure and count one, two. Repeat the pressure as at the beginning, and continue to do so without appreciable pause at the rate of twelve to fifteen times per minute. When natural breathing is established, cease the artificial

movements unless the breathing again ceases. Artificial respiration should be commenced as soon as the patient is removed from the water. When natural breathing is established, efforts should be made to promote warmth and circulation by the application of heat, warm drinks, etc.

21. Choking.—Articles of food may stick in the gullet or windpipe and prevent air entering the lungs. The symptoms are very urgent and should be dealt with promptly. Sometimes a vigorous blow on the back, by producing a forced expiration, will dislodge the obstruction. If this fails, an attempt should be made to pass the forefinger down one side of the throat and, bending the point of the forefinger to act as a blunt hook, endeavour to dislodge the obstruction upwards. Pass the finger along one side of the cheek and keep to the same side of the throat, and endeavour in this way to get below the object. If this manœuvre is not successful, try to induce vomiting.

22. Bites from Rabid Animals.—Fortunately rabies has disappeared from this country owing to effective legislation. If a person is bitten by an animal, the bite should be cauterised by a red-hot wire or by a drop of pure carbolic acid. The animal should not be destroyed, but be placed under observation. If there is any question that it may be rabid, the patient should be sent to the nearest Pasteur Institute for treatment.

23. Bites from Snakes and Adders.—In Britain adder-bites are the most common, but are seldom fatal

to man. Two minute punctures are visible on the skin, and these should be dealt with at once. The limb should be grasped above the wound and a tourniquet (see Bleeding) firmly applied ; this prevents the poison entering the general circulation. The wound should then be freely incised with a knife and sucked by a person whose lips and mouth have no abrasions or cracks. The wound is freely washed, and if available crystals of permanganate of potash are rubbed in. In tropical countries snake-bites are frequently fatal, but prompt treatment on the above lines has saved innumerable lives.

Most sportsmen in the tropics carry a lancet and permanganate of potash with them. Free stimulation with alcohol is regarded by many as a valuable aid to treatment.

24. INSECT STINGS.—Should the sting be visible, remove it by the pressure of a watch-key over it, then apply dilute ammonia. When the mouth or tongue has been stung, great swelling may result and even produce suffocation. The mouth should be washed out frequently with equal parts of whisky and water. If any faintness or weakness occurs, stimulate with alcohol.

25. CONCUSSION OF THE BRAIN.—This occurs when a person is stunned by a fall or a blow on the head.

Treatment.—Keep the patient on his back, raise the head slightly, loosen tight clothing, and apply cold to the head. Send for a doctor to decide whether any injury to the skull or brain has taken place.

26. EPILEPSY.—Commonly called "fits." Force the handle of a key between the patient's teeth to prevent the tongue being bitten. Merely guide the convulsive movements to prevent the patient injuring himself. When the fit has passed, if the patient is drowsy let him sleep.

27. SUNSTROKE.—Sunstroke may show itself by mere giddiness or faintness, with sickness and weakness, or the person may fall to the ground insensible, with a flushed face.

Treatment.—Remove to a shady spot, raise head and shoulders, remove outer clothing, and douche head, chest, and back with cold water.

In hot weather, to avoid sunstroke, a suitable hat should be worn. The nape of the neck should also be protected.

28. FAINTING.—Place the patient on his back with the head lower than the body. Loosen tight clothing and admit fresh air. Give a small quantity of spirits and water, or half a teaspoonful of sal volatile in water.

29. POISONING.—Act promptly. Avoid appearance of hurry or excitement. Give an emetic, consisting of a tablespoonful of mustard to a tumblerful of tepid water or two tablespoonfuls of salt to the quantity of water. Follow this by a handful of flour made into a cream with water or two or three eggs beaten up.

INDEX

For Product Safety Concerns and Information please contact our EU representative GPSR@taylorandfrancis.com Taylor & Francis Verlag GmbH, Kaufingerstraße 24, 80331 München, Germany

Batch number: 08153795

Printed by Printforce, the Netherlands